Advances in Entrepreneurial Finance

Rassoul Yazdipour

Advances in Entrepreneurial Finance

With Applications from Behavioral Finance and Economics

Springer

Rassoul Yazdipour
California State University
Fresno, CA,
USA
ryazdipour@aoef.org

ISBN 978-1-4419-7526-3 e-ISBN 978-1-4419-7527-0
DOI 10.1007/978-1-4419-7527-0
Springer New York Dordrecht Heidelberg London

Library of Congress Control Number: 2010938798

Printed on acid-free paper

Springer is part of Springer Science+Business Media (www.springer.com)

Foreword

The study of entrepreneurship is vital to continued growth and innovation in our society. At its most basic level, entrepreneurship is a means for individuals to lift themselves out of poverty and to create jobs for others. The new businesses that are started each year offer the promise of wealth and independence to the entrepreneurs who take on the inherent risks. At a broader level, however, the entrepreneurs who bring truly new and innovative products and services to the market offer something even more important to all members of the community. These are the new businesses that are responsible for much of the economic growth in our economy and the progress in our standard of living. The long history of new business ideas that changed our daily lives is familiar to all of us. From the radio and the television to the personal computer and new medical technologies, these innovations benefited – and continue to benefit – many more people than the entrepreneurs and their employees. Innovations promise greater prosperity for society as a whole.

A greater understanding of entrepreneurship and its drivers is critical to the continued growth of our economy. It is only through the study of new businesses and their founders that we will identify the motivation to start a business and understand the entrepreneurial process, the financing of these businesses, the challenges entrepreneurs face, and the policies and institutions that encourage greater entrepreneurial activity. The Ewing Marion Kauffman Foundation has devoted significant resources toward this effort at an academic level, working with economists and others who study this important phenomenon. In addition to supporting research on the topic, we have sponsored new efforts to collect data on entrepreneurial activity.

These initiatives have proven fruitful. There has been increased attention to entrepreneurship among academics in recent years. The strength of the work in this book testifies to the growing interest in this work among academics from a variety of perspectives. Furthermore, the summary of statistical databases for small business financial research, the discussions of data sources within individual chapters, and the use of new data herein suggest that efforts to improve data sources for the study of entrepreneurship are progressing as well. This book, in fact, includes an analysis of Kauffman Firm Survey data, a panel study of businesses founded in 2004 that tracks them over their early years of operation.

Empirical research on entrepreneurship has much to offer us from a policy perspective. Among many other topics, economists have elucidated a great deal about firm formation, growth, and death; the financing of new businesses; the institutional influences on entrepreneurship; the demographic characteristics of entrepreneurs; and the important role of entrepreneurship in economic growth. The Academy of Entrepreneurial Finance community has contributed significantly to our understanding of how new businesses are financed, and this book presents an important summary of the current state of this knowledge.

This volume is evidence of the importance of interdisciplinary works on entrepreneurship that bring together insights from different perspectives. The focus here is at the intersection of psychology and neuroscience and economics, an important junction as entrepreneurs' and investors' decisions do not always seem to follow traditional economic models. Among other topics, these chapters bring to light the importance of exploring entrepreneur–investor relations from a cognitive perspective, suggest that emotion and heuristics play an important role in entrepreneurs' and investors' risk perceptions, identify some common psychological characteristics of entrepreneurs (and the non-pecuniary benefits of entrepreneurship), and indicate that broader approaches to financial risk metrics are necessary. The contributions from neuroscience in this book allow for a more direct examination of the "internal landscape" of decision making.

Ultimately, the works in this book bring out the human element of firm decision-making, and bring the teaching of psychology and neuroscience to bear on it. This understanding certainly pushes us toward a new understanding of entrepreneurship, and it reminds us that bringing together a wide range of disciplines will allow us to achieve both a broader and deeper understanding of this important topi

Robert Strom, Ph.D.
Director of Research and Policy, Ewing Marion Kauffman Foundation

Contents

Contributors

Richard W. Ackley Ph.D.
Professor, The Chicago School of Professional Psychology, Chicago, IL, USA

Richard L. Constand Ph.D.
California State University, Fresno, CA, USA

William Dunkelberg Ph.D.
Temple University, Philadelphia, PA, USA
and
National Federation for Independent Businesses, Nashville, TN, USA

Philip Garcia Ph.D.
Professor, University of Illinois at Urbana – Champaign, Chicago, IL, USA

Lukasz M. Konopka Ph.D., ECNS, BCIA-EEG
Professor, Loyola Stritch School of Medicine and The Chicago School of Professional Psychology, Chicago, IL, USA

Fabio Mattos Ph.D.
Professor, University of Manitoba, Winnipeg, MB, Canada

William P. Neace Ph.D.
Professor, University of Hartford, West Hartford, CT, USA

Robert A. Olsen Ph.D.
Decision Research, Eugene, OR, USA

Charles Ou Ph.D.
Office of Advocacy, The US Small Business Administration, Washington, DC, USA

Jonathan A. Scott Ph.D.
Professor, Temple University, Philadelphia, PA, USA

Martin Sewell
University of Cambridge, Cambridge, UK

Hersh Shefrin Ph.D.
Santa Clara University, Santa Clara, CA, USA

Robert Strom Ph.D.
Director of Research Entrepreneurship Research and Policy, Ewing Marion Kauffman Foundation, Kansas City, MO, USA

Peter Wirtz Ph.D.
Professor, Université Lumière, Lyon 2, France

Rassoul Yazdipour Ph.D.
California State University, Fresno, CA, USA
and
The Academy of Entrepreneurial Finance, Los Angeles, CA, USA

Chapter 1
Introduction

Rassoul Yazdipour

... the theoretical firm is entrepreneurless...,

William J. Baumol (1968)

I ran across Baumol's famous statement as brought in above for the very first time almost 25 years ago. That thought not only stayed with me over the years, but it probably, and possibly subconsciously, might have even helped trigger the launching of the Academy of Entrepreneurial Finance 3 years later and the publication of the *Advances in Small Business Finance* (Yazdipour 1991) around the same time. So Baumol's point was a natural opener for this section; except for the fact that given the subtitle of the book – *behavioral finance* – it needed some added element. For this, I visited NASA's Knowledge Management site to see if I could improve upon the quotation; and there I saw Alan Kay's "It's the people, stupid." But that was telling the same thing except for saying it more emphatically. Then I remembered Herbert A. Simon's characterization of the version of economic rationality that he refers to as the Olympian model and then goes on to define it as a model that "... serves, perhaps, as a model of the mind of ..., but certainly not as a model of the mind of man" (Simon 1983). And that is exactly what I was looking for: economic rationality does not serve as a model of the mind of man!

Given above, there was no need to change anything; and now that we know about the theme behind the present book, let us continue with the rest of the introduction as follows.

A quick review of the literature on entrepreneurship and small and medium-sized enterprises (SMEs) reveals the existence of a relatively substantial body of knowledge on the subject matter. But a closer examination of the said literature demonstrates that a great majority of such work addresses issues that fall under the general classifications of management, strategy, and marketing; or what is collectively

R. Yazdipour (✉)
California State University, Fresno, CA, USA
and
The Academy of Entrepreneurial Finance, Los Angeles, CA, USA
e-mail: ryazdipour@aoef.org

R. Yazdipour, *Advances in Entrepreneurial Finance: With Applications from Behavioral Finance and Economics*, DOI 10.1007/978-1-4419-7527-0_1,

referred to as general entrepreneurship in the business administration discipline. Additionally, energized by Baumol's statement just mentioned in above, attempts have been made by some economists and entrepreneurship scholars, especially over the past 20 years or so, to develop "a theory of entrepreneurship." If and when developed, such theories should be able to explain the decision processes that are used in start-up entry and exit judgments, venture investment decisions, firm growth, and expansion evaluations; and at a macro level, economic development, growth, and job creation. However, "there continues to be a lack of consensus about what constitutes entrepreneurship theory and no generally accepted theory of entrepreneurship has emerged" (Alvarez 2005).

A similar review of the literature in the field of finance depicts even a less moving picture for both academics and practitioners. This especially is not encouraging for entrepreneurs and investors because the financial side of entrepreneurship – entrepreneurial finance – deals with the "life line of a business." Additionally, even if we consider one of the most elegant and most applied models that the standard finance theory has ever produced – the Agency Theory, and its main by-product, Financial Contracting – according to a very recent and comprehensive study, "...evidence supporting theory's predictions is mixed and weak" (Bitler et al. 2009).

In sum, both the financial economics and the general entrepreneurship disciplines have little to say regarding the dynamics of decision making and risk taking by entrepreneurs and venture capitalists (VCs). For example, and by design, the principal agent or agency theory cannot address the venture entry/exit decisions. And as we just saw in above, entrepreneurship researchers are still discussing "what constitutes entrepreneurship theory."

However, by building upon the new developments from the fields of cognitive psychology and neuroscience, we may be closer than ever to developing real-life risk/uncertainty models that could explain the decision processes that are used as road maps in key entrepreneurial actions. Entrepreneurial actions that require decision making under conditions of extreme risk and uncertainty; including entry/exist judgments, venture capital investment decisions, growth and expansion evaluations, economic development and job creation measures, etc. And this is exactly where the present book comes in. The volume presents the latest research and findings from the fields of finance, psychology, entrepreneurship, and neuroscience; and illustrates how such disciplines can shed new lights on the central questions in entrepreneurial finance and the related decision processes. What then follows is a brief overview of what is ahead in this volume.

1.1 Part I: The Theoretical Foundation of Entrepreneurial Finance

The chapters in the present volume are organized into three main sections. Part I contains contributions that address the theoretical foundation of entrepreneurship and entrepreneurial finance. The common thread in all five chapters in Part I is the risk and uncertainty phenomenon; as pricing of risk lies at the heart of the finance discipline, and naturally its offspring, entrepreneurial finance. Pricing of risk becomes even more of a challenge in entrepreneurial finance because the opaque nature of entrepreneurial and venture capital markets make the search for objective "information" extremely difficult, if not impossible. However, as you will see, especially in Chaps. 2 and 4, and this may sound counterintuitive to traditional financial economists, that type of "information" that is normally discussed and used in conjunction with Agency and Information Asymmetry models may not even be the major problem in the first place.

Chapter 2, written by this author, starts with discussing how some of the behavioral finance theories like the Prospect Theory and the Affect heuristic can be applied to the three central decision problems identified in entrepreneurial finance. In this respect, the author focuses his attention on one of the three key decision problems that has received very little to no attention at all in both the finance and economics literature – the actual launching of a new venture that requires two sets of decisions by both an entrepreneur and a VC. Chapter 2 then attempts to provide a risk model, though a rather preliminary one, to help better understand the elusive nature of risk and uncertainty in an entrepreneurial environment. The rationale for the work throughout Chap. 2, Part I, and the whole book can be summarized in the form of the following question: If we cannot define risk and uncertainty, and consequently cannot measure it in a meaningful way, then how can we ever price it?[1]

Chapter 3 addresses the shortcomings of the Agency Theory relative to the key issues in entrepreneurial finance. By adding a cognitive perspective (a cognitive conflict) to the theory, Wirtz further extends such a theory. Specifically, he argues that the principal agent's incentive and monitoring solutions fall short of explaining and predicting success for the involved ventures. He introduces a new agency-related cost that is incurred as a result of the theorized cognitive conflict, the "cognitive cost," and argues that such a cost should also be factored in along with the other traditional principal agent costs. "Such conflicts are not rooted in mutually inconsistent interests and thus cannot be tackled by the means of interest aligning alone, as the traditional agency theory would have it." Like all other contributions in this book, Wirtz's approach to making the Agency Theory and other traditional finance theories more relevant to common entrepreneurial finance problems is the type of research that our field needs more of.

[1]Needless to say that we may never be able to completely measure risk, especially in entrepreneurial environments. However, with our newly found knowledge from the fields of psychology and neuroscience, we should be able to increase our understanding of the risk phenomenon and consequently improve our decision making processes. This follows the line of reasoning that "understanding the problem is half of the solution."! And as you will further see, especially in Chap. 4 by Olsen, although we now have identified the two main sources of risk/uncertainty – the "real world" where actual transactions take place, and our psyche which defines our "real world" where different people have different pictures of their "real world" – we still are at the start of the road in making risk operational. And, by the way, this is where the real opportunity is for all types of future research and experimentation.

Olsen's Chap. 4 is truly a "game changer" especially when it comes to the analysis of risk and uncertainty – the central concern in any type of decision making and regardless of whether the underlying assets under consideration are publicly traded or privately managed. Olsen states that risk is not an evidence-based phenomenon like standard deviation, beta, or other variations thereof that can be measured and used in financial decision making.[2] Put differently, risk does not exist "out there" so that we (a) observe it, (b) measure and analyze it, and (c) use it as an input in our calculations. Olsen specifically states that, "all risk that is acted upon must be perceived risk because perception is based upon sensory data. We can only sense the 'real world' because we have no other way of being informed."[3] This effectively means risk is a phenomenon that is created in our psyche – the "in here" risk versus the "out there risk" phrase that at times we use in this book. Regarding entrepreneurial risk taking, Olsen states: "In entrepreneurial environments we see the full influence of the dual decision process and how it can lead to biased risk perceptions. Entrepreneurs don't appear to have significantly higher risk tolerance, they just judge the perceived risks to be less threatening."

Although the truth about risk most probably lies somewhere between "in here" (our psyche) and "other there" ("the real world"), but Olsen's well documented and precedence-setting contribution has not only catapulted discussions on risk to a new level, but it has also created a fresh research environment in which more realistic risk models can be conceived, developed, and tested. My rather preliminary attempt in Chap. 2 represents one such example.

Contributions of neuroscience to financial decision making, with direct implications for new research in entrepreneurial finance, is the subject of Chap. 5 by Konopka and Ackley. In this chapter, authors address key questions like: What is the nature of decision-making? How does the brain generate choice outputs? What are the inputs? What are the throughputs? How are decisions rendered? Moreover, the significance of Chap. 5 lies in the fact that it directly examines the two related issues of decision making and information processing in the brain. As the authors show, the brain operates at two different levels – the unconscious level and the conscious level. Although each brain pays attention to different types of information, but they both work in tandem to attend to different decision problems.

More importantly, "Applied neuroscience studies have identified a more elemental process which identifies the affective process where intuition is dominant."

---

[2]Needless to say that the standard finance theory definitions of risk have no relevance at all to a great majority of entrepreneurial finance problems where there is little or no historical data "out there" to be measured in the first place! For example, in case of start-ups, almost all the data are projected data and are contained in a highly guarded business plan, if such a business plan exists at all. In places like Silicon Valley, it is not unusual to hear that the back of a napkin being used as the initial business plan for an actual launch.

[3]See Chap. 4, Olsen.

This finding validates the important role that heuristics (mental shortcuts) play in complex decision environments. A key conclusion of the chapter is that "due to the existence of the dopaminergic system and the working of the dopamine neurons that give rise to reward prediction errors, different individuals like entrepreneurs and venture capitalists may perceive risk and uncertainty differently." Findings such as these are certainly critical to our better understanding of the *real sources of risk* and, consequently, our ability to better manage them.

Chapter 6 by Neace discusses decision making under conditions of uncertainty from a rather new perspective. By building upon the extant literature on risk, probability judgment, and choice, the chapter first identifies three main sources of uncertainty. They are, (a) incomplete information,(b) Inadequate understanding of the situation under consideration, and (c) undifferentiated (or undifferentiable) alternatives due to the complexity surrounding a given decision problem. Needless to say that all these three sources are present in almost all entrepreneurial endeavors.

The author then continues with proposing a "psychological discomfort" model to study risk and uncertainty. Neace hypothesizes that "uncertainty under any conceptualization has the potential to create a state of 'psychological discomfort,' and it is the need to reduce such discomfort that motivates the decision maker to move forward in the decision making process." Interestingly enough and from a neuroscientific perspective, Konopka and Ackley arrive at a similar hypothesis in Chap. 5.

1.2 Part II: Issues in Financing Start-ups and SMEs

The first paper in this section is written by Dunkelberg and Scott, and it focuses on the extent to which the landscape of SME financing has changed over the past 20 years. The chapter also offers a summary of the current state of knowledge about small firm financing. More importantly, by analyzing data from some of the key data sets in the USA – including National Federation of Business' Small Business Economic Trends Survey, the Kauffman Firm Survey and Panel Study of Entrepreneurial Dynamics, and the Board of Governor's Survey of Small Firm Finances – the authors examine some of the most important concerns in small firm financing. Such concerns include (a) small firm credit availability, (b) the effect of bank consolidation and changes in market structure on small firm access to credit, (c) the role of market structure on availability and pricing of small firm loans, and (d) the unique role of community banks in facilitating small firm finance. Of particular importance are the results of two 2008/2009 surveys that contradict the conventional wisdom that a pervasive small business credit access problem exists in the USA.

As we saw in our brief discussion earlier in this introduction, pricing risk lies at the heart of every financial decision; including those by entrepreneurs and venture capitalists. Also as we alluded to in above, and will see in much detail in part

I of this volume, individuals use a set of heuristics (simple rules, mental shortcuts) to make judgments in complex and uncertain situations. However, although heuristics can simplify decision problems and speed up decision making processes, but they can also lead to biases and errors in judgment. Consequently, knowledge about such biases, along with the ability to minimize their negative effects, becomes very valuable to every decision maker. By studying real-life decision making by a group of CME traders who specialize in agricultural contracts and risk their own capital, Mattos and Garcia provide a rather unique test of the Prospect Theory and its application to individual decision making. The experiment is unique because through their test they are able to measure the degree to which behavior can change in the presence of probability weighting – a process of Prospect Theory's evaluation mechanism. This is important because probability weighting is a decision point where all types of biases can enter the evaluation and judgment process.

Mattos and Garcia's contribution in Chap. 8 results in three findings. First, the decision makers, in this case the entrepreneurs/traders, exhibit probability weighting in their judgments. This is important because it supports Prospect Theory's premises regarding individual decision making. Second, probability weighting has substantial effect on behavior; another support for the theory. Third, and this is a major characteristic of entrepreneurs, risk-averse and risk-seeking behavior is more intense under conditions of uncertainty.

The last chapter in this section, Chap. 9, an empirical contribution by Shefrin, provides new insights into the psychological profiles of entrepreneurs. The motivation behind Shefrin's work can be summarized in the form of the following question. If entrepreneurs earn suboptimal risk-adjusted returns – working more and earning less than non-entrepreneurs as documented by prior research – then why do people choose to become entrepreneurs? This question is an important one for at least two main reasons. First, if a VC knows the true motivation(s) behind a given entrepreneur's business plan, then the decision-making process for the VC becomes much simpler as a careful screening of funding applicants will eliminate the less serious (lifestyle) entrepreneurs.[4] Second, and by the same token, if an entrepreneur knows about her own true motivation(s) behind the launching of a given venture, then she might be able to become more cognizant of the choices and resources available to her and consequently make more effective decisions.

By analyzing the data obtained from responses to four sets of carefully selected psychological surveys, Shefrin concludes that "Taken together, these findings suggest that the non-pecuniary benefits that entrepreneurs experience are substantial." Achieving greater control over their working environments is one such benefit for entrepreneurs that Shefrin discusses in the chapter.

[4]This may sound like the traditional finance's Signaling Theory, but the root causes in the present work are psychological.

1.3 Part III: Issues in Growth and Beyond

Chapter 10 by Constand and Yazdipour on firm failure has three distinct parts. First, the authors make a convincing argument that the literature on financial distress and failure prediction has totally ignored the *cause* of failure, the managers and owner-managers, and instead has almost exclusively focused on the *effect* of failure, the financial data. This is true for both large and small firms. Second, the authors conduct a comprehensive review of the literature on the topic, as well as the statistical tools that range from MDA and LOGIT and PROBIT models to even more sophisticated Artificial Intelligence (AI) and Expert Systems (ES) approaches. Not surprisingly, such review reveals that very little work has been done with SMEs in mind. Furthermore, the authors conclude that "it should be noted that despite all the sophisticated models and methodologies used in studies of the effects of firm failure, it is not surprising that a comprehensive review of the related literature concludes that after 35 years of academic research into bankruptcy prediction, there is 'no academic consensus as to the most useful method for predicting corporate bankruptcy". Third, Chap. 10 argues that especially in the case of entrepreneurial companies and SMEs, failure researchers need to focus their attention on the decision maker, the entrepreneur and/or the manager, in addition to the financial data. "Zeroing in on the commerce (effect) side of failure, as has been the case for almost all the research up to this point, only reveals to us a half-image of the foundation of the firm under consideration. To see the whole foundation we must also consider information about the decision maker and especially her/his predisposition toward the known heuristics."

After briefly reviewing the foundation of risk and uncertainty and discussing the evolutionary aspects of psychology, Sewell, in Chap. 10, details five key psychological phenomena that can lead to cognitive biases and error in judgment. They are: Overconfidence and Optimism, Representativeness, Availability, Under- and Over-Reaction, and Herding. He then discusses the effect of cognitive biases on both entrepreneurs and venture capitalists. Almost all of the five sets of biases listed and discussed play key roles in success or failure of especially entrepreneurs. Sewell concludes that "success of both entrepreneurs and VCs will likely depend on the degree to which their probabilistic reasoning is calibrated and the degree to which their decision making is consistent with the normative expected utility theory."

Finally, statistical databases for research on the financing of SMEs is the subject of Ou's contribution in Chap. 12. Availability of dependable data continues to be a major problem in entrepreneurial finance research; and here lies the importance of Chap. 12. Ou discusses all the major US databases that can be used for entrepreneurial finance research. He also provides additional comments on the strengths and/or weaknesses of each of the six major databases detailed in the chapter.

Included in Chap. 12 are, The Kauffman Firm Survey (KFS), Panel Study of Entrepreneurial Dynamics (PSED II), and Survey of Business Owners (SBO) 2002.

Moreover, detailed information is provided in the chapter on the Survey of Small Business Finances (NSSBF, 1987 and 1993 and SSBF, 1998), Loans to small businesses by depository institutions, Consumer Finance Survey (by the Board of Governors of the Federal Reserve System), Tax return data from the Statistics of Income (SOI) division of the Internal Revenue Service (IRS), and The National Federation of Independent Business (NFIB) studies of Credit, Banks, and Small Business, a survey of a special group of small firms – the members of the NFIB.

At the end, and before we proceed to the rest of the book, I have to say that although the focus of the present volume is on the financial aspects of the entrepreneurial companies, but one can easily extend the discussions presented especially in Part I to larger business entities and even the publicly traded companies. This should come natural because regardless of the size of a given firm, the decision makers are *individuals* with "*... a bunch of emotions, prejudices, and twitches... (who) do not necessarily have a complete portrait of themselves, warts and all, in their own mind, but they do have the ability to stop abruptly when their intuition and what is happening Out There are suddenly out of kilter.*"[5]

References

Alvarez, S.A. 2005. Two theories of entrepreneurship: Alternative assumptions and the study of entrepreneurial action. Max Planck Institute Discussion Papers on Entrepreneurship, Growth and d Pubic Policy 19, Jena, Germany, p. 2.

Baumol, W.J. 1968. Entrepreneurship in economic theory. *American Economic Review* 58(2): 68.

Bitler, M.P., T.J. Moskowitz, and A. Vissing-Jorgensen. 2009. Why do entrepreneurs hold large ownership shares? Testing agency theory using entrepreneur effort and wealth. Working Paper. Graduate School of Business, University of Chicago, p. 1.

Simon, H.A. 1983. *Reason in human affairs*, 34. Stanford: Stanford University Press.

Slovic, P. 1972. Psychological study of human judgment. *Journal of Finance* 27(4): 779–799.

Yazdipour, R. 1991. *Advances in small business finance*. Dordrecht: Kluwer Academic.

[5]Adam Smith, *The Money Game*- as quoted in Slovic (1972).

Part I
Theoretical Foundation

Chapter 2
A Behavioral Finance Approach to Decision Making in Entrepreneurial Finance

Rassoul Yazdipour

By 'uncertain' knowledge, let me explain,... We simply do not know.

J.M. Keynes (1937)

Humans have an additional capability that allows them to alter their environment as well as respond to it. This capacity both creates and reduces risk.

Paul Slovic (1987)

All risk that is acted upon must be perceived risk because perception is based upon sensory data. We can only sense the 'real world' because we have no other way of being informed.

Robert Olsen (2010)

Understanding a problem is half of the solution

Unknown

Abstract Three central decisions in entrepreneurship and entrepreneurial finance – entry/seed funding, financing/investment, and growth/exit – are discussed and case is made for applying the behavioral finance theories and concepts to better understand the involved decision processes, and consequently, to help improve the decision-making process for both entrepreneurs and venture capitalists. The behavioral finance approach is important because the traditional finance has remained silent on the first issue, and the Agency Theory (financial contracting), which is effectively the only theory that is applicable to issues in entrepreneurial finance, has produced mixed empirical results. (See for example Bitler et al. [Bitler MP, Moskowitz T J, Vissing-Jorgensen A (2009) Why do entrepreneurs hold large ownership shares? Testing agency theory using entrepreneur effort and wealth. Working Paper. Graduate School of Business, University of Chicago].) Attempts are also made in this chapter to

R. Yazdipour (✉)
California State University, Fresno, CA, USA
and
The Academy of Entrepreneurial Finance, Los Angeles, CA, USA
e-mail: ryazdipour@aoef.org

R. Yazdipour, *Advances in Entrepreneurial Finance: With Applications from Behavioral Finance and Economics*, DOI 10.1007/978-1-4419-7527-0_2,

introduce some new concepts – "Perception Asymmetry," "Resident Risk," and a preliminary behavioral risk framework – that as complements to the existing constructs could be used in discussions on decision making under risk and uncertainty. Although the focus is on individual decision making under highly uncertain entrepreneurial environments, the suggested risk framework and the related discussions can be extended to decision making in other uncertain environments.

2.1 Introduction

In general, there are three types of problems that require decision making on part of the entrepreneurs and investors. They are

1. Entry/Seed Funding Decisions
2. Financing/Investment Decisions, and
3. Growth/Exit Decisions

Given our approach in this chapter is on the application of theory, I have stated the above problems in such a way that they involve two decision makers that are needed to conclude a transaction. Throughout this writing, such two decision makers are entrepreneurs and investors, also known as venture capitalists or VCs.

Additionally, regardless of one's association with either of the two finance paradigms, traditional finance or behavioral finance, uncertainty, and return remain to be the determining factors in all the three decision problems listed in above.[1]

Moreover, although the traditional finance and economic theories have had some successes in providing some solutions to the last two problems, they have had little to say on how entrepreneurs decide to start a new venture and how investors select such ventures for investment purposes.[2] By design, the dominant traditional theory, the Agency Theory, cannot make any predictions regarding firm entry or exit issues. Furthermore, such paucity of research on the subject should not be surprising at all because in the standard finance and economic theory, problems have to be definable in mathematical terms to be considered for any type of analysis and application. The rational construct assumes that economic agents – investors, managers of all kind, and entrepreneurs – are "capable of understanding vastly complex puzzles and conduct

[1]In this chapter, and especially where both traditional and behavioral finance paradigms are discussed, we intentionally use the terms risk and uncertainty interchangeably. As will be seen soon, some leading scholars have shifted the whole notion and source of risk and uncertainty away from evidence-based risk, as defined by statistical tools, to perception-based uncertainty. Chapter 4, written by Professor Olsen, mainly deals with the latter notion of risk.

[2]Two points should be mentioned in here:

(a) I use the word "some" because as will be seen in this writing, traditional finance models such as Agency Theory continue to have their own shortcomings in explaining and predicting behavior. For details see Bitler et al. 2009 and Kaplan and Stromberg (2002); and

(b) On related research we have to mention Camerer and Lovallo's work (1999) where they use overconfidence to explain failure.

endless instantaneous optimizations" (Montier 2006, p. xiii). Also the standard finance theory has built its whole foundation after a human brain that in H.A. Simon's words "... serves, perhaps, as a model of the mind of God, but certainly not as a model of the mind of man" (Simon 1983, p 34). Therefore, to the traditional financial economists, uncertainty – a truly *perceptual* and *personal* phenomenon – does not fall in such a category and therefore cannot be operationalized in any "meaningful" way.[3]

On the other hand, over the past 30 years or so psychologists, and more recently neuroscientists, have helped us to better understand the human decision-making processes; and more specifically, how we as individuals perceive risk and uncertainty and how we take the required actions at the judgment time.[4] Scientific breakthroughs in those fields have also given rise to the new subfield of behavioral finance.[5] It is through such behavioral lenses that we believe attempts should be made to address the three central questions listed in above. Our main focus in this chapter involves the application of behavioral finance and economic theories to the least explored of such three decisions; that is, the Entry/Seed Funding decisions. Given we first need to communicate with each other in this rather unfamiliar territory, attempts are made in this chapter to introduce some new concepts – which include "Perception Asymmetry," "Resident Risk," and a behavioral risk model – that as complements to the existing concepts and tools could be used in any discussion on decision making under risk and uncertainty.

Section 2 provides a brief background on the decision problems that entrepreneurs and their financial backers, venture capitalists or VCs, face in the course of their business. Section 3 discusses some new concepts along with an attempt to provide a preliminary behavioral risk model; believing that if we better understand the uncertainties that are involved in and around the problems, we will have a better chance of providing more effective solutions to them. Section 4 summarizes the chapter and provides some suggestions for future research.

2.2 The Entry/Seed Funding Decisions: Problems and Existing Solutions

2.2.1 Central Questions in a Launch Decision

As said in above, our main focus here is on the application of behavioral finance and economics theories to entry/seed funding decisions – jointly defined as launch decisions. Such joint decisions involve two separate but related decisions by both

[3]For detailed discussion on this issue see Chap. 4, Olsen.

[4]The most authoritative work advanced in this regard is Kahneman and Tversky's Prospect Theory which is presented as an alternative to the Expected Utility theory and is outlined in this section and the Appendix. Another equally significant work is Slovic et al.'s (2002) and Finucane et al. (2000) Affect Heuristic which is outlined in this section and the Appendix.

[5]For a comprehensive review of the key issues in Behavioral Finance, see Richard H. Thaler's *Advances in Behavioral Finance*, Vol I and II (Thaler 1993 and 2005).

an entrepreneur and a VC. The reason for discussing and analyzing the two decisions together is a practical necessity. That is, the decision to enter a business by an entrepreneur alone does not mean much; unless, she can convince a VC to fund her start-up. With this in mind, there are two central questions that both entrepreneurs and VCs face in a launch decision.

(a) What are the decision processes for entrepreneurs in a launch decision, and what are the decision criteria in that regard?
(b) What are the decision processes for venture capitalists in investing in a launch, and what are the decision criteria in that regard?

2.2.2 *Markets for Venture Capital*

In free enterprise systems, the role of efficient capital markets is to facilitate the flow of funds between the suppliers and the demanders of capital. Well-functioning capital markets also ensure that funds are raised and invested at competitive and reasonable rates. Operational transparency is among the most important requirements for the smooth working of such markets. Efficient market mechanisms certainly support innovation, job creation, economic development, and business growth. Inefficient capital markets will have the opposite effects. In the US and other free market economies, transparent and public capital markets, which serve large corporations have played such a role with unprecedented success in history.

However, markets for venture capital, broadly defined in this chapter as those markets that serve the capital needs of small firms ranging from start-ups to pre-IPO companies, are certainly not among the well-functioning capital markets. This is true even in the USA, the birthplace of venture capital. The opaqueness of these markets is the main reason behind their operational inefficiency. Naturally, such inefficiency translates into increased levels of risk and uncertainty, and consequently increased costs of doing business for small and entrepreneurial companies, which such markets serve.

2.2.3 *Traditional Finance and Economics' Response to Launch Decisions*

To resolve the problems that arise in the opaque venture capital markets that we just described, traditional finance theory has offered a relatively large body of literature and theories that are based on the classical Principal-Agent and Information Asymmetry theories. Under one version of the Information Asymmetry (IA) for example, the opaqueness of the IPO markets is addressed and a solution like Signaling Theory is provided. Other IA problems addressed range from corporate debt financing to dividend policy and corporate takeovers.[6] Under Principal-Agent, or Agency Theory (AT), the presumed conflict of interest between owner–managers and investors is addressed[7] (this is also called "interest asymmetry") and "optimum" financial contracts are offered to compensate for the assumed conflicts of interest and other additional risks and uncertainties.[8]

However, even with so much work done in the area of financial contracting, a recent study (Bitler et al. 2009) states, "an extensive theoretical literature examines the principal-agent problem, ... yet, evidence supporting theory's predictions is mixed and weak." Besides, Treating entrepreneurs as agents and venture capitalists as principals, as it is the case in AT, is a questionable start because by definition entrepreneurs are the opposite of agents who are good at taking orders. Entrepreneurs on the other hand are independent individuals, again by definition, because they want to be their "own bosses"! In fact, a great majority of entrepreneurs cannot even work within a corporate structure just like a regular employee or an agent.

And this now takes us to the main topic of this chapter as discussed in the following section.

2.3 A Behavioral Approach to Decision Making in Entrepreneurial Finance

The approach that we have taken in this chapter and especially this section is based on the belief that if we can better understand the types of risks and uncertainties that are involved in and around the entrepreneurial finance problems listed at the beginning of the chapter, we will have a better chance of understanding the related decision processes. Moreover, we also believe that such an understanding alone would bring more transparency for all parties in any given transaction, like a financial contract, and consequently, improve their decision processes. However, the attempt will not end here as we also try to put together "pieces of the risk puzzle" and see if a meaningful risk framework can emerge for any future use and analysis. With these in mind, we now continue with such a plan and as follows.

[6]For a literature review and a related test of the theory see Cai et al. (2007).

[7]For a good discussion and a literature review on Agency Theory and an empirical test of the said theory using data from the VC market, see Kaplan and Stromberg (2002).

[8]If there is one branch of standard finance that has relevance to the world of entrepreneurs and venture capitalists, it must be the financial contracting branch.

2.3.1 Perception Asymmetry

We introduce the Perception Asymmetry as a counterpart to standard finance theory's Information Asymmetry as described in below. But before defining and further discussing the proposed imbalance, it would be helpful if we refresh our memory about the Prospect Theory and the affect heuristic, which are discussed in more details in the Appendix.

According to Prospect Theory (PT), there are two distinct phases to each decision-an initial phase called editing or framing; and a second phase called evaluation phase. The editing phase includes a number of operations that simplify decision problems before they are sent for evaluation. Options are evaluated via the value function so that a final decision can be made regarding the decision problems under consideration.

According to Affect theory, subjective impressions of "goodness" or "badness" can act as a heuristic, capable of producing fast perceptual judgments. For example, stocks perceived as "good" are judged to have *low* risks and *high* returns and stocks perceived as "bad" are judged to have *low* returns and *high* risks.

By building upon the Prospect Theory and the affect heuristic as just mentioned, and using our example of entrepreneurs and venture capitalists for illustration, we propose that the perceptions of both entrepreneurs and venture capitalists, and consequently their judgments, will be shaped by the triple effects of:

1. The Prospect Theory's editing operations, which include Coding, Combination, Segregation, and Cancelation,
2. The Prospect Theory's value function where "probability weights" are assigned, and
3. The affect heuristic's capability of producing perceptual judgments.

In addition to above, the working of the brain would add the fourth effect; but for now, we will limit our coverage to the key psychological phenomena.[9]

We now define Perception Asymmetry as the situation under which a perception gap exists for at least one party to a transaction. More specifically, in case of our present discussion, we define Perception Asymmetry (PA) as the situation under which a perception gap exists between an entrepreneur and a venture capitalist (VC) regarding the same business opportunity, its gain and loss potentials, and consequently the opportunity's perceived value. Furthermore, the only situation in which such a gap will not exist is when both the entrepreneur and the VC in question share the same psyche; something that is not physically possible.

---

[9]I am not specifically discussing other heuristics and biases for two main reasons. First, the Prospect Theory and Affect cover most, if not all, of such heuristics and biases. Second, given this is a preliminary framework, I'd rather to stay on the central issues to prevent any confusion. For detailed discussion of these biases see the Appendix.

We suspect the proposed imbalance would help create a better understanding for both parties regarding each other's views on a transaction like a seed funding deal. Such an understanding may minimize the Perception Asymmetry and consequently bring the parties closer to a mutually beneficial decision and ultimately conclusion of a deal.

2.3.2 *Resident Risks and Behavioral Risks: Toward a Behavioral Risk Model*

Some behavioral finance scholars, especially Slovic and Olsen, have advocated that risk is not "something out there." By that, they mean risk is not an evidence-based phenomenon like standard deviation, beta, or other variations thereof that can be measured and used in financial decision making.[10] Put differently, risk does not exist "out there" so that we (a) observe it, (b) measure and analyze it, and (c) use it as an input in our Expected Utility (EU)–based calculations. Slovic (1987) attributes business risk to individual survival risk where he says, "Humans have an additional capability that allows them to alter their environment as well as respond to it. This capacity both *creates* and reduces risk" (Slovic 1987, p 280 [Emphasis is mine]). He further adds that the "concept risk means different things to different people" (Slovic 1987, p 283). Moreover, as we will see in this chapter, affect plays one of the most important roles in the perception of risk by individuals.[11] For example, if a person has a positive affect regarding a given venture, she/he may perceive the risk in that venture much less than the risks perceived by other individuals with a lower level of affect for the same exact venture under otherwise the same exact circumstances.

Olsen specifically states that, "all risk that is acted upon must be perceived risk because perception is based upon sensory data. We can only sense the 'real world' because we have no other way of being informed."[12] This effectively means risk is a phenomenon that is created in our psyche- the "in here" risk versus the "out there risk" phrase that we use in this chapter.

However, and especially from a more applied point of view, we argue that risks and uncertainties are not completely perceived "in here" either (in our psyche). This can be seen clearly when we break down the notion of total risk and uncertainty

[10]Needless to say that the standard finance theory definitions of risk have no relevance at all to a great majority of entrepreneurial finance problems where there is little or no historical data "out there" to be measure in the first place! For example, in case of startups almost all the data are projected data and are contained in a highly guarded Business Plan.

[11]According to Olsen, culture, including trust, is another source of risk. However, in this writing we will limit our discussions to the factors stated in above.

[12]See Chap. 4, Olsen.

into its components and discuss "Resident Risks" below. We then believe the truth about the sources of risks probably lie somewhere between "out there" and "in here." To get our discussion started, we define risk and uncertainty as follows.

$$\text{Total (Perceived) Risk and Uncertainty} = \text{Resident Risks} + \text{or} - \text{" Behavioral Risks "}$$

2.3.2.1 Resident Risk: Risk as the "Other Side of a Business Opportunity Coin"

First, note that due to the nature of the topic, I use the terms risk and uncertainty interchangeably throughout this writing. Second, for simplicity and illustration, I use the decision to launch a brand new business venture, a business opportunity, as an example. Now think of "Resident Risks" as the type of risks that actually *resides* in, or are native to, a given business opportunity; without which the opportunity would be riskless. (Riskless in the sense of a short-term US Treasury Bill.) In other words, in our example, risk is the "other side of a *business opportunity coin.*"

I especially use the coin analogy to make the point that resident risk (RR) automatically comes with any selected and implemented business opportunity; just like throwing a coin that comes with it known odds of success/fail. Of course, measuring success/failure rates in business is much more complicated; but still doable. Another analogy for the definition is water and the wetness of water. That is, one cannot exist without the other; and you know if you throw yourself in the water, you will get wet, and the odds are 100% in your favor! Just like tossing a coin with well-defined outcomes, we can also define the possible outcomes in a launch decision. For example, success can mean reaching $5 M sales in three years and failure can mean not reaching that sales threshold by the third year.

Additionally, dissecting Total Perceived Risk as such has another theoretical and empirical advantage. It allows us to have a significant portion of the total risk measurable and concentrate on its elusive component – the behavioral risk component.

2.3.2.2 Determinants of Resident Risk

In anticipation of making the resident risk component operational and consequently measurable, we can proceed as follows. Imagine yourself as an entrepreneur who has not only found a unique business opportunity, but has also developed a non-working prototype of her product and wants to launch the business by first perfecting the prototype and then mass producing and selling the finished product. She also needs capital to do all the above. You may also imagine yourself at the other side of the transaction and as a venture capitalist who is considering funding such an entrepreneur. Given this background, we can list and define the following factors as the key determinants of residual risk.

1. Commercialization and Technology risk factor – the risk of taking an opportunity or a prototype and turning it into a fully functional product or service that consumers will pay to use it,
2. Market risk factor – whether or not a profitable and sustainable market will emerge for the envisioned product/service,
3. Management risk factor – whether or not the entrepreneur behind the opportunity and her team will succeed in executing the envisioned business strategies
4. Financing risk factor – whether or not the entrepreneur and her team can raise the needed capital on a timely basis to execute the envisioned business strategies, and finally,
5. Macro risk factors – including regulatory risks, environmental risks, etc.

The above risks certainly exit "out there" in and around *any* business opportunity. However, they do *not* exist in vacuum as there must be a real asset in the physical world to contain such native risks. And that is exactly why I refer collectively to these risks as resident risks.[13]

2.3.2.3 Behavioral Risks

The "Behavioral Risk" component is mainly shaped by the editing, evaluating, and affect processes as described earlier in this chapter. As shown by the risk equation, behavioral risks can either increase or decrease the total risk. The increase part seems very intuitive by the standards of the traditional finance; although that is not the case for the decrease part as it can easily be ignored as a behavioral "anomaly"! To a behavioral economist, however, the decrease is a result of the affect heuristic.

Furthermore, according to the proposed risk framework and the theories behind it – Prospect Theory and affect heuristic – the behavioral risk portion of the total risk is our own creation. In other words, when we consider a set of opportunities for evaluation and final selection, we automatically, and possibly unknowingly, *construct* a portion of the risks that involve all those opportunities. Given the current state of brain technology, this is the type of risk that is very hard, if not impossible, to quantify.

2.3.2.4 Behavioral Risk Processes

Although discussion on making the behavioral risk component operational is well above and beyond the present writing, however, we can still list and describe the four underlying processes that produce it as follows.

[13]Resident Risks can become *the only* risks, and therefore the only *"real" risks*, if we take all the heuristics out of the simple equation suggested in this section. In such a case, Total Risk is equivalent to the Total Risk under standard finance paradigm, and measurable. But again, to take the behavioral risk component out is equivalent to assuming a "mind of God" for a normal earth-bound human being.

1. Framing processes
2. Evaluation processes
3. Affective processes, and
4. Other non-Affect processes like Overconfidence, Availability, Anchoring, etc.

All the above processes are as described in this chapter.

2.3.3 Individual Decision Making in Highly Uncertain Entrepreneurial Settings: A Discussion and Some Final Thoughts

By building upon the Prospect Theory and affect heuristic, we argued how the editing and evaluation phases, coupled with affect's capability of producing perceptual judgments, can influence the perception and judgment of the entrepreneurs and VCs regarding the business opportunities that they consider in the course of their businesses. Moreover, by building upon Slovic and Olsen's notion of risk that all risks are perceptual, and introducing the real-life aspects of risk and risk taking into the discussion, we proposed a two-component risk formula that contained both objective and subjective elements of risk.

Based on what was said above, and given my own personal experiences as a real-life entrepreneur, investor, and consultant to hundreds of entrepreneurs in California, we argue that an entrepreneur:

(a) Bases her final decision mainly on the perceived gains and losses of the venture opportunity that she has eventually selected as a result of her search for similar opportunities; and more importantly,
(b) The finalized and selected business opportunity *already* has a level of risk and uncertainty residing in it that the entrepreneur feels comfortable about.

Proposition "a" is based on the Prospect Theory; and proposition "b" is based on both the now familiar affect heuristic and the "Homeostasis Principle," or "Comfort Hypothesis," as mentioned in below.

Moreover, proposition "b" is a simple extension of the two-component risk equation just mentioned and discussed in details earlier. Built in proposition "b" is the observation that in the real life, business risks automatically come with business opportunities; just like the coin toss analogy.[14]

More importantly, we may already have support from the fields of psychology and neuroscience especially for the more significant proposition "b." Specifically, on the neuroscience side, Konopka and Ackley (2010) state that "actions are initiated

[14]Another fact regarding risk taking in real life goes like this, and every honest venture consultant will tell the same to her/his clients: "The only way to *know the risk* is to *take the risk*!"

to maintain an individually defined level of homeostasis. In other words, one may try to answer questions such as: What is my level of discomfort?" And on the psychology side and along the same line, Neace (2010) argues that "… uncertainty creates a state of psychological discomfort that motivates the decision maker to move the decision from a state of uncertainty toward a state of certainty in order to reduce the discomfort created …."[15]

2.4 Summary and Some Suggestions for Future Research

In this chapter, we discussed three central decisions in entrepreneurial finance and made the case for applying the behavioral finance theories and concepts to better understand these decisions and the underlying processes. We also introduced some new concepts such as "Perception Asymmetry," "resident risk," and a preliminary behavioral risk framework to further facilitate discussions on related risks and uncertainties. This was done with the belief that if we can better understand the issues, we would have a better chance of improving the decision-making processes.

Although the discussions in this chapter did not lead to any specific model, we certainly hope the theory- and experience-based thoughts and concepts provide a starting point for future theoretical and empirical works on the topic. What follows are some suggestions for future research relative to the stated problems.

(a) One immediate and relatively easy-to-implement work is to survey a group of entrepreneurs and see if they behave as hypothesized in this chapter. My instinct and first-hand experiences tell me that they do; however, I never conducted a formal study.
(b) The same exact experiment in above can be conducted in case of VCs. Again, my view is that VCs also behave as proposed in this chapter; but this needs to be verified too.
(c) Related to item above and as compared with entrepreneurs, I suspect VC's Total Risk is much influenced by the resident risks than the behavioral risks. In other words, VCs are expected to be less affective when it comes to investment decisions. On the other hand and by definition,[16] entrepreneurs behave the opposite way; that is, more affectively.
(d) Finally, and this is where the real challenge is, work can be done to make the proposed risk equation operational so that it could be tested for further analysis and possible use in decision making. Selection and/or development of a suitable

[15] See Konopka and Ackley, Chap. 5, and Neace, Chap. 6, both in this book.

[16] This follows from the fact that entrepreneurs are passionate individuals. Such notion of passion is consistent with the use of the term "baby" in the English language to describe one's project or initiative. Moreover, passion is a key factor that experienced VCs look for in an entrepreneur when they consider different venture proposals.

methodology that can process both objective and subjective risks and uncertainties is a first major step in such direction. A possible starting point on methodology is Lewis' (1980) "The Principal Principle"[17]

2.5 Appendix 1: The Prospect Theory

According to the Prospect Theory (PT), there are two distinct phases to each decision – an initial phase called editing or framing; and a second phase called evaluation phase.

2.5.1 *The Editing or Framing Phase*

According to Kahneman and Tversky (KT) (1979) and Tversky and Kahneman (1981), framing effects in decision situations arise when *different* imagery and descriptions of the *same problem* highlight different aspects of the decision outcomes. Choices often depend on the *manner in which alternatives are framed (described) and presented to us;* something not allowed in the Expected Utility (EU) theory. The role of the initial editing phase is to organize the possible options for the purpose of simplifying the evaluation phase and consequently making it easier to select the final option that has the highest value to the decision maker.

In other words, framing leads to a representation of the acts, outcomes, and contingencies that are associated with a particular choice problem like the choice to pursue a specific venture opportunity by an entrepreneur. Moreover, often the entrepreneur does not have the basic information about different choices available to her/him; or at least all the available choices are not that clear to him. In such cases, she has to actually figure out and possibly *mentally construct* what her options are; a process that is referred to as the *Opportunity Recognition* phase in the traditional entrepreneurship literature and practice.[18]

---

[17]I want to thank Martin Sewell for suggesting Lewis' work.

[18]In a working paper on this topic I argue that by mentally constructing different opportunities and in preparation for the next phase of evaluation – where she/he select a specific opportunity for starting a business based on the chosen opportunity – the entrepreneur is effectively, knowingly or knowingly, creating the matching risk that she/he will be comfortable with when and if the envisioned venture is actually launched; pending the needed financing. Otherwise, she/he will not take the next steps of actually starting the venture, including starting his search for a financial backer. Moreover, such constructed and perceived risk – which is unique to the entrepreneur behind the given opportunity – will be discussed along with the *real* uncertainty that certainly exists in the selected opportunity; the risk that is referred to in the literature as "risk out there." For the lack of a better term, I refer to this "risk out there" as the "resident risk" or the risk that resides in any new opportunity; as there is no such a thing as riskless opportunity. I will also argue that the new term (new as far as I know) is not a tautological argument as it is the next natural step in better understanding how at least entrepreneurs make decisions in the real life and how their financiers would have their own perceived risk which will be different from the one seen by the entrepreneurs and possibly different from the "resident risk" or "native risk." Finally we hypothesize that the VC's envisioned/perceived risk is closer to the real risk- the "resident risk" or "native risk" – than that of the entrepreneur.

2.5.2 Editing Operations

The editing phase also involves the application of a number of operations by the decision maker as briefly outlined in below.

Coding. Coding is simply the categorization of the outcomes in terms of gains and losses; and not as final states of wealth, which is an underlying assumption used by the EU model. Furthermore, gains and losses are defined relative to the status quo or the reference point. Ruling out any "psychic income" for entrepreneurs and VCs, the reference point for them corresponds to their current assets or their current value of their portfolios. Moreover, by moving the reference point, outcomes may be categorized.

Combination. This refers to the tendency to add together the probabilities of choices that present identical outcomes. For example, the prospect (500,.25; 500,.25) is reduced to (500,.50) to facilitate evaluation.

Segregation. This is where the riskless component of a prospect is separated from its risky component.

Cancelation. This is the tendency to discard common outcome-probability choices. For example, and using KT's example, the choices (200, 0.2; 100, 0.5; 20, 0.3) and (200, 0.2; 300, 0.4; –50, 0.4) can be reduced to choices (100, 0.5; 20, 0.3) and (300, 0.4; –50, 0.4).

2.5.3 The Evaluation Phase

A second phase where acts, related contingencies, and outcomes for each decision choice are evaluated. In this phase, the edited prospects, such as business opportunities, are evaluated and the business opportunity with the highest value is selected. The value function as formulated in what follows will be used to assign values to each prospect or opportunity.

To see this, consider a gamble with two outcomes: x with probability p, and y with probability $1-p$; where $x \geq 0 \geq y$. Also assume an initial level of wealth (W) is our reference point in this example. According to PT, value of the gamble (or prospect) is $V = \pi(p)v(x) + \pi(1-p)v(y)$; where π is a probability-weighing function and v is value of an outcome. KT's value function is shown in Fig. 2.1.

The value in PT is defined in terms of expected *gains and losses* and not in terms of expected *level of final* wealth. Furthermore, the probability-weighting function $\pi(p)$ is not the same thing as original probability p; as can be seen from Fig. 2.2 that follows. The probability-weighting function transforms original probabilities into subject probabilities that follow a nonlinear pattern as shown in Fig. 2.2.

2.6 Appendix 2: The Affect Heuristic

According to Finucane et al., the affect heuristic refers to the way in which subjective impressions of "goodness" or "badness" can act as a heuristic, capable of producing fast perceptual judgments, and also systematic biases. For example, as Ganzach has demonstrated,

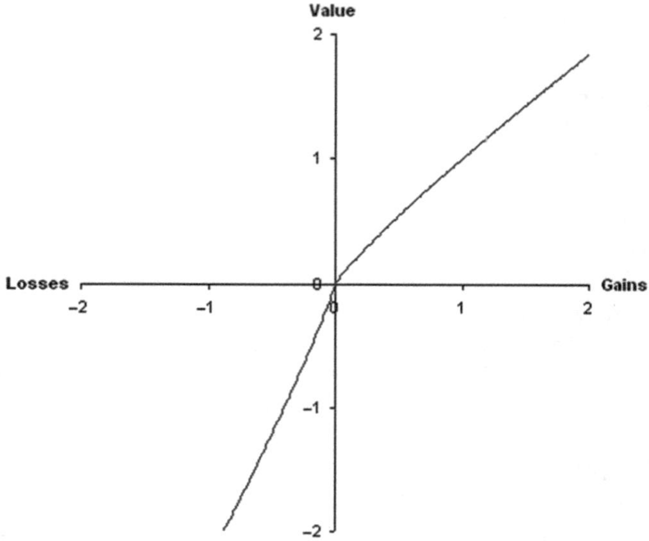

Fig. 2.1 A hypothetical value function. *Note:* The value function is defined by gains and losses on deviations from a reference point, where the function is concave for gains and convex for losses. This function is steeper for losses than gains (loss aversion). This means a loss causes a greater feeling of pain than a joy caused by the same amount of gain (Reproduced with permission from Martin Sewell and behaviuoralfinance.net)

- Stocks perceived as "good" were judged to have *low* risks and *high* return
- Stocks perceived as "bad" were judged to have *low* return and *high* risks

That is, for *unfamiliar* stocks, perceived risk and perceived return were *negatively* correlated, as predicted by the affect heuristic. For *familiar* stocks, perceived risk and perceived return were positively correlated; riskier stocks were expected to produce higher returns, as predicted by ordinary economic theory.

2.7 Appendix 3: Other Heuristics and Biases

When faced with huge amount of data and information and an array of decision problems, people do not do and in fact are not humanly capable of doing the rather complex optimization calculations that are expected of them under standard finance theory. Instead, they rely on a limited number of cognitive strategies or heuristics that will simplify the complex scenarios faced by them in making decisions. We can think of heuristics as information-processing shortcuts that mainly result from one's experiences in a field of work. Of course, such simplifying shortcuts are productive, until we consider that heuristics, by nature are imperfect, and, consequently, will result in *biases and errors*.

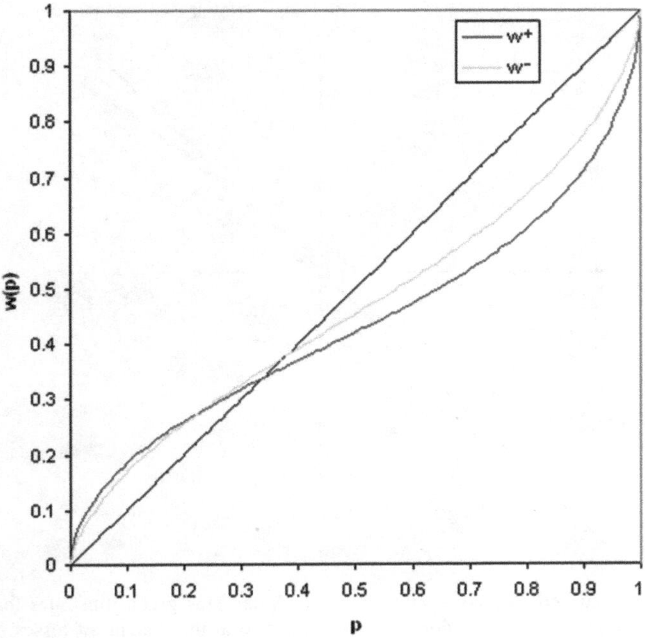

Fig. 2.2 A hypothetical probability-weighting function for gains ($w+$) and losses ($w-$). *Note:* According to Prospect Theory, a probability p has a decision weight $w(p)$. Probability-weighting functions overweight low probabilities and underweight high probabilities (Reproduced with permission from Martin Sewell and behaviuoralfinance.net)

We furthermore have to add that, in traditional theory, unsystematic biases are expected to average out at the market level and consequently have no effect on asset prices. However, the behavioralists argue that both heuristics and biases are in fact *systematic*, thereby potentially lasting for long periods of time and affecting prices accordingly.

Tversky and Kahneman (1974), as well as other new researchers, have brought to the attention of the finance professionals a number of such systematic biases as follows (Fig. 2.3).

2.7.1 Representativeness (Similarity)

According to TK (Tversky and Kahneman 1974), many of the probabilistic questions that people are concerned with can be characterized by, "What is the probability that object A belongs to class B? What is the probability that event A originates from process B? etc." To answer questions like these, people utilize the representative heuristics, in which probabilities are evaluated by the degree to which A resembles B.

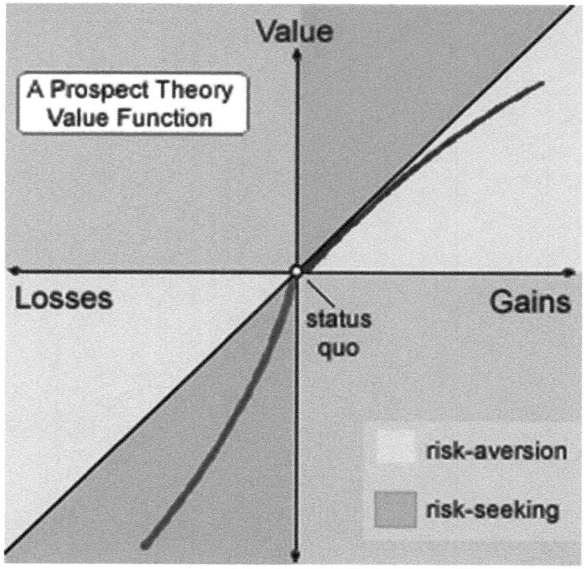

Fig. 2.3 Kahneman and Tversky's value function. *Note:* This graph illustrates that people are generally risk averse in the gains domain but loss averse in the domain of losses. Furthermore, losses cause greater feelings of pain than joys caused by the same amount of gain (Courtesy of Professor Ralph Byrns)

For example, when A is highly representative of B, the probability that A originates form B is judged to be high.

In such cases, the representative heuristic assists in evaluating the *probabilities* dealing with objects or processes A and B. As an example, when A is highly representative of B, the probability that A originates from B is judged to be high; and so forth. The problem is that representativeness (similarity) *should not* affect the judgment of probability. What *should be* considered in the judgment to probability is "prior probability" or "base rate." However, the latter is not the case in practice. (violation of Bayes' rule).

The Representativeness Heuristic in a Nutshell

- The "representativeness heuristic" is a built-in feature of the brain for producing rapid probability judgments, rather than a consciously adopted procedure.
- As humans, we are not aware of substituting judgment of *representativeness* for judgment of *probability*.

2.7.2 Availability

To understand this judgment heuristic, we just need to know that people disproportionately recall the salient events, those that are very recent and/or those that are/were emotionally involved with especially in the recent past. The more salient an event is, the more likely the probability that we can recall that event. The result is that this sort of bias prevents us from considering other potential and related outcomes. For example, one may assess the risk of getting mugged in New York City (NYC) by recalling such incidences among friends and family. Under availability, people search their memories for relevant information.

The problem, however, is that not all memories are equally retrievable/available and this leads to error in judgment. For example, more recent incidences and more salient events (getting mugged in NYC) will weigh more heavily and will lead to prediction biases and distort the judgment or estimate.

The Availability Heuristic in a Nutshell: Biases implicit in the availability heuristic affect estimates of risk.

2.7.3 Anchoring, Adjustment, and Contamination

According to TK (1974), when forming estimates and predictions, people usually start with some initial arbitrary value and adjust away from it. Also, people make estimates by starting from an initial value that is adjusted to yield the final answer. The initial value may be suggested by the formulation of the problem or it may be the result of a partial calculation. Regardless, TK argue that "adjustments are typically insufficient," and "*Different starting points yield different estimates which are biased toward the initial value.*" This is anchoring. Anchoring happens when the starting point is given to the subject; as well as when the subject bases her estimate on the result of some incomplete computation.

The Anchoring Heuristic in a Nutshell

- Information that is *visibly* irrelevant still anchors judgments and contaminates guesses. When people start from information known to be irrelevant and adjust until they reach a plausible-sounding answer, they under-adjust.
- People under-adjust more severely in cognitively busy situations and other manipulations that make the problem harder.
- People deny they are anchored or contaminated, even when experiment shows they are.
- These effects are not diminished or are only slightly diminished by financial incentives, explicit instruction to avoid contamination, and real-world situations.

Contamination Effects. It turns out that almost *any* information could work its way into a cognitive judgment. (Chapman and Johnson 2002); and you cannot decrease Anchoring or Contamination effects either (Tversky and Kahneman 1974).

2.7.4 Overconfidence Heuristics and Calibration

People typically have great confidence in judgments based upon them. For example, events to which subjects assigned a probability of 2% happened 42.6% of the time!

2.7.5 *Hindsight Heuristics*

Hindsight bias is when subjects, after learning the eventual outcome, give a much higher estimate for the *predictability* of that outcome than subjects who predict the outcome without advance knowledge. Hindsight bias is sometimes called the I-knew-it-all-along effect. Hindsight bias is important in legal cases, where a judge or jury must determine whether a defendant was legally negligent in failing to foresee a hazard (Sanchiro 2003).

2.7.6 *Others: Black Swan Phenomenon*

As Taleb has coined the term and discussed this phenomenon in much detail, sometimes *most of* the variance in a process comes from exceptionally rare, exceptionally huge events. Consider a financial instrument that earns $10 with 98% probability, but loses $1000 with 2% probability; it is a poor net risk, but it looks like a steady winner. As another example, why did Long-Term Capital Management (LTCM) borrow leverage of $125 billion against $4.72 billion of equity, almost ensuring that *any* Black Swan would destroy them?

Heuristics and Biases: Evidence and Implications – some examples

- Implication for performance-based management contracts: People/managers will prefer performance-based incentives schemes more often than standard theory predicts. This can be attributed to the overconfidence trait. Due to overconfidence, managers prefer riskier projects because they think they can beat the odds. This goes against the standard theory, which predicts that, as output variance increases, principals should offer less output-sensitive contracts to agents because, under standard theory, agents are assumed to dislike risk. According to Camerer and Lovallo (1999), there is some evidence in support of this phenomenon.
- Implication for stock selections due to availability bias: People easily recall the information that has recently arrived, especially in the media and corporate releases; and their memory is fresh with their broker's/advisor's recommendations. According to a study, stocks with very high level of press coverage underperformed in the subsequent 2 years.
- Implication for asset valuation due to anchoring bias**.** In a study done in the field of real estate, subjects were asked to give their opinions on the appraisal value, appropriate listing price, and the lowest price they would accept if they were the seller. This was done after they had been given detailed and identical information about the house they had been shown for such a purpose. The only information that was changed in this study was the asking price (the anchoring factor). The result of this study showed individual valuations of houses were directly related to the asking price given to them.

References

Bitler, M.P., T.J. Moskowitz, and A. Vissing-Jorgensen. 2009. Why do entrepreneurs hold large ownership shares? Testing agency theory using entrepreneur effort and wealth. Working Paper. Graduate School of Business, University of Chicago.

Camerer, C., and D. Dan Lovallo. 1999. Overconfidence and excess entry: an experimental approach. *The American Economic Review* 89(1): 306–318.

Chapman, G.B., and Johnson, E.J. 2002. Incorporating the irrelevant: Anchors in judgments of belief and value. In T. Gilovich, D. Griffin, & D. Kahneman (Eds.), Heuristics and biases: The psychology of intuitive judgment (pp. 120–138). Cambridge: Cambridge University Press.

Cai, C.X. 2007. A new test of signaling theory. *Finance Letters* 5(2): 1–5.

Finucane, M., A. Alhakami, P. Slovic, and S. Johnson. 2000. The affect heuristic in judgments of risks and benefits. *Journal of Behavioral Decision Making* 13(1): 1–17.

Kahneman, D., and A. Tversky. 1979. Prospect theory: an analysis of decision under risk. *Econometrica* 47(2): 263–291.

Keynes, J.M. 1937. The General Theory of Employment. Quarterly Journal of Economics, 51: 209–23.

Kaplan, S.N., and P. Stromberg. 2002. Financial contracting theory meets the real world: an empirical analysis of venture capital contracts. *Review of Economic Studies* 00: 1–35.

Lewis, D. 1980. A subjectivist's guide to objective chance. In *Studies in inductive logic and probability Richard, Vol II, Chap. 13*, ed. C. Jeffrey, 263–293. Berkeley: University of California Press.

Montier, James. 2006. *Behavioural finance: insights into irrational minds and markets*. Chichester: Wiley.

Olsen, R. 2010. Financial risk perceptions: a behavioral perspective. In ed. R. Yazdipour, Springer.

Sanchiro, C. 2003. Finding error. *Michigan State Law Review* 1189.

Simon, H.A. 1983. Why should machines learn? In *Machine learning: an artificial intelligence approach*, ed. R.S. Michalski et al., 34. Palo Alto: Tioga.

Slovic, P. 1987. The perception of risk. *Science* 23(4): 280–285.

Spence, A.M. 1974. *Market signaling: informational transfer in hiring and related screening processes*. Cambridge: Harvard University Press.

Thaler, R. (ed.). 1993 and 2005. *Advances in behavioral finance, Vol I and II*. New York: Princeton University Press and Russell Sage Foundation.

Tversky, A., and D. Kahneman. 1981. The framing of decisions and the psychology of choice. *Science, New Series* 211(4481): 453–458.

Tversky, A., and D. Kahneman. 1974. Judgment under uncertainly: heuristics and biases. *Science, New Series* 185(4157): 1124–1131.

Chapter 3
Beyond Agency Theory: Value Creation and the Role of Cognition in the Relationship Between Entrepreneurs and Venture Capitalists*

Peter Wirtz

Abstract This chapter explores entrepreneur–investor relations from a cognitive perspective. I show that entrepreneurs' and investors' specific mindsets matter for the perception and realization of strategic opportunity. Differences in cognitive structure and process thus influence value creation beyond economizing on agency costs. I define and add concepts of cognitive cost and cognitive value to a basic agency model, which allows me to explain why some entrepreneur–investor relations create more value than others, although they may have the same level of agency costs. This enhanced framework also helps understand why external funding may not be available to certain ventures, even if agency conflicts can be kept under control through proper incentive alignment. The concepts of cognitive cost and value are shown to be especially relevant in the context of entrepreneurial finance, where uncertainty is typically high, and knowledge about value creation opportunities is ambiguous. An investor's appreciation of the value of entrepreneurs' knowledge about strategic opportunity depends on the closeness of their respective mindsets. Some investor types such as venture capitalists (VCs) share certain of the entrepreneurs' mental features and develop specific skills to identify valuable ventures at a low cognitive cost while adding cognitive value through strategic advice and mentoring, especially when entrepreneurs are still inexperienced.

3.1 Introduction

3.1.1 Background and Overview

For many years, finance scholars have examined the relationship between founder/managers and external investors within the agency framework (Jensen and Meckling 1976), where information asymmetry and conflicting interests between entrepreneurs

* I am indebted to Rassoul Yazdipour for helpful comments on an earlier version of this chapter.

P. Wirtz (✉)
Université Lumière, Lyon 2, France
e-mail: peter.wirtz.fcs@gmail.com

R. Yazdipour, *Advances in Entrepreneurial Finance: With Applications from Behavioral Finance and Economics*, DOI 10.1007/978-1-4419-7527-0_3,

and external shareholders lead to agency costs. Under such theory, agency costs may be controlled by putting in place the appropriate monitoring and incentive mechanisms to better align the entrepreneur's behavior with investors' interests. Hence, the retention of a significant ownership stake by the entrepreneur may reduce the risk of consuming perquisites and of expending low managerial effort (Jensen and Meckling 1976; Bitler et al. 2006). Moreover, according to the agency literature, the identity of the external shareholder matters too in as much as certain investor types may have developed superior monitoring and incentive mechanisms to reduce agency costs and hence contribute to value creation. This is supposedly the case of private equity firms (Baker and Wruck 1989; Jensen 1993). Consequently, beyond the degree of ownership concentration, investor type seems to matter when controlling for agency costs in funding entrepreneurial ventures.

Among all sorts of investor types, venture capitalists (VCs) are an especially important source of finance for funding young entrepreneurial firms. Empirical studies on the relationship between venture capitalists (VCs) and entrepreneurs, while describing the existence of specific monitoring mechanisms helping to minimize the downside risk on value due to agency conflicts, also document a more direct contribution of these professional shareholders to a firm's upside potential (Cumming and Johan 2007), and hence to venture success. This added service

Exhibit 3.1 Agency costs and cognitive costs in entrepreneur-stakeholder relations

Agency costs (Jensen and Meckling 1976)	**Cognitive costs**
Monitoring aims at reducing information asymmetry (e.g. through a well informed independent board of directors).	**Mentoring** efforts undertaken by certain stakeholders, such as venture capitalists, may influence an entrepreneur's mindset and enable him to engage in relationships with different stakeholder groups (e.g. financial investors).
Bonding is the activity whereby managers convey credible (and thus costly) signals that they will behave in accordance with external shareholders' interests.	**Externalizing** tacit knowledge (Nonaka et al. 2001) consists of an entrepreneur's efforts to transform his tacit knowledge into explicit knowledge which can be communicated to external stakeholders, such as potential investors. The costs of externalization are different from bonding costs. The latter's role is to convince shareholders that the manager's interests are aligned with shareholder interests, whereas externalization of partially tacit mindset is aimed at convincing (potential) stakeholders of the intrinsic quality of strategic projects.
Residual loss is due to the fact that information asymmetry can never be completely eliminated and that interest alignment is never perfect.	**Cognitive heterogeneity** persists because mindsets are specific and path-dependent and, thus, never perfectly aligned, in spite of mutual interaction. Thus, some degree of mutual misunderstanding may always persist.

potentially comes at two levels: (1) the identification or conception of a proper strategy where VCs may act as a sounding board in the strategy formulation process (Rosenstein et al. 1993) and (2) the professionalization of managerial capabilities (Hellman and Puri 2002). Hence, the contribution of VCs goes beyond the supply of funding and objective financial discipline through monitoring and incentives to include some more specifically cognitive resources, such as new strategic ideas, knowledge, and skills. Strategy formulation and skill acquisition imply cognitive structures and processes that are more complex than the mere transfer of objective information through monitoring mechanisms to overcome information asymmetry as traditionally prescribed by agency theory.

In this chapter, we propose an extended conceptual framework of entrepreneur–VC relationship, which integrates both agency costs and cognitive costs (Exhibit 3.1) derived from the strategy literature and the dynamic capabilities approach to better understand the overall impact of venture financing on value creation (Penrose 1959; Barney 1986; Wernerfelt 1984; Teece et al. 1997). Integrating cognitive cost and value into an extended agency framework thus may help resolve some potential problems for both entrepreneurs and investors. One important implication is a better understanding of the reasons for which certain VC–entrepreneur relationships are more successful than others, even in cases where agency costs are relatively low. In fact, our framework makes predictions on venture success based on the respective cognitive attributes of VC firms and entrepreneurs. These predictions are consistent with Gompers et al. (2006), who empirically study the impact of matching different levels of VC skills with different levels of entrepreneurs' skills on venture success. They find that a skilled VC contributes significant (cognitive) value only where the entrepreneur's prior experience in starting a venture is either low or has been a failure. In the latter case, skilled VCs can identify more easily than unskilled VCs, the promising entrepreneurs, in spite of the latter's prior failures or lack of experience and help them acquire enhanced management skills.

The second section of this Chapter explains why traditional agency theory stops short of explaining the value creation potential inherent in VC–entrepreneur relationships. Sect. 3 then proposes a general framework of investor–entrepreneur relationships, emphasizing the potential cognitive role played by certain investor types. Sect. 4 applies such framework to the specific case of young entrepreneurial firms funded by venture capitalists, yielding some empirical implications.

3.2 Entrepreneurial Ventures and Value Creation in an Agency Setting

Jensen and Meckling (1976) made the seminal contribution to positive agency theory, which has become the dominant theoretical framework for analyzing shareholder–manager relationship and its impact on the financial performance of the firm. The starting point in Jensen and Meckling's analysis is an entrepreneurial firm, where the founder is the shareholder and the manager at the same time. In this situation, agency conflicts are absent because the entrepreneur completely internalizes the value impact of his decisions. Things change when the entrepreneur sells outside equity because such a scenario creates an incentive for the founder/manager to pursue his or her personal interests to the detriment of the new shareholders. Consequently, when a new shareholder enters, agency costs arise. Such an increase can however be reduced by putting in place the appropriate monitoring and incentive mechanisms.

The question arises, however, why the entrepreneur should open up his or her venture to investors in the first place since this brings about agency costs, which will be anticipated and priced by the potential external shareholders anyway. Jensen and Meckling's answer is in the recognition of the entrepreneur's personal budget constraint. That is to say that the sale of outside equity may be the only means to capture certain value enhancing investment opportunities, simply by loosening the firm's budget constraint. Thus, outside equity brings the firm on a value enhancing "expansion path", as long as the incremental value generated from expansion exceeds the marginal agency costs induced by the decrease of the entrepreneur's ownership stake. Consequently, in the Jensen and Meckling model, the possibility to create value through a relationship between the entrepreneur and external shareholders (e.g. venture capitalists) depends on the relative amount of the value supplement inherent in a new investment project and the added agency costs due to the more diffuse ownership structure. Leaning on the ownership structure model initially developed by Roe (2002) and extended by Charreaux (2002), we can note that selling an ownership stake to an outside shareholder creates value, as long as

$$V_d - A_{mi} > 0,$$

where V_d is the value created as a result of expanded investment opportunity and when the budget constraint is loosened by bringing in new investors. A_{mi} is agency cost in a traditional sense, which has its root causes in the entrepreneur-manager's pursuit of his or her personal interests under conditions of asymmetric information (perks, leisure, overinvestment). Consequently, the value created by an external shareholder, say a private equity firm, stems from the funds it contributes and its capacity of controlling managerial agency costs by devising the appropriate incentive and control mechanisms. In discussing the O.M. Scott LBO for instance, Baker and Wruck (1989) make a case for the private equity firm's ability to design governance mechanisms (remuneration design, management participation, board of director functioning, covenants), which help decrease agency costs. According to traditional agency theory, value can hence be created in entrepreneur–investor relationships by widening the $V_d - A_{mi}$ spread. It should however be noted that, in the initial agency model, the outside shareholders play no role in constructing the investment opportunity set itself. The latter is given, and the role of outside shareholders is restricted to bringing in financial capital and to supporting the residual risk, while controlling the objective attributes of their investments by maintaining transparency on information flows. In such a model, outside shareholders' impact on the performance of the firm is restricted to the amount of financial capital they put on the table and to their monitoring skills.

3.3 Cognitive Cost and Cognitive Value Inherent in Entrepreneur–Investor Relations

Agency theory focuses on controlling costs of conflicting interests when information is asymmetrically distributed. Value can hence be created by crafting the appropriate monitoring and incentive mechanisms to eliminate such costs. Monitoring reduces information asymmetry, whereas incentives align the entrepreneur's interests with those of external shareholders. Jensen (1993) considers the governance mechanisms developed by certain private equity firms as especially efficacious when it comes to economizing on agency costs. Though this may be one important explanation for the success of certain ventures, in many cases, the success of entrepreneurial ventures is not due to financial incentives and monitoring alone. In fact, one major shortcoming of agency theory lies in its implicit assumptions about the origin and the recognition of opportunities to create value. The origin of strategic opportunities and the recognition of their value creation potential are actually exogenous to the theory, and it is simply assumed that good (positive NPV) and bad (negative NPV) projects somehow exist. They are given by the environment, and to maximize value, it is important to have access to information about the good projects, to give incentives to the entrepreneur to choose the good ones and to make him or her expend optimal effort.

The strategic management literature however has a longstanding tradition in recognizing that making a competitive strategy is as much about cognition (Hambrick and Mason 1984; Huff 1990; Walsh 1995), vision (Fransman 1994; Witt 1998), and difficult to imitate capabilities (Penrose 1959; Teece et al. 1997), as it is about mere information. What an entrepreneur perceives as the best strategy depends on his or her specific mindset. The same goes for an investor. Mindsets are influenced by individual and collective learning processes, which may be highly specific and path dependent. Part of such learning is tacit in nature and thus difficult to communicate to others. One implication of the cognitive nature of strategy formulation is the fact that many value creation opportunities do not exist independently of the people who conceive them in specific organizational contexts. The art of strategy is not simply about choosing the objectively best strategy in a predefined menu. Strategy is created in processes of individual and organizational learning (Nonaka et al. 2001), which rely on capabilities that go beyond the control of conflicting interests.

Fransman (1994) illustrates the central importance of knowledge in creating and realizing the potential of corporate success. He actually draws a clear distinction between information, as it is present in agency theory, and knowledge, as employed in strategic management and evolutionary economics (Nelson and Winter 1982). Information is in fact defined as objective data about states of the world and state-contingent outcomes. As such, it is a closed set. It may be asymmetrically distributed, but its transfer from one stakeholder to another is possible, albeit at a cost (monitoring costs). In such a context, an information's meaning is unambiguous. Things change when the precise meaning of any given information depends on people's mindsets. Thus, even if knowledge evolves with the acquisition of information, there is "loose coupling" between the two concepts, which is to say that the interpretation of any piece of information in terms of value creation is not self evident but depends on people's mental patterns at the time they receive the information. The latter may then have an impact on mental patterns and belief structures, but these change in a highly path-dependent way so that the knowledge gained from new information is sometimes very different from one person to another. In fact, Fransman defines knowledge as dynamic mental constructs. So, in comparison to agency theory's conception of information, knowledge is an open set. It is created in an ongoing learning process, part of which is tacit (Nonaka et al. 2001).

Beyond their privileged access to information in the above-defined sense, top managers' specific knowledge structures can hence be crucial in an effort to create value. In their work on upper echelons, Hambrick and Mason (1984) actually consider a firm's strategy to be a reflection of its top managers' cognitive base and values. Since there is only loose coupling between objective information and knowledge gained, some people perceive opportunities for value creation and others do not, even if information is distributed symmetrically. In such a situation, monitoring and incentive alignment alone are insufficient to increase a firm's value. This is because information from the environment is perceived through the lens of an entrepreneur's specific mindset. The latter influences strategy formulation and, ultimately, a firm's performance (Hambrick and Mason 1984).

One important implication is that there may be a conflict between an entrepreneur and his firm's investors about the best strategy to follow, independently of any problem of conflicting interests. As Conner and Prahalad (1996) put it: "[...] truthful individuals honestly may disagree about the best present and future course of action for their business activities. Or, the parties may possess different mindsets generally. Discord fundamentally derives from personal knowledge that cannot be communicated fully to others at the time of the disagreement." (p. 483). Consequently, our understanding of entrepreneur–investor relations may gain from admitting the existence of cognitive (or knowledge) asymmetry, which is different in nature from mere information asymmetry.

Such cognitive asymmetry is likely to induce conflicts due to mutual misunderstanding among stakeholders (e.g. the entrepreneur and certain external shareholders). Such conflicts are not rooted in mutually inconsistent interests and thus cannot be tackled by the means of interest alignment alone, as traditional agency theory would have it. Their resolution depends on stakeholders' initial skills and knowledge, as well as on their willingness and capability to learn. Thus, cognitive conflicts cause costs, which may be labeled as cognitive costs.

The costs stemming from cognitive conflicts are different in nature from costs rooted in agency conflicts. They are related to the various efforts undertaken by stakeholders to overcome differences in the perception of opportunities, to convince others of the relevancy of their conceptions (e.g. an innovative business model), as well as to eventual losses of efficiency due to lasting differences in understanding. Exhibit 3.1 sketches out different types of potential cognitive costs in comparison with the traditional agency costs.

The above presentation of cognitive costs characterizing the relationship between entrepreneurs and external stakeholders, such as venture capitalists, shows that these costs are linked to learning processes that potentially lead to a transformation of strategic knowledge (which may reduce the gap between different mindsets) and to an acquisition of new managerial capabilities. It is however important to emphasize that cognitive conflict differs from traditional agency conflict in a fundamental way. In fact, agency conflict is always value reducing, and as long as the marginal cost of monitoring and bonding remains inferior to the marginal reduction in residual losses, the latter's minimization will maximize value. Not so with cognitive heterogeneity, which can actually be value enhancing (Forbes and Milliken 1999; Hambrick et al. 1996), in as much as it opens up new strategic perspectives and allows to sustain an ongoing process of learning and innovation. Consequently, the specific mindsets of external stakeholders, different from the entrepreneur's own, not only generate cognitive cost, but may also contribute cognitive value by bringing in new perspectives and valuable experience.

Recognizing that certain shareholder types play more roles than just assuming risk, Charreaux (2002) proposes an extension of Roe's model of ownership structure by introducing two concepts derived from the above-mentioned literature on knowledge and capabilities in strategic management. He does so by adding cognitive cost A_c and cognitive value V_c to the basic agency model. This is to recognize that certain shareholder types may contribute specific knowledge in the process of strategy formulation. For example, a venture capitalist can act as a sounding board to the entrepreneur who proposes different strategic initiatives. He may also help the firm acquire enhanced management skills (e.g. management control, human resource management …), which is a manifestation of mentoring. On the other hand, an external shareholder's acquisition of a significant ownership stake may raise costs due to cognitive conflict A_c. The closer the entrepreneur's cognitive base to a specific investor's mindset, due to common educational background or shared professional experience, the lower the degree of cognitive cost should be.

Hence, the entry of a new shareholder creates value if $V_d + V_c - A_{mi} - A_c > 0$, that is value created through loosening the budget constraint and knowledge/skill added by new shareholders, exceeds the sum of managerial agency cost and cognitive cost. This can help explain the breakdown of certain agency relationships, even in situations where managerial agency costs are low.[1] In fact, traditional agency theory

[1] This is when an entrepreneur is isolated in his perception of a unique business opportunity for the realization of which he needs external funding. Hence for value to be created the venture needs funds, but financial investors just do not get the point, even though they may have ways to achieve interest alignment (by acquiring only a minority stake, imposing incentive contracts...). So in spite of agency costs being absent or very low, investors do not enter the venture because V_d actually exists in the entrepreneur's perception only. This situation is captured by the model through prohivitive cognitive costs. This means that because of inconsistent mindsets, A_c simply offsets V_d. Giving an investor access to the entrepreneur's perception of opportunities would translate into the model by lowering A_c.

would always predict an ownership structure to be viable, as long as $V_d > A_{mi}$, which is the case when the entrepreneur keeps a significant ownership stake (Bitler et al. 2006). However, our discussion of knowledge asymmetry shows that certain potentially value creating ventures may never have access to external finance, although $V_d > A_{mi}$ through proper incentive alignment, because cognitive cost is excessively high. Achieving low cognitive cost likely depends on the relative closeness of entrepreneurs' and shareholders' cognitive structure and ways of reasoning. In other words, when incentives are properly aligned, entrepreneurs should have less difficulty in raising external finance when addressing investors with mental patterns close to their own, due to shared educational background and/or professional experience. In addition, even if incentives are properly aligned through high ownership concentration and monitoring (A_{mi} low) and if mental patterns are relatively close (A_c low), there still may be significant differences in firm performance due to investor relations, because all shareholders do not necessarily make the same contribution to cognitive value (V_c), where different mentoring skills may imply different degrees of venture professionalization.[2]

3.4 Conditions of Value Creation in Entrepreneur-VC Relationships

Cognitive structures and processes should be particularly relevant in the context of entrepreneurship. In fact, according to Krueger (2003, p. 105), "understanding entrepreneurial cognition is imperative to understanding the essence of entrepreneurship, how it emerges and evolves. This is especially true if we wish to move from descriptive research to theory-driven research." Our understanding is that this argument made for entrepreneurship in general applies to entrepreneurial finance likewise. Forbes (1999) advances two arguments in support of the idea that the understanding of cognitive structures and processes should be crucial in coming to grips with the dynamics of entrepreneurial ventures. First, entrepreneurship typically takes place in a context of high uncertainty, where resource-output-performance relations are very ambiguous. In such a setting, special cognitive features may be required to take effective action, such as the use of specific heuristics (Alvarez and Busenitz 2001; Busentiz and Barney 1997) and nonlinear processes of reasoning. Entrepreneurial cognition, thus different in nature from cognition of managers in large established firms, may be a key to understanding why entrepreneurs perceive opportunities where others see nothing. Beyond the entrepreneur's own perception, the capacity of representing the perceived opportunities to stakeholders is also crucial in the effort to assemble the strategic resources to realize the venture (Barney 1986; Forbes 1999). The latter aspect, however, has received less attention in the

[2] V_c is the specific cognitive input made by the investor: new ideas, more professional managerial capabilities...

literature on managerial cognition. The present chapter can be seen as a tentative contribution to bridge this gap, in as much as our concept of cognitive cost relates to the learning effort necessary to obtain shared representations of opportunities by entrepreneurs and key stakeholders such as potential contributors of equity finance.

Secondly, the relatively small size of new ventures gives special significance to the entrepreneur's specific mindset, probably more so than in the typical large managerial firm. "The implication of individual-level and group-level cognition [...] may be more direct and immediate in the context of new venture creation than is the case in more conventional organizational settings. Most new ventures have only one or a few key managers at their core [...] Thus, their beliefs and decision-making processes are likely to be more concentrated than those of large organizations." (Forbes 1999). Because of this concentration, the potential of cognitive conflict may be especially strong in young entrepreneurial ventures, with the inexperienced entrepreneur often being isolated and having a hard time communicating his or her original strategic ideas to investors from a different background than his or her own. The early stage in a firm's lifecycle can thus be considered to be a particularly appropriate setting to study the concepts of cognitive cost and value in an extended model of agency relationships.

The cognitive dimension of the investor–entrepreneur relationship may be especially important at an early stage in a firm's lifecycle, when an entrepreneur's managerial experience is low. In this case, the entrepreneur's perception of strategic opportunities is likely to depend significantly on tacit (hard to communicate) knowledge. The latter may be an outcome of nonlinear processes of heuristic-based reasoning, which Busenitz and Barney (1997) consider to be a typical feature of entrepreneurs' cognitive process. An investor's ability to ascertain the strategic value of knowledge gained from such process is likely to depend on his or her own specific knowledge and on his or her ability to penetrate the entrepreneur's specific mode of reasoning. Cognitive conflict between entrepreneurs and certain investor categories is thus potentially strong, if the latter lack the requisite mental skills and training. For example, traders at large institutional investors (IIs) are trained to make investment decisions based on the assumptions of rationality implicit in traditional financial economics. This very analytical approach to decision making may thus be at a great distance from the typical entrepreneur's approach to decide on strategic opportunities. Consequently, traditional investors are likely to have a hard time in appreciating the value creation potential of entrepreneurial ventures. Monitoring skills developed to control conflict of interests (source of traditional agency costs) are not of any help in this matter because they suppose that good (positive NPV) and bad (negative NPV) investment projects can easily be distinguished by the investor. Where they cannot, even though V_d as perceived by the entrepreneur may be potentially high, the traditional large institutional investor whose perception of strategic opportunity is at a long distance from the entrepreneur's will not fund the venture, even when A_{mi} (traditional agency costs) are low. The reason is the strong effort necessary to engage in learning, which would ultimately improve mutual understanding. It would simply be too time consuming and too costly in relation to the financial stake. In such a situation, A_c (the cognitive cost due to a lack of mutual understanding) is very high, whereas V_c (the specific cognitive value this investor is able to bring to the venture) is typically low so that $V_d + V_c^{II} < A_{mi}^{II} + A_c^{II}$. This relationship is thus not viable, the prime cause not being prohibitive agency costs, but a cognitive mismatch between entrepreneurs and those investors who invest at arm's length.

Those young firms where a strong competitive advantage crucially hinges on tacit knowledge derived from entrepreneurs' personal experience and heuristic-based reasoning may thus have few possibilities to raise external finance, even if one could effectively control problems of interest alignment and information asymmetry in a traditional sense (A_{mi}). Rather than mere information asymmetry, these firms face problems inherent in cognitive asymmetry. Monitoring is insufficient to overcome the latter because of the loose coupling between information and knowledge (Fransman 1994). As a matter of consequence, arm's length finance is not available, because tacit knowledge cannot be readily traded at arm's length (Forbes 1999). The sharing of tacit knowledge requires specific mental skills and a certain learning effort.

Certain investors, however, such as venture capitalists and business angels, may possess or develop these specific cognitive skills that allow them to enter into a relationship with an entrepreneur at a low cognitive cost. Those are investors capable of recognizing the potential of promising young ventures, because they are able to cope with entrepreneurial cognition. If the entrepreneur lacks managerial experience, these investors may not only enter at a low cognitive cost (A_c), but also have a strong potential cognitive input (V_c). This is the case, for example, when venture capitalists (VCs) play a strong role in professionalizing managerial functions in young ventures (Hellmann and Puri 2002). Hence, the inequality becomes

$$V_d + V_c^{VC} > A_{mi} + A_c^{VC}.$$

One testable implication is that venture capitalists should typically be expected to invest where the entrepreneurs' cognition is close to their own. In fact, closeness of mental patterns and cognitive process reduces cognitive cost. This theoretical prediction is consistent with empirical evidence, according to which venture capitalists prefer to invest when there is a certain degree of cognitive similarity with the entrepreneur (Murneiks et al. 2007).

The management literature on strategic resources, managerial capabilities, and learning, however, teaches us that knowledge structures and skills are not static but change as a result of dynamic path-dependent processes. This implies that the concepts of cognitive cost and value are themselves dynamic and time dependent. As a venture matures, the inherent value creation potential becomes more explicit, and even shareholders without the specific cognitive skills of VCs and business angels may see an interest in contributing financial capital to further growth. The firm may then be taken public without arm's length investors facing special problems of cognitive cost any more.

The entrepreneur's own cognitive structure may also evolve due to the accumulation of experience with the maturing venture and due to certain shareholders' mentoring efforts. Consequently, the potential to create cognitive value (V_c) should be higher with inexperienced entrepreneurs than with serial entrepreneurs, which is consistent with empirical evidence from Gompers et al. (2006). The latter actually show that experienced VCs have higher success rates than their less experienced competitors, only in cases where the venture is started by a first-time entrepreneur. With serial entrepreneurs, success rates are not significantly different between high-experience and low-experience VCs. This is consistent with our model in as much as it can be supposed that the success of serial entrepreneurs is a positive signal with respect to the quality of their entrepreneurial capabilities, which can be readily observed by almost any professional investor. Such a signal hence decreases potential cognitive cost on a wide scale. Not so with first-time entrepreneurs. In the latter case, the fit between the entrepreneurs' and the VCs' cognition should be particularly relevant in achieving low cognitive cost. That is because their long experience of interacting with entrepreneurs (some of them first-time) likely helps established VCs to develop an intimate understanding of successful entrepreneurs' cognitive structure and process. Hence, it can be supposed that experienced VCs have developed specific mindsets, which help them track the existence of potentially value creating tacit knowledge, even in the absence of an explicit track record. So, in comparison with their inexperienced counterparts, the better VCs experience lower cognitive cost when choosing to invest alongside entrepreneurs without a track record. It is also in such a situation that potential cognitive value from mentoring can be supposed to be highest, whereas serial entrepreneurs are likely to have already acquired such value through the experience with their previous ventures.

3.5 Conclusion and Implications

This conceptual chapter has set out to demonstrate that entrepreneurial finance may gain explanatory power with respect to entrepreneur–investor relations, by integrating the concepts of cognitive cost and value derived from the management literature in an extended model of agency. In fact, issues of cognition have been shown to be particularly relevant in the context of entrepreneurship (Alvarez and Busenitz 2001; Busenitz and Barney 1997; Forbes 1999; Krueger 2003). Our model predicts that arm's length financing is not an option for most entrepreneurs, even if there was a check on agency costs due to sound monitoring and interest alignment mechanisms, because the average arm's length investor faces high cognitive cost[3] while contributing low cognitive value.[4] In fact, potential shareholders' identity matters, in as much as it determines their cognitive structure and process. The latter have an impact on

[3] High cognitive cost is due to the investor's lack of understanding of the entrepreneur's specific mindset and to the learning effort necessary to gain access to the entrepreneur's perception of strategic opportunity.

[4] Cognitive value may only be derived from certain investors' specific expertise and know-how which would enhance a venture's managerial capabilities and/or strategic perspective.

cognitive value added and cognitive cost due to more or less inconsistent mindsets. We have shown that the traditional instruments of value optimization derived from agency theory (interest alignment and transparent monitoring) are insufficient to fully exploit the value potential to be gained from entrepreneurial cognition.

References

Alvarez, S., and L. Busenitz. 2001. The entrepreneurship of resource based theory. *Journal of Management* 27: 755–775.

Baker, G.P., and K.H. Wruck. 1989. Organizational changes and value creation in leveraged buyouts: The case of the O. M. Scott & Sons company. *Journal of Financial Economics* 25: 163–190.

Barney, J.B. 1986. Strategic factor markets: Expectations, luck, and business strategy. *Management Science* 32(10): 1231–1241.

Bitler, M.P., T.J. Moskowitz, and A. Vissing-Jørgensen. 2006. Why do entrepreneurs hold large ownership shares? Testing agency theory using entrepreneur effort and wealth. Working paper. http://papers.ssrn.com/sol3/papers.cfm?abstract_id=352480. January.

Busenitz, L., and J. Barney. 1997. Differences between entrepreneurs and managers in large organizations: Biases and heuristics in strategic decision making. *Journal of Business Venturing* 12: 9–30.

Charreaux, G. 2002. L'actionnaire comme apporteur de ressources cognitives. *Revue Française de Gestion* 28(141): 77–107. November–December, Special Issue.

Conner, K.R., and C.K. Prahalad. 1996. A resource-based theory of the firm: Knowledge versus opportunism. *Organization Science* 7(5): 477–501. September-October.

Cumming, D., and S. Johan. 2007. Advice and monitoring in venture finance. *Financial Markets and Portfolio Management* 21: 3–43.

Forbes, D. 1999. Cognitive approaches to new venture creation. *International Journal of Management Review* 1: 415–439.

Forbes, D., and F. Milliken. 1999. Cognition and corporate governance: Understanding boards of directors as strategic decision making groups. *Academy of Management Review* 24(3): 489–505.

Fransman, M. 1994. Information, knowledge, vision and theories of the firm. *Industrial and Corporate Change* 3(3): 713–757.

Gompers, P., Kovner, A., Lerner, J., Scharfstein, D. 2006. Skill vs. luck in entrepreneurship and venture capital: Evidence from serial entrepreneurs, working paper, Harvard University, July.

Hambrick, D.C., T.S. Cho, and M. Chen. 1996. The influence of top management heterogeneity on firm's competitive moves. *Administrative Science Quarterly* 41(4): 659–684.

Hambrick, D.C., and P.A. Mason. 1984. Upper echelons: The organization as a reflection of its top managers. *Academy of Management Review* 9: 193–206.

Hellmann, T., and M. Puri. 2002. Venture capital and the professionalization of start-up firms: Empirical evidence. *Journal of Finance LVII* 1: 169–197.

Huff, A. 1990. *Mapping strategic thought*. Chichester: Wiley.

Jensen, M. 1993. The modern industrial revolution, exit, and the failure of internal control systems. *Journal of Finance* 48(3): 831–880.

Jensen, M., and W. Meckling. 1976. Theory of the firm: Managerial behavior, agency costs, and ownership structure. *Journal of Financial Economics* 3: 78–133.

Krueger, N. 2003. The cognitive psychology of entrepreneurship. In *Handbook of entrepreneurship research*, ed. Z. Acs and D. Audretsch, 105–140. Boston: Kluwer.

Murneiks, C., Haynie, J., Wiltbank, R., and Harting, T. 2007. I like how you think: The role of cognitive similarity as a decision bias, paper presented at the Academy of Management Annual Meeting, Best Empirical Paper Award, Philadelphia.

Nelson, R.R., and S.G. Winter. 1982. *An evolutionary theory of economic change*. Cambridge: Harvard University Press.

Nonaka, I., R. Toyama, and P. Byosière. 2001. A theory of organizational knowledge creation: Understanding the dynamic process of creating knowledge. In *Handbook of organizational learning and knowledge*, ed. M. Dierkes, A. Berthoin-Antal, J. Child, and I. Nonaka, 491–517. Oxford: Oxford University Press.

Penrose, E.G. 1959. *The theory of the growth of the firm*. Oxford: Blackwell.

Roe, M. 2002. Corporate law's limits. *Journal of Legal Studies* 31: 233–271.

Rosenstein, J., A. Bruno, W. Bygrave, and N. Taylor. 1993. The CEO, venture capitalists, and the board. *Journal of Business Venturing* 8: 99–113.

Teece, D.J., G. Pisano, and A. Shuen. 1997. Dynamic capabilities and strategic management. *Strategic Management Journal* 18(7): 509–533.

Walsh, J. 1995. Managerial and organizational cognition: Notes from a trip down memory lane. *Organization Science* 6: 280–321.

Wernerfelt, B. 1984. A resource-based view of the firm. *Strategic Management Journal* 5: 171–180.

Witt, U. 1998. Imagination and leadership: The neglected dimension of an evolutionary theory of the firm. *Journal of Economic Behavior & Organization* 35: 161–177.

Chapter 4
Financial Risk Perceptions: A Behavioral Perspective

Robert A. Olsen

Abstract The generally accepted financial risk metrics, such as variance and Beta, are axiomatic mathematical constructions. They have mathematical validity but can be questioned on behavioral grounds. This chapter suggests a broader alternative approach. First, perception involves experiential content acquired as a result of human/world interaction. It is not merely the product of a passive internal "brain process." Second, financial risk is hypothesized to be primarily a perception of potential loss as fabricated by an evolutionary dual decision-making process that embraces both affect and formal cognitive analysis. Thus of necessity, perceptions of risk contain both cognitive and affective attributes. Because man is by nature a social creature, perceived risk also entails risk attributes that manifest group concerns. These hypotheses are supported by a comprehensive literature review. Evidence is presented suggesting that this alternative perspective parsimoniously explains many current "risk/return" market anomalies.

4.1 Introduction

Defining financial risk has become much like defining pornography. There is no universal agreement about the content but all believe that they "know it when they see it". Alternative approaches to financial risk involve objective probability distributions, Knight (1921), subjective probability distributions, Savage (1954), confidence in estimated probability distributions, Keynes (1936), and ambiguity about probability distributions, Ellsberg (1961). Using "Support Theory," Tversky and Koehler (1994), replaced subjective probabilities with "felt confidence" while Pennington and Reid (1993) suggested that probabilities are a function of the consistency, completeness, and coherence of "stories" about possible future events. Others have suggested that risk is more a function of outcomes rather than probabilities. *Shackle (*1952*)*, suggested that outcomes should be modeled as

R.A. Olsen (✉)
Decision Research, Eugene, OR, USA
e-mail: olsenbfin@msn.com

R. Yazdipour, *Advances in Entrepreneurial Finance: With Applications from Behavioral Finance and Economics*, DOI 10.1007/978-1-4419-7527-0_4,

"anticipations of possible surprise" while others have suggested that risk is more appropriately associated with potential loss (loss aversion) rather than variability in future outcomes, Shapira (1995). Many researchers have identified financial risk as a combination of probabilities and outcomes, Kahneman and Tversky (1992). More comprehensive risk theories hypothesize that financial risk is a multi attribute psychological phenomenon that involves other attributes besides probabilities and outcomes. Such attributes include dread, feelings of knowing, trust, fairness, voluntarism, and even one's "worldview," Slovic (2000). Last but not least, it has been suggested that formal "Fuzzy Logic" might be of use in understanding and integrating the many conflicting definitions of perceived risk, Lopes (1997), Reyna (2004).

This chapter attempts to cut the definitional "Gordian Knot" of financial risk by focusing on the risk perceiver rather than the financial hazard per se. This chapter discusses the wellsprings of risk perceptions by reviewing the latest neuroscience and decision-making literature suggesting that the human mind operates as a dual process system. One system is more primitive, more affective, intuitive and rapid. The second system is of a more recent evolutionary origin, but is more analytical, conscious, and slower in operation. Recent research suggests that the brain has been evolutionarily "cobbled together" such that these two systems simultaneously interact. Thus, perceptions of risk are not only likely to have affective and analytical attributes but they may be expected to contain pluralistic or community focused attributes as well.

The financial risk literature is extensive, and this essay is not meant to be an encyclopedic review, and so I apologize for not mentioning all the excellent studies that make up the literature. The more limited objective of this chapter is to make a start at developing a more comprehensive and integrated risk paradigm.

4.2 Neoclassical Financial Risk: A Prequel

Neoclassical finance has tended to treat financial risk as a set of attributes of a financial hazard; attributes independent of the investor. This chapter takes a broader view wherein perceived risk also incorporates the cognitive and affective mental processing of the perceiver. As Slovic (1987) has noted "Risk does not exist out there independent of our minds and cultures waiting to be measured. Instead humans invented the concept to help them understand and cope with the dangers and uncertainties of life. Risk assessments are subjective, assumption laden and depend upon judgment."

While there is little doubt that financial decision makers are made uneasy by the unpredictable nature of the future, there is no necessary psychological basis for assuming that one's mental unease is uniquely captured by some particular statistical metric such as variance or standard deviation of the distribution of possible outcomes. Nevertheless, this has been the path embraced by neoclassical finance. In addition, neoclassical finance has promoted a false dichotomy between objective risk, that which deals with known probability distributions and uncertainty, that which exists in the realm of imperfect knowledge. In particular, quantum theory and omplexity theory have demonstrated that complete deterministic knowledge is humanly impossible, Hardin (2003), Peat (2002) and that all perceived risk is subjective because we can only experience the "real world" through the filter of our brain.

More recently, it has been argued that perception is not just a process in the brain whereby a perceptual system constructs an internal representation of the world. Instead perceptual experience is intrinsically active whereby the perception acquires content, thanks to the perceiver's activity and experience, Noe (2004). Therefore, just as a newly sighted formerly blind person can still exhibit experiential blindness because of an inability to integrate sensory stimulation with thought-based experience, individual's risk perceptions may be absent or faulty because they are not able to integrate sensory stimulation with the experiences of uncertain outcomes. Perception is not like the content of a picture where the scene is given to us all at once. To perceive is to be able to interpret the situation relative to one's experience with the world. Perception is an "enactive" experience. Support for this argument is provided by the many experimental studies, which indicate that investors place much greater weight on concrete experienced risk-related attributes such as the "experience of loss" and "feelings of understanding" rather than abstract statistical metrics such as return variance and Beta.

Consciousness research suggests that perceived risk is phenomenological as well as psychological, Chalmers (1996), Thompson (2007). The phenomenological state of mind refers to how something "feels" rather than its simple "perception." For example, the redness of a rose and the melancholy of regret have a qualitative feel to them that is something quite apart from the perception of the color or mental condition. For this reason, the "feel" is referred to as the qualia of the perception. Where qualia come from is still a matter of debate. However, qualia seem to be neurologically associated with the pleasure and pain centers of the brain. Qualia can be accompanied by both cognition and emotion but are usually more associated with emotional affect. Qualia seem to be more akin to bodily sensations that arise from some primal internal process designed to alert the decision maker to the quality of their thoughts. The influence of qualia is especially obvious in situations where the decision maker reports that a decision must "feel right" as well as "look right." Recent neurological studies suggest that decision makers' "feelings of knowing" or "familiarity," usually interpreted as being thought based, are often qualia and involuntary, Burton (2008). The importance of qualia for risk perception is suggested by investors' statements that financial risk has a qualitative feel of unease or discomfort to it, apart from the obvious formal outcome, Gardner (2008), Loewenstein and Weber (2001).

I would suspect that most financial professionals are so accustomed to thinking about risk in statistical terms that they are almost unaware that the use of variance (or it's square root, standard deviation) as an operational measure of perceived risk initially resulted from a purely axiomatic mathematical derivation. Specifically, variance was the mathematical outcome of combining five standard axioms of utility theory (completeness, transitivity, independence, measurability, ranking) with the assumptions of non satiation and risk aversion, Alexander and Francis (1986).

In this context, it is crucial to remember that the risk aversion assumption does not say anything about how investors perceive and experience risk. It merely states that investors prefer a sure thing to a fair gamble with an equivalent expected value. Statistical variance, now utilized as the primary metric of perceived risk, was mathematically derived from a Taylor series expansion on a utility of wealth function. It was not derived from psychological assumptions about how people mentally perceived or physically "felt" uncertainty. As such, the term does not necessarily have psychological validity. It has only mathematical validity. Whether people actually do think, or even should think, in such terms is clearly open to conjecture and empirical verification. Portfolio theory has further obscured the statistical arrogation of risk by piling on additional assumptions about investors' abilities and need to take proper notice of correlation between asset returns such that they might choose efficient portfolios.

It is well recognized by psychologists that to make a decision, emotion is the necessary trigger. Emotions make choices possible. In fact, emotion is what mattering actually means when a choice is made and an outcome is experienced! A central problem with standard statistical risk metrics is that as metrics they have no inherent affective or emotional content. They are merely axiomatically derived abstractions. On the other hand, how people feel and behave toward uncertainty about the future is primarily the result of an evolutionary process that has led to ways of feeling and acting that are adaptive and increase the odds of survival. It is of course possible that some mathematical abstractions might become "marked" with affective content through experience. Unfortunately, neoclassical finance rashly implies that such should be the case for the metrics variance and Beta.

4.3 Fear: The Foundation of Perceived Risk

In order to examine the notion of perceived financial risk, some basic information about the brain, and its processes, cognition (thinking) and emotion, needs to be discussed. To begin, a meaningful definition of "risk perception" must imply emotional content. This follows because investment decisions are physical responses and emotions are the triggers or instigators of action. That is, emotions are responsible for the implementation of action tendencies oriented toward the attainment of some goal. Assuming that the goal of the investor is to become better off in the future (or at least not worse off), it seems reasonable to assume that perceptions of financial risk must have to do with the possibility of not realizing this goal. There are three primary emotions associated with negativity. These are anger, sadness, and fear. Of the three, fear appears to be the most likely candidate as the motivator of thoughts of negative future outcomes. While, ex post, we may experience anger or sadness with the results of our investment choice, fear is the ex ante negative emotion associated with coming up short.

While fear can be apportioned into finer emotional subcategories such as dread, worry, anxiety etc., it is important to be aware that what is commonly called fear is the internal "feeling" of bodily sensations that are triggered by stimuli associated with danger. Emotions come first and give rise to sensations that we call "feelings," Damasio (1999, 2003), Johnston (1999). Sometimes emotions and their feelings can even be triggered by stimuli outside of our conscious awareness, Berridge and Winkielman (2003). These "background" emotions can be vague and influence our conscious decision process in ways that we are unaware of, Erb and Bioy (2002). Also, felt emotions are very often difficult to verbalize.

The term emotion is still widely misunderstood and usually viewed as the antithesis of cognition or rational thought. However, such is not the case, and in fact, much of what we call cognition or thinking is actually modulated emotion, Gray (2004). For example, humans appear to rely extensively on "feelings of knowing or similarity" especially in complex decision situations and where time is short. These "feelings" mimic sensations of knowledgeable contemplation but are instead affective responses to the unconscious recognition of previous similar situations, Burton (2008). These feelings of knowing are akin to intuition, Reber (1993), Hogarth (2001). As the neuroscientist Antonio Damasio (1999) has noted "Emotion probably assists reasoning, especially when it comes to personal and social matters involving risk and conflict. Well targeted and well deployed emotion seems to be a support system without which the edifice of reason cannot operate properly."

The basic emotions such as fear, anger, joy, etc. are not something that "will to occur." Also different emotions are associated with somewhat separate brain subsystems, Elliot and Friston (2000), Breiter and Aharon (2001), Hamann and Ely (2002), Smith and Dickout (2002), Berns and Chappelow (2006). Neurologically, the emotion of "fear or risk of loss" does not appear to be the neurological flip side of the emotion associated with the "anticipation of gain," as Lopes (1997), had correctly anticipated. Emotions evolved over time to allow humans to adapt and reproduce. Thus, emotions might be viewed as the products of "evolutionary wisdom" and from this perspective they are not necessarily adaptively irrational, Gilbert (1998), Gaulin (2001). In addition, much emotion is nonconscious, just as is most cognition, Geary (2005). It is important to note that emotions not only have visceral effects but they also cause neural electrochemical changes in the brain that can alter cognition in many unrecognized and subtle ways, Harlow and Brown (1990), Lane and Nadel (2000), Erb and Bioy (2002), Gray (2004), Kosfield and Heinrich (2005).

The old view of emotion was one where the process progressed as: stimulus-feeling- response. Currently, the debated process is: stimulus- appraisal- feeling-response, Fisher and Shaver (1990). Appraisal is the focus of much current emotion theorizing. Nevertheless, emotion gives rise to an "action tendency," which has valence (feelings of goodness or badness) sometimes called "Affect," which leads to a moving toward or away from some stimulus. It is still generally believed that emotion has primacy over (can come first) and can be independent of (exist without) cognition.

The stimuli that trigger fear were originally natural and would have alerted humans to dangers from predators, unsafe activities, etc. However, humans and other animals can develop "learned triggers," which are not natural but will also unleash fear feelings and responses. That is people can be "conditioned" to respond with fear just as Pavlov's dog was conditioned to respond to the sound of a bell. In addition, culture may also have an effect on the emotion of fear in that: (1) It can alter what constitutes an adequate inducement of fear, (2) It can shape the expression of fear and (3) It can influence the behavioral response to fear. The usual fear responses include withdrawal, immobility, defense, and submission. The investment behaviors of panic selling, holding on to unprofitable assets for too long, purchasing fixed return annuities, and adopting a buy and hold strategy appear suggestive of these typical responses.

In summary, much emotional processing is unconscious just as is most cognition. What is different are the mental processing structures that are involved. The fear response involves the transmission of electrochemical signals along two separate pathways to the Amygdala, a key brain organ associated with fear and alarm. The fear stimuli can go either the "high road" through the cerebral Cortex, where it will be subject to more extensive cognitive processing and analysis and then to the Amygdala or it can go the "low road" straight to the Amygdala, LeDoux (1996). The primary advantage of the "low road" is a quicker behavioral response. The advantage of the high road is a more complete analysis of the situation and a more nuanced response. Evolution has provided humans with the alternative routes because in some cases, reaction to a snake for example, a quick fear response is the better alternative, while in other cases, the decision maker may benefit from a little more careful thought. Conscious emotional thought (recognition of feelings) and conscious cognition (thinking) both involve the use of the working memory, a key contributor to consciousness. A principal distinction of emotion, however, is that it involves physical feelings and changes in mental processing that have been evolutionarily inbred to automatically trigger adaptive behaviors. However, it is most important to remember that both emotion and cognition appear to be necessary for the execution of good conscious decisions, Damasio (1999), Firth (2007)

In closing this section, it is important to note that the brain does not have a special system devoted to "perception". The term perception describes in a general way what the many sensory neural systems are doing when we experience the world. It is in this sense that I use the word risk perception to refer to the way in which investors experience the dangers of investing. How risky they perceive an investment to be is a function of the amount and form of the data as well as the context within which it is presented. The use of statistics and probabilities is just one alternative way of presenting information, a form that is not evolutionarily natural and one that would not be expected to be associated with much emotion unless "statistical triggers" had been inculcated through conditioned learning. However, even in this case, the learned triggers may not have much emotional force unless emotional "as if" loops have been created that allow the decision maker to mentally emote the bodily feelings of a naturally risky situation. Incidentally, creating "as if" loops is what "method actors" attempt to do in order to theatrically portray emotional states.

4.4 Dual Decision Processes: Thinking and Feeling

The previous section summarized findings from brain research by neuroscientists and evolutionary biologists. In general, the picture presented was of a brain not designed as a "general problem solver," such as a computer, but instead physically cobbled together to handle many specific tasks such as mate selection, locomotion, etc., Campbell (1989). Brain architecture consists of interacting neural subsystems and there is little evidence that optimization and efficiency were evolutionary objectives, Restak (1994), Goldberg (2001). Mental function just had to be sufficient to allow some humans to survive and reproduce. Emotional brain structures such as the amygdala, hypothalamus, and the basal forebrain appear to be older than other structures that are generally associated with the type of cognition that we call "rational thought." As mentioned before, most of what the brain does is not available to the conscious mind and the brain often perceives and responds to stimuli that are not consciously sensed. For example, how many times have you driven your car without consciously having to think about each action necessary to arrive at your planned destination?

In this section, we will examine evidence provided by psychologists and decision researchers suggesting that the human brain functions in such a manner that it appears to be utilizing two separate but integrated decision processes; one process more intuitive and emotionally focused and the other more conscious and analytical. While no one suggests that decision makers actually switch back and forth between pure forms of these two processes, the hypothesis of two alternative processes has helped decision theorists to understand and predict how decision makers are likely to act under varying circumstances.

There is an extensive dual decision process literature, Hammond (1996), Over and Jonathan St Evans (1996), Over (2003), Chaiken and Trope (1999), Forgas (2000), Gigerenzer and Selten (2001), Gray (2004), Montague (2006). However, I will confine my comments to dual process research that is relevant to risk perception and choice under uncertainty.

Most dual decision process models are based on a common set of general observations about decision making. First, they emphasize that perception and sensation are distinct and that the mind actively imposes meaning on sensory data. That is, "knowledge" is a mental creation. Nevertheless, decision makers generally don't experience judgment as a "construction". Second, because the world is complex, decision makers extensively utilize categorization procedures to simplify and sort data. Third, motives direct perception. In effect, people most often see what they are ready to see and different people may interpret the same data differently. Nevertheless, cultural values and norms constrain and condition alternative perceptions, judgments, and choices. Fourth, decision makers don't seek absolute truth as much as they seek to terminate doubt by having their world appear satisfactorily consistent. This creates tendencies to avoid ambiguity and discordant data and to see new experiences as being similar to those already incurred. Fifth, the default decision process tends to be heuristic (based on so called rules of thumb) because it conserves effort, accelerates the decision process, and is generally perceived to yield acceptable results in a less than fully understandable and predictable world. Decision makers may make use of more effortful and systematic information processing in some circumstances but when they do, heuristic processing usually occurs simultaneously. Time, cognitive capacity, and felt need generally determine whether more systematic and effortful decision-making processes are utilized.

At one end of the decision process, continuum is a decision process usually called "associative" or "experiential." The associative or experiential process generates what are experienced as intuitive and affective responses. It is reproductive rather than productive in the sense that it uses cues mentally retrieved from similar past events when processing information. The experiential system encodes information in the form of concrete exemplars, images, and narratives. It appears to be relatively nonsymbolic and not linguistic. For this reason, it is speculated that experiential processing is evolutionarily much older than "rational" thought. In general, experiential information processing tends to be holistic, context sensitive, and flexible. Most importantly, experiential processing is emotionally driven and motivated by anticipated affect. For this reason, decision makers often feel that they are "compelled" to make a decision that "feels right" as opposed to one that "looks right". In fact, there is substantial evidence that decision makers often use "rationally derived" information as a cover for their more experientially based inclinations.

At the other end of the decision process continuum is the process called "rule based" or "rational". A defining feature of the rule-based or rational decision process is that it uses symbolically represented knowledge in processing. Processing rules are culturally based and socially learned. Information is evaluated and integrated using logical analysis as opposed to informal associations. The rational processing system requires greater mental focus and therefore tends to be used where greater accuracy is an important consideration. The rational system is more effortful and time consuming. Also, it performs well only where the decision situation is relatively simple and there is a unique goal or objective. Affect plays little or no role in this decision-making process although some have suggested that affect may be conceptualized as "deliberative" and thus treated as a rational element.

The two decision processes appear to act simultaneously but with different weights depending upon the situation. Evidence of simultaneous operation is abundant. It ranges from such obvious evidence as people expressing irrational fears while at the same time being aware that the fears are not realistic, to carefully controlled laboratory experiments where lack of experiential input leads to poor judgment even where rational processes are fully implemented.

Grossberg and Gutowski (1987), Hanoch (2002) and Reyna (2004) have developed theoretical models suggesting how the two decision systems operate in tandem. Grossberg calls his model "Affective Balance Theory" and he describes how learning can instill affective influences into cognitive representations. Hanoch suggests that emotion influences reason in three particular ways. First, emotions restrict the range of options considered. Second, emotions focus attention on specific parameters of the decision situation and third, emotions assist in terminating any evaluation process. Reyna calls her model "Fuzzy Trace Risk Theory". She suggests that risk perceptions are represented in two alternative memory forms. The first is a more computational, abstract, and individual in form. The second is more "gist" oriented where the gist captures the emotion of the situation and embraces the consistency that people seek by relating the risk in a particular situation to other similar situations. She hypothesizes that gist, and thereby affect, gets the greater weight in complex decisions. In general, there seems to be common agreement that greater decision complexity leads to increased perceptions of risk and a tendency to rely on more holistic and affective evidence.

Other risk perception implications of the dual process have been suggested. Gonzach (2000) and Weber and Siebermorgen (2005) note that familiarity leads to greater emphasis on affective risk attributes. Investors perceive less risk in companies that they recognize and feel positive about. Loewenstein and Weber (2001) also suggest that different decision attributes trigger different risk attributes. For example, cognitive perceptions of risk are related to probabilities whereas emotional or affective attributes are related to outcome vividness and salience. Brandstatter and Kubberger (2002) finds that, in general, emotion leads to the over weighting of low probabilities and the under weighting of high probabilities. Forlani (2002) finds that positive affect arising from feelings of control leads to lower risk perceptions and increased risk taking while, Moreno and Kida (2003) notes that, in general, positive affect induces risk taking.

The relationship between ambiguity and perceived risk has been the focus of a number of studies by Sarin and Weber (1992), Hogarth and Kunreuther (1995), Huber (1995), Ghosh and Ray (1997), Lauriola (2001), and Ho and Keller (2002). They find that risk perceptions vary directly with ambiguity and that risk perceptions tend to increase with perceived decision complexity. Alhakami and Slovic (1994), Jordan and Kass (2002) and Finucane and Holup (2006) note that risk perceptions often are inversely related to expectations of return because of affect. Good (bad) things are seen as being low (high) in risk and high (low) in return. Eiser (2002) suggests that trust can have this effect as a positive affective risk attribute but that affective and cognitive risk dimensions appear to have independent effects on hazard acceptance.

Perhaps the most important conclusion from studies of the simultaneous operation of the two decision-making systems is that because the experiential system can operate outside of normal awareness, the rational system can be significantly influenced because it is unaware that there is any affective influence, Berkowitz (2000), Frijida and Manstead (2000), Erb and Bioy (2002). A rather obvious example of this can be seen in the situation where the experiential system directs attention to more salient information and the rational system logically analyzes the information unaware that the information selection process was biased from the start.

Decision makers' ability to think "rationally" appears to increase with training. It has been suggested that experts' lesser perceptions of risk in their domain of expertise are a function of their greater ability to focus on statistical facts, with less affective interference, Barke (1995). Sjoberg (2002) disputes this contention. He contends that experienced decision makers are similarly influenced by the same mix of affective and analytical influences as nonexperts. He concludes that positive affect is the primary reason that experts rate risks as less in their domains of expertise. That is what they do as work is seen as "good," and what is "good" is usually seen as less risky.

4.5 Risk: For Me or for Others Also?

To this point, I have examined the neural underpinnings of perceived risk and have discussed the decision-making processes that would carry its influence. I have implicitly assumed that risk perceptions would manifest attributes reflecting the singularly selfish goals of the decision maker. In this section, I will briefly survey research suggesting that an individual's risk perceptions might also contain attributes that are pluralistic or group focused.

Man is a social animal and it would be surprising not to find traces of sociality in his perceptions of risk. In particular, where personal survival and the transmission of one's genes to the next generation are partially a function of group support, it would appear likely that perceived risk might contain "group traces".

Research from Evolutionary Biology and Neuroscience suggests that humans have a significant proclivity to cooperate as well as compete and have evolved neural hardware to enhance survival through "evolutionary and psychological altruism," Cashdan (1990), Pfaff (2007), Wang and Johnson (1995), Ridley (1996), Sober and Wilson (1998). As a consequence, humans seem to have some inborn ability to detect social cheaters and free riders through observations of facial features, body posture, and speech patterns. There is also speculation that the naturally occurring emotions such as anger and fear, outrage, etc. serve important roles in encouraging social behaviors and norms that support group relationships and non-zero sum reciprocity. Shunning, ostracism, and disdain for hoarders are examples of such derivative enforcement mechanisms. Humans also demonstrate a significant ability to become empathetic by internally simulating the experiences of others. Also humans have a strong innate predisposition to be socially influenced and to imitate others, Dugation (2000). In this regard, "herding" and a type of "swarm logic" become especially prevalent in complex and uncertain situations and there is brain imaging evidence to suggest that it may be partly "hardwired," Rizzolatti and Craighero (2004).

Game theorists also point to evidence that cooperation seems to be a natural state Axelrod (1997), Wright (2001), Skyrms (2004). Experimental results from "prisoner dilemma" type games indicate that in more natural settings, cooperation rather than defection seems to be normal. Even more significant is the fact that in environments that contain some irreducible uncertainty, game outcomes with cooperation are evolutionarily stable. That is, free riding and selfish behavior do not force cooperation into extinction.

Finally, it has been argued that from an evolutionary perspective, humans appear to have developed a feeling for a "logic of appropriate behavior," Freeman (1997). Based upon these considerations, it might be expected that individual's risk attributes might be associated with group concepts such as fairness, trust, equality, etc. A number of studies have found elements of these concepts in risk perceptions, Weber and Hsee (1998), Lupton (1999), Renn and Rohrnan (2000), Nisbett (2003), Fehr and Fischbacher (2005), Olsen (2008).

At the most general level, a person's "worldview" appears to influence risk perceptions. Studies by Bouyer and Bagdassaian (2001) and Slovic (1993) find that that people with a more egalitarian or individualistic worldview tend to perceive hazards as riskier than those with hierarchical or fatalistic worldviews. Wang and Johnson (1995), Wang and Simons (2001) note that risk perceptions are related to the size and relatedness of the group facing a hazard. Large group size and lack of social relatedness are associated with lower perceived risk. In a related study, Scherer and Cho (2003) find that people with stronger social linkages have more similar perceptions of risk. Viklund (2003) finds that trust is related to perceived risk. Where group trust is greater, people perceive risk to be lower. Siegrist and Cvetkovich (2000) find that people trust most those who share their values. Renn (2004) and Slovic (1987, 2000) note that perceived risk is a function of other social factors such as perceived fairness, voluntarism, effect on future generations, and group control.

4.6 Amplification

There is a growing body of literature revealing that information about hazards can interact with psychological, social, and institutional processes in ways that can amplify or attenuate perceptions of risk and return, Pidgeon and Kasperson (2006). Amplification can occur at two points: in the transfer of information and in the response of the receiver. Amplified risk perceptions in turn lead to behavioral responses that can have secondary impacts such as requirements for new regulations or financial impacts on unrelated firms. Sometimes information about a perceived risk, such as the failure of Enron, has an amplified financial repercussion that far exceeds the local impact, while at other times attenuation occurs. Attenuation of perceived risk appears to have been the case with the failure of Long-Term Capital Management, which went almost unnoticed by most investors yet it threatened the survival of the US financial system.

In communication theory, amplification (attenuation) takes place in the information transmission stage. Each message not only has a factual content but also inferential, value related, and symbolic content. These additional dimensions have independent influences on how a message is interpreted. For example, if the financial information comes from a highly respected and knowledgeable source, and concerns an issue that is important to the investing public, the impact is likely to be more significant than otherwise. Also, if a message is heard many times from a variety of sources, or comes from a personal friend, the impact is likely to be greater. Conversely, if the information is disputed, not very dramatic, or concerns some marginalized group, the impact is likely to be attenuated. It is especially important to note that amplification is not just due to media repetition. More important is the degree to which one is personally perceived to be at risk and that the message comes from a trusted source. In extremely negative situations, the perception of risk can be raised to such levels that a stigma may become attached to entire classes of activities or financial assets. This may be seen in the labeling of lower grade bonds as "junk bonds" and in the negative characterization of "hedge funds" by many investors.

As just mentioned, risk amplification primarily takes place at the information transmission stage. Because transmission depends upon the dynamics of the information network, it is important to be clear how the financial information network is structured (it's topology). If it takes what is called a "small world" form with many "weak" informational ties, we would find that information would travel fast but be subject to considerable amplification.

First, a small world financial network describes a situation where there is a hub and spoke arrangement in which many nodes (investors) are clustered around informational hubs (advisors, financial institutions) that act as opinion leaders. In addition, there would be many "weak ties" (professional organizations and associations) that bring distant hubs into more frequent contact. Hubs tend to lower the threshold of new information absorption and increase retransmission velocity. Belief synchronization resulting in herd mentality and groupthink are enhanced in the small world network as a result of sequential information transmission and positive feedback. In addition, preferential attachment, wherein those hubs that appear superior gain the most followers, exacerbates contagious behavior within the network. Loss aversion, in the form of regret avoidance, also increases the tendency for network compaction. The information amplification in the small world network arises from positive feedback and path dependency. The significant macro financial market result would be nonlinear price behavior wherein informational influences would result in stock price fluctuations that were nonproportional to the initial informational content. That is security markets would exhibit excess volatility. Most standard economic models do not assume a small world network. Alternatively, they assume random networks where information is independently evaluated by investors. In the standard economic model, investors' preferences are exogenous and not influenced by the "mind of the market" as formed by network dynamics. Network influence is implicitly neutral.

Second, there is structural and market behavior evidence that financial information networks are "small world networks" and subject to significant price amplification.

1. Given the complexity of the investment process, most nonprofessional investors rely heavily upon the advice of those seen to be experts. In this regard, trust in the form of ability and integrity is given great weight. Affective information is generally given greater weight than quantitative data. Portfolio Diversification is generally insufficient (concentration in "good prospects"), and investment horizons are usually short, (less than 3 years). Capon (1996), Clark-Murphy (2004), DeBondt, (1998), Waynered (2001).
2. Professional investors are very well connected through a web of educational, social, and business associations. This milieu tends to result in beliefs and methods

of analysis that are quite homogenous. They scrutinize competitors' investment behavior in the attempt to generate superior performance. The relative ease with which funds can flow between financial institutions creates a relatively short investment mind set. Professionals make greater use of formal analytical techniques but affect plays a significant role due to time pressure, informational complexity, and few if any audited "fool proof" valuation/management techniques. Abolafia (1996), Fenton-O'Creevy (2005), Cetina (2005), Smith (1999).
3. Empirical market data reveal that asset returns tend to follow power laws indicating lack of randomness and conformity with small world network dynamics. Asset returns also exhibit excess volatility that is consistent with market over reaction, herding, and momentum investing arising from amplification. Ormerod (2000), Shiller (1989).
4. Survey data indicate that professional investors herd, momentum invest, over extrapolate trends, exhibit wishful thinking, and over estimate the return/risk ratio for investments believed to be familiar from an affective vantage point. In addition, they tend to be overconfident and give less weight to disconfirming evidence. Cooper (2005), Dennis (2002), Karceski (2002), Sias (2004).

In conclusion, it is most likely that information amplification will influence investment valuations. Because there appears to be an inverse affective relationship between perceived risk and expected returns in the minds of many investors and because affect is a significant influence in asset valuation, it is likely that positive investment information will result in upwardly amplified market valuations. Expected return will be biased upward while risk will be biased downward. Negative information should have the reverse effect. However, the amplification of negative information is subject to two complicating influences. Loss averse investors usually react more strongly to identified negative information but investors often underestimate the potential of negative information because of "desirability bias" (positive outcomes are seen as more likely than negative outcomes), Olsen (1997a).

4.7 Implications and Evidence

By now, it may appear that the variable called "perceived financial risk" might present market modelers with an iconoclastic nightmare. However, there are a few identifiable overarching general implications. This section will identify those important themes and briefly identify some of the more representative supporting research.

First and foremost, perceptions of financial risk are dominated by fear of loss. Although variability in potential return is also sometimes mentioned as a risk attribute, more detailed probing reveals that people are not especially troubled by unexpected gains but instead by the low side of the return distribution. Rode and Wang (2000) present theory and evidence suggesting that this predisposition is an evolutionary adaptation. In fact, animal studies identify loss aversion as a "common denominator" underlying animal foraging behavior and investment selection, Olsen (2008). The desire to avoid loss is also indicated in the tendency to prefer outcome distributions with positive skew and an extreme dislike for return distributions exhibiting the potential for very large losses, even where the chance of the loss is very low.

Loss can be manifested in different ways. Sometimes loss is perceived in absolute terms, such as in dollars lost or a particular low percentage return. At other times, it is expressed in qualitative terms, such as a future opportunity that would have to be forgone. On other occasions, it is perceived in relative terms whereby the loss is expressed as that of falling below some desired target or aspiration level. Finally, it might be expressed as a fear of experiencing future regret, as in making a choice that yields an outcome that would be disappointing or embarrassing, Landman (1993). Much has been made of the observation that in some experimental situations described as "loss situations" investors tend to act as "risk takers". That is, they prefer the more risky gamble that might put them much deeper into a financial hole if a positive alternative does not materialize. Examination of this behavior in "real world" settings suggests that the decision maker is still attempting to avoid a loss. He/she is usually trying to avoid an existing bad situation but one that has not as yet yielded the "final blow". Thus, the risk-taking behavior actually represents a last ditch effort to avoid the impending calamity, which is not perceived as being made significantly worse by any additional negative results. When one has his/her "back to the wall," behavior that would be inappropriate in more normal situations is often quite rational. For example, military combat, firefighting, and even important athletic contests are rife with such behavior.

Some of the earlier studies of importance with regard to the avoidance of loss are those by Alderfer and Bierman (1970) Gooding (1976),Cooley(1977), Laughunn and Payne (1980). Later studies include those of Solt (1989), Harlow and Rao (1989), Unser (2000), Ippolito (1992), March and Shapira (1992), Holtgrave and Weber (1993), Shapira (1995), Olsen (1997a), Williman and O'Creevy (2002), Kermer and Driver-Linn (2006).

The second major implication of risk perception studies is that most investors' risk perceptions simultaneously contain affective and cognitive elements. By affective elements, I mean risk attributes that reflect the investor's feelings of goodness or badness toward an investment. These feelings can be nonconscious or conscious. In general, good (bad) feeling leads to perceptions of lower (greater) risk. This affective influence can also give rise to a negative, as opposed to a positive statistical correlation between perceived risk and expected return. Usually, affect has the most significance where the decision situation is complex and effortful, information is perceived to be incomplete or unreliable, the decision maker feels less confident, is female, and the time for evaluation is short. Cognitive risk attributes, such as statistics, tend to be more commonly used by experts and those who have been trained to think in more abstract terms. However, it is not the case that experts are uninfluenced by affective considerations.

Finally, it is important to note that current financial theory emphasizes the importance of correlation for risk control in a portfolio context. That is investors should diversify by investing in assets that have returns that are less than perfectly positively correlated. Nevertheless, studies of nonprofessional investors indicate that people do not follow this advice, Benartzi and Thaler (1995), Fisher and Meir (1997). The reasons appear to be twofold. First, humans do not well understand the formal concept of covariance in nonnatural and abstract circumstances. Humans do not appear to recognize covariance unless it occurs in very repetitive and concrete circumstances. Second, humans tend to mentally compartmentalize decisions by goal and context. Thus, when they formulate an investment plan, they do not visualize the task as a whole but instead see a need to make separate investments for retirement, the children's education, etc. Therefore, the risk level of the individual's portfolio becomes a random byproduct instead of a managed attribute, Shefrin (2000). "Total perceived risk" is not a naturally meaningful concept because it entails multiple goals, timelines, and information types.

It is interesting to consider how affective risk attributes might offer the most parsimonious explanation of many of the risk/return anomalies that have arisen from tests of current financial theories,(the CAPM in particular). Take for instance the observation that firm size and the ratio of book value to market value appear to be risk proxies, Fama and French (1993), Fama and French (1996), Jensen and Johnson (1997). More specifically, common stocks of small firms and those with high book to market values appear to yield excessively high ex post returns, after standard (Beta) risk adjustments. There is evidence that small firms yield higher compensatory equilibrium returns because they are associated with increased negative affect due to difficulty of evaluation, Olsen and Troughton (2000). Assuming risk aversion, these more negatively perceived firms require a higher compensatory risk premium resulting in a lower market value. Thus, these more negatively affected firms, with their higher BV/MV, yield higher conventionally risk-adjusted ex post returns.

The observation that investors are subject to "home bias," a predilection for the stocks of "local" companies, has been widely noted, Huberman (2001), Grinblatt and Keloharju (2001). Again, positive affect may be a reason for this behavior. Affect research shows that decision makers see as more positive, and hence less risky, those financial assets that are more familiar, Gonzach (2000), Weber and Siebermorgen (2005), Cao (Cao et al. 2008). Thus, even if the "home firm" is cognitively seen as identical to a nonhome equivalent, the home firm is likely to be favored because of the positive sentiment associated with familiarity.

There are many other anomalies that may result from affective influence, Thaler (2005) Shefrin (2000). Herding and over reaction are likely related to the observed positive affect and lower perceived risk associated with crowd following and group membership, Wang and Johnson (1995), Wang and Simons (2001); Scherer and Cho (2003). Likewise, the disposition effect is likely associated with the negative affect associated with the formal acknowledgment of loss, Landman (1993). Similarly, large IPO premiums quite probably are affect related. As an example, expectations of gain may have an amplified influence on stock prices due to the affectively induced inverse ex ante relationship between expected gain and perceived risk.

Most of the studies that have investigated perceived financial risk from both affective and cognitive perspectives are of more recent origin. Much of this research has not received extensive publicity because of the traditional finance emphasis on statistical risk metrics. Nevertheless, important affective/cognitive financial risk perception research involving experts and novices, and utilizing many different research designs can be found in Farrelly and Reichenstein (1984) MacCrimmon and Wehrung (1986), Harlow and Brown (1990), Goszcznyska (1991), Shapira (1995), Jungerman (1997), Lopes (1997), Olsen (1997b), Olsen and Troughton (2000), Olsen (2001, 2002, 2004, 2008), Jianakoplous and Bernasek (1998), Macgregor and Slovic (1999), Williams and Voon (1999), Gonzach (2000), Diacon and Ennew (2001), Bohner and Zeckhauser (2004), Dunn (2005), Koonce and Gascho (2005), Weber and Siebermorgen (2005).

The third important implication of risk perception research is that risk perceptions can be influenced by cultural and group factors. That is investors' perceptions of what is risky involves cultural values as well as considerations of the distribution of loss among group members. In this regard, studies by Renn and Rohrnan (2000), Slovic (1993) find risk attributes, such as fairness, voluntarism, effect on future generations, are important. Bouyer and Bagdassaian (2001) and Peters and Slovic (1996) find world views to be important. Those who see the world from a more egalitarian or individualistic perspective see hazards as posing greater risks than those who believe in a more hierarchical society or whom are more fatalistic. Wang and Johnson (1995), Wang and Simons (2001) find that risks are perceived as greater by small close-knit groups while Scherer and Cho (2003) find that individual risk perceptions tend to become more similar as group interaction increases. Nisbett (2003) notes that Asians are more likely to perceive risk in a more affective fashion, be less overconfident in belief, less inclined to believe in continuity of returns over time, and more likely to follow group convention than Westerners. Finally, Viklund (2003) and Olsen (2008) note a strong inverse relationship between personal trust and perceived risk. Siegrist and Earle (2003) note that as decisions become more complex, trust appears to become the preferred affective substitute for risk estimated in a more probabilistic fashion.

Johnson and Grayson (2005) note that investors' trust in their financial advisors appears to be influenced by both cognitive and affective attributes. "Cognitive trust" is based upon perceptions of competence and reliability whereas "Affective trust" is based upon care, concern, and familiarity.

4.8 Entrepreneurs: Confirmation About the Risk Perception Process

Most discussions of entrepreneurial behavior are heavily weighted toward the subject of risk because the activity is viewed as involving a willing acceptance of greater financial uncertainty. Earlier literature suggested that entrepreneurs had a high personal tolerance for risk that accounted for their risk proclivity. More recent research has shown that risk tolerance has little explanatory value. Instead, it appears that the nature of entrepreneurial activity causes budding entrepreneurs to select and weigh information in such a way that risk perceptions are very often "low side biased," Krueger (2003).

The entrepreneurial milieu skews the decision process toward the use of more affective decision rules that result in more favorably perceived risk/return opportunities. A critical element in this process is the affective tendency to equate opportunities with high expected return with lower levels of risk, Alhakami and Slovic (1994), Jordan and Kass (2002), Finucane and Holup (2006). In addition, there is evidence that entrepreneurs tend to give greater weight to expected outcomes as opposed to prospective risk in investment decisions because of the affective influence of time constraints, incomplete information, and ambiguity, Baron (1998), Palich and Ray Bagby (1995). Additional research has suggested that cognitive errors associated with overconfidence, feelings of control, and a belief in the "law of small numbers" further exacerbate the downward affective risk bias, Mitchell and Busenitz (2002), Simon and Houghton (1999). In entrepreneurial environments, we see the full influence of the dual decision process and how it can lead to biased risk perceptions. Entrepreneurs do not appear to have significantly higher risk tolerance; they just judge the perceived risks to be less threatening.

4.9 Conclusion

In an earlier chapter, I discussed how neoclassical finance has become descriptively hobbled and normatively suspect by adopting assumptions that are now scientifically untenable, Olsen (2001). Neoclassical Finance incorrectly assumed that humans were, or at least could become, axiomatically rational optimizers, as implied by the now outdated psychology of behaviorism. Second, it assumed a deterministic reality that could be fully deciphered through reductionism; an assumption that has also been overturned by complexity theory and quantum theory. Until recently, with the reawakened interest in behavioral economics and the new "behavioral finance," finance appears not to have sought the necessary nourishment from its social science roots while constructing elegant but fragile mathematical edifices.

The quantification of risk is operationally convenient and necessary for developing theories of market behavior. However, inattention to the more complex affective side of risk perception is now limiting a more profound understanding of risk-driven investment behavior. Individual investors, industry, and government are constantly looking for better ways to measure, communicate, and contend with financial risk. Normative processes leading to better investment results cannot be developed and enacted without understanding the psychology and limits of the investing mind. Hopefully, this chapter will stimulate further research along these lines.

References

Abolafia, M. 1996. *Making markets*. Cambridge: Harvard University Press.

Alderfer, C.P., and H. Bierman. 1970. Choices with risk: Beyond the mean and variance. *Journal of Business* 43(3): 341–353.

Alexander, G., and J.C. Francis. 1986. *Portfolio analysis*. Englewood Cliffs: Prentice Hall.

Alhakami, A.S., and P. Slovic. 1994. A psychological study of the inverse relationship between perceived risk and benefit. *Risk Analysis* 14(6): 1085–1096.

Axelrod, R. 1997. *The complexity of cooperation*. Princeton: Princeton University Press.

Barice, Richard, and Hank, Jenkins-Smith. 1995. Risk perceptions of men and women scientists, Eugene Oregon, Decision Research paper.

Baron, R. 1998. Cognitive mechanisms in entrepreneurship: Why and when entrepreneurs think differently than other people. *Journal of Business Venturing* 13: 275–294.

Benartzi, S., and R. Thaler. 1995. Myopic risk aversion and the risk premium puzzle. *Quarterly Journal of Economics* 110(1): 73–92.

Berkowitz, L. 2000. *Causes and consequences of feelings*. Cambridge: Cambridge University Press.

Berns, G., and J. Chappelow. 2006. Neurobiological substrates of dread. *Science* 312: 754–758.

Berridge, K., and P. Winkielman. 2003. What is an unconscious emotion? *Cognition and Emotion* 17(2): 181–211.

Bohner, I., and R. Zeckhauser. 2004. Trust, risk and betrayal. *Journal of Economic Behavior and Organization* 55: 467–484.

Bouyer, M., and S. Bagdassaian. 2001. Personality correlates of risk perception. *Risk Analysis* 21(3): 457–465.

Brandstatter, E., and A. Kubberger. 2002. A cognitive-emotional account of the shape of the probability weighting function. *Journal of Behavioral Decision Making* 15: 79–100.

Breiter, H., and I. Aharon. 2001. Functional imaging of neural response to expectancy and experience of monetary gains and losses. *Neuron* 30: 619–634.

Burton, Robert. 2008. *On being certain*. New York: St. Martin Press.

Cetina, K.K. 2005. *The sociology of financial markets*. Oxford: Oxford University Press.

Cao, H. Henry, et. al. 2008. Fear of the unknown: Familiarity and economic decisions. Working paper, Beijing, China, Cheung Kong Graduate School of Business.

Cashdan, Elizabeth. 1990. *Risk and uncertainty in tribal and peasant economies*. San Francisco: Westview Press.

Chaiken, S., and Y. Trope. 1999. *Dual process theories in social psychology*. New York: Guilford Press.

Chalmers, D. 1996. *The conscious mind: In search of a fundamental theory*. Oxford: Oxford University Press.

Cooley, P. 1977. A multidimensional analysis of institutional investor perceptions of risk. *Journal of Finance* 32(1): 27–45.

Cooper, M. 2005. Changing names with style. *Journal of Finance* 60(6): 2825–2858.

Damasio, A. 2003. *Looking for Spinoza: Joy, sorrow, and the feeling brain*. New York: Harcourt Brace.

Damasio, A. 1999. *The feeling of what happens*. New York: Harcourt Brace.

Dennis, P. 2002. Who blinks in volatile markets, individuals or institutions? *Journal of Finance* 57(5): 1923–1949.

Diacon, S., and C. Ennew. 2001. Consumer perceptions of financial risk. *Geneva Paper on Risk and Insurance* 26(3): 389–409.

Dugation, L. 2000. *The imitation factor: Evolution beyond the gene*. New York: Free Press.

Eiser, J.R. 2002. Trust, perceived risk and attitudes toward food technologies. *Journal of Applied Social science* 32(11): 2423–2433.

Elliot, R., and K. Friston. 2000. Dissociable neural responses to human reward systems. *Journal of Neuroscience* 16: 6159–6165.

Ellsberg, D. 1961. Risk, ambiguity and the savage axioms. *Quarterly Journal of Economics* 75(3): 643–699.

Erb, H.-P., and A. Bioy. 2002. Choice preferences without inferences: Subconscious priming of risk attitudes. *Journal of Behavioral Decision Making* 15: 251–262.

Fama, E., and D. French. 1996. Multifactor explanations of asset pricing anomalies. *Journal of Finance* 51(1): 55–84.

Fama, E., and D. French. 1993. Common risk factors in the returns on stocks and bonds. *Journal of Financial Economics* 33(1): 3–56.

Farrelly, G., and W. Reichenstein. 1984. Risk perceptions of institutional investors. *Journal of Portfolio Management* 10(4): 5–12.

Fehr, E., and U. Fischbacher. 2005. *Neuroeconomic foundations of trust and social preference: Initial evidence*. Zurich: Switzerland Institute for Empirical Research in Economics.

Fenton-O'Creevy, M. 2005. *Traders*. Oxford: Oxford University Press.

Finucane, M., and J. Holup. 2006. Risk as value: Combining affect and analysis in risk judgments. *Journal of Risk Research* 9(2): 141–164.

Fisher, K., and P. Shaver. 1990. How emotions develop. *Cognition and Emotion* 4(2): 81–127.

Fisher, K., and S. Meir. 1997. The mean variance optimization puzzle: Security portfolios and food portfolios. *Financial Analysts Journal* 53(4): 41–50. July/August.

Forgas, J. 2000. *Feeling and thinking: The role of affect in social cognition*. Cambridge: Cambridge University Press.

Forlani, D. 2002. Risk and rationality: The influence of decision domain and perceived outcome control on managers' high risk decisions. *Journal of Behavioral Decision Making* 15(2): 125–140.

Freeman, Steven. 1997. *Good decisions: Reconciling human rationality, evolution and ethics*. Cambridge: Sloan School, MIT.

Frijida, N., and A. Manstead. 2000. *Emotions and beliefs: How feelings influence thought*. Cambridge: Cambridge University Press.

Firth, C. 2007. *Making up the mind*. Massachusetts: Malden.

Gardner, D. 2008. *Risk: The science and politics of fear*. London: Virgin Press.

Gonzach, Y. 2000. Judging risk and return of financial assets. *Organizational Behavior and Human Decision Processes* 83(2): 353–370.

Gaulin, S. 2001. *Psychology: An evolutionary approach*. Prentice Hall: Saddle River New Jersey.

Geary, David. 2005. *The origin of mind: Evolution of the brain, cognition and general intelligence*. New York: Psychology Press.

Ghosh, D., and M. Ray. 1997. Risk, ambiguity and decision choice: Some additional evidence. *Decision Science* 28(1): 81–103.

Gigerenzer, G., and R. Selten. 2001. *Bounded rationality: The adaptive toolbox*. Cambridge: MIT Press.

Gilbert, P. 1998. The evolved basis and adaptive functions of cognitive distortions. *British Journal of Medical Psychology* 71: 447–463.

Gooding, A. 1976. Some preliminary findings regarding the nature of investment risk. *Financial Review* 11: 21–35.

Goszczynyska, M. 1991. Risk perception in Poland: A comparison with other countries. *Journal of Behavioral Decision Making* 4(3): 153–175.

Gray, J. 2004. Integration of emotion and cognitive control. *Current Directions in Psychological Science* 13(2): 46–49.

Grinblatt, M., and M. Keloharju. 2001. How distance, language and culture influence stockholdings and trades. *Journal of Finance* 56(3): 1053–1073.

Grossberg, S., and W. Gutowski. 1987. Neural dynamics of decision making under risk. *Psychological Review* 94(3): 300–318.

Hamann, S., and T. Ely. 2002. Ecstasy and agony: Activation of the human amygdala in positive and negative emotion. *Psychological Science* 13(2): 134–141.

Hammond, K. 1996. *Human judgment and social policy*. Oxford: Oxford University Press.

Hanoch, Y. 2002. Neither an angel nor an ant: Emotion as an aid in bounded rationality. *Journal of Economic Psychology* 23: 1–25.

Hardin, R. 2003. *Indeterminacy in society*. Princeton: Princeton University Press.
Harlow, W.V., and K. Brown. 1990. *The role of risk tolerance in the asset allocation process: A new perspective*. Charlottesville: CFA Research Foundation.
Harlow, W.V., and R. Rao. 1989. Asset pricing in a generalized mean lower partial moment framework: Theory and evidence. *Journal of Financial and Quantitative Analysis* 24(3): 285–311.
Ho, J., and R. Keller. 2002. Effects of outcome and probabilistic ambiguity on managerial choice. *Journal of Risk and Uncertainty* 24(1): 47–74.
Hogarth, R. 2001. *Educating intuition*. Chicago: University of Chicago Press.
Hogarth, R., and H. Kunreuther. 1995. Decision making under uncertainty: Arguing with yourself. *Journal of Risk and Uncertainty* 10(1): 15–36.
Holtgrave, D.R., and E. Weber. 1993. Dimensions of risk perception for financial and health risks. *Risk Analysis* 13(5): 553–558.
Huber, O. 1995. Ambiguity and perceived control. *Swiss Journal of Psychology* 54(3): 200–210.
Huberman, G. 2001. Familiarity breeds investment. *Review of Financial Studies* 14(3): 659–680.
Ippolito, R. 1992. Consumer reactions to measures of poor quality: Evidence from the mutual fund industry. *Journal of Law and Economics* 35(1): 45–70.
Jensen, G., and R. Johnson. 1997. New evidence on the size and price to book effects in stock returns. *Financial Analysts Journal* 53: 34–42. November/December.
Jianakoplous, N.A., and A. Bernasek. 1998. Are women more risk averse? *Economic Inquiry* 36: 620–630.
Johnson, D., and K. Grayson. 2005. Cognitive and affective trust in service relationships. *Journal of Business Research* 58: 500–507.
Johnson, J., and A.C. Bruce. 1998. Risk strategy under task complexity. *Journal of Behavioral Decision Making* 11: 1–17.
Johnston, Victor. 1999. *Why we feel: The science of human emotions*. Reading: Perseus Books.
Jordan, J., and K. Kass. 2002. Advertising in the mutual fund business. *Journal of Financial Services Marketing* 7(2): 129–140.
Jungerman, H. 1997. Reasons for uncertainty: From frequencies to stories. *Psychologische Beitrag* 39: 126–139.
Kahneman, D., and A. Tversky. 1992. Advances in prospect theory: Cumulative representations of uncertainty. *Journal of Risk and Uncertainty* 5(4): 297–323.
Karceski, J. 2002. Returns chasing behavior, mutual funds, and beta's death. *Journal of Financial and Quantitative Analysis* 37(4): 559–593.
Kermer, D., and E. Driver-Linn. 2006. Loss aversion in an affective forecasting error. *Psychological Science* 17(8): 649–652.
Keynes, J.M. 1936. *The general theory of employment, interest and money*. New York: Harcourt Brace.
Knight, F. 1921. *Risk, uncertainty and profit*. Chicago: University of Chicago Press.
Koonce, L., and M. Gascho. 2005. Judging the risk of financial instruments: Problems and potential remedies. *Accounting Review* 80(3): 871–895.
Kosfield, M., and M. Heinrich. 2005. Oxytocin increases trust. *Nature* 152(2): 671–676.
Krueger, Norris. 2003. The Cognitive Psychology of Entrepreneurship. In *Handbook of entrepreneurship research*, ed. Acs and Audretsh. Great Britain: Kluwer.
Landman, Janet. 1993. *Regret: The persistence of the possible*. Oxford: Oxford University Press.
Lane, R., and L. Nadel. 2000. *Cognitive neuroscience of emotion*. Oxford: Oxford University Press.
Laughunn, R., and J. Payne. 1980. Managerial risk preferences for below target returns. *Management Science* 26(12): 1238–1249.
Lauriola, M., and I. Levin. 2000. Relating individual differences in attitude toward ambiguity to risky choice. *Journal of Behavioral Decision Making* 14: 107–122.
Ledoux, J. 1996. *The emotional brain*. New York: Touchstone.
Lopes, L. 1997a. Between hope and fear: The psychology of risk. *Advances in Experimental Social Psychology* 20: 225–295.
Lopes, L. 1997b. Risky choice with fuzzy criteria. *Psychologische Bietrag* 39: 56–82.

Loewenstein, G., and E. Weber. 2001. Risk as feeling. *Psychological Bulletin* 127(2): 267–286.
Lupton, D. 1999. *Risk*. London: Routledge.
Maccrimmon, K., and D. Wehrung. 1986. *Taking risks: The management of uncertainty*. New York: Free Press.
Macgregor, D., and P. Slovic. 1999. Perception of financial risk: A survey study of advisors and planners. *Journal of Financial Planning* 12(8): 68–86.
March, J., and Z. Shapira. 1992. Variable risk preferences and the focus of attention. *Psychological Review* 99(1): 172–183.
Mitchell, R., and B. Lowell. 2002. Toward a theory of entrepreneurial cognition: Rethinking the people side of entrepreneurship research. *Entrepreneurship Theory and Practice – Winter* 27(2): 93–104.
Moreno, K., and T. Kida. 2003. The impact of affective reaction on risky decision making in an accounting context. *Journal of Accounting Research* 40(5): 1331–1349.
Nisbett, R. 2003. *The geography of thought*. New York: Free Press.
Noe, A. 2004. *Action in perception*. Cambridge: MIT Press.
Olsen, R. 1997a. Desirability bias among professional investment managers. *Journal of Behavioral Decision Making* 10: 65–72.
Olsen, R. 1997b. Investment risk: The expert's perspective. *Financial Analysts Journal* 53: 62–66. March/April.
Olsen, R., and G. Troughton. 2000. Are risk premiums caused by ambiguity? *Financial Analysts Journal* 56: 24–31. March/April.
Olsen, R. 2001. Professor Burrell's proposal for a behavioral finance. *Journal of Behavioral Finance* 2(1): 54–56.
Olsen, R., and C. Cox. 2001. The influence of gender in the perception and response to investment risk: The case of professional investors. *Journal of Behavioral Finance* 12(1): 29–36.
Olsen, R. 2002. Professional investors as naturalistic decision makers: Evidence and market implications. *Journal of Behavioral Finance* 3(3): 161–167.
Olsen, R. 2004. Trust, complexity and the 1990s market bubble. *Journal of Behavioral Finance* 5(4): 186–191.
Olsen, Robert. 2008. Animal foraging, hunter gatherer diets and investors' portfolios: Why the similarity ? Working paper, Decision research.
Olsen, R. 2008. Trust as risk and the foundation of investment value. *Journal of Socio-Economics* 37: 2189–2200.
Ormerod, P. 2000. *Butterfly economics*. New York: Basic Books.
Over, D., and B.T. Jonathan St Evans. 1996. *Rationality and reasoning*. New York: Psychology Press.
Over, D. 2003. *Evolution and the psychology of thinking*. New York: Psychology Press.
Palich, L., and D. Ray Bagby. 1995. Using cognitive risk theory to explain entrepreneurial risk taking: Challenging the conventional wisdom. *Journal of Business Venturing* 10: 425–438.
Peat, F.D. 2002. *From certainty to uncertainty: The story of science and ideas in the twentieth century*. Washington: Joseph Henry Press.
Pennington, N., and Hastie Reid. 1993. Reasoning in explanation based decision making. *Cognition* 49(1): 123–136. and Sons.
Peters, E., and P. Slovic. 1996. The role of affect and world views as orienting dispositions in the perception and acceptance of nuclear power. *Journal of Applied Psychology* 26: 1427–1453.
Pfaff, D. 2007. *The neuroscience of fair play*. Washington: Dana Press.
Pidgeon, N., and R. Kasperson. 2006. *The social amplification of risk*. Cambridge: Cambridge University Press.
Reber, A. 1993. *Implicit learning and tacit knowledge*. Oxford: University of Oxford Press.
Renn, O., and B. Rohrnan. 2000. *Cross cultural risk perception: A survey of empirical studies*. Boston: Kluwer.
Renn, O. 2004. The perception of risk. *Toxicology Letters* 149: 405–413.

Reyna, V. 2004. How people make decisions that involve risk: A dual process approach. *Current Directions in Psychological Science* 13(2): 60–66.
Ridley, M. 1996. *The origins of virtue: Human instincts and the evolution of cooperation*. New York: Penguin Press.
Rizzolatti, G., and L. Craighero. 2004. The mirror neuron system. *Annual Review of Neuroscience* 27: 169–192.
Rode, C., and X.T. Wang. 2000. Risk sensitive decision making examined within an evolutionary framework. *American Behavioral Scientist* 43(6): 926–939.
Sarin, R., and M. Weber. 1992. Recent developments in modeling preferences: Uncertainty and ambiguity. *Journal of Risk and Uncertainty* 5(2): 602–615.
Savage, L. 1954. *The foundations of statistics*. New York: Wiley.
Scherer, C., and H. Cho. 2003. A social contagion theory of risk perception. *Risk Analysis* 23(2): 261–267.
Shackle, G. 1952. *Expectation in economics*. Cambridge: Cambridge University Press.
Shapira, Z. 1995. *Taking risks: A managerial perspective*. New York: Russell Sage Press.
Shefrin, H. 2000. *Beyond greed and fear*. Cambridge: Harvard Business School Press.
Shiller, R. 1989. *Market volatility*. Cambridge: MIT Press.
Sias, R. 2004. Institutional herding. *Review of Financial Studies* 17(1): 165–206.
Siegrist, M., and G. Cvetkovich. 2000. Salient value similarity, social trust, and risk/benefit perception. *Risk Analysis* 20(3): 353–362.
Siegrist, M., and T. Earle. 2003. Test of a trust confidence model. *Risk Analysis* 23(4): 705–716.
Simon, M., and S. Houghton. 1999. Cognitive bias, risk perception, and venture formation: How individuals decide to start companies. *Journal of Business Venturing* 15: 113–134.
Sjoberg, L. 2002. The allegedly simple structure of experts' risk perceptions. *Science, Technology and Human Values* 27(4): 443–459.
Skyrms, B. 2004. *The stag hunt and the evolution of social structure*. Cambridge: Cambridge University Press.
Slovic, P. 1987. The perception of risk. *Science* 23(4): 280–285.
Slovic, P. 1993. Perceived risk, trust and democracy. *Risk Analysis* 13(6): 675–682.
Slovic, P. 2000. *The perception of risk*. London: Earthscan.
Smith, C. 1999. *Success and survival on wall street*. Oxford: Rowman and Littlefield.
Smith, K., and J. Dickout. 2002. Neuronal substrates for choice under ambiguity, risk, gains and losses. *Management Science* 48: 711–718.
Sober, E., and D.S. Wilson. 1998. *Unto others: The evolution and psychology of unselfish behavior*. Cambridge: Harvard University Press.
Solt, M. 1989. Good companies, bad stocks. *Journal of Portfolio Management* 15(4): 39–44.
Thaler, R. 2005. *Advances in behavioral finance*, vol. 2. New York: Russell Sage.
Thompson, E. 2007. *Mind in life*. Cambridge: Harvard University Press.
Tversky, A., and D. Koehler. 1994. Support theory: A non extensional representation of subjective probability. *Psychological Review* 101(4): 547–567.
Unser, M. 2000. Lower partial moments as measures of perceived risk: An experimental study. *Journal of Economic Psychology* 21(3): 253–280.
Viklund, M. 2003. Trust and risk perception in Western Europe: A cross national study. *Risk Analysis* 23(4): 727–738.
Wang, X.T., and V. Johnson. 1995. Perceived social context and risk preference. *Journal of Behavioral Decision Making* 8: 279–293.
Wang, X.T., and F. Simons. 2001. Social cues and verbal framing in risky choice. *Journal of Behavioral Decision Making* 14: 1–15.
Weber, E., and R. Milliman. 1997. Perceived risk attitudes: Relating risk perception to risky choice. *Management Science* 43(2): 123–144.
Weber, E., and C. Hsee. 1998. Cross cultural differences in risk perception but cross cultural similarities in attitudes toward perceived risk. *Management Science* 44(9): 1205–1217.

Weber, E., and N. Siebermorgen. 2005. Communicating asset risk: How name recognition and the format of historic volatility information affect risk perception and investment behavior. *Risk Analysis* 25(3): 597–609.

Williams, S., and Y. Voon. 1999. The effects of mood on managerial risk perceptions: Exploring affect and the dimensions of risk. *Journal of Social Psychology* 139(3): 268–287.

Williman, P., and M.F. O'Creevy. 2002. Traders, managers and loss aversion in investment banking. *Accounting, Organizations and Society* 27: 85–98.

Wright, R. 2001. *The logic of human destiny*. New York: Vintage Books.

Chapter 5
Contribution of Neuroscience to Financial Decision-Making

Richard W. Ackley and Lukasz M. Konopka

Abstract The apparent limitations of rational decision-making have become increasingly important phenomena that are unexplained by traditional economic models. Initial research found that these anomalies were not just random deviations from normative models, but actually, systematic physiologically driven psychological processes. Behavioral Finance and Economics that emerged as biopsychological fields began to explain how people actually use information when making financial decisions. In the past, behavioral economic research has relied on extrapolation. Choice could only be inferred from observed outcomes through behavior. Recently, neuroscience, as powered by in-vivo brain imaging and our understanding of brain biology, has allowed scientists to more directly examine the internal landscape of decision-making. A literature review of applied clinical neuroscience and neuroeconomics yields a new perspective on decision-making – one that is driven by objective data. These data are generated by means of newly developed tools. However, these tools come with well-defined strengths and weaknesses. Understanding the technological constraints is critical to appropriate data interpretation and future model building. This review addresses two different and independent brain operations: the reflexive automatic process and the reflective deliberate process. The meso-limbic and meso-cortical systems, which underlie each operation, are essential to understanding decision-making in the light of the emotional, learning, memory, and executive processes involved in decision-making. A significant amount of work has been devoted to studies of the neurotransmitter system involving Dopamine (DA). Dopamine seems to emerge as a key player in decision-making due to the association it holds with reward, attention, motivation, and error assessment brain processes. In addition, DA, in concert with other neurotransmitters and neuro-modulators, influences affective states that play a significant role in regulating physiological and psychological homeostasis. An individual's intrinsic processes that are genetically influenced and modulated to regulate homeostasis will consequently impact acute sensitivities as related to rewards

R.W. Ackley (✉)
The Chicago School of Professional Psychology, Chicago, IL, USA
e-mail: rackley@thechicagoschool.edu

R. Yazdipour, *Advances in Entrepreneurial Finance: With Applications from Behavioral Finance and Economics*, DOI 10.1007/978-1-4419-7527-0_5,

and punishments. Thus, the threshold and tolerance for reward and punishment are strongly associated with the decision-making. In line with the growing body of neuroeconomic research, this review presents the neuroscientific underpinnings of information processing and decision-making. The conclusions are not about the rational decision model being wrong, but rather about its potential limitations in light of new biologically driven data.

5.1 Introduction

Over the past 50 years, anomalies in economic data have taxed the classical interpretations of economic behavior. In an effort to amend their models, economists' attention has increasingly turned to explanations that psychology can offer. In the 1950s, Herbert Simon initially offered economic refinements with his ideas of "bounded rationality." The later work of Richard Cyert and James March in the 1960s further elaborated and developed the rationality theory. The real turning point in the field of economics arose in 1978 when Daniel Kahneman and Amos Tversky offered the prospect theory. As psychologists, their stance toward examining decision-making behavior was quite different than the previous investigators. They expanded the focus from "how people should behave" to "how people actually do behave." Through a series of studies, they were able to reveal cognitive biases and heuristics that often contaminate decisions made by real people. This led to a new wave in economic thinking, which came to be called behavioral economics. As a founding developer of behavioral economics, Richard Thaler played an influential role in establishing this subfield. Other important and key players who have contributed to the behavioral field include: Colin Camerer, Drezac Prelec, Matthew Rabin, and George Lowenstein. Their revolutionary work resulted in cross-disciplinary contributions from fields such as psychology, which helped to further investigate the behavioral inconsistencies that present in decision-making. This new wave of economic approach has recently forayed into the application of psychological theory in efforts to facilitate clarity within the tenets of behavioral economics. With applications from the fields of cognitive psychology and neuroscience, research has now produced a new reality for the understanding of inference and choice. Assumptions that were previously considered de rigueur in economics and finance are now speculative under the light of recent contributions from the neuroscience field. What was once just inferred through mathematical models can now be observed directly through brain imaging. Previous subjective examinations of outward behavior can now be objectively measured through the understanding of brain activity.

This chapter will examine the contributions that neuroscience provides for financial decision-making. Our purpose is to discuss an overview of the findings that will be informative for behavioral economics and finance. Given that many of the field's contributions revolve around the considerations concerning the nature and dynamics of gains and losses, we will focus on the reward and punishment systems in the brain. Relevant and associated neurobiological processes will be discussed in depth. We will also fully examine the impact that the dopaminergic system has on individual perception, deliberation, and action as relevant to decision-making. Our ability to investigate these effects comes from the utilization of brain-imaging modalities. To appreciate the findings from a neuroscience perspective, it is essential to understand the mechanisms involved in the most popular brain-imaging techniques. In Sect. 5.2 we will explore an overview of the technologies and methods that are employed by the neuroscience field to measure brain activity. This will include highlights of the strengths, weaknesses, and limitations of individual approaches. In Sect. 5.3 we will emphasize two major brain processes and their role in decision-making. Importantly, these processes involve differentiating sources of motivation and therefore rely upon different types of neuronal networks and inputs. Further, building on these concepts, in Sect. 5.4, we will examine the impact that cognition and affect have on decision-making. As dopamine (DA) is critical to understanding the operations of cognition and affect, we will explain its role in the decision-making processes. With this foundation, in Sect. 5.5, we will look at the systematic types of biases, heuristics, and errors that arise in decision-making and further identify how these are related to cognition, affect, and dopamine regulation. Sect. 5.6 presents comprehensive summary and relevant conclusions.

5.2 Overview of Technologies and Methods

5.2.1 Methods

Due to the advent of imaging tools, questions regarding the biological basis of behavior can be determined with greater insight and confidence. The recent shift in thinking has shed light on new possibilities that question the validity of old paradigms. In this section, we will address the availability and utility of imaging tools, primarily focusing on the technologies that may be practically employed in the investigation of decision-making.

The human brain depends on very complex neuronal networks that coordinate activities for problem solving, mood regulation, and behavioral presentation. Given these underlying brain driven processes we must focus our understanding on the associated neuronal interactions. Neurons communicate with one another through complex electrical signaling identified as action potentials. This chemically mediated process is an all or nothing occurrence. Meaning, if a certain threshold is not met for firing, the neuron will cease communication. Further, this chemical process involves graded characteristics that are based upon the interactions we define as neurotransmitters (NT) and neuromodulators (see Fig. 5.1). These chemicals, when

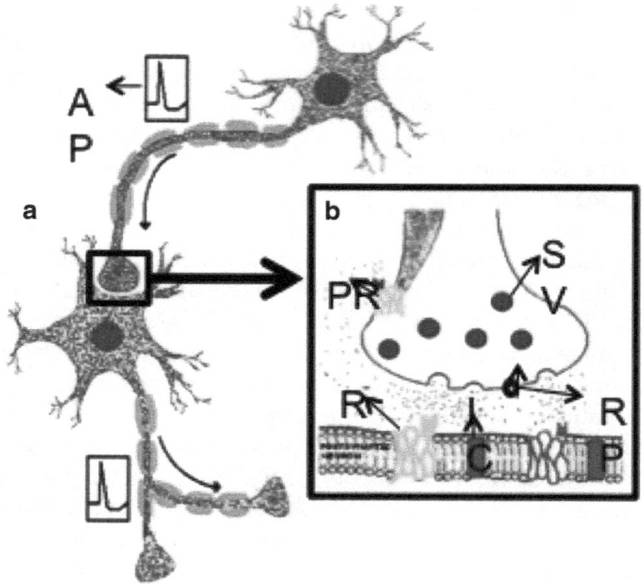

Fig. 5.1 Interaction of two neurons (**a**) via synaptic contact (**b**). This figure represents two hypothetical neurons interacting by synaptic contact, action potentials (AP), and chemical transmission. The enlarged section B provides a simplified schematic of the pre and post-synaptic structures composed of the pre-synaptic terminal with synaptic vesicles (SV) containing neurotransmitter (NT), re-uptake pump (RP) where cocaine binds and prevents re-absorption of the NT, pre-synaptic receptors (PR) that limit NT available for release, synaptic cleft, post-synaptic membrane with receptors (R), and ion channels (IC)

released, bind to receptor proteins and, in most instances, generate an electrical event. The amplitude of these events depends on the number of NT molecules released and the number of available receptors. In many cell types, we can record synchronized neuronal activity from this active brain region. Many synchronized, electrical, neuronal events can be recorded through EEG, then mapped in three dimensional space by Functional Magnetic Resonance Imaging (fMRI), and further quantified by nuclear medicine techniques such as SPECT and/or PET imaging (see Fig. 5.3). It is estimated that normal human brain contains approximately 100 billion neurons and that each neuron, as based on its function and location, will receive 10–50 thousand inputs.

Magnetic Resonance Imaging (MRI) technology is currently the golden standard for structural brain imaging. This method allows for highly defined structural definitions of brain anatomy that may be used for quantitative analyses. Due to well-defined and visualized morphological detail of the human brain, imaging allows us to generate hypotheses that relate brain volume to function (see Fig. 5.3). For instance, significant data has shown that chronic stress is highly correlated with a decrease in hippocampal volume (Bremner et al. 1995). This is particularly true in patients diagnosed with post-traumatic stress disorder (Gianaros et al. 2007; Lupien et al. 2009). This literature argues that hippocampal volume decrease is directly related to observable and measurable behavioral consequences.

Functional Magnetic Resonance Imaging (fMRI) is a technique related to MRI studies. This technique allows for the functional assessment of the biological substrates that are related to one's behavior. First, an individual brain template is created for the patient and it is then superimposed onto a functional or normative template. Blood Oxygenation Level Dependency (BOLD) is the critical and differentiating function in this imaging modality. Brain changes in BOLD are directly related to neuronal activity levels. There are significant advantages to this popular method. For instance, the potential neuronal networks that are involved in a given task can be clearly observed through the co-registration of functional data into well-defined anatomical substrates. This data contributes to the understanding of the biological basis underlying a performed task. Subsequent to evaluation, theories related to structural and functional abnormalities can be generated. Another advantage of fMRI method is that the subject can be repetitively exposed to a task. Variations in task techniques can occur. Additionally the method is relatively safe to the participants. The utility of MRI/fMRI assessments are only limited by the participant's ability to be focused, motivated, and motionless. In addition, an fMRI can be used in a single subject design paradigm. This enables the researcher to compare an individual to themselves under different behavioral conditions. This paradigm provides significant importance to experimental designs that allow for the evaluation of individual variability. MRI/fMRI data can also be averaged across subjects, which can lead to more generalizable inferences related to the behavioral outcome.

At several levels, we need to address the drawbacks of MRI studies and how the involved quantitative analysis relates to behavior: First it is unclear how much structural variability is present in the general population. Also, specific differences have yet to be determined on the basis of age and gender. Further, we lack normative, gender-specific databases that control for volumetric variability. The studies described above were reliant on controlled populations that were recruited by individual labs. Thus, generalizability of these data could be questionable. Also, this technology only indirectly assesses neuronal activity patterns due to poor temporal resolution in fMRI techniques. Neuronal activity has a time resolution in the millisecond range whereas the BOLD signal reflects changes in seconds. In addition, functional imaging requires significant subject cooperation, as the participant must remain motionless during the designed task. Patients may find themselves relatively uncomfortable in the tight space of the MRI magnet, and in some cases, this provokes a significant emotional shift. During the MRI acquisition period, the participant is exposed to loud clicking, which may disrupt brain processes (see Fig. 5.2). One can manipulate these variables by accommodating the patient's needs and masking the sound. However, because only a subpopulation may tolerate the MRI, this may impact the experimental design and undermine the ability to generalize the findings. In addition, the fMRI signal is often only acquired from focal neuroanatomical sites. Therefore, other brain regions and structures may be activated during a given task and not adequately accounted for. This can lead and contribute to potentially erroneous interpretations. Moreover, during data acquisition, it is impossible

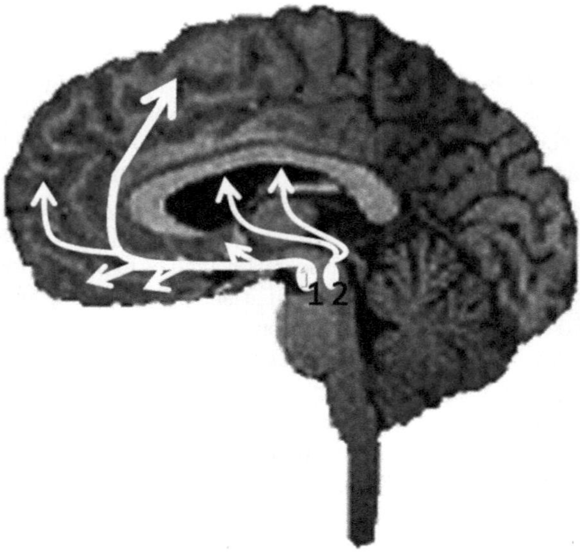

Fig. 5.2 Sagittal section through the brain with mapped DA pathways originating in region 1 and 2. This figure is based on the MRI sagittal section through the human brain. Two main regions are identified. Region 1 represents axons from dopamine containing neurons projecting from the ventral tegmental area (VTA) via the meso-limbic and meso-cortical pathways. These paths provide Dopamine input to the limbic system and include the reward area of the nucleus accumbens (mesolimbic). The meso-cortical pathway supplies input into the executive brain regions called the frontal lobes. Area 2 (substantia nigra) contains DA neurons DA neurons projecting to the striatum

to assess the data's quality. Only post-acquisition processing exposes the potential weakness in the acquired data. Due to these shortcomings, the subjects must follow precise instructions and remain motionless during data acquisition. Very recent developments in the software and hardware of fMRI systems facilitate online evaluation of the data quality as well as control for movement artifact.

Photon emission based imaging tools are another measurement strategy. Studies that utilize this type of technique rely on injecting a ligand into the participant's vascular system. The effect of the ligand is used to measure the process. For instance, if we want to measure the utilization of glucose (see Fig. 5.3d), we can either measure specified protein receptor binding, or bold flow. These techniques are invasive because they involve direct injection of a foreign radio-labeled compound into the subject's vascular system. The shorter-lived ligands, whose life cycle is in minutes, can be utilized. However, these studies are limited by the scarce availability of these ligands and one's proximity to a cyclotron (laboratory devoted to synthesis of radiochemicals called ligands) facility. In addition to this technique's invasiveness, one must consider the radiation exposure. The results of the studies using nuclear medicine techniques can be analyzed in a similar way as the data is acquired in the fMRI method. The conditions can be compared in the within subject

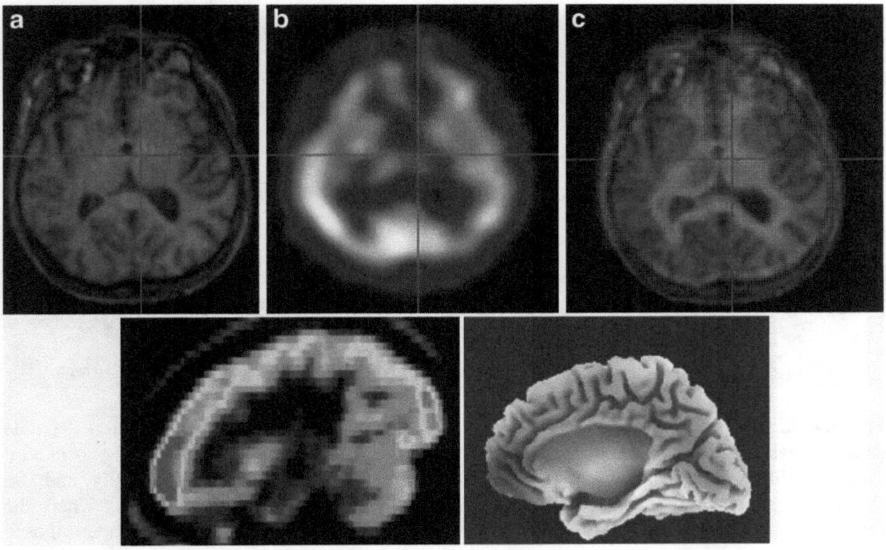

Fig. 5.3 Three imaging modalities following cocaine abuse: MRI (**a**), SPECT (**b**), MRI and SPECT on the same image (**c**), PET (**d**), and EEG (**e**) LORETA. Images were acquired with MRI, SPECT, PET and EEG. The **a**, **b**, and **c** images were obtained from two subjects. The first image sets may be superimposed by co-registration so not only structure but activity may be evaluated. The second set, **d** and **e**, were obtained from an individual who abused cocaine and presented with significant clinical anxiety. The increased activity in the frontal lobes is shown with PET. Increased glucose uptake and beta EGG activity are seen in the same brain region

as well as between group design. Structural imaging may be enriched by nuclear medicine techniques such as PET or SPECT methods where co-registration of these techniques provides for additional information (see Fig. 5.3b and c).

Another technique that is currently gaining wide use is quantitative electroencephalography (qEEG). This technique allows for the measurement of cortical electrophysiology in true-time resolution. The method quantifies a summation of postsynaptic and pre-synaptic action potentials that are derived from the neuron's electrical activity. This activity is measured in milliseconds, providing for high temporal resolution. Historically, these measures informed us about the scalp distribution of electrical activities; however, new developments in electrical source analysis give us the ability to represent surface electrical activity maps in a three dimensional space that is defined by MRI. A particular tool that can be utilized for this purpose is a low-resolution brain electromagnetic tomography (LORETA). This new software allows for surface activity to be analyzed in the MRI space (see Fig. 5.2a and b) (Fig. 5.4). Given that electrical activity analysis can be displayed on the MRI template, we can directly compare this modality to other functional and structural modalities such as MRI, fMRI, PET, and SPECT (see Fig. 5.3d and e). In the field of applied neuroscience, these techniques have facilitated our current studies and allowed us the ability to evaluate the theoretical validity of the proposed hypothesis.

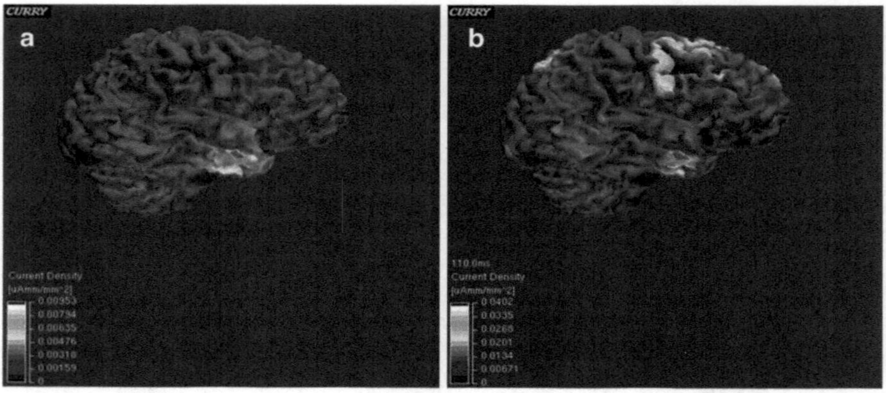

Fig. 5.4 Mapping of the auditory response to low (**a**) and high intensity stimulation (**b**). The figure shows mapping of electrical brain activity from a subject who was listening to neutral sounds of different intensities. **a** represents the brain response to 60 Db (mild intensity) and 100 Db (startling intensity). Increased brain activity is seen in response to high intensity where the subject's brain activated the regions involved in movement. The electrical activity is superimposed on the MRI scan

5.3 Brain Process Involved in Decision-Making

To fully understand how the brain makes decisions, we have to first look at how the brain processes information. The brain operates on two different levels. Each has a different "motivation," meaning that they actually pay attention to different types of information. Thus, they are processed through differentiating pathways. First, we will fully examine each, and next move on to how they operate in tandem to address different types of problems.

5.3.1 The Unconscious Brain

Here we will use a computer analogy. The automatic system in the brain is the default setting of the organism. This system operates in an "off-line" fashion. Using a categorical type framework, the automatic system can quickly sort issues into go/no-go alternatives (Zajonc 1998). Thus, the organism is seemingly unaware of the actions that are being processed through this automatic system. These reflexive, intuitive, and subconscious processes are located underneath the cerebral cortex. Specifically, they can be found in the basal ganglia and limbic system (see Fig. 5.3). The striatum's neural sensitivity allows for identifying and seeking out what we recognize as rewarding. Operating as our interface between the cortex and the limbic system, the striatum mediates the reception of the stimuli and the analysis of what to do about it at a very primitive level (mesolimbic).

The primary drive of the unconscious system is based on implicit memory processes. In evolution, decisions often needed to be made quickly. Thus, implicit memory is instrumental to survival in many situations. Clear evidence exists supporting this notion. Studies (Libet 1985, 1990; Libet et al. 1979) have shown that electrophysiological events occur in response to a given situation without our cognitive realization. For instance, a well-trained athlete may respond to the sound of the starting gun before he or she consciously recognizes it. In other situations, we may act without being unable to explain our choice. This unconscious process indicates our inability to evaluate behavioral consequences as they occur. The sense of urgency demanded by a threatening situation often results in a feeling of perceived internal alarm. These described types of solutions demand intuition rather than normative axioms of choice.

The unconscious system maintains a vigilant watch and gives instant alarm when confronted with deviation from the expected. There are many events monitored by this unconscious system. To ensure diligence, the reflexive system uses parallel processes. Different components of the brain may be working on the same task. Simultaneously, similar neurons may be working on different tasks. There is a great deal of work and a high degree of coordination needed. However, the unconscious system is vulnerable; the affective states such as depression, anxiety, and acute conditions of drug use may modify the integration of this systemic process (see Fig. 5.3c and d).

5.3.2 The Conscious Brain

The conscious brain is our "on-line" experience. The reflective processes of deliberation and calculation are key functions of the conscious brain. The prefrontal cortex and anterior cingulate gyrus are the core cortical components that are involved in formulating advice and shaping long term planning. Picking through experiences and ramifications, the reflective system makes calculated choices. It relies on explicit memory, which is the impression related to previous experience. Explicit memory is bilaterally represented in the frontal lobes; episodic memory (the recollection of events) relies on the right frontal and temporal lobes. Semantic memory (remembering and recognizing old friends, events, etc.) involves the left fronto-temporal regions. If resources of the conscious mind are overwhelmed, it will ask the reflective brain for additional input and perhaps even refer the decision to the unconscious brain for an intuitive response.

Repetitive and automated behaviors are the most effective for the brain. The conscious brain is plodding and slows as it expends a lot of effort to accomplish its deliberative tasks. As such, learned behaviors are more efficient than unpracticed ones. When compared to the learned processes, the data indicates that novel behaviors use significantly more brain resources. Learning depends on how one perceives reward. There are also potential factors related to how one uses common neurotransmitter systems. Researchers have shown that dopamine (DA) plays a significant role in the pleasure of achievement, anticipation of rewards, and avoidance of punishment. Additionally, DA neurons are directly activated via substances such as cocaine or amphetamines (see Fig. 5.3d and e).

Previous researchers believed that brain growth ended as one entered adulthood. It is now known that our brains can continue to grow and generate new neurons throughout the lifespan. Plasticity is a principle that holds as activities are practiced and reinforced. This influences the strength of neural connections. Also, the associated pathways become more dominant. The subsequent result is improved performance. Even the decision-making of experts can be considered a skill in this arena. But expertise can be highly domain specific. For instance, Gobet and Simon (1996) investigated the behavior of chess masters. When the researchers presented the chessboards with games in action to the chess masters they were able to remember the positions quickly. In fact, de Groot (1965) showed that a grand master could recall 100,000 different configurations of games. But Gobet and Simon also found that when pieces were randomly placed on boards, experts were little better than non-experts in recalling their placement. The brain is quite similar to other muscles. Expertise attained through exercise and practice can result in the strengthening of specific critical areas. Draganski et al. (2006) studied German medical students 3 months prior to their medical exam, and then again after. They found that, in comparison to controls, the medical students showed significant increases in their parietal cortex and posterior hippocampus. Maguire et al. (2006) produced MRI data to show that London cab drivers had increased hippocampal mass compared to controls, likely due to the occupational demand for memory. In examining musicians, Gaser and Schlaug (2003) were able to show that those who practiced at least an hour a day had increased volume in the parietal cortex and temporal areas as compared with non-musicians. Elbert et al. (1995), using magnetic imaging, showed that string players had larger cortical areas associated with the digits of their left hand. This was associated with the appendages needed for the stringed instrument. In the linguistic field, Mechelli et al. (2004) found that bilingual subjects had larger parietal cortex masses than monolingual subjects. Lo and Repin (2002) looked at expert behavior in foreign exchange traders. More experienced traders were much less aroused by market reversal, as measured by skin conductance and cardiovascular activity, than less experienced traders. Thus, the well-trained individual may have developed tolerances to emotionally challenging cues. Over a host of domains, the evidence is substantial that brain circuits can develop, consolidate, and increase efficacy with increased practice and use.

5.4 How Decisions Are Made

If decisions are the outputs generated by the brain, we need to answer two prior questions. First, how is the information input handled? Next, how is throughput processed once the initial information is received?

The cognitive focus of economics and finance has emphasized "homo economicus." This idea assumes that people, given the available information, will behave rationally and act within their own self-interest. People make deliberative decisions to maximize their expected utility. Decisions can be mathematically formulated to predict behavior. The cognitive nature of humans cannot be denied. Analysis, planning, and decision-making are strong capacities that humans possess. In fact, some of the critical reasons why we have evolved to this point are based in these capacities. Where economics has viewed the mind as a black box, cognitive processes and observable products of the mind have been of most interest. What decision did the person make and what were the data points that the person used to make that decision? Applied neuroscience studies have identified a more elemental process which identifies the affective process where intuition is dominant.

We may define motivation either as an activity driven toward reward, or as a means to avoid punishment. As we have said, the brain evaluates potential behavior outcomes based on expectation, experience, and genetics. The learning process is mediated by the frontal lobe, the executive function controller. Additionally, the prefrontal cortex is a critical but elusive component to the equation. A malfunctioning prefrontal cortex results in severe disruption of motivation and attention driven behaviors. Actions are initiated to maintain an individually defined level of homeostasis. In other words, one may try to answer questions such as: What's my level of discomfort? Can I tolerate it? Thus, there is a hierarchy of urgency. Individuals who do not have their basic needs of food and water satisfied will be unlikely to pursue a higher need that may be mediated, for example, by a sexual drive. However, once those basic needs are satisfied, sex can be pursued. Beyond the "basic" drives, motivation may be understood to be an intrinsically derived process that combines emotional and cognitive components. Sometimes this can promote non-intuitive actions. For instance, one investor may purchase and hold onto speculative stocks that have underperformed for a long period. Only if the investors are able to realize the consequences of their risk are they able to initiate the painful act to rectify their losing position. The fear of loss may provide the prompt to extricate them before a total loss. Subsequently, this action will provide them with the rush of having survived. Often, we see this sensation seeking behavior in patients who engage in risky behaviors such as tobacco use, illegal substance use, unprotected sexual activities, gambling, risky investing, etc. Sensation seeking behaviors are associated with DA system deregulation (see Fig. 5.3). Studies have shown a significant association with D2 type receptor (see Fig. 5.1) binding in the right insula and novelty seeking traits (Suhara et al. 2002). Further using the investment analogy, another investor may be intolerant of risk and never purchase speculative stocks. Their reward may be based on avoiding potential harm and feeling in control. So we then have to ask the question, what makes the two scenarios different?

5.4.1 Do People Act Primarily in Regards to Cognition?

Behavioral neuroscience has called the primacy of cognition into question. While not rejecting the role of cognition, neuroscience has relegated deliberation to a secondary activity. The initial access to incoming stimuli has been shown to occur below cognitive awareness. Zajonc (1998) has shown that people have an affective reaction to something before they can state what it is. People often have physiological feelings of stress about negative situations before the events register in the conscious mind (Bechara et al. 1994). Unfortunately, the nature of affect is often misunderstood. Usually the definition of affect relates to "emotional" meaning. As such, it has a connotation of evaluation related to how we feel about something. However, this is an incomplete description. While affect does assign valences (weights of positive and negative) its purpose is to prompt action. Affect may be generated rapidly. Also there may be involvement from a direct connection between the thalamus and amygdala (Ledoux 1996). This neuroanatomical connection may help us understand the affective labels we associate with objects and concepts (Greenwald 1992). Affect regulation may be rapidly adjusted based on changes in environmental cues. There may be effects on our use of language, which has been seen to happen in individuals suffering from depression. Thus, the emotions and drives are continually interacting with variable equilibrium.

Moreover, affect is the source of motivation. The word motivation comes from the Latin word "movere," which means literally "to move." Affect involves basic emotions such as joy, disgust, sadness, and rage. Further, our drive states are equally imperative in the executive of affective states. Thirst, hunger, and sex are prompts to action that mitigates affect. Homeostasis is the condition of equilibrium on the biological plane. Many biological functions have set points. These operate as reference points. As long as they are within tolerances, we do not have to attend to them. Once deviations occur, we are prompted to restore equilibrium. These deviations can operate below conscious awareness and create actions that are attempting to restore homeostasis to be misinterpreted as intentionally purposive. In humans, data indicates that frontal lobe myelination occurs much later than in any other species (Fuster 2002). This discrepancy indicates that the limbic system dominates significant parts of human maturation and learning. A brain system loaded with implicit behaviors will be adapted to pure survival and thus may not be suitable for "normal life." This is because, in light of the long-term consequences, our capacity to delay gratification may be jeopardized. In this situation, the prefrontal cortex loses its influence over the emotive, primitive, and survival-directed brain networks (Drabant et al. 2009).

5.4.2 The Interaction of Affect and Cognition

The key is to recognize these affective labels and develop cognitive processing pathways to re-categorize them. For instance, although we may have very negative and emotional responses to stock fluctuations, acting on these impulses may have detrimental consequences. Thus, we need to engage higher cognitive processes to avoid disaster. From an evolutionary standpoint, our ability to engage these processes is regulated by the frontal lobes. The frontal lobe's role in decision-making is well documented. The clearest and most well established example of the frontal lobe's role in managing emotive behavior is the famous case of the Phinias Gage. Mr. Gage suffered from an accidental lobotomy (the severing of neuronal connections to the frontal lobes). The accident left him seemingly as a different person; he became impulsive and unable to perceive the consequences of his behavior.

In addition to the frontal lobes, the amygdala plays a significant role in decision-making; this subcortical structure functioning with regards to fear of an anticipated outcome. It is well accepted that the amygdala is chronically scanning the environment for potential danger. This brain structure then relays this information to the autonomic nervous system and subsequently the rest of the brain. In potentially threatening situations, we all experience sudden sympathetic activation due to the stimulation of the amygdala. An increased heart rate and shortness of breath exemplify this sympathetic response. Fortunately, to override this response, the amygdala also receives inputs from the cortex. In animal studies, it has been shown that after an investigator pairs a tone or light with an aversive stimulus, such as a shock, one can easily elicit the fear response through the associated stimulus (the light or tone). Conversely, one can also unlearn this process by eliminating the shock over a number of trials. One may interpret this data to mean that the connection of the amygdala and cortex were severed. However, after one exposure to the aversive stimulus the learned pattern can return (LeDoux 2000). Perhaps we can interpret this data by saying that the fear response was not previously eliminated at all, but rather masked by higher order cognitive processing.

Over the past decade, much research has been undertaken to examine a dual system in the brain that mediates the experience of reward and punishment. Kuhnen and Knutson (2005) have shown that there are actually two systems connected with rewards. One is a gain prediction system that is associated with the nucleus accumbens. The second is a loss prediction system that is associated with the anterior insula. Knutson et al. (2008) examined this in a consumer experiment. He gave the buyers a choice between different products with different prices. They found that the products increased activity in the nucleus accumbens while the prices stimulated the insula. Purchase decisions were ultimately determined by which was more activated. McClure et al. (2004) concluded that two different systems are involved in choice. The limbic system is preferentially activated when confronted with immediate rewards. But the prefrontal cortex and posterior parietal cortex are uniformly engaged with delayed choices no matter what the timing may be. Berridge and Robinson (1998) found that with their incentive sensitization model it can be postulated that "wanting" and "liking" systems are inherently independent. It is possible to get what you "want" but not "like" it. Bernheim and Rangel (2004) expanded on this notion by looking at a hedonic forecasting mechanism and concluded that addictive substances disrupt forecasting and thus impede cognitive control.

Recently, Matsumoto and Hikosaka (2009) have challenged the model of bimodal firing related to reward generation. They have shown that in different areas of the mid-brain (see Fig. 5.3), neurons actually increase their firing to both reward and punishment. Since we operate on the premise of rewards and punishments, reward-based learning is important. By interfering with DA activity, Sevy et al. (2006) demonstrated that there is associated impairment in emotionally based decision-making. He found shortsightedness in the inability to resist short-term rewards despite long-term consequences. In naturally defined dopamine levels, we are not identical. This variation may explain why individuals vary in their responses to a reward versus a punishment. As measured by PET scans, subjects with higher striatum baseline DA levels showed better reversal relearning to unexpected rewards than subjects with lower levels of DA (Cools et al. 2009). This data is consistent with the studies of patients diagnosed with Parkinson disease, as they have been shown to elicit difficulties (see Fig. 5.3) in reward-based learning (Cools et al. 2006).

5.4.3 Dopamine: The Neurotransmitter of Reward

Decision-making depends on the communication between different parts of the brain. Brain communication depends on the coordination of complex neuronal networks. Communication is highly dependent on chemical messengers. Dopamine (DA) is a neurotransmitter that appears to play a significant role in the actions of interest to behavioral finance. Thus, it is the neural messenger we will focus on. Dopamine derives from the neuronal synaptic terminals that transform Tyrosine (a precursor molecule) into the neurotransmitter DA. Cells that generate and release DA are called dopaminergic neurons. Once dopaminergic neurons release DA, there is an interaction between receptors that are located on adjacent nerve cells. There are many different types of dopamine receptors labeled as D1, D2, D3, etc. These are grouped into families that are related by the effects they have on the biochemical events in the receiving cells. Once DA is released, its action must be terminated. Excess dopamine must be recalled from the synapse to prevent over-stimulation of the receiving cell. Recall primarily involves the re-uptake of dopamine back into pre-synaptic neuron, where it is repackaged for reuse. The re-uptake efficacy determines the quantity of the neurotransmitter's availability in the synapse. This process points to the precise regulation of the NT content in the synaptic regions. The receiving cell receptors are dynamically regulated. Chronic exposure to DA will desensitize the cells and, conversely, the absence of DA will sensitize them (see Fig. 5.1).

Dopamine is an old neurotransmitter and has been well preserved by evolution. For example, many studies on the famous fruit fly, referred to as *Drosophila*, have demonstrated that DA is used to modulate aversive reinforcement (punishment) circuitry in the nervous system (Riemensperger et al. 2005). In the mammalian brain, the primary source of DA comes from the brain area called the mid-brain, specifically, the substantia nigra and ventral tegmental region. These areas contain neuronal cell bodies that produce DA as a primary neurotransmitter and send axons to many brain regions. These regions include the basal ganglia, which regulates movement; limbic system, which regulates emotions; and frontal lobes, which play an important role executive functioning (see Fig. 5.3). Due to the axonal projections, dopamine plays a significant role in a variety of human and animal behaviors, one being the experience of pleasure (see Fig. 5.3). Some studies have compared the rewarding properties of DA in relation to the continuation of substance use by chronic abusers. A recent meta-analysis by Le Foll et al. (2009) focused on the D1 and D2 receptors within families who engage in addictive behaviors. They reported that DA receptors might play a critical role in the expression of different types of addiction phenotypes. Breiter et al. (2001) showed that reward and punishment, as related to money, stimulate the DA neurons. The potential gain of money (the reward) activates the brain like any other physiological reward. Its impact is as strong as addictive substances. It may also be related to basic drives such as food, drink, sex, and safety.

Dopamine's role is also well studied in rodents, primates, and human. Significant data has pointed to DA's involvement in mammalian reward reinforcement (Schultz 2002). In classical learning paradigms, a stimulus is presented and a reward follows. The stimulus then becomes a cue for the reward. Expectation studies were initially preformed by Schultz et al. (1997) based on electrophysiological recordings from the midbrain. The midbrain DA neurons showed surprisingly high increases in firing during reward and surprisingly low levels in firing when the reward was withheld. It was as if the dopamine neurons anticipated the reward and showed disappointment if their expectation was not met. Once the patterns are learned, the system becomes quite sensitive to it. If rewards follow the cue, the dopamine neurons remain active. But if the reward does not follow the cue, the dopamine neurons become deactivated. When rewards are non-conforming, there is an error in detecting negativity. We may see this biphasic modulation of DA neurons as a teaching signal that modifies the striatum modification of synaptic connections. The striatum has been linked to reward-based learning (Schonberg et al. 2007).

When neurons do not receive the expected rewards, error detection negativity can be seen. The error detection mechanism is located medially in the brain. The focal research point has been an area of the brain that has a high concentration of dopamine neurons, which is the anterior cingulate. This brain structure allows for the comparison of anticipated outcome to reality. It employs an empirical testing process to look for regularity in the delivery of rewards. The anterior cingulate mediates the communication between the conscious brain and the unconscious brain. The cingulate cortex communicates with the hypothalamus and is involved in the unconscious autonomic regulation in the periphery. For instance, the sympathetic activation constricts our blood vessels and inhibits peristalsis. A racing heart and excited skeletal muscles prepare us to confront imminent dangers. In addition to the role of autonomic nervous system regulation, the anterior cingulate plays a role in memory functions. Upon detecting errors, anterior cingulate remembers what the dopamine neurons have just experienced. A pattern map is revised. As with other the brain systems, learning occurs at the cellular level, as the neurons are better able to predict a pattern more efficient they become in identifying rewards. Rangel et al. (2008) have clarified the process with a computational version of reward prediction errors and reinforcement prediction errors. This function is critical for effective decision-making. Kennerley et al. (2006) have shown the effects that damage to the anterior cingulate cortex has on decision-making. Monkeys with damage to the anterior cingulate cortex were unable to sustain learning in a foraging task. Initial learning of a new task was not impaired. However, the maintenance of the behavior was significantly lower when compared to controls. The described implication suggests that learning from negative reinforcement may be different than learning form positive reinforcement.

5.5 Looking at the Biases, Errors, and Distortions That Impact Decision-Making

Neuroscience research has provided evidence that suggests the particular brain regions and neural processes that are used to make decisions. Some of the errors that might occur in decision-making have been discussed but the focus will now turn to a more direct discussion of the specific errors that occur in decision-making together with the associated neurobiological underpinnings.

Behavioral neuroscience has demonstrated the neurobiological substrate of unconscious and conscious behavioral patterns. A critical system involved is the dopaminergic system. In this system the primary messenger is the neurotransmitter (NT) dopamine (DA). The impact of dopamine on both the limbic system and the frontal cortex has been shown to influence the nature of errors in reward prediction. In light of this background, errors in reward prediction significantly impact the conscious and unconscious processes that are involved in decision-making.

Certainly, some errors may stem from limits in one's cognitive capacity. Recent data has shown that cognitive loading may modulate frontal lobe activity. Shiv and Fedorikhin (1999) found that higher cognitive loading in the frontal region was negatively correlated with rational decision-making. Thus, as loading within the frontal region increased, there was a significant decline in one's ability to rationally conclude on how to proceed in a given scenario. Substance use or sexual arousal may also modulate frontal lobe functioning (Giordano et al. 2002). As stress level and physiological arousal increase, our decision-making capacities become limited. For instance, if we are making decisions while in a stable physiological state of calmness, the process is simple. However, when the same decision is made while we are in a state of hyperarousal, the rational response may cognitively unavailable.

Additionally, further errors have been found to stem from more systemic processes in which there is an over-reliance on information that is either incomplete or mistaken. Loss aversion, as described by Kahneman and Tversky (1979), states that losses have a more profound impact than gains. In contrast to expected utility theory, they emphasized "weights," rather than probabilities, and a personal reference point that differentiates gains and losses. The reference point determines where you are now. The value curve for prospect theory is s-shaped and passes through the reference point. Losses have a steeper curve than gains. Gains have small incremental value and losses have relatively large incremental value. Thus, we are adverse to large anticipated effect of losses and our financial decisions can be affected. This can be directly applied to the influence that dopamine has in error prediction of rewards. Tom et al. (2007) found that when consumers make decisions they exhibit a greater sensitivity for losses than for gains. Specifically, behaviorally endorsed loss aversion was matched by neural loss aversion in the ventral striatum and the prefrontal cortex (see Fig. 5.3). They found that midbrain dopaminergic activity was heightened for potential gains and showed decreased activity for potential losses.

In reward prediction, dopamine neurons operate in the assessment of when and where rewards will come. The aversion to loss may be altered by variables influencing our current equilibrium. In general, when positive gain is expected, DA neuronal activity increases. However, when we anticipate loss, the DA activity is reduced. Effectiveness comes from the ability to see patterns that are emerging and allow for us to act on them. How do we conclude that a pattern is present? With heuristics we can create mental short cuts that will save much mental effort. According to Kahneman and Tversky, availability bias arises when we draw upon very small samples of data to make our decisions. Our pattern seeking behavior can make us particularly susceptible to errors. Huettel et al. (2002) have suggested that neurons begin to sense a pattern after only several exposures. This implies that actions often do follow patterns. By assuming regularity in events we can operate more efficiently. If there is randomness, our plans and methods do not work quite as well. Many of the cognitive biases and inferential errors that we commit are connected to our lack of respect for randomness. Our tendency is to act as if regularity exists across the experiential board. We can leap to conclusions with an amazingly small degree of conscious evidence.

Rogan et al. (2005) investigated learned safety as a psychological tool to effect mood. In a classical learning paradigm, they taught mice to reduce learned and instinctive fear responses through a conditioned stimulus that was explicitly unpaired with an aversive stimulus. After training, the mice were placed into an open field. Mice typically stay near the walls in open spaces to avoid predators. However, the conditioned auditory sound prompted the animals to move to the center of the field. The safety signal from the auditory tone produced risky exploration. The EEG results revealed that this exploration was associated with decreasing activity in the amygdala and increased activity in the striatum providing evidence of decreased influence of amygdala.

In a subsequent test, mice were exposed to a stressful environment. Rogan et al. (2005) placed the mice into a pool of water. The physiological distress felt by the mice was moderated in the safety-conditioned group. In fact their responses were comparable to untrained mice that were placed in the condition while on the medication used for treatment of anxiety and depression (fluoxetine) (Pollack et al. 2008). We may conclude that the safety conditioning regulated the amygdala which plays a role in mood modulation.

If safety conditioning can modulate affect in the face of danger, could self deception be promoted if associated with the wrong stimuli? Libet (1985) has shown that we become consciously aware of events only after we unconsciously process them. With this delayed accessibility of conscious awareness, we can misinterpret the cause and effect relationships for our behaviors and over-emphasize personal control. Misattributions often arise. We have a sense of control but it is not often real. Our ability to learn from mistakes is compromised. This may be associated with another type of error, one that stems from overconfidence. The concept of overconfidence was demonstrated in numerous studies (Fischoff et al. 1977; Camerer and Lovallo 1999; Harvey 1997). Generally, overestimation of personal abilities eventually reduces behavioral and cognitive flexibility and leads to less objective decisions. Overconfidence may stem from reward prediction error. As rewards accrue with greater regularity, the neurons are primed to continue in the pattern that has been established. Randomness is not something tolerated well. Distinct patterns may be perceived even if none actually exist. If the illusion of control is established, then feeling safe might encourage one to commit riskier actions. Dampening the operation of the amygdala may foster confirmation bias and hindsight bias.

The disposition effect appears to be related to the aversion of loss and reward prediction errors. Investors are prompted to sell their winners too soon and keep their losers too long. Investors are less disposed to recognize paper losses and more willing to recognize paper gains. Barberis and Xiong (2008) found that the utility of realized gains and losses posed the most parsimonious explanation for the disposition effect. “Avoiding regret and seeking pride” is how Nosfinger (2001) posed the dilemma. Leal et al. (2008) looked at the Portuguese stock market and found significant support for the disposition effect. At the individual level, market sophistication as based on trade frequency, volume, and portfolio value acted to protect sophisticated investors more than the unsophisticated. At the market level they found the disposition effect more pronounced in bear market conditions rather than in bull markets. Weber and Welfens (2008) conducted a controlled experiment and produced evidence that there are actually two different brain systems acting within the disposition effect. “A preference for cashing in gains” and a “loss aversion realization” operate independently of each other. Others (Leal et al. 2008; Weber and Welfens 2008) have found results that seem to be in line with the previous discussion that describes how losses are related to insula activity and gains are associated with mid-brain stimulation through two different operating systems (Knutson et al. 2005; McClure et al. 2004).

The Endowment Effect occurs when we place a higher value on an asset than others because we own the asset. There is a difference between our willingness to accept payment for our own and our willing to pay for the same. This difference has been shown to have a neuropsychological foundation. Knutson et al. (2008) examined the endowment effect with fMRI data under buying, choosing and selling. Preferred products were found to generate increased nucleus accumbens activity in both buying and selling. Medial prefrontal cortex activity was greater when low prices were prominent in buying and selling. Susceptibility to the endowment effect was found in the insular activity for preferred products. Roth and Ockenfels (2002) examined auction behavior and found that experienced traders who were aware of the endowment effect sniped more than less experienced buyers who were more likely to participate in multiple bidding. In a study looking at reference dependent choices, De Martino et al. (2009) asked subjects to act as buyers and sellers in a market exchange of lottery tickets. They found that subjects uniformly gave higher value to tickets they owned than to those they did not. With fMRI results, they showed that activity in ventral striatum scaled the degree to which stated prices varied from a reference point. Status quo bias thus creates the unwillingness to change unless the reason is compelling.

Temporal Discounting is the tendency for people to view rewards that are closer to now as being more desirable. In psychological terms, the delay of gratification is compromised. This notion has been shown to have a neurobehavioral foundation. Xu et al. (2009) looked at the differences between discounting losses and gains. Using event related fMRI, they found that the pre-frontal cortex and posterior parietal cortex operate in discounting future losses and gains. The effect was stronger when discounting losses. With immediate losses, the dorsal striatum and insula were activated. This then indicated that discounting losses might involve negative emotions. With immediate options the posterior cingulate cortex and medial prefrontal cortex were activated. The authors concluded that there may be two different processes for discounting losses and gains, which may explain why future losses are less significantly discounted than future gains. Hariri et al. (2006) examined delayed discounting on a computerized task using positive and negative feedback with a monetary reward. With fMRI measurements of ventral striatum activity, they found that delayed discounting related to ventral striatum activity in both positive and negative feedback conditions. For individuals who showed the greatest preference for immediate versus delay rewards there was greater ventral striatum activity. This is in accordance with Delgado et al. (2000); Thut et al. (1997); and Knutson and Cooper (2005). For Harari et al., this may indicate a general over-sensitivity in the ventral striatum of individuals predisposed to addiction.

Mental accounting has also been shown to have a neural basis. The artificial asset valuation prompts people to treat the assets differently and take investments of varying risks based on the segmentation. For example, money won at a casino is treated as "house money" and treated more speculatively than money in the pocket. Also, money inherited can be treated differently than money earned (Holroyd and Coles 2002). Postponed payment, or even pre-paid expenses may affect consumption levels. Credit card purchases have been shown to decrease activity in anterior insula (Knutson et al. 2005). Categorical differences between cash payment and credit card payment have a basis at the neurobiological substrate.

There are other biases and cognitive distortions that occur in economic decision-making and behavioral finance: problems like under-reaction, over-reaction, and herding. Market sentiment may be related to the reward system (bubbles) or to loss aversion (collapses), but the evidence is as of yet abundant (Leal et al. 2008, Fisher and Statman 2000). These are important issues but we will leave them until the research has caught up.

The systematic errors in decision-making have been examined by behavioral neuroscience. Not only do the cognitive processes have a role in ineffective decision-making, but also the psychological states. Personality has a homeostatic threshold that is connected to the underlying neurobiological substrate.

Acute mania is characterized by euphoria and grandiosity. Some of the classic examples involve highly impulsive behavior, e.g., spending sprees and sexual promiscuity, and extreme risk-taking, e.g., excessive gambling and high danger activities. Mania has been found to be associated with overactive dopaminergic activity in the brain, particularly in the mesolimbic system (see Fig. 5.3).

Dopamine is also related to other effects of personality. One example is a clever study of dopamine and the placebo effects on suggestion. Researchers exposed the subjects to a paradigm involving anticipated response effects to analgesia. Pain relief from the placebo was shown to have individual differences related dopamine activity. There were individual differences in terms of novelty seeking and harm avoidance, as measured by the Temperament and Character Inventory (TCI) (Cloninger 1987a), which showed an inverse relationship to dopamine activity.

Dopamine levels in the amygdala have also been shown to modulate the processing of aversive stimuli in the dorsal cingulate region. This modulation has been associated with individual differences in the anxious temperament (Kienast et al. 2008). Acute anxiety has been associated with chronic stimulation of the loss aversion center (see Fig. 5.3c and d). Hypervigilance and heightened sensitivity to risk have been noted, and, at the extreme end of the continuum, panic. As much as the under-regulation of behavior, i.e., impulsivity is a problem. The other side of the spectrum is as problematic. Over-regulation is found with people who cannot let themselves go, so to speak. This is illustrated by observing the over-planned indecisive who procrastinates and gets stuck when choices need to be made. Other examples can be seen in hoarders who cannot part with useless items, or individuals with anorexia who cannot gain weight, or workaholics who literally cannot "not work." Compulsive behavior has been connected to dopamine dysfunction. People who are suffering from Parkinson's disease have been found to be susceptible to compulsive gambling and overactive sex behavior when put on dopamine agonists.

5.6 Summary and Conclusions

What is the nature of decision-making? How does the brain generate choice outputs? What are the inputs? What are the throughputs? How are decisions rendered? These were the questions that were addressed in this chapter. We looked at the methods and technologies that allow us to look into the brain and observe its functions that impact decision-making. The goal was to examine the elements and circuitry of the brain and their impact on different types of decisions. Both animal and human data were evaluated. We discuss the nature of the unconscious mind and its ability to intuitively react to environmental input, and the conscious brain and its ability to logically evaluate ongoing unconscious operations. In addition we showed how the dynamics of affect and cognition impact decision-making processes.

For the first time, economic and financial theories of decision-making can be tested directly. Some of the information presented in this chapter provides evidence that new imaging techniques facilitate inquiry into human brain functions supported by animal models. In this chapter, the focus was on reward systems, how gains and losses are processed. Overwhelming data has shown that DA participates in many behavioral aspects of our lives. Each one of us is endowed with a genetically defined system that has an optimal performance range and an intrinsically established equilibrium. Throughout our lives, we are exposed to life events, and these become memories. When well practiced, these events find a place in the implicit memory systems. We respond to the environment with well-established, fast-acting processes that involve powerful, mostly unconscious limbic system. The initial perception and even the responses may not reach our consciousness, resulting in potentially irrational actions. With practice and maturity, expertise is attainable through our abilities to recognize and modulate the initial responses. This is supported by brain plasticity that continues through lifespan. By optimizing the relationship between the limbic (emotional) and cortical (rational) systems, more advantageous decisions and adaptation to the widest range of life events can occur.

As neuronal networks can be mapped based on defined brain regions, with synaptic activity and receptor sites, we can begin to answer questions about the function of specific neurotransmitter systems. The focus in this chapter was DA based networks. It must be remembered there are other neurotransmitters, e.g., serotonin and glutamate that may influence decisions. Glutamate has particularly profound implications for improving decision making, with its effect on long-term potentiation reflecting learning at the cellular levels. There are also a host of hormones, such as cortisol and testosterone, that impact human behavior and decision-making. Description of these processes is outside of the scope of this chapter.

The issues of personal causation and self-consistency have long been of interest to psychology. Control seems to be a prominent drive. Control implies that we need to find ways to reduce uncertainty. If events are deemed to be predictable and orderly, control can be asserted. The heuristics and cognitive biases appear to be attempts for people to control events. For instance, heuristics can be looked at as a way to deal with cognitively complex problems by answering a simpler one first. It is a process that allows us to reach a conclusion, although it might be non-optimal, but allow for control to be maintained. The theories of cognitive dissonance and attribution theory have helped to articulate the dynamics in personal, interpersonal, and social decision-making. Their connections to the cognitive biases that interest behavioral economics and finance are apparent. But they have long been neglected. With the reward and punishment systems in the light of individualized homeostasis levels, it is possible to better understand how these systems operate leading to possible understanding, and inference.

The interface of neuroscience, psychology, economics, and behavioral finance is consolidating. As the work of neuroscience expands, the exchange of information across the fields will make each stronger. It seems as though the model of brain circuitry may be strongly applicable for our professional lives.

Acknowledgments Scientific and academic endeavors require extraordinary effort and timeless devotion. Because we all have a limited lifespan, families often make significant sacrifices for these endeavors. These authors would like to acknowledge these sacrifices by families given in the pursuit of academics and science. In addition, our gratitude goes out to the scientists, researchers in-training, and our graduate students, in particular Lord T. Giddie, MA.

References

Barberis, N., and Xiong, W. (2008). Realization utility. NBER Working Paper Series, Vol. w14440, 2008. Available at SSRN: http://ssrn.com/abstract=1289674.

Bechara, A., A.R. Damásio, H. Damásio, and S.W. Anderson. 1994. Insensitivity to future consequences following damage to human prefrontal cortex. *Cognition* 50: 7–15.

Bernheim, B.D., and A. Rangel. 2004. Addiction and cue-triggered decision processes. *American Economic Review* 94(5): 1558–1590.

Berridge, K.C., and T.E. Robinson. 1998. What is the role of dopamine in reward: Hedonic impact, reward learning, or incentive salience? *Brain Research Review* 20(3): 309–369.

Breiter, H.C., I. Aharon, D. Kahneman, A. Dale, and P. Shizgal. 2001. Functional imaging of neural responses to expectancy and experience of monetary gains and losses. *Neuron* 30: 619–639.

Bremner, J.D., P. Randall, T.M. Scott, R.A. Bronen, J.P. Seibyl, S.M. Southwick, et al. 1995. MRI-based measurement of hippocampal volume in patients with combat-related post- traumatic stress disorder. *American Journal of Psychiatry* 152(7): 973–981.

Camerer, C., and D. Lovallo. 1999. Overconfidence and excess entry: An experimental approach. *The American Economic Review* 89(1): 306–318.

Cloninger, C.R. 1987a. A systematic method for clinical description and classification of personality variants. A proposal. *Archives of General Psychiatry* 44(6): 573–588.

Cloninger, C.R. 1987b. Neurogenetic adaptive mechanisms in alcoholism. *Science* 236: 410–416.

Cools, R., L. Altamirano, and M. D'Esposito. 2006. Reversal learning in Parkinson's disease depends on medication status and outcome valence. *Neuropsychologia* 44(10): 1663–1673. doi:S0028-3932(06)00107-2[pii] 10.1016/j.neuropsychologia.2006.03.030.

Cools, R., M.J. Frank, S.E. Gibbs, A. Miyakawa, W. Jagust, and M. D'Esposito. 2009. Striatal dopamine predicts outcome-specific reversal learning and its sensitivity to dopaminergic drug administration. *Journal of Neuroscience* 29(5): 1538–1543. doi:29/5/1538 [pii] 10.1523/JNEUROSCI.4467-08.2009.

de Groot, A.D. 1965. *Thought and choice in chess*, 1st ed. The Hague: Mouton Publishers.

De Martino, B., D. Kumaran, B. Holt, and R. Dolan. 2009. The neurobiology of reference-dependent value computation. *The Journal of Neuroscience* 29(12): 3833–3842. doi:10.1523/JNEUROSCI.4832-08.2009.

Delgado, M.R., L.E. Nystrom, C. Fissell, D.C. Noll, and J.A. Fiez. 2000. Tracking the hemodynamic responses to reward and punishment in the striatum. *Journal of Neurophysiology* 84: 3072–3077.

Drabant, E.M., K. McRae, S.B. Manuck, A.R. Hariri, and J.J. Gross. 2009. Individual differences in typical reappraisal use predict amygdala and prefrontal responses. *Biological Psychiatry* 65(5): 367–373. doi:S0006-3223(08)01098-6 [pii] 10.1016/j.biopsych.2008.09.007.

Draganski, B., C. Gaser, G. Kempermann, H.G. Kuhn, J. Winkler, C. Buchel, and A. May. 2006. Temporal and spatial dynamics of brain structure changes during extensive learning. *Journal of Neuroscience* 26(23): 6314–6317.

Elbert, T., C. Pantev, C. Wienbruch, B. Rockstroh, and E. Taub. 1995. Increased cortical representation of the fingers of the left hand in string players. *Science* 270(5234): 305. doi:10.1126/science.270.5234.305.

Fischoff, B., P. Slovic, and S. Lichtenstein. 1977. Knowing with certainty: The appropriateness of extreme confidence. *Journal of Experimental Psychology: Human Perception and Performance* 3: 552–564.

Fisher, K.L., and M. Statman. 2000. Investor sentiment and stock returns. *Financial Analysts Journal* 56: 16–23.

Fuster, J.M. 2002. Frontal lobe and cognitive development. *Journal of Neurocytology* 31(3–5): 373–385. doi:5123790 [pii].

Gaser, C., and G. Schlaug. 2003. Brain structures differ between musicians and non-musicians. *Journal of Neuroscience* 23(27): 9240–9245.

Gianaros, P.J., R.J. Jennings, L.K. Sheu, P.J. Greer, L.H. Kuller, and K.A. Mathews. 2007. Prospective reports of chronic life stress predict decreased grey matter volume in the hippo campus. *Neuroimage* 35: 795–803. doi:10.1016/j.neuroimage.2006.10.045.

Giordano, L.A., W.K. Bickel, G. Loewenstein, E.A. Jacobs, L. Marsch, and G.J. Badger. 2002. Mild opioid deprivation increases the degree that opioid-dependent outpatients discount delayed heroin and money. *Psychopharmacology (Berlin)* 163(2): 174–182. doi:10.1007/s00213-002-1159-2.

Gobet, F., and H.A. Simon. 1996. Recall of random and distorted positions: Implications for the theory of expertise. *Memory & Cognition* 24: 493–503.

Greenwald, A.G. 1992. New look 3. Unconscious cognition reclaimed. *American Psychologist* 47(6): 766–779.

Hariri, A.R., S.M. Brown, D.E. Williamson, J.M. Flory, H. de Wit, and S.B. Manuck. 2006. Preference for immediate over delayed rewards is associated with magnitude of ventral striatal activity. *The Journal of Neuroscience* 26(51): 13213–13217.

Harvey, N. 1997. Confidence in judgment. *Trends in Cognitive Sciences* 1: 78–82.

Holroyd, C.B., and M.G. Coles. 2002. The neural basis of human error processing: Reinforcement learning, dopamine, and the error-related negativity. *Psychological Review* 109(4): 679–709. doi:10.1037//0033-295X.109.4.679.

Huettel, S.A., P.B. Mack, and G. McCarthy. 2002. Perceiving patterns in random series: Dynamic processing of sequence in prefrontal cortex. *National Neuroscience* 5: 485–490.

Kahneman, D., and A. Tversky. 1979. Prospect theory: An analysis of decision under risk. *Econometrica* 47: 263–291.

Kennerley, W.S., M.E. Walton, T.E. Behrens, M.J. Buckley, and M.F. Rushworth. 2006. Optimal decision making and the anterior cingulate cortex. *Natural Neuroscience* 9(7): 940–947.

Kienast, T., A.R. Hariri, F. Schlagenhauf, et al. 2008. Dopamine in amygdala gates limbic processing of aversive stimuli in humans. *Nature Neuroscience* 11: 1381–1382. doi:doi:10.1038/nn.2222.

Knutson, B., and J.C. Cooper. 2005. Functional magnetic resonance imaging of reward prediction. *Current Opinion in Neurology* 18: 411–417.

Knutson, B., J. Taylor, M. Kaufman, R. Peterson, and G. Glover. 2005. Distributed neural representation of expected value. *The Journal of Neuroscience* 25(19): 4806–4812. doi:10.1523/jneourosci.0642-05.2005.

Knutson, B., E.G. Wimmer, S. Rick, N.G. Hollon, D. Prelec, and G. Loewenstein. 2008. Neural antecedents of the endowment effect. *Neuron* 58: 814–822. doi:10.1016/j.neuron.2008.05.018.

Kuhnen, C.M., and B. Knutson. 2005. The neural basis of financial risk taking. *Neuron* 47: 763–770. doi:10.1016/j.neuron.2005.08.008.

Le Foll, B., A. Gallo, Y. Le Strat, and P. Gorwood. 2009. Genetics of dopamine receptors and drug addiction: A comprehensive review. *Behavioral Pharmacology* 1: 1–17.

Leal, C.C., M.J. Armada, and J.L. Duque. (2008). Are all individual investors equally prone to the disposition effect all the time? New evidences from a small market. Retrieved online on December 16, 2009 from SSRN: http://ssrn.com/abstract=1024763

LeDoux, J. 1996. *The emotional brain: The mysterious underpinnings of emotional life*. London: Simon & Schuster.

LeDoux, J.E. 2000. Emotion circuits in the brain. *Annual Review of Neuroscience* 23: 155–184. doi:10.1146/annurev.neuro.23.1.155.

Libet, B. 1985. Subjective antedating of a sensory experience and mind-brain theories: Reply to Honderich (1984). *Journal of Theoretical Biology* 114(4): 563–570.

Libet, B. 1990. Subjective perception. *Science* 247(4943): 727.

Libet, B., E.W. Wright Jr., B. Feinstein, and D.K. Pearl. 1979. Subjective referral of the timing for a conscious sensory experience: A functional role for the somatosensory specific projection system in man. *Brain* 102(1): 193–224.

Lo, A., and D. Repin. 2002. The psychophysiology of real-time financial risk processing. *Journal of Cognitive Neuroscience* 14(3): 323–339.

Lupien, S.J., B.S. McEwen, M.R. Gunnar, and R. Heim. 2009. Effects of stress throughout the lifespan on the brain, behavior and cognition. *Nature Reviews Neuroscience* 10: 434–445. doi:10.1038/nrn2639.

Maguire, E.A., K. Woollett, and H.J. Spiers. 2006. London taxi drivers and bus drivers: A structural MRI and neuropsychological analysis. *Hippocampus* 16: 1091–1101.

Matsumoto, M., and O. Hikosaka. 2009. Two types of dopamine neuron distinctly convey positive and negative motivational signals. *Nature* 459(7248): 837–841. doi:nature08028 [pii] 10.1038/nature08028.

McClure, S.M., D.I. Laibson, G. Loewenstein, and J. Cohen. 2004. Separate neural systems value immediate and delayed monetary rewards. *Science* 306(5695): 503–507. doi:10.1126/science.1100907.

Mechelli, A., J.T. Crinion, U. Noppeney, J. O'Doherty, J. Ashburner, R.S. Frackowiak, et al. 2004. Neurolinguistics: Structural plasticity in the bilingual brain. *Nature* 431(7010): 757.

Nosfinger, J.R. 2001. *Investment madness: How psychology affects your investing- and what to do about it.* Upper Saddle River: Pearson Education.

Pollack, D.D., F.J. Monje, L. Zuckerman, C.A. Demny, M.R. Drew, and E.R. Kandel. 2008. An animal model of a behavioral intervention for depression. *Newron* 60: 149–161.

Rangel, A., C. Camerer, and P.R. Montague. 2008. A frame work for studying the neurobiology of value-based decision making. *Nature Reviews Neuroscience* 9: 545–556. doi:10.1038/nrn2357.

Riemensperger, T., T. Voller, P. Stock, E. Buchner, and A. Fiala. 2005. Punishment prediction by dopaminergic neurons in Drosophila. *Current Biology* 15(21): 1953–1960. doi:S0960-9822(05)01112-7 [pii] 10.1016/j.cub.2005.09.042.

Rogan, M.T., K.S. Leon, D.L. Perez, and E.R. Kandel. 2005. Distinct neural signatures for safety and danger in the amygdala and striatum of the mouse. *Neuron* 46: 309–320.

Roth, A.E., and A. Ockenfels. 2002. Last-minute bidding and the rules for ending second-price auctions: Evidence from eBay and Amazon auctions on the Internet. *The American Economic Review* 92(4): 1093–1103.

Schonberg, T., N.D. Daw, D. Joel, and J.P. O'Doherty. 2007. Reinforcement learning signals in the human striatum distinguish learners from nonlearners during reward-based decision making. *Journal of Neuroscience* 27(47): 12860–12867. doi:27/47/12860 [pii] 10.1523/JNEUROSCI.2496- 07.2007.

Schultz, W. 2002. Getting formal with dopamine and reward. *Neuron* 36(2): 241–263. doi:S0896627302009674 [pii].

Schultz, W., P. Dayan, and P.R. Montague. 1997. A neural substrate of prediction and reward. *Science* 275(5306): 1593–1599.

Sevy, S., Y. Hassoun, A. Bechara, E. Yechiam, B. Napolitano, K. Burdick, et al. 2006. Emotion-based decision-making in healthy subjects: Short-term effects of reducing dopamine levels. *Psychopharmacology (Berlin)* 188(2): 228–235. doi:10.1007/s00213-006-0450-z.

Shiv, B., and A. Fedorikhin. 1999. Heart and mind in conflict: Interplay of affect and cognition in consumer decision making. *Journal of Consumer Research* 26: 278–282.

Suhara, T., F. Yasuno, Y. Sudo, M. Yamamoto, M. Inoue, Y. Okubo, and K. Suzuki. 2002. Dopamine D2 receptors in the insular cortex and the personality trait of novelty seeking. *Neuroimage* 13(5): 891–895.

Thut, G., W. Schultz, U. Roelcke, M. Nienhusmeier, J. Missimer, R.P. Maguire, and K.L. Leenders. 1997. Activation of the human brain by monetary reward. *NeuroReport* 8: 1225–1228.

Tom, S.M., C.R. Fox, C. Trepel, and R.A. Poldrack. 2007. The neural basis of loss aversion in decision-making under risk. *Science* 315: 515–518.

Weber, M. and Welfens, F. (2008). Splitting the Disposition effect: Asymmetric reactions towards 'selling winners' and 'holding losers. Retrieved online in December 16, 2009 from SSRN: http://ssrn.com/abstract=1176422.

Xu, L., Z. Liang, K. Wang, S. Li, and T. Jiang. 2009. Neural mechanism of inter temporal choice: From discounting future gains to future losses. *Brain Research* 1261: 65–74. doi:10.1016/j.brainres.2008.12.061.

Zajonc, R.B. 1998. Emotion. In *The handbook of social psychology*, ed. D.T. Gilbert, S.T. Fiske, and G. Lindzey. Boston: McGraw-Hill.

Chapter 6
Uncertainty Is Psychologically Uncomfortable: A Theoretic Framework for Studying Judgments and Decision Making Under Uncertainty and Risk

William P. Neace, Kate Deer, Steven Michaud, and Lauren Bolling

Abstract A novel theoretic framework for examining judgments under uncertainty and risk is proposed based on literature examining how decision makers subjectively represent the concept of uncertainty, and how that representation influences the decision-making process. The literature suggests that "uncertainty" is conceptualized differently than is implied from the perspective of formal models such as the expected utility model. The literature further suggests that strategies used to cope with uncertainty are contingent upon how uncertainty is conceptualized, and also suggests that both cognitive and affective components of the decision influence how information is processed during decision making. The theoretic framework presented in this chapter postulates that uncertainty creates a state of psychological discomfort that motivates the decision maker to move the decision situation from a state of uncertainty toward a state of certainty in order to reduce the discomfort created by uncertainty, and ultimately, to make a decision. Given uncertainty is the main characteristic of an entrepreneurial environment, the present chapter has direct implications for both entrepreneurs and venture capitalists. Both theoretic and practical implications for future research suggested by the theoretic framework are outlined.

6.1 Introduction

Decision making can be broadly characterized as a complex series of processes involving four steps: Setting goals, selecting options relevant for goal satisfaction, assessing the selected options, and finally making a choice among the options (e.g., Beach 1993; Byrnes 1998; Gilotti 2002). We are faced with making decisions in an uncertain world every day; and the entrepreneurs and venture capitalists (VCs) are

W.P. Neace (✉)
University of Hartford, West Hartford, CT, USA
e-mail: Neace@hartford.edu

R. Yazdipour, *Advances in Entrepreneurial Finance: With Applications from Behavioral Finance and Economics*, DOI 10.1007/978-1-4419-7527-0_6,

the best examples when it comes to decision making in the world of business and finance. Traditionally, a judgment is defined as an assessment of the likelihood of the occurrence of some outcome where that likelihood is bounded between 0 and 1. Judgments are made under conditions of uncertainty (the objective probabilities of event occurrence are unknown), or they can be made under conditions of risk (outcome probabilities are known). The structure of a judgment is traditionally formalized by probability theory and its axioms. Judgments under uncertainty are deemed rational if they are coherent (i.e., do not violate probability theory's axioms) or are well calibrated (i.e., correspond to actual event probabilities). Choices made under conditions of risk are rational if they lead to decisions that maximize expected value (under an economic model) or that maximize expected utility or subjective expected utility (under a psychological model).

While early research indicated that people make their judgments and choices in accord with probability theory (e.g., Edwards 1968; Peterson and Beach 1967), more recent research has found that neither probability theory nor its constituents (expected utility-based and subjective expected utility-based models) provide satisfactory descriptive models of human judgment and decision making. Violations of normative probability models abound in the judgment and decision-making literature with respect to both judgments under uncertainty (see Kahneman et al. 1982 for a comprehensive overview), and choices made under risk (e.g., Birnbaum and Beeghley 1997; Birnbaum and Martin 2003; Birnbaum et al. 1999; Diederich and Busemeyer 1999; Luce 2003; Kahneman and Tversky 1979; Tversky and Kahneman 1992). Indeed, the trend in judgment standards has moved from the purely "rational" criteria implied by formal models toward examining the "adaptive rationality" aspects of judgments and decisions (e.g., Mellers et al. 1998; Gigerenzer 2008; Payne and Bettman 2001; Payne et al. 1992; Todd and Gigerenzer 2007; and Shafir and LeBoeuf 2002). Alternatively, rationality can be viewed as a matter of degree that depends upon the recognition and application of appropriate reasoning principles most relevant to the given decision problem (Reyna 2004; Reyna and Brainerd 1995; Reyna and Ellis 1994). Moreover, process models of decision-making are needed to advance our understanding of how decisions and choices are made (Johnson et al. 2008).

One important contribution to the field of judgment and decision making is to propose a decision-making framework that elaborates on several key processes that may underlie decisions under uncertainty.

Given the nature of this book and its main focus on the entrepreneur, the main focus of our literature review will be on decision making under uncertainty. However, we will also examine research on decisions under risk where informative. Moreover, given the breadth of the theoretic framework developed in this chapter, our literature review will necessarily be selective. First, we begin by examining how decision makers internally represent the decision problem. Specifically, we examine how they subjectively represent the concept of uncertainty, and how subjective representation influences later stages of the decision-making process. We then examine the types of decision strategies that are used to cope with uncertainty as conceptualized from the decision maker's perspective and the contingent nature of the strategy selection process. Next, we outline a novel theoretic framework for examining judgments under uncertainty. As will be seen in the chapter, the proposed theoretic framework hypothesizes that: (1) uncertainty creates a state of psychological discomfort, and (2) the decision maker is motivated to move the judgment situation from a state of uncertainty toward a state of certainty with the goal of reducing the discomfort created by uncertainty. Finally, we end the chapter with practical implications of the proposed framework regarding decision making under risk, as well as some suggestions for future research.

6.2 Forming a Subjective Problem Representation

How do people conceptualize "uncertainty?" Is it seen as "chance?" As "probability?" As "insufficient information?" Differences in conceptualizations of uncertainty imply that people may not always agree with "uncertainty" as defined by a formal model such as expected utility (EU). Indeed, at times, people may use some rudimentary form of probabilistic reasoning, demonstrating an intuitive understanding of certain probabilistic concepts (e.g., Nisbett et al. 1983). Alternatively, people may see the world as fundamentally deterministic (e.g., Einhorn 1986), in which case their conceptualization of "uncertainty" may drastically differ from its more formal characterization as probability. The point is that the manner in which uncertainty is communicated by an information source (e.g., an entrepreneur) may affect how it is conceptualized by the receiver (e.g., a VC). Related to this is the issue of how people conceptualize the source of uncertainty, and how the perceived source of uncertainty bears on the subjective representation of what is adopted by the decision maker (e.g., Kahneman and Tversky 1982; Lagnado and Sloman 2004).

The main theoretical issue here relates to the manner in which people conceptualize "uncertainty." Naïve conceptualizations of uncertainty may differ from formal ones; that is, those given to us by probability theory and associated formal models such as EU theory, subjective EU theory, and their variants. More specifically, while formal models of uncertainty characterize it as a unidimensional construct based on either relative frequency of event occurrence given some sample space or as degrees of belief that take on values between 0 and 1, "uncertainty" from a psychological view may well be a multidimensional construct that impacts our degree of confidence in making causal assertions about event occurrence. Several lines of evidence provide converging support for the notion that decisions under uncertainty are subjectively represented differently, and characterized more broadly than is implied by formal models.

Kahneman and Tversky (1979) provide a comprehensive critique of the EU theory and offer prospect theory as an alternative description for decision making under risk. Among the inconsistencies between EU theory and choice behavior that their research uncovers are (1) the certainty effect – the underweighting of outcomes that are probable in comparison with those that occur with certainty; and (2) the isolation effect – people generally disregard shared components in choice alternatives and focus on the unique aspects of the choices. Certainty effects contribute to risk aversion (for gains) and risk seeking (for losses), and isolation effect leads to inconsistency in preference when different aspects of the same choice are made more or less salient by the manner in which the choice is described. Prospect theory is developed to account for these (and other) violations of EU theory. In particular, prospect theory postulates that value is assigned to changes in asset states (gains, losses) relative to a reference point, replacing "utility for final outcomes" as the maximization criterion for choice. Prospect theory also postulates that decision weights replace stated objective probabilities in evaluating given choice alternatives. Both subjective value (v) and decision weights (π) represent psychological parameters in prospect theory. This reflects a significant departure from EU theory's assumptions that the probability of outcome (p) and utility of outcome (u) serve to represent how information is encoded and combined in the decision process.

Decision weights are predicted to change as a function of changes in the description of the choice problem, and also as a function of the context of the choice situation. Choices may depend upon consideration of factors other than stated probabilities. Thus, prospect theory represents a fundamental change in scientific thinking about how people assess risk by underscoring the difference between the objective statement of the decision problem and its attendant psychological representation. The importance of investigating the manner in which the decision situation is internally represented was reiterated in a recent review by Maule and Villejoubert (2007), who also point out that choice depends on factors that go beyond the given information, such as the content and context of the decision problem (see also Pitz and Sachs 1984). Moreover, they review literature suggesting that different decision strategies result in different choices, and may reflect differences in the evaluation operations performed on the internal representation of the decision situation.

One such contextual factor influencing how an event's uncertainty is subjectively represented may be related to its perceived "psychological distance." Drawing on construal level theory (Liberman et al. 2007; Wakslak et al. 2006) proposed that low-probability events are mentally represented by their more central, abstract, and general features (i.e., represented at a high construal level), and that high-probability events are mentally represented by their more concrete, specific features (i.e., represented at a low construal level). Psychological distance is created when an event is not part of one's "direct experience," that is, events that belong to the past or future rather than the present; that happen to others rather than to ourselves; or that take place in foreign countries rather than in our homeland, and are perceived as distant. By extending such logic, the authors propose that an uncertain event can seem more distant than a certain event. For example, when the probability of receiving a job offer from a prestigious company is low, one may feel as though they will "never get the job." On the other hand, when the probability of the job offer is high, one may feel as though they will get a call "at any moment now."

More fundamentally, the authors suggest that perception is integral to the determination of value, and that probability will have an influence on the value assessment aspect of decision making that is systematically related to how the decision situation is mentally represented, and which influences the processing orientation that is used to make the decision. Accordingly, the authors hypothesize that low-probability events are processed more abstractly and high-probability events are processed from a more concrete orientation. In a series of seven studies using multiple operationalizations of construal level and multiple methods of manipulating event probability, Wakslak et al.'s (2006) findings consistently supported the hypothesis.

In a more direct test of construal-level theory as related to decision-making, Todorov et al. (2007) examined how the probability of winning a prize influences the manner in which the attributes of choice alternatives are weighted. According to the authors, the attributes of a judgment situation can be characterized along two dimensions: desirability of the prize (result), and feasibility of obtaining the prize (result). The authors hypothesized that decisions would be based on desirability of the prize (the "what" aspect) rather than the feasibility of obtaining it when the probability of winning was low. However, when the probability was high for winning it, feasibility became more important, giving rise to a preference reversal.

The main implication from other studies (Wakslak et al. (2006), Todorov et al. (2007), and Keren and Roelofsma (1995)) is that the subjective experience of "uncertainty" can be created by more than simply changing the probability of outcomes. People seem to represent a choice differently depending upon whether its occurrence is perceived as imminent or more distant, and temporal distance in the decision situation can also impact choice behavior in ways similar to the impact of manipulating outcome probability in other studies of intertemporal choice and discounting (e.g., Herrnstein 1990; Loewenstein and Thaler 1989; Loewenstein and Prelec 1992). Together, the findings from these studies suggest that "uncertainty" may be conceptualized by the decision maker as something that goes beyond its more "obvious" probabilistic definition. The findings suggest that participants use probability information as another piece of evidence to be incorporated into their causal model of the given situation, and that such information is used as a basis for providing a deterministic response. This type of reasoning suggests that "uncertainty" might be interpreted as meaning "degrees of ignorance" related to an internal source of uncertainty (Kahneman and Tversky 1982) that prompts the search for additional information upon which to base a "yes, no" response (whether such additional information is useful or not). When participants were given an opportunity to select additional information, some of their selections reflected deterministic rather than probabilistic reasoning strategies, suggesting that "uncertainty" might be characterized as insufficient information in an otherwise causally based decision model.

Perhaps the strongest evidence that people use deterministic or causal reasoning under uncertainty comes from a series of experiments conducted by Krynski and Tenenbaum (2007). The authors proposed a three-stage process to describe judgments under uncertainty. In stage 1, people construct a causal model that structures the relationships between variables stated in the problem description. In stage 2, people set the values for the variables in their model using the statistical information provided in the problem statement. In stage 3, people make their probability judgment, via Bayesian inference over the variables in the model (i.e, by combining the statistical information in a manner consistent with the logical structure of the causal model).

Two other areas of research that bear upon the issue of how "uncertainty" is understood and used to structure decision problems comes from studies investigating differences between verbal and numeric labels used to express probabilities, and whether uncertainty is presented in the context of the problem as probabilities or as frequencies. Findings from these two lines of research are reviewed next.

6.2.1 Verbal Versus Numeric Probability Labels and the Meaning of "Uncertainty"

Research in the area of linguistic interpretation of numeric probabilities indicates that verbal expressions of uncertainty (e.g., unlikely, quite possible, almost certain) and numeric probability labels (e.g., .20, .70, .90) do not share the same meaning. Research in this area indicates that there is a large between-subject variability in how both verbal and numeric expressions of probability are interpreted (Beyth-Marom 1982; Wallsten et al. 1986a), but that such variability is smaller around the anchor points of 0, .5, or 1 (Wallsten et al. 1986a). Moreover, verbal expressions of numeric probabilities are highly context dependent (Brun and Teigen 1988; Wallsten et al. 1986b), and influence the types of inferences that are based on them (Moxey and Sanford 2000; Teigen and Brun 1999). Even precise numeric statements of probability (e.g., 70% chance) have been found to be context-sensitive in their interpretation (e.g., Flugstad and Windschitl 2003; Windschitl and Weber 1999).

The implications of these findings are that people have a generally vague notion of the meaning conveyed by either a verbal probability expression or a more precise numeric one, and that their understanding of "uncertainty" is subjectively represented best and understood most at the extreme ends of the probability scale.

Also noteworthy is that the meaning of both numeric and verbal probability expressions varies over contexts. This suggests that something other than "probability" is being judged about the given information. Wallsten et al. (1986a) suggest that attributes associated with the perceived reliability of the given information might be reflected in a membership function used to map verbal probability expressions onto a range of numeric probabilities (firm "uncertainty" might produce a monotonic, sharply peaked function while more diffuse "uncertainty" might produce a more broadly shaped, single-peaked function). Sykes and Johnson (1999) suggest that subjective probability estimates given numerically do not fully capture the degree of belief in an assertion, and provide evidence that indirect measures of subjective probability such as surprise and difficulty imagining the truth of a counterfactual may more accurately assess subjective degree of belief. Their findings also imply that greater weight is given to evidence based on a factual assertion about an uncertain event than is evidence framed as probability (e.g., the evidence suggests that X is liable versus there is an 80% chance that X is liable), and that the difficulty of imagining the counterfactual event may underlie a preference for concrete reasoning.

6.2.2 *Problem Format: Frequency Versus Probability and the Meaning of "Uncertainty"*

Probabilities can be expressed as proportions (e.g., .30), as percentages (e.g., 30%), or as frequencies (e.g., three out of ten). While these different forms are mathematically equivalent, evidence suggest that people make better judgments when information is provided to them in the form of frequencies than when the same information is presented in the form of probabilities (Cosmides and Tooby 1996; Fiedler 1988; Gigerenzer and Hoffrage 1995; Hetwig and Gigerenzer 1999; Tversky and Kahneman 1983). One explanation for the frequency effect is that information regarding event occurrence in the natural environment comes to us in the form of non-normalized frequencies (i.e., simple counts of events) that are experienced directly (so-called natural frequencies as discussed at length by Hoffrage et al. (2002)). According to the natural frequency view (Cosmides and Tooby 1996; Gigerenzer and Hoffrage 1995), frequency information represents the mode of information acquisition to which the human mind has become attuned through evolution. Moreover, the label "probability" is a vague linguistic term because it carries more than one interpretation, for example, as degree of evidentiary support, or as the plausibility of an assertion (Fiedler 1988; see also Gigerenzer 1994 and Hertwig and Gigerenzer 1999 for a detailed discussion of this issue), and may foster a single-event problem representation over a more distributional one (e.g., Hertwig and Gigerenser 1999; Reeves and Lockhart 1993). Thus, presenting information in the form of frequencies facilitates probabilistic reasoning because frequencies are ecologically valid information formats (Brase 2002; Brase and Barbey 2006; Cosmides and Tooby 1996; Gigerenzer 1994; Hoffrage et al. 2002), and asking for frequencies is more likely to elicit a mathematical rather than nonmathematical interpretation of the judgment task (Fiedler 1988; Hertwig and Gigerenzer 1999).

Contradictory evidence and alternative explanations for the frequency effect have been offered (Evans et al. 2000; Griffin and Buehler 1999; Macchi 2000; Mellers and McGraw 1999; Neace et al. 2008; Sloman et al. 2003; Yamagishi 2003). In particular, the nested-sets hypothesis (e.g., Sloman et al. 2003) suggests that frequency effects may be an indirect consequence of inducing a set-inclusion problem representation, which contributes to making the problem's logical structure transparent, and thus easily solvable. Tversky and Kahneman (1983) offered such an explanation for why conjunction errors are less common when frequency versions of probability problems were given to their participants. Both Neace et al. (2008) and Sloman et al. (2002) provide evidence that presenting information in a manner that makes set–subset relationships salient facilitates reasoning regardless of whether probabilities or frequencies are used. Other evidence suggests that frequency problem formats facilitate mathematical rather than statistical reasoning (e.g., Griffin and Beuhler 1999; Neace et al. 2008), and make the judgment problem computationally simpler (e.g., Evans et al. 2000; Johnson-Laird et al. 1999. For an alternative view, see Brase 2002 and Brase and Barbey 2006). This line of research provides evidence that problem format (frequency vs. probability) is less important than problem structure in facilitating probabilistic reasoning.

In sum, the literature suggests that "uncertainty" is a multidimensional construct, and that the manner in which a decision problem is presented results in making different aspects of "uncertainty" more or less psychologically salient. Reasoning about decisions differs depending upon which aspect of uncertainty is made particularly salient in the description of the decision situation or the manner in which probabilities are communicated. Moreover, deterministic reasoning appears to be the default mode used when making predictions under uncertainty or in explaining the occurrence of an uncertain event, and people appear to be more sensitive to certainty (represented by probabilities of 0 and 1) than to varying degrees of uncertainty. The manner in which uncertainty is conceptualized by the decision maker should have an influence over the types of decision strategies and actions that are taken to cope with it during the decision-making process. We turn our attention to strategy selection in the next section.

6.3 Decision Strategies and Coping with Uncertainty

In their review, Payne et al. (1992) call attention to several lines of evidence culled from the risk, probability judgment, and choice literatures that converge in support of their conclusions that (1) decision strategies are contingent upon task characteristics and decision-making context, and (2) that decision makers actively construct preferences during the decision-making process. They also point out that researchers often assume decision makers take the information they are given at face value but point out some evidence suggesting that given information is actually restructured during the process of deciding. As noted earlier, decision makers may not adopt the same definition of uncertainty that is often taken for granted by researchers as being obvious – that is, the unidimensional operationalization of probabilistic uncertainty as conceptualized by decision researchers may not reflect the multidimensional nature of "uncertainty" as conceptualized by the decision maker. In extending Payne et al.'s (1992) view of contingent decision strategy used to include how uncertainty is subjectively represented, it is both theoretically and practically meaningful to examine the relationship between how "uncertainty" is conceptualized and the various strategies that are used to cope with "uncertainty" as defined from the point of view of the decision maker.

Lipshitz and Strauss' (1997) proposed that uncertainty can be broadly defined as "… a sense of doubt that blocks or delays action" (p. 150). Further, they proposed that the type of uncertainty with which decision makers must cope depends upon the decision-making model that they adopt. The authors broadly characterize decision-making models according to the types of action they entail: Consequentialist actions (those actions that address a set of questions related to identifying what the choice alternatives are, what the outcomes of each alternative are, and what consequences are associated with the outcomes of the choice alternatives – the focus of traditional decision research), and obligatory actions (those actions that address a set of questions related to understanding the current decision situation, what the decision maker's role might be in the situation, and what actions might be "required" in such situations as dictated by social norms or prescribed rules). The authors also propose that different types of uncertainty can be classified along two dimensions: The issue of uncertainty (what the decision maker is uncertain about), and the source of the uncertainty (what causes the uncertainty). Issues include uncertainty about outcomes, situation, alternatives, and source includes uncertainty related to incomplete information, inadequate understanding of the situation, and to undifferentiated alternatives (i.e., conflict between similar choices in which one choice does not clearly dominate the other).

Evidence to support their proposals comes from the narratives of participants who were asked to write about one personal experience of decision making under uncertainty. The definition of "uncertainty" was left up to the participants. The study's findings indicated that participants' conceptualizations of "uncertainty" fell into three main categories: Inadequate understanding, conflict among alternatives (i.e., undifferentiated alternatives), and lack of information. The findings also suggested that participants' conceptualizations of uncertainty lie mostly within the domains of lacking a complete understanding of the situation or lack of clarity as to what role they should play in the situation, rather than uncertainty being related to the outcomes and their consequences as maintained by the expectancy-based theories (e.g., EU, SEU, and their variants). Only one-third of the participants mentioned using a "pros-and-cons" strategy, and those that did based it on a qualitative rather than a quantitative assessment of outcome likelihood and consequences. Moreover, most participants' responses indicated that they were either uncertain about the situation or about their role in the situation, compared to about one-third of participants whose responses reflected uncertainty about outcomes and their consequences. Of particular interest is that participants' responses favored qualitative assessments of uncertainty over quantitative ones (indeed, no participant's response indicated any form of quantification of uncertainty). This suggests that assessments of uncertainty take a primarily qualitative form, which runs contrary to the focus of many traditional decision-making models that tend to quantify uncertainty.

Five coping strategies were identified from participants' responses: Reduction of uncertainty, putting off the decision ("forestalling"), assumption-based reasoning (filling in gaps in available information with reasonable assumptions), weighting pros and cons (a strategy more in line with traditional judgment and decision-making theories, such as multiattribute choice models), and otherwise ignoring or failing to deal directly with uncertainty. Most of the coping strategies participants engaged in centered on seeking additional information about either the situation or their role in the situation, rather than involving a quantitative assessment of outcome likelihood. The data also indicated that different coping strategies were used depending upon the type of uncertainty that was incorporated into the participant's subjective representation: Inadequate understanding was most often managed by uncertainty reduction (operationalized as collecting additional information, seeking advice from others, or relying on standard operating procedures or social norms);

incomplete information was most often managed by assumption-based reasoning (operationalized as constructing a mental model that is constrained by what is firmly known while incorporating other information that goes beyond what is given but which is logically constrained by the decision situation); and conflict was most often managed by weighting pros and cons (operationalized as evaluating the potential gains vs. losses associated with the choice alternatives).

Based on such findings, Lipshitz and Strauss (1997) criticize the way in which traditional judgment and decision-making theories have viewed the process of making a decision under uncertainty. Of particular relevance is that the authors point out that traditional judgment and decision-making theories do not address the qualitative nature of conceptualizing "uncertainty" from the decision maker's perspective. In addition, they argue that mainstream judgment and decision-making theories often fail to acknowledge that different conceptualizations of uncertainty are related to different strategies that are used to cope with it. The implications of such criticisms are that subjective representations of uncertainty are linked to specific corresponding actions taken to move forward in the decision process, and that additional research is needed to more fully explore the issue of how decision makers' strategies are contingent upon how they represent uncertainty in the decision problem. Moreover, such criticisms have implications for the types of interventions that might be used to assist people in improving their decision making. There is evidence that decision aids traditionally recommended typically meets with resistance, skepticism, and appear untrustworthy (e.g., Dawes et al., 2000; Yates et al. 2003). If a better understanding of how uncertainty is conceptualized can be achieved, then research could work toward decision aids that formalize uncertainty in a manner that takes into consideration the needs of the decision maker, and informs strategies that people naturally use to cope with uncertainty. That is, decision aids could be made more "user-friendly."

6.4 Uncertainty and Psychological Discomfort

Mainstream judgment and decision-making research has recently begun to acknowledge the role that affect, mood, and emotions play in the decision-making process (e.g., Loewenstein et al. 2001; Schwarz 2002; Slovic et al. 2002). Affective states experienced during and after the decision-making process are important additions to the cognitive components of decision making. Examining the role that affect plays in decision making highlights some of the consequences of the psychological discomfort that uncertainty may create. A short list of some of these consequences includes regret and disappointment (e.g., Bell 1982, 1985; Loomes and Sugden 1986), loss aversion (Tversky and Kahneman 1991), anxiety created by disproportionately allocating attention to the least probable outcome (Wu 1999), worry that influences decisions regarding follow-up medical testing (e.g., Gurmankin et al. 2004), fear of negative side effects associated with choosing a medical treatment (Amsterlaw et al. 2006), and doubt about what action to take that may leave the decision maker indecisive for a prolonged period (Lipshitz and Strauss 1997).

In the mainstream judgment and decision-making theories have incorporated affect into expectancy-based choice models by arguing that they carry value for the decision maker in addition to the usual outcome utility, and that standard decision-making models need to be revised to reflect the consideration given to affect in order to more accurately describe decision-making processes (e.g., Wu 1999). That is, mainstream judgment and decision-making theories have attempted to model affective components of decision making by incorporating them into consequentialist models (cf. Loewenstein et al. 2001). Consequentialist models assume that decision makers carefully consider all aspects of the decision situation (including anticipated affect) before arriving at a choice. In contrast, other theorists view affect in the decision process from a nonconsequentialist perspective, in which affective reactions may diverge from cognitive appraisals to directly effect choice behavior (Loewenstein et al. 2001), or in which affect may serve as the basis for evaluating information or to guide subsequent decision processes (by determining what features of the decision situation becomes salient) in the absence of careful cognitive assessment (Bechara et al. 2000; Peters et al. 2006a; Schwarz 2002; Slovic et al. 2002).

Elaydi (2006) proposed and tested one such model of nonconsequentialist decision making. In his view, a nonconsequentialist decision-making process is one in which a decision is made in order to cope with negative emotions that are experienced as part of trying to make a decision without regard to the attendant consequences of the choice. The author argues that concurrent negative emotions experienced during the decision-making process (which may be more aptly described as affective states such as regret, dread, fear, angst, anxiety) can lead the decision maker to change the focus of the decision-making process from careful consideration of the choices (a cognitive evaluation) to managing the negative emotions being experienced (an affective evaluation). One way to manage such emotions is to make a premature decision as a way of coping with the negative emotions being experienced without regard to the consequences of the choice.

Drawing from past research suggesting that decision difficulty has a direct effect on choosing an option just to manage the negative emotions experienced (e.g., Janis and Mann 1977; Lazarus and Folkman 1984), the author proposed a model in which direct relationship is fully mediated by indecisiveness. The author defines indecisiveness as a state that occurs when "… the decision maker becomes stuck in the decision-making process (undecided) while experiencing concurrent negative emotions …" (p. 46). Therefore, difficult decisions can lead to indecisiveness (which is really an emotionally unpleasant state to tolerate), and the decision maker attempts to reduce the state of indecisiveness by making a decision based on the need to reduce negative concurrent emotions rather than based on a carefully reasoned assessment of the decision situation.

The findings indicated that only anticipated regret was significantly and positively correlated with indecisiveness, suggesting that the other hypothesized components of decision difficulty (e.g., preference instability, poor decision structure) were not predictive of indecision. The findings also indicated that the relationship between anticipated regret and nonconsequentialist dysfunctional coping behaviors (e.g., shifting responsibility, biased information seeking, narrowly focusing on options that promise immediate relief to the negative emotional state) was fully mediated by indecisiveness. Thus, the findings indicated that anticipated regret produces a negative emotional state that creates indecisiveness, and the decision maker is motivated to attend to the emotional state at the expense of a more careful cognitive assessment of the choice alternatives and their consequences.

Although decision processes can be influenced by purely cognitive assessments on the one hand, and purely affective assessments on the other, their effects may blend during decision making (see, for example, Peters et al. 2006b). Evidence that affect and cognition interact during decision making comes from studies showing that risk-averse and risk-seeking behavior (cognitive elements of prospect theory discussed earlier) can emerge in the absence of a deliberative decision strategy (Franken et al. 2006), and that affective reactions can have a greater impact on choices than do purely cognitive assessments (Rottenstreich and Hsee 2001). Peters and Slovic (2000) found that participants placed more weight on immediate outcomes (gains and losses) in a simulated gambling task than they did on the expected value of the choice alternatives, suggesting that affective reactivity to those outcomes influenced choice behavior more than did deliberative cognitive strategies.

Evidence indicates that positive affect is related to heuristic processing, and that negative affect is related to more systematic processing (e.g., Bless et al. 1990; Schwarz and Bless 1991), suggesting that information processing differs along an affective valence dimension (good, bad; happy, sad). Other evidence indicates that the level of uncertainty produced by particular affective states influences the depth of cognitive processing along an emotional certainty–uncertainty dimension regardless of the affect's valence. Tiedens and Linton (2001) produced evidence that the certainty–uncertainty appraisal of an emotional experience influenced the certainty with which participants felt about their predictions regarding an unrelated future event, and also influenced the depth of information processing they used. An affective state related to emotional uncertainty (e.g., fear) produced systematic processing while an affective state associated with certainty (e.g., anger) produced greater heuristic processing. The authors suggested that people might prefer certainty over uncertainty, and that their certainty preference might motivate them to resolve the uncertainty by processing the available information more deeply.

Decisions have both affective and cognitive components, and these components may be weighted differentially in the decision-making processes. Moreover, there appears to be a tension between cognition and affect that impacts the manner in which information is processed, and ultimately, should influence what decision is made. Such tension may even underlie the manner in which the decision situation is psychologically represented, and especially how uncertainty is conceptualized by the decision maker. The psychological impact of uncertainty forms a central element in the theoretical treatment of decisions under uncertainty that is proposed in this chapter. In the final section, we propose a theoretical framework that attempts to tie together the various aspects of the decision-making process that are identified from the foregoing literature review. We then suggest avenues for future research that are implied by such a framework.

6.5 A Proposed Theoretic Framework for Studying Judgments Under Uncertainty

Figure 6.1 presents a preliminary theoretical framework for more extensively examining decision-making processes under uncertainty in light of issues raised in our literature review in this chapter. The proposed framework begins with the assumption that information is provided to the decision maker, and that posing the decision problem marks the start of the decision-making process. In any given decision situation, people have at their disposal information that they may use to form a judgment and, ultimately, to make a decision. The given information must then be encoded to form a subjective representation of the decision situation. The subjective representation need not necessarily recognize "uncertainty" as an element of the decision. When "uncertainty" is made part of the subjective problem representation, however, it must be conceptualized or defined by the decision maker. "Uncertainty" may be conceptualized in a variety of ways. It may be subjectively represented as a lack of information, as a lack of clarity as to one's role in a situation, or as doubt about what action to take in a given situation, reflecting epistemic uncertainty. Uncertainty may also be characterized as an acknowledgement of "chance" processes that reflects a rudimentary understanding of "probability."

The theoretic framework proposes that uncertainty under any conceptualization has the potential to create a state of "psychological discomfort," and it is the need to reduce such discomfort that motivates the decision maker to move forward in the decision-making process.

The framework further proposes that the "discomfort" must be resolved by moving the decision problem from a state of uncertainty toward a state of certainty.

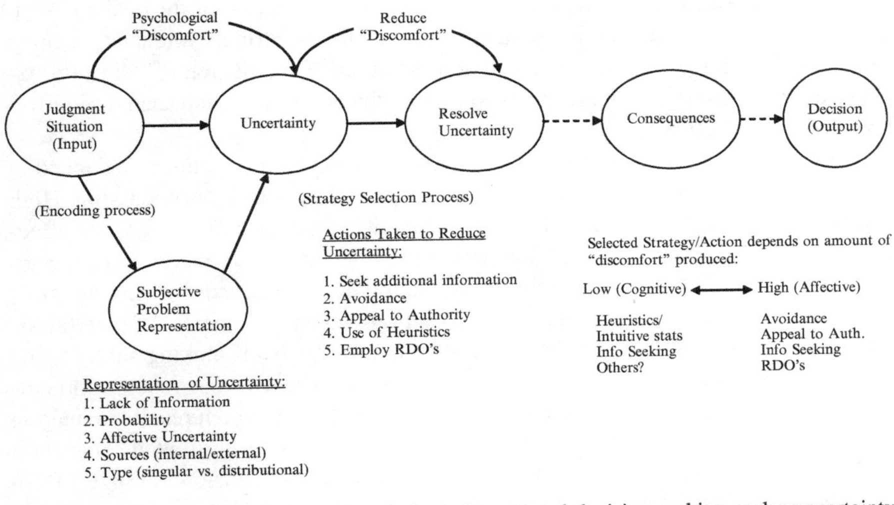

Fig. 6.1 A proposed theoretic framework for judgment and decision making under uncertainty and risk

This proposal comes from evidence that decision makers tend to view "uncertainty" as an impediment in an otherwise causal assessment of the decision problem. When the uncertainty cannot be resolved, the decision maker's default is to maintain the status quo or otherwise avoid making a choice altogether by, for example, forestalling or seeking alternatives not explicitly mentioned in the choice set.

The proposed process relating uncertainty to psychological discomfort should not be mistaken as a form of cognitive dissonance that was originally proposed by Festinger (1957), see also Festinger and Carlsmith (1959), or as has been revised over the years (see the recent review by Harmon-Jones and Harmon-Jones (2007). In dissonance theory, an unpleasant cognitive state is created by a general inconsistency between two relevant but opposing attitudes, or between a behavior and an attitude that are inconsistent. Such dissonance motivates an individual to reduce the inconsistency by changing the behavior, by changing the attitude, or both to make them more congruent with one another. In contrast, the psychological discomfort proposed within the present theoretical framework is created simply by the perception of "uncertainty" in the given decision situation, and the need to cope with that uncertainty in order to make a decision.

The theoretic framework also proposes that actions taken to reduce the psychological discomfort created by uncertainty depend, in part, upon how the decision maker conceptualizes "uncertainty." Such actions may be contingent upon the perceived source of uncertainty, with internal uncertainty leading to actions that increase the amount of available information or that otherwise clarify the relationship between the choice alternatives and their consequences, and external uncertainty leading to actions that attempt to control or to mitigate undesirable consequences in the choices offered. Where there is no clear solution, the decision maker may attempt to appeal to an authority (e.g., an experienced entrepreneur or advisor) for advice. This process of reducing psychological discomfort may or may not contain components of both a consequentialist perspective (i.e., a cognitive appraisal of the decision situation) and nonconsequentialist elements (appeal to authority, avoidance, seeking information in a biased manner, etc.), depending upon the degree of "discomfort" experienced by the decision maker, as well as on the degree to which such discomfort produces an affective state.

Accordingly, the present theoretical framework posits a continuum balanced at one end by cognitive processing and at the other end by affective processing. High levels of psychological discomfort move the decision maker more toward the affective end of the continuum, while low levels move the decision maker more toward the cognitive end, thereby providing a psychological mechanism for linking "hot" and "cold" decision-making processes to actions taken to cope with uncertainty. Affective states may be a significant component of decision making under some circumstances, leading to the experience of negative affect whose resolution takes precedence over more reasoned, cognitive assessments, and which results in making choices or decisions without regard to their consequences (hence the dotted connection in the link between resolve, uncertainty, consequences, and decision in Fig. 6.1). On the other hand, lack of affect may be detrimental to decision making since evidence indicates that affect might serve as a signal that directs subsequent information processing (e.g., efficient use of limited attentional resources). Cognitive components may predominate in the decision-making process under other circumstances, which may result in selecting strategies differently than primarily affect-directed processing by influencing the manner of information processing that ensues. The interplay between affect and cognition has implications for the weight given to these components, which in turn may influence the types of strategies that are used to resolve uncertainty during decision making.

The proposed "psychological discomfort" might be analogized as a "mental itch" – some form of (cognitive) annoyance that is persistent, and which must be attended to until it is resolved. This notion is akin to a physiological itch. There are levels of physiological itches that, while experienced as uncomfortable, are nonetheless experienced at levels below what might be experienced as "pain." Such "itches" are nevertheless intense and persistent. Using the physical analogy, the present conceptualization of "psychological discomfort" might be described as "an intense and persistent psychological state that requires attention." Like a physical itch, the "mental itch" persists until it is resolved. Also like a physical itch, the "mental itch" may become intense enough to invoke an affective state but need not always have an affective component.

The theoretic framework proposes that "uncertainty" causes the mental itch, and its resolution is what motivates the decision maker to take some type of action to resolve it (whether such action is searching for additional information, appealing to authority for an "answer," avoidance, and other actions listed in Fig. 6.1). How the "mental itch" is "scratched" depends, in large part, upon the manner in which uncertainty is subjectively represented (e.g., issue/source from Lipshitz and Strauss 1997; as internal or external, namely, Kanheman and Tversky (1982); or as invoking a distributional vs. a singular representation as in the "inside" vs. "outside" view proposed by Legnado and Sloman (2004)), and the attendant reasoning processes (probabilistic vs. deterministic) that such representations invoke.

When causal reasoning fails (i.e., when uncertainty or risk in the decision situation is unavoidable), then uncertainty may create a disruption in the decision maker's sense of certainty, and this disruption may underlie the attendant "psychological discomfort." In that case, we believe that the "discomfort" motivates the decision maker toward reducing the "uncertainty" by bolstering elements of their internal "causal model" representation, which may lead to nonconsequentialist decision strategies (as proposed by Elaydi (2006)) even in the absence of concurrent negative emotions, depending upon where the decision maker is located along the cognitive-affective continuum.

6.6 Implications of the Proposed Framework and Some Suggestions for Future Research

The theoretic framework proposed for judgment and decision making under risk and uncertainty in Fig. 6.1 has both theoretical and practical implications. Theoretically, developing and testing models of the decision processes that people use adds significantly to our basic understanding of the psychology of judgment and decision making by making explicit assumptions that have not been empirically tested, and by identifying gaps in our present knowledge of those underlying decision processes. Practically, increasing our understanding of how people make decisions under uncertainty and risk can be used to increase the efficacy of those decisions. Some of these implications are highlighted below.

6.6.1 Implications for the Subjective Representation of Uncertainty

The manner by which people internally represent the given information in a decision problem is an important aspect of the initial decision-making phase that should not be overlooked. In particular, it is important not to make assumptions about how "uncertainty" is conceptualized from the decision maker's perspective. The need to address the process by which given information is encoded and internally represented is made explicit in the proposed theoretic framework, and points to an area of research that has not received sufficient empirical attention. We derive three implications regarding how people subjectively represent uncertainty.

One implication is that "uncertainty" may be a multidimensional construct whose psychological representation is quite different than its formal one (i.e., psychologically, "uncertainty" is more than a value in the range of 0–1). "Uncertainty" means different things in different contexts, and it can represent different aspects of the same decision problem depending upon how that problem is presented. A related issue is the extent to which two individuals like an entrepreneur and a VC share a common representation of the decision, and how their representation may differ relative to the circumstances surrounding the decision. Such theoretical understanding becomes of practical importance when we decide to raise capital for a venture, invest in a new venture, seek the advice of experts, etc. Moreover, individual differences related to gender, age, education level, professional training, and others (e.g., Stanovich and West 2000) might impact the encoding process, and influence the manner in which uncertainty is represented and understood by different people. It is important to consider such differences in order to more fully understand how best to make a decision. Moreover, this points to the need for developing a shared understanding of the decision situation among all parties involved.

A second implication is that people have a rather vague understanding of what "uncertainty" means; whether such uncertainty is conveyed by a verbal probability expression or by a more precise numeric statement. Understanding "uncertainty" appears to be best at the extreme ends of the probability scale, with probabilities near 0 reflecting psychological certainty that an event will not occur, and probabilities near 1 reflecting psychological certainty about an event's occurrence. People tend to be insensitive to probabilities in the mid-range of the scale, except at the .5 anchor point, where, psychologically, it reflects epistemic uncertainty rather than "even odds." That is, people may translate information about probabilities (formal uncertainty) onto a psychological "certainty" scale, and adjust mid-range probabilities toward one of these three psychologically meaningful anchor points (a process that differs from the anchor-and-adjustment heuristic described by Tversky and Kahneman (1974)). The adjustment process may be driven, in part, by the degree of psychological discomfort experienced. People may feel less discomfort, for example, with probabilities of .7 or .3 than they do with probabilities of .5 because the high and low probabilities can be adjusted to create a sense a certainty, whereas the .5 probability anchor offers no opportunity to reduce uncertainty.

Understanding this implied adjustment process is of practical importance when people must decide on a course of action or make a choice among several options that carry unwanted consequences but that differ by mid-range probabilities to which people appear insensitive. Part of the difficulty in making trade-offs, for example, may lie with being forced to choose the best of a set of bad alternatives, or in trying to choose among alternatives that, on the surface, appear equally acceptable. Such choices may become clearer, in part, by making the small differences in probabilities psychologically meaningful.

A third implication is that people seem to use deterministic reasoning to structure their representation of the decision problem, even when it should be clear from the problem statement that no causal mechanism exists to explain outcome occurrence. As a result, they may place undue weight on information that is irrelevant to predicting an outcome, underweight relevant information, or overlook altogether information that would, if used properly, lead to better choices and decisions. Gaining a better understanding of how the information in a decision problem is subjectively structured, and what factors influence the degree to which casual reasoning is used to make decisions under uncertainty, is an important first step toward explaining why people often fail to use statistical reasoning. Practically, such understanding can be used to develop and assess decision aids whose implementation has traditionally met with resistance. It is therefore important to more fully examine how types of information input (verbal or numeric; frequency or probability) are related to the manner in which given information is structured. By gaining a better understanding of these processes, relevant information that might otherwise be discounted or ignored can be presented in a way that makes it more useful for the decision maker.

6.6.2 *Implications for Strategy Selection During Decision Making*

Strategy selection is another key element of the decision-making process that is highlighted in the proposed theoretic framework. Choices and decisions are purposeful in the sense that the termination of the decision process results in the decision maker taking some form of action or settling for inaction that still results in consequences. "Uncertainty" may be seen as an impediment to decision making that must be resolved before a choice is made. Thus, selection of decision strategy to cope with uncertainty is closely linked to how uncertainty is conceptualized by the decision maker in the proposed theoretic framework. Three implications are derived from this notion.

First, by building upon existing evidence that decision makers actively construct preferences during decision making, and that their strategies tend to be contingent upon task characteristics (e.g., number of alternatives, imposed time constraints, etc., see Payne et al. 1992), one implication is that strategy selection may also be contingent upon how a decision maker conceptualizes uncertainty. A preliminary list of strategies for coping with uncertainty consists of using heuristics to simplify the decision (e.g., Kahneman et al. 1982), seeking additional information (e.g., Konold 1989; Huber et al. 2001), appealing to an authority (e.g., experienced entrepreneur, financial advisor, etc.), taking action to reduce uncertainty or taking precautions in preparing for the worse case (Huber et al. 2001), weighting positive and negative aspects of the choices, or otherwise ignoring or failing to directly deal with uncertainty (avoidance, maintaining the status quo, etc.; e.g., Anderson 2003; Lipshitz and Strauss 1997). Understanding the circumstances under which each of these strategies is used, either individually or in combination, in relation to how people conceptualize the decision problem is theoretically meaningful. At a more practical level, additional research in this area has the potential to identify which strategies tend to be successful, and the circumstances under which they work best for the decision maker. On the other hand, such research can also determine when, and under what circumstances, unsuccessful or potentially deleterious strategies are used, thus providing practical guidelines for assisting decision makers with moving forward in the decision-making process.

A second implication is that strategies tend to result from qualitative, rather than quantitative, assessments of the decision situation. Of theoretical interest is to examine factors that move strategy selection toward cognitive assessments, and how those assessments bear upon the types of choices that are made. Further, comparing the efficacy of cognitive (quantitative) versus affective (qualitative) assessments on aspects of decision quality and satisfaction with outcomes is important in order to increase our understanding of what works best from the point of view of the decision maker, and to uncover circumstances under which each predominates during the process of decision making. Determining factors that influence how much weight is given to quantitative versus qualitative information, and under what circumstances, becomes practically important when decision makers must combine available information in the process of making a final choice or decision, and likely impacts the type of strategy they use in that process.

A third implication regarding strategy selection is that different types of personality characteristics might be more or less prone to use a particular strategy. For example, differences in locus of control or in need for cognition might be related to the degree to which people adopt an information-seeking strategy or appeal to authority in attempting to reduce uncertainty. Moreover, such personality characteristics might be related to how uncertainty is subjectively represented and understood, which may in turn influence the types of strategies that are used to cope with it during the decision-making process. It would be meaningful to examine such differences.

6.6.3 *Implications for Cognitive Versus Affective Components in Decision Making*

Decisions can have both cognitive and affective components, and these components may be weighted differently in the process of deciding on a course of action or in anticipation of the consequences of making a choice. Moreover, the degree to which these components are weighted may impact the nature of information processing that ensues during the decision-making process as proposed in many dual-processing theories (e.g., Chaiken et al. 1989; Kahneman and Frederick 2002; Petty and Cacioppo 1986; Reyna et al. 2003; Sloman 1996; Stanovich and West 1998). The potential polarization of cognitive and affective components may create a tension in the decision maker, and such tension may underlie the manner in which the decision situation is subjectively represented, especially affecting how uncertainty is conceptualized. Uncertainty may then give rise to a state of psychological discomfort for the decision maker. The psychological impact of uncertainty forms a central element linking the subjective representation component of the proposed theoretic framework to the strategy selection process. The psychological discomfort is what we believe largely motivates the decision maker to select a strategy to cope with uncertainty. The decision maker ultimately selects the strategy that reduces their level of discomfort, and by extension, the perceived uncertainty in the situation, in order to make a decision. Three implications derived from this aspect of the theoretic framework are outlined below.

One implication is that decisions can follow from purely consequentialist processes in which the decision maker carefully weighs all aspects of the decision situation (both cognitive and affective components) and potential consequences associated with the choice alternatives, or they can be the result of purely nonconsequentialist processes in which the decision maker attempts to manage the attendant affect created by the decision situation (i.e., makes a purely "emotional decision") at the expense of a more "reasoned" choice. More likely, however, is that both cognitive and affective components play a role in decision making, and the degree to which one or the other predominates during the decision making process may be influenced by the degree of psychological discomfort that is experienced by the decision maker. Examining the role that psychological discomfort plays in the decision-making process informs theory regarding the degree to which affective considerations might tend to outweigh cognitive considerations, and how that impacts the strategy selection aspect of the decision-making process. More practically, research can provide useful information on the extent to which people will go to avoid experiencing a negative outcome, such as regret or disappointment, and the extent to which they will go to maintain the promise of a positive outcome by holding on to hope or prolonging the experience of anticipation. Such information can be used to set reasonable limits on decision-making activities, and to provide for a reasonable stopping point in the decision-making process. One source of worry or anxiety might be in not knowing when to stop and make a decision.

A second implication is that decisions will differ depending upon the degree to which affective and cognitive components are consistent with one another.

Where consistent, the decision maker may experience a sense of certainty about their decision (e.g., Tiedens and Linton 2001). Where inconsistent, however, people may have a sense that "I know I should do one thing but I feel as though I should do another." It is theoretically meaningful to examine the nature of interplay between cognition and affect in order to more fully understand their relative influence on decisions. Choices that appear irrational from one perspective (cognition) may appear to be rational from another (affective). Theoretically, then, new and different standards of assessing rationality might be gleaned from research investigating the interaction between affect and cognition on the decision-making process. On a more practical level, bringing affective and cognitive components into synchrony may be one way to resolve the psychological discomfort associated with uncertainty, and allow the decision maker to move forward in the decision process by alleviating the nagging sense of unease that might otherwise prevent them from making a choice. Here, cognitive dissonance theory (Festinger 1957) and the proposed theoretic framework may share a small piece of common ground. It would be interesting to determine whether dissonance reduction occurs during the process of aligning cognitive and affective elements of the decision.

A third implication is that differences in perceived source of the uncertainty (e.g., internal vs. external) might produce different levels of psychological discomfort. People might experience less discomfort if they perceive the source of uncertainty as internal (i.e., lack of information, knowledge) because they may believe they have control over such uncertainty. They can always seek additional information or turn to an authority for advice. On the other hand, where uncertainty is perceived to be external, there might be a perceived loss of control and, as a result, more psychological discomfort will be experienced.

6.7 Conclusion

We hypothesize that the desire to live in a certain world, and the inevitability of encountering uncertainty, can create a tension that manifests itself as psychological discomfort. Such discomfort resonates throughout the decision-making process, from initially representing the decision situation and selecting strategies to cope with it, to managing the interplay between affect and cognition that drives us toward making our decisions and living with the consequences of our choices. At two extremes, the said discomfort can also end up with either inaction or total chaos for individuals. In most cases however, the psychological discomfort, if not managed satisfactorily, can lead to incorrect decisions in life and in business. We hope that the theoretic framework developed in this chapter provides a fresh perspective in the area of judgment and decision making under uncertainty. We also hope that the proposed framework stimulates research to address the gaps in our present understanding of these decision processes.

References

Amsterlaw, J., B.J. Zikmund-Fisher, A. Fagerlin, and P. Ubel. 2006. Can avoidance of complications lead to biased healthcare decisions? *Judgment and Decision Making* 1: 64–75.

Anderson, C.J. 2003. The psychology of doing nothing: Forms of decision avoidance result from reason and emotion. *Psychological Bulletin* 129: 139–167.

Beach, L.R. 1993. Broadening the definition of decision making: The role of prochoice screening of options. *Psychological Science* 4: 215–220.

Bechara, A., D. Tranel, and A.R. Damasio. 2000. Poor judgment in spite of high intellect: Neurological evidence for emotional intelligence. In *The handbook of emotional intelligence: Theory, development, assessment, and application at home, school, and in the workplace*, ed. R. Bar-On and J.D. Parker, 192–214. San Francisco: Jossey-Bass.

Bell, D.E. 1982. Regret in decision making under uncertainty. *Operations Research* 30: 961–981.

Bell, D.E. 1985. Disappointment in decision making under uncertainty. *Operations Research* 33: 1–27.

Beyth-Marom, R. 1982. How probable is probable? A numerical translation of verbal probability expressions. *Journal of Forecasting* 1: 257–269.

Birnbaum, M.H., and D. Beeghley. 1997. Violations of branch independence in judgments of the value of gambles. *Psychological Science* 8: 87–94.

Birnbaum, M.H., and T. Martin. 2003. Generalizations across people, procedures, and predictions: Violations of stochastic dominance and coalescing. In *Emerging perspectives on judgment and decision research*, ed. S.L. Schneider and J. Shanteau, 84–107. New York: Cambridge University Press.

Birnbaum, M.H., J.N. Patton, and M.K. Lott. 1999. Evidence against rank-dependent utility theories: Violations of cumulative independence, interval independence, stochastic dominance, and transitivity. *Organizational Behavior and Human Decision Processes* 77: 44–83.

Bless, H., G. Bohner, N. Schwarz, and F. Strack. 1990. Mood and persuasion: A cognitive response analysis. *Personality and Social Psychology Bulletin* 16: 311–345.

Brase, G.L. 2002. Which statistical formats facilitate what decisions? The perception and influence of different statistical information formats. *Journal of Behavioral Decision Making* 15: 381–401.

Brase, G.L., and A.K. Barbey. 2006. Mental representations of statistical information. In *Advances in psychology research*, vol. 41, ed. A. Columbus, 91–113. New York: Nova Science.

Brun, W., and K.H. Teigen. 1988. Verbal probabilities: Ambiguous, context-dependent, or both? *Organizational Behavior and Human Decision Processes* 41: 390–404.

Byrnes, J.P. 1998. *The nature and development of decision making: A self-regulation model.* Mahwah: Lawrence Erlbaum.

Chaiken, S., A. Liberman, and A.H. Eagly. 1989. Heuristic and systematic information processing within and beyond the persuasion context. In *Unintended thought*, ed. J.S. Uleman and J.A. Bargh, 212–252. New York: Guilford.

Cosmides, L.J., and J. Tooby. 1996. Are humans good intuitive statisticians after all? Rethinking some conclusions from the literature on judgment under uncertainty. *Cognition* 58: 1–73.

Dawes, R.M., D. Faust, and P.E. Meehl. 2000. Clinical versus actuarial prediction. In *Heuristics and biases: The psychology of intuitive judgment*, ed. T. Gilovich, D. Griffin and D. Kahneman, 49–81. Cambridge, UK: Cambridge University Press.

Diederich, A., and J.R. Busemeyer. 1999. Conflict and the stochastic-dominance princiole of decision making. *Psychological Science* 10: 353–359.

Edwards, W. 1968. Conservatism in human information processing. In *Formal representation of human judgment*, ed. B. Kleinmutz, 17–51. New York: Wiley.

Einhorn, H.J. 1986. Accepting error to make less error. *Journal of Personality Assessment* 50: 387–395.

Elaydi, R. 2006. The development and testing of a nonconsequentialist decision-making model. *International Journal of Organizational Analysis* 14: 43–66.

Evans, J.St B.T., S.J. Handley, N. Perham, D.E. Over, and V.A. Thompson. 2000. Frequency versus probability formats in statistical word problems. *Cognition* 77: 197–213.

Festinger, L. 1957. *A theory of cognitive dissonance*. Standford: Stanford University Press.

Festinger, L., and J.M. Carlsmith. 1959. Cognitive consequences of forced compliance. *Journal of Abnormal and Social Psychology* 58: 203–210.

Fiedler, K. 1988. The dependence of the conjunction fallacy on subtle linguistic factors. *Psychological Research* 50: 123–129.

Flugstad, A.R., and P.D. Windschitl. 2003. The influence of reasons on interpretations of probability forecasts. *Journal of Behavioral Decision Making* 16: 107–126.

Franken, I.H.A., I. Georgieva, P. Muris, and A. Dijksterhuis. 2006. The rich get richer and the poor get poorer: On risk aversion in behavioral decision-making. *Judgment and Decision Making* 1: 153–158.

Gigerenzer, G. 1994. Why the distinction between single-event probabilities and frequencies is relevant for psychology (and vice versa). In *Subjective probability*, ed. G. Wright and P. Ayton, 129–161. New York: Wiley.

Gigerenzer, G. 2008. Why heuristics work. *Perspective on Psychological Science: Special issue: From philosophical thinking to psychological empiricism* 3: 20–29.

Gilotti, K.M. 2002. *Making decisions that matter: How people face important life choices*. Mahwah: Lawrence Erlbaum.

Gigerenzer, G., and U. Hoffrage. 1995. How to improve Bayesian reasoning without instruction: Frequency formats. *Psychological Review* 102: 684–704.

Griffin, D., and R. Buehler. 1999. Frequency, probability and prediction: Easy solutions to cognitive illusions? *Cognitive Psychology* 38: 48–78.

Gurmankin, A.D., J. Baron, and K. Armstrong. 2004. Intended message versus message received in hypothetical physician risk communications: Exploring the gap. *Risk Analysis* 24: 1337–1347.

Harmon-Jones, E., and C. Harmon-Jones. 2007. Cognitive dissonance theory after 50 years of development. *Zeitschrift für Sozialpsychologie* 38: 7–16.

Herrnstein, R.J. 1990. Rational choice theory: Necessary but not sufficient. *The American Psychologist* 45: 356–367.

Hertwig, R., and G. Gigerenzer. 1999. The "conjunction fallacy" revisited: How intelligent inferences look like reasoning errors. *Journal of Behavioral Decision Making* 12: 275–305.

Hoffrage, U., G. Gigerenzer, S. Krauss, and L. Martignon. 2002. Representation facilitates reasoning: What natural frequencies are and what they are not. *Cognition* 84: 343–352.

Johnson, E.J., M. Schulte-Mecklenbeck, and C. Martijn. 2008. Process models deserve process data: Comment on Brandstätter, Gigerenzer, and Hertwig (2006). *Psychological Review* 115: 263–272.

Huber, O., C. Beutter, J. Montoya, and O.W. Huber. 2001. Risk-defusing behavior: Towards an understanding of risky decision making. *European Journal of Cognitive Psychology* 13: 409–426.

Janis, I.L., and L. Mann. 1977. *Decision making: A psychological analysis of conflict*. New York: Free Press.

Johnson-Laird, P.N., P. Legrenzi, V. Girotto, M.S. Legrenzi, and J.-P. Caverni. 1999. Naive probability: A mental model theory of extensional reasoning. *Psychological Review* 106: 62–88.

Kahneman, D., and S. Frederick. 2002. Representativeness revisited: Attribute substitution in intuitive judgment. In *Heuristics and biases: The psychology of intuitive judgment*, ed. T. Gilovich, D. Griffin, and D. Kahneman, 49–81. New York: Cambridge University Press.

Kahneman, D., P. Slovic, and A. Tversky. 1982. *Judgment under uncertainty: Heuristics and biases*. New York: Cambridge University Press.

Kahneman, D., and A. Tversky. 1979. Prospect theory: An analysis of decision under risk. *Econometrica* 47: 263–291.

Kahneman, D., and A. Tversky. 1982. Variants of uncertainty. In *Judgment under uncertainty: Heuristics and biases*, ed. D. Kahneman, P. Slovic, and A. Tversky, 509–520. Cambridge: Cambridge University Press.

Keren, G., and Roelofsma. 1995. Immediacy and certainty in intertemporal choice. *Organizational Behavior and Human Decision Processes* 63: 287–297.

Konold, C. 1989. Informal conceptions of probability. *Cognition and Instruction* 6: 59–98.

Krynski, T.R., and J.B. Tennenbaum. 2007. The role of causality in judgment under uncertainty. *Journal of Experimental Psychology: General* 136: 430–450.

Lagnado, D.A., and S.A. Sloman. 2004. Inside and outside probability judgment. In *Blackwell handbook of judgment and decision making*, ed. D.J. Koehler and N. Harvey, 157–176. Malden: Blackwell.

Lazarus, R.S., and S. Folkman. 1984. *Stress appraisal and coping*. New York: Springer.

Liberman, N., Y. Trope, and E. Stephan. 2007. Psychological distance. In *Social psychology: Handbook of basic principles*, 2nd ed, ed. A.W. Kruglanski and E.T. Higgins, 353–381. New York: Guilford.

Lipshitz, R., and O. Strauss. 1997. Coping with uncertainty: A naturalistic decision-making analysis. *Organizational Behavior and Human Decision Processes* 69: 149–163.

Loewenstein, G., and D. Prelec. 1992. Anomolies in intertemporal choice: Evidence and an interpretation. In *Choice over time*, ed. G. Loewenstein and J. Elster, 119–145. New York: Sage.

Loewenstein, G., and R. Thaler. 1989. Anomolies: Intertemporal choice. *The Journal of Economic Perspectives* 3: 181–193.

Loewenstein, G.F., E. Weber, C.K. Hsee, and N. Welch. 2001. Risks as feelings. *Psychological Bulletin* 127: 267–286.

Loomes, G., and R. Sugden. 1986. Disappointment and dynamic consistency in choice under uncertainty. *Review of Economic Studies* 53: 271–282.

Luce, D. R. 2003. Rationality in choice under certainty and uncertainty. In *Emerging perspectives on judgment and decision research*, ed. S. L. Schneider, and J. Shanteau, 64–83. Cambridge, UK: Cambridge University Press.

Macchi, L. 2000. Partitive formulation of information in probabilistic problems: Beyond heuristics and frequency formats. *Organizational Behavior and Human Decision Processes* 82: 217–236.

Maule, J., and G. Villejoubert. 2007. What lies beneath: Reframing framing effects. *Thinking & Reasoning* 13: 25–54.

Mellers, B.A., and P. McGraw. 1999. How to improve Bayesian reasoning: Comment on Gigerenzer and Hoffrage (1995). *Psychological Review* 106: 417–424.

Mellers, B.A., A. Schwarz, and A.D.J. Cooke. 1998. Judgment and decision making. *Annual Review of Psychology* 49: 447–477.

Moxey, L.M., and A.J. Sanford. 2000. Communicating quantities: A review of psycholinguistic evidence of how expressions determine perspectives. *Applied Cognitive Psychology* 14: 237–255.

Neace, W.P., S. Michaud, L. Bolling, K. Deer, and L. Zecevic. 2008. Frequency formats, probability formats, or problem structure? A test of the nested-sets hypothesis in an extensional reasoning task. *Judgment and Decision Making* 3: 140–152.

Nisbett, R.E., D.H. Krantz, C. Jepson, and Z. Kunda. 1983. The use of statistical heuristics in everyday inductive reasoning. *Psychological Review* 90: 339–363.

Payne, J.W., J.R. Bettman, and E.J. Johnson. 1992. Behavioral decision research: A constructive processing perspective. *Annual Review of Psychology* 43: 87–131.

Payne, J.W., and J.R. Bettman. 2001. Preferential choice and adaptive strategy use. In *Bounded rationality: The adaptive toolbox*, ed. G. Gigerenzer, 123–145. Cambridge: The MIT Press.

Peters, E., I. Lipkus, and M.A. Diefenbach. 2006a. The functions of affect in health communications and the construction of health preferences. *The Journal of Communication* 56: S140–S162.

Peterson, C.R., and L.R. Beach. 1967. Man as intuitive statistician. *Psychological Bulletin* 68: 29–46.

Peters, E., K.D. McCaul, M. Stefanek, and W. Nelson. 2006b. A heuristics approach to understanding cancer risk perception: Contributions from judgment and decision-making research. *Annals of Behavioral Medicine* 31: 45–52.

Peters, E., and P. Slovic. 2000. The springs of action: Affective and analytical information processing in choice. *Personality and Social Psychology Bulletin* 26: 1465–1475.

Pitz, G.F., and N.J. Sachs. 1984. Judgment and decision: Theory and application. *Annual Review of Psychology* 35: 139–163.

Reeves, T., and R.S. Lockhart. 1993. Distributional versus singular approaches to probability and errors in probabilistic reasoning. *Journal of Experimental Psychology: General* 122: 207–226.

Petty, R., and J. Cacioppo. 1986. *Communication and persuasion: Central and peripheral routes to attitude change*. New York: Springer.

Reyna, V.F. 2004. How people make decisions that involve risk: A dual-processes approach. *Current Directions in Psychological Science* 13: 60–66.

Reyna, V.F., and C.J. Brainard. 1995. Fuzzy-trace theory: Some foundational issues. *Learning and Individual Differences* 7: 145–162.

Reyna, V.F., and S.C. Ellis. 1994. Fuzzy-trace theory and framing effects in children's risky decision making. *Psychological Science* 5: 275–279.

Reyna, V.F., F.J. Lloyd, and C.J. Brainard. 2003. Memory, development, and rationality: An integrative theory of judgment and decision making. In *Emerging perspectives on judgment and decision research*, ed. S.L. Schneider and J. Shanteau, 201–245. New York: Cambridge University Press.

Rottenstreich, Y., and C.K. Hsee. 2001. Money, kisses, and electric shocks: On the affective psychology of risk. *Psychological Science* 12: 185–199.

Schwarz, N. 2002. Feelings as information: Moods influence judgments and processing strategies. In *Heuristics and biases: The psychology of intuitive judgment*, ed. T. Gilovich, D. Griffin, and D. Kahneman, 534–547. New York: Cambridge University Press.

Schwarz, N., and H. Bless. 1991. Happy and mindless, but sad and smart? The impact of affective states on analytical reasoning. In *Emotion and social judgment*, ed. J.P. Forgas, 55–72. New York: Pergamon.

Shafir, E., and R.A. LeBoeuf. 2002. Rationality. *Annual Review of Psychology* 53: 491–517.

Sloman, S.A. 1996. The empirical case for two systems of reasoning. *Psychological Bulletin* 119: 3–22.

Sloman, S.A., Over, D., Slovak, L., & Stibel, J.M. 2002. Frequency illusions and other fallacies. *Organizational Behavior and Human Decision Processes* 91: 296–309.

Sloman, S.A., D. Over, L. Slovak, and J.M. Stibel. 2003. Frequency illusions and other fallacies. *Organizational Behavior and Human Decision Processes* 91: 296–309.

Slovic, P., M. Finucane, E. Peters, and D.G. MacGregor. 2002. The affect heuristic. In *Heuristics and biases: The psychology of intuitive judgment*, ed. T. Gilovich, D. Griffin, and D. Kahneman, 397–420. New York: Cambridge University Press.

Stanovich, K.E., and R.F. West. 1998. Cognitive ability and variation in selection task performance. *Thinking & Reasoning* 4: 193–230.

Stanovich, K.E., and R.F. West. 2000. Individual differences in reasoning: Implications for the rationality debate? *The Behavioral and Brain Sciences* 23: 645–726.

Sykes, D.L., and J.T. Johnson. 1999. Probabilistic evidence versus the representation of an event: The curious case of Mrs. Prob's dog. *Basic and Applied Social Psychology* 21: 199–212.

Teigen, K.H., and W. Brun. 1999. The directionality of verbal probability expressions: Effects on decisions, predictions, and probabilistic reasoning. *Organizational Behavior and Human Decision Processes* 80: 155–190.

Tiedens, L.Z., and S. Linton. 2001. Judgment under emotional certainty and uncertainty: The effects of specific emotions on information processing. *Journal of Personality and Social Psychology* 81: 973–988.

Todd, P.M., and G. Gigerenzer. 2007. Environments that make us smart: Ecological rationality. *Current Directions in Psychological Science* 16: 167–171.

Todorov, A., A. Goren, and Y. Trope. 2007. Probability as psychological distance: Construal and preferences. *Journal of Experimental Social Psychology* 43: 473–482.

Tversky, A., and D. Kahneman. 1974. Judgment under uncertainty: Heuristics and biases. *Science* 185: 1124–1131.

Tversky, A., and D. Kahneman. 1983. Extensional versus intuitive reasoning: The conjunction fallacy in probability judgment. *Psychological Review* 90: 293–315.

Tversky, A., and D. Kahneman. 1991. Loss aversion in riskless choice: A reference-dependent model. *Quarterly Journal of Economics* 106: 1039–1061.

Tversky, A., and D. Kahneman. 1992. Advances in prospect theory: Cumulative representation of uncertainty. *Journal of Risk and Uncertainty* 4: 297–324.

Wakslak, C.J., Y. Trope, N. Liberman, and R. Alony. 2006. Seeing the forest when entry is unlikely: Probability and the mental representation of events. *Journal of Experimental Psychology: General* 135: 641–653.

Wallsten, T.S., D.V. Budescu, A. Rapoport, R. Swick, and B. Forsyth. 1986a. Measuring the vague meanings of probability terms. *Journal of Experimental Psychology: General* 115: 348–365.

Wallsten, T.S., S. Fillenbaum, and J.A. Cox. 1986b. Base rate effects on the interpretations of probability and frequency expressions. *Journal of Memory and Language* 25: 571–587.

Windschitl, P.D., and E.U. Weber. 1999. The interpretation of "likely" depends on the context, but "70%" is 70% - right? The influence of associate processes on perceived certainty. *Journal of Experimental Psychology. Learning, Memory, and Cognition* 25: 1514–1533.

Wu, G. 1999. Anxiety and decision making with delayed resolution of uncertainty. *Theory and Decision* 46: 159–198.

Yamagishi, K. 2003. Facilitating normative judgments of conditional probability: Frequency or nested sets? *Experimental Psychology* 50: 97–106.

Yates, F.J., Veinott, E.S., and Patalano, A.L. 2003. Hard decisions, bad decisions: On decision quality and decision aiding. In *Emerging perspectives on judgment and decision research*, ed. S.L. Schneider, and J. Shanteau, 13–63. Cambridge, UK: Cambridge University Press.

Part II
Issues in Financing Startups and Small Firms

Chapter 7
The Changing Landscape of Small-Firm Finance

William Dunkelberg and Jonathan A. Scott

Abstract This chapter reflects on the changes in financing small firms during the past 25 years by reviewing the extant literature on how small businesses are financed at their inception, how continuing operations are financed, and how changing technologies have shaped capital markets for small firms. Our review of a unique small firm time series data set shows that many of the obstacles small firms faced in the early 1980s have mostly disappeared. New firm formations continue to depend on owner savings, friends, and family, while venture capital remains a microscopic proportion of total new firm financing in any given year. Once operating, small firms depend primarily on banks for operating support and capital investment, but the use of credit cards (business and personal) and nonbank sources (finance/leasing companies) is increasing in importance. We end with a discussion of two current issues in small firm finance: the cumulative impact of banking consolidation in the USA and the effect of the current financial crisis in the USA on small firm access to capital.

7.1 Introduction

The financial crisis in the USA that began in the summer of 2007 provides a reminder of the importance to small business of external capital from the banking system.[1] Start-up firms always rely heavily on personal savings and family, with

[1] The Small Business Administration (SBA) defines a small business as one that employs less than 500. According to the SBA Office of Advocacy, small firms represent 99.7% of all employer firms, employ over half of all private sector employees, pay 44% of total US private payroll, have generated 64% of net new jobs since 1993, and created more than half of non-farm private gross domestic product (see http://web.sba.gov/faqs/faqindex.cfm?areaID=24).

W. Dunkelberg (✉)
Temple University, Philadelphia, PA, USA
and
National Federation for Independent Businesses, Nashville, TN, USA
e-mail: wdunk@aol.com

R. Yazdipour, *Advances in Entrepreneurial Finance: With Applications from Behavioral Finance and Economics*, DOI 10.1007/978-1-4419-7527-0_7,

external equity injections a rare occurrence – even for ventures that have highly valuable but uncertain growth opportunities (Reynolds and Curtin 2008; Robb et al. 2009). Although banks are not the direct primary source of capital for starting a new firm, they are the primary source of funds for small firms once started, providing working capital and funding for investment in plant and equipment (Berger and Udell 1998). The ongoing consolidation of the US banking industry since the early-1990s, however, continues to raise concerns about the availability of bank financing for small firms because the merged bank generally devotes a small percentage of total assets to small business loans (Peek and Rosengren 1998). Yet during the past 15 years the number of new charters expanded by over 1,500 and the total number of bank offices increased as a result of a boom in branch openings. In addition, a small group of large banks expanded their lending to small firms via another channel – credit cards – while other large banks focused on mid-market lending to replace the lower interest margins from highly competitive large-company financing.

Since the mid-1990s, scholars directed their attention to the financing of small firms through two distinct channels. The first channel is the special role banks play in resolving the information asymmetry associated with small firm lending that can otherwise lead to credit rationing (Stiglitz and Weiss 1981). While the intellectual foundations of this literature date back to Diamond's (1984) idea of a delegated monitoring role for banks, much of the work since then is empirical. Beginning with Berger and Udell (1995), the idea of relationship banking was established, where banks accumulate private hard and soft information to mitigate the inherent information asymmetry associated with lending to information-opaque small firms. They empirically documented how stronger relationships – using length of time at their primary bank as a proxy for relationship strength – can improve the credit availability and pricing for information-opaque small firms. This paper was also one of the first, along with Petersen and Rajan (1994, 1995), to use the newly initiated Board of Governor's of the Federal Reserve System Survey of Small Business Finances (SSBF). An entire literature subsequently developed based largely, but not exclusively, on the SSBF surveys that examines the role of private information acquisition, bank size, and bank distance on small firm credit availability and pricing.

The other channel is the role of venture capital in financing innovation. This work, mostly the legacy of pioneering work by Gompers (1995), Gompers and Lerner (1996) and Lerner (1994, 1995), began by addressing such issues as the structure of limited partnership funds, the staging and syndication of investments and the performance of venture-backed IPO offerings. More recent studies rely on hand-collected data to perform more firm-level analysis, addressing such questions as characteristics of term sheets (Kaplan and Stromberg 2003; Kaplan and Strömberg 2004), venture-capital returns (Kaplan and Schoar 2005), the evolution of companies from start to becoming public, (Kaplan et al. 2007), and the geography of venture-capital expansion (Chen et al. 2009). Although the supply of venture capital continues to grow – especially with institutional demand for alternative investments, the number of principals per firm remains constant and the total number of principals has been stagnant since 2000 (Metrick, Chap. 2). With less attractive exit economics (attributable by many to Sarbanes-Oxley) and the low returns in the 2000s (NVCA 2010), VC financing is likely to remain a very limited channel for financing entrepreneurial firms.

The operating environment for small firms is much different than in the mid-1990s when scholars began a serious investigation into the special challenges of small firm finance. Deregulation (e.g., Riegel-Neal, Gramm-Leach-Bliley), new regulation (e.g., Sarbanes-Oxley), the growth in entrepreneurship programs at universities, along with scholarly documentation of their role in the job generation process (Birch 1979, 1981) attracted the interest of policy makers. Unlike the securities markets where comprehensive secondary market data is widely available for analysis (e.g., CRSP, Dealscan, etc.), no such source exits for small business finance that allows analysis of the effect of changes in regulation or macroeconomic conditions on small firm financing. This interest dramatically increased in 2009 because of concerns in the USA and elsewhere about the ability of small firms to obtain the credit they need (Spors and Flandez 2008; Eckblad 2009; Thirwangadam 2009; Chan 2010).

The primary sources of data on small firm financing are panel studies and periodic surveys of various small firm populations. The Fed's SSBF surveys conducted in 1987, 1993, 1998, and 2003 are the most comprehensive sources of information on existing firms but the surveys have been discontinued because of the cost. Although US bank call reports (FFIEC, Consolidated Reports of Condition and Income) have a line item for small business lending, these data only allow scholars to look at aggregate changes, without the ability to relate changes to local market conditions or the credit quality of the borrowers. In addition, the definition of "small" for the loan size categories includes two loan size categories: under $100,000 and $100,000 to $1 million. Given that the average loan sizes in the SSBF have generally been under $50,000, loans in the latter category are likely to be capturing the activity of firms that do not fall within the typical definition of a small- and medium-sized enterprise. The Panel Study of Entrepreneurial Dynamics, (PSED) (Reynolds and Curtin 2008), has a wealth of data on nascent entrepreneurs, that is, those in the start-up process. More recently, the Kauffman Foundation launched a panel study of new firms with a focus on high-technology businesses (Robb et al. 2009). The National Federation of Independent Business (NFIB) conducts monthly surveys of its membership (since late 1973) that ask questions about credit availability and terms, as well as periodic surveys of its membership on issues related to bank credit. Venture-capital data sources are largely aggregate numbers (e.g., National Venture Capital Association), although some research uses hand-assembled confidential data sets (e.g., Kaplan and Strömberg 2004; Kaplan and Schoar 2005) to investigate both the structure of term sheets and rates of return on private equity investments.

This chapter summarizes the current state of knowledge about small firm finances and then offers some perspectives on future research opportunities. Our focus is primarily on empirical studies and data sets, but we also identify key theoretical work that forms the basis for many of the most widely cited empirical papers. We begin with an historical analysis of small firm credit availability (over the past 35 years) using the National Federation of Business' *Small Business Economic Trends* survey. We provide a perspective on the current policy debates regarding small firm credit availability with a time series analysis of the experience of over 500,000 small firms. This section also provides a chronological review of new firm financing panel studies, including the Kauffman Firm Survey and Panel

Study of Entrepreneurial Dynamics, as well as the key trends identified in the Board of Governor's SSBF. This section also addresses the evolution of credit cards (both business and personal) as a source of funds, the role of real estate collateral in shaping small business credit availability, and the limited, but special, role of venture capital (including angel financing). Finally, we examine current issues in small firm finance. Among the topics addressed are the effect of bank consolidation and changes in market structure on small firm access to credit, the role of market structure on availability and pricing of small firm loans, the increasing distance of small firms from their primary lenders, the unique role of community banks in facilitating small firm finance, and recent survey evidence on the impact of the credit crisis of 2007–2009 on small firm credit availability.

7.2 Time-Series Perspective on Credit Availability and Cost

The National Federation of Independent Business (NFIB) began economic surveys of its membership in 1973. Since that time, a virtually identical three-page questionnaire is mailed to a sample of the NFIB's small business owner members: from October of 1973 through 1985 the survey was mailed on the first day of every quarter and since January 1986, the survey is mailed on the first day of every month. The yield is between 1,300 and 2,300 responses in the first month of each quarter and 500–900 in each of the following 2 months. A report based on the findings of the survey, "Small Business Economic Trends" (SBET), is produced each month and is available from the NFIB at nfib.com/research. These data are meaningful because they apply to about half a million employer firms (out of an estimated 6 million employer firms) and NFIB members have been shown to be reasonably representative of the population of small business in the USA (Dunkelberg and Scott, 1983).

The SBET includes a number of questions related to credit availability: (1) "If you borrow regularly, at least once a quarter, are loans easier or harder to get than they were 3 months ago?" (2) "Do you expect to find it easier or harder to obtain your required financing during the next 3 months?" (3) "During the last 3 months was your firm able to satisfy its borrowing needs?," and (4) "What is the most important business problem facing your business today (with "financing and interest rates" as one of ten choices provided)?" The survey also asks regular borrowers how the interest rate on their most recent loan compares to 3 months ago and the rate they are paying on loans for maturities of 1 year or less. Figures 7.1 through 7.5 show the time-series responses to these questions.

Figure 7.1 reports the percent of owners who reported borrowing at least once a quarter (which includes accessing lines of credit). Regular borrowing activity was highest during the pre-1983 period when exceptionally high nominal interest rates and inflation that created a need for borrowing because of the pressure that high inflation rates (input prices) put on cash flows. Even with interest rates near 20%, small firms continued to borrow to operate their businesses but endured much lower margins.

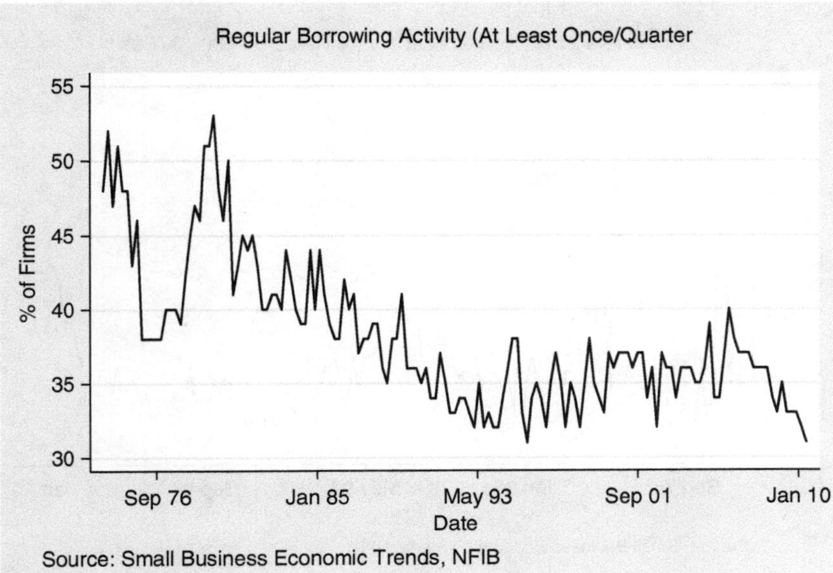

Fig. 7.1 Regular borrowing activity (at least once/quarter) (Small Business Economic Trends NFIB)

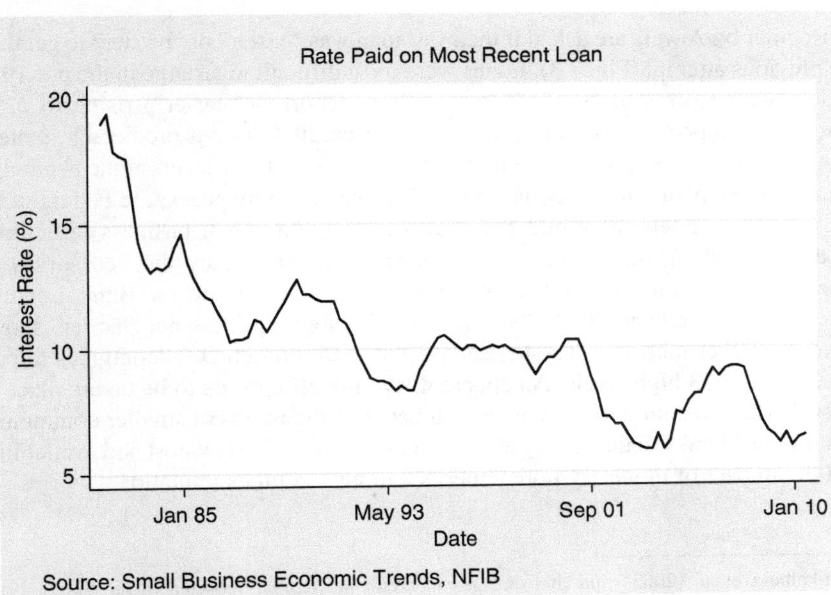

Fig. 7.2 Rate paid on most recent loan (Small Business Economic Trends NFIB)

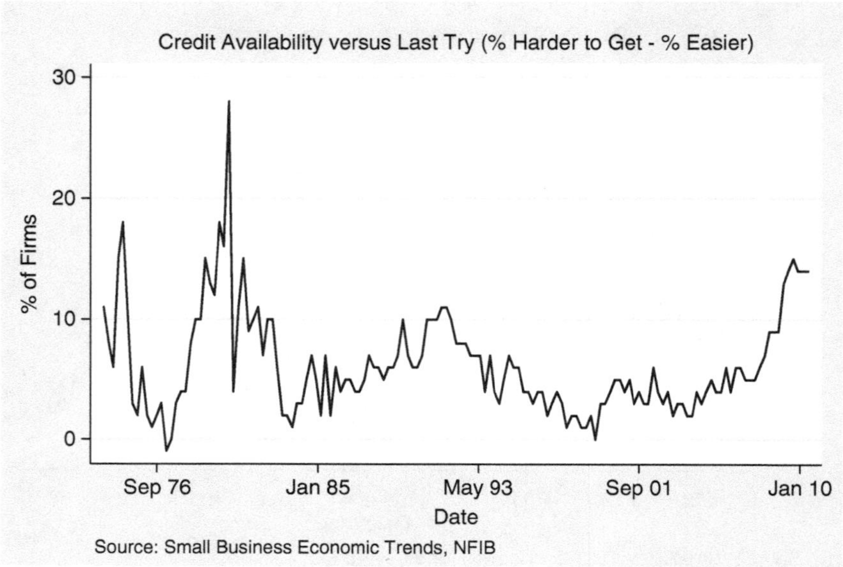

Fig. 7.3 Credit availability versus last try (% harder to get – % easier) (Small Business Economic Trends NFIB)

As inflation declined, nominal interest rates fell, profit margins and cash flow improved, and the number of firms borrowing on a regular basis fell (Figs. 7.1 and 7.2).

Regular borrowers are asked if their last loan was "easier" or "harder" to get than the previous attempt (Fig. 7.3). Loans were most difficult to arrange in the pre-1983 period, with reports of "harder" (net of those reporting "easier") rising to 27%. Since then, reports of difficulty in accessing credit follow a predictable pattern shown in Fig. 7.3. Reports of credit problems start off at low levels at the beginning of an expansion and then become "harder" as the economy peaks, the Fed tightens, and a recession sets in. While not shown in Fig. 7.3, small business difficulties accessing credit generally lag reports of credit tightening by the Fed survey of money center banks (Senior Loan Officer Opinion Survey on Bank Lending Practices).[2] The recent (2007–2009) increase in those reporting net "harder" shows a much quicker increase since the early-1980s and through 2009 continues to persist at post-1983 high levels. An apparent leveling off appears to be taking place in early 2010. The nature of the connection between thousands of smaller community and regional banks to the money center banks in terms of credit cost and availability and the impact of monetary policy merits a more careful examination.

[2]Dunkelberg et al. (2003) find that changes in credit availability reported in the Senior Loan Officer Survey takes about 17 quarters to have its maximum effect on credit availability for small firm owners.

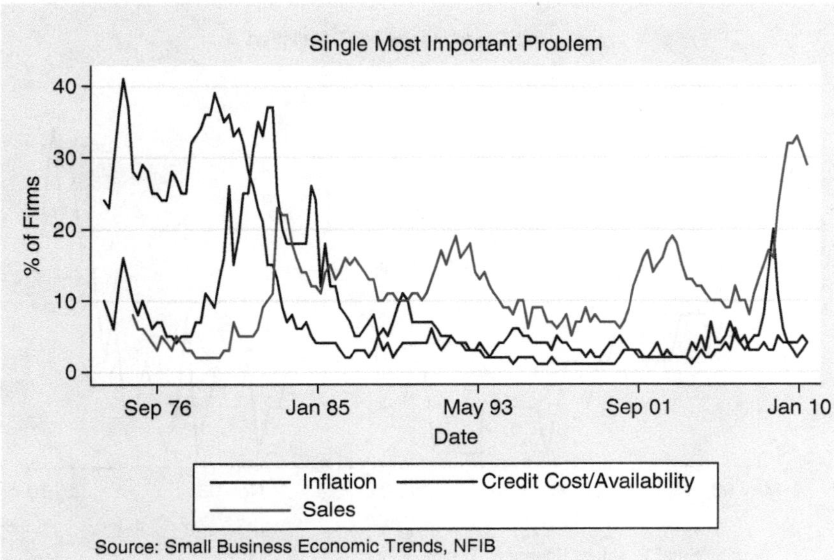

Fig. 7.4 Single most important problem (Small Business Economic Trends NFIB)

All small firms are asked to report the most important problem facing their business. Figure 7.4 shows that financing and interest costs are barely on a small firm's radar. Even as credit became harder to obtain in the last two economic slowdowns (1991 and 2001), financing costs and difficulties did not rise to the top of their list of concerns. The data in Fig. 7.4 clearly indicate that in the recent recession (2007–2009), the state of the economy as reflected in weak sales is threatening small business survival, not the fragile condition of many banks and the financial markets in general.

Starting in 1993, the survey asked owners if all of their credit needs were met in the prior quarter (Fig. 7.5). Unfortunately, this series covers only one recession, 2001, that was a rather mild event. Focusing on the percent of owners who reported "No," the incidence of complaints did not move out of the recent historical range until the first quarter of 2009. At its worst in 2009, only 10% reported that all their credit needs were not met (turned down or didn't receive all the credit the desired or credit terms were unsatisfactory). Still, the percent reporting needs not meant doubled in a very short period of time. The true number is likely to be higher (in all periods) if discouraged borrowers could be identified, that is, those who did not apply for fear of being turned down. For the remaining 90% of owners, they either received the credit they wanted or didn't want to borrow.

Overall, the SBET data suggest that many of the problems small firms faced in the early-1980s have largely disappeared. Much of the improvement is due to a more stable macroeconomic environment with lower inflation and less severe cyclical contraction – at least until 2008–2009. The number of competitors in many markets is much greater because of deregulation that began with the lifting of many branching

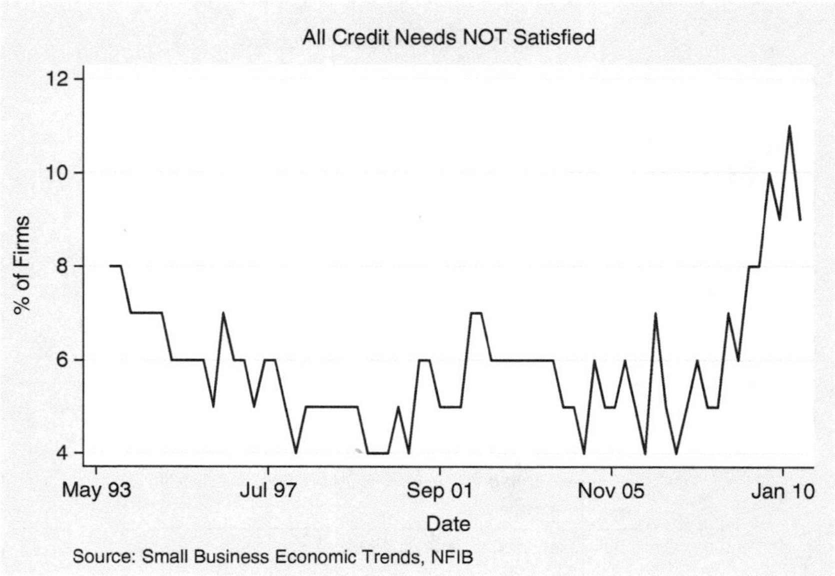

Fig. 7.5 All credit notes NOT satisfied (Small Business Economic Trends NFIB)

restrictions in the 1980s. Although the number of charters has fallen dramatically and deposit concentration has been increasing in some markets, new charters continue to provide alternatives for small firms. And finally, advances in information technology have opened several new channels of borrowing for small firms, of which business credit cards are the most important. We address these topics in more detail below.

7.3 Current Sources of Funding

Any analysis of funding in the context of entrepreneurial finance needs to distinguish between nascent firms, that is, firms in the start-up process as described by Reynolds and Curtin (2008), new firms, and existing (or established) firms. Even with this classification, a further cut of new/existing firms should be based on "growth opportunities." The term growth opportunity generally differentiates entrepreneurial finance from small business finance, but a widely accepted definition of entrepreneurial finance remains elusive. With these caveats in mind, we begin this section with a summary of the findings (in chronological order) related to start-up financing, regardless of whether the firm is nascent (PSED) or established (Kaufmann and NFIB surveys), and present conclusions about the availability of start-up financing. Next, we summarize the trends for existing small firm financing from the Fed's Survey of Small Business Finances with a focus on the importance of credit cards versus direct bank lending.

7.3.1 Start-up Financing

In a 1979 NFIB study of how new firms were financed, Dunkelberg and Cooper (1983) report that 47% of the owners cited personal savings as the major source of capital ("major" is not defined as a percentage), with 28% depending on financial institutions and 13% on friends and relatives.[3] Only 4% cite independent investors as their major capital source. For owners reporting more than one source, personal savings accounts for 63% of the major financing sources (as reported by the owner), financial institutions for 47% and friends, and relatives for 26%. Reports of venture-capital use are virtually nonexistent and government sources accounted for 1%.

In 1985, the National Federation of Independent Business undertook a panel study of all its members who reported starting a business within the past 18 months (Cooper et al. 1990). In the panel's first year, of the 3,951 eligible survey respondents, 71% start their business from "scratch" and 29% start by purchasing an existing firm. For those starting from scratch, 49% provide at least 50% of the start-up investment from their own funds (primarily savings).[4] Thirty percent report bank loans as the major source of funding (since banks are not venture capitalist, these loans are likely secured by personal assets).

The Panel Study of Entrepreneurial Dynamics II, which began in 2004, tracks the sources of informal and formal funding for emerging firms. Reynolds and Curtin (2008) report that informal financing of 882 nascent firms is most likely from personal savings (84%), followed by personal credit card, bank, and mortgage loans (27%), and then personal, family, and friend loans (23%). Thirteen percent of these firms report no financing for their nascent firm. Formal financing for 435 established firms, that is, after a firm is legally registered, is led by personal loans from team and family members (39%), followed by additional team equity (27%), and financial institution lending via credit cards, bank loans, or working capital loans (20%). SBA-guaranteed loans, which are through bank lenders, are reported by 26% of new firms. Reynolds and Curtin (2008) note that the firms with the largest outside funding are not closely associated with significant growth opportunities, for example, a technology focus or market innovation. His observation is another piece of evidence illustrating the difficulty of identifying entrepreneurial finance opportunities ex-ante.

The Kauffman Firm Survey (Robb et al. 2009) may come closest to identifying entrepreneurial start-up firms but with a focus on high-technology status, which excludes most "Main Street" types of businesses. But their choice of North American Industrial Classification System codes includes some rather prosaic industries such as chemicals and allied products (identified as high tech) and

---

[3]These data were obtained from a survey of the membership of the National Federation of Independent Business.

[4]The amount invested was defined as the total amount of funds invested in the firm at the time the first dollar of revenue was received.

cigarettes (identified as medium tech). Commercial bank lending plays an important role for the firms in this survey as well, confirming the findings in the PSED and NFIB panel studies. Forty-five percent of over 4,000 start-up firms in 2004 reported outside debt with an average amount of $85,681 (Robb and Robinson, 2008). Most of this debt is bank-related (either business/personal loans or business/personal credit cards), with very few respondents reporting a nonbank loan or reporting a government business loan. The low incidence of government loans stand in contrast to the high incidence of SBA-guaranteed loans in the PSED. Many of the bank loans reported in the Kaufmann survey are SBA guaranteed but may not be reported as such. The average business bank loan is $9,357 ($150,704 for those reporting a loan), while the average credit line is $3,237 ($62,156 for those reporting a line). Personal bank loans to the owners (survey respondent plus other owners) almost equal the total for business bank loans with an average of $147,932. During the first year of operations, 48% report new personal debt, while 28% report new business debt.

Despite the difficulties involved in direct data comparisons, several conclusions can be drawn from the above studies. First, start-up businesses rely heavily on owner (and founding team) equity, along with significant contributions from what is affectionately known as "family, friends, and fools." Second, both business and personal credit cards have become an important source of financing for start-ups. And third, banks continue to remain an important source of external capital outside of credit cards, either through working capital lines, asset-backed (mortgage) loans on business property, or other loans (e.g., equipment).

All of the panel studies report a very low incidence of venture capital as a source of financing. In 2004 (the base year of the Kauffman and PSED II surveys), there were only 192 seed/start-up deals, 862 early-stage investments, 1,205 expansion investments, and 765 late-stage investments (PWC Moneytree 2009). The 192 seed investments pale in comparison to the over 600,000 business starts for 2004 estimated by the SBA, as well as the total venture-capital investments – just over 3,000 – compared to some 6 million small firms with employees in 2005 (SBA). Another source of early-stage capital is angel funding. Shane (2008) reports that angel investment was approximately $23 billion per year between 2001 and 2003, an amount that is very close to the $21.8 and $19.7 billion invested by venture capitalists in 2002 and 2003, respectively. The typical angel investment is $10,000, usually an early-stage investment, and frequently placed in companies not considered to have high growth opportunities. For example, Shane (2008) reports that 25% of the angel investments made between 2001 and 2003 went into retail firms and 12.5% into personal services firms.

7.3.2 Ongoing Small-Firm Financing

The Board of Governor's Survey of Small Business Finances (SSBF) is the most comprehensive and most recent source of information about ongoing small firm financing. These surveys, conducted in 1987, 1993, 1998, and 2003, focus on small firm sources and uses of financial services along with data on firm and owner characteristics. Although the structure of financial markets changed dramatically since the first Fed survey in 1987, small firms continue to rely on commercial banks as their primary source of external capital. Ou and Williams (2009) report that almost 90% of small businesses in 2003 use some form of credit, with 48% using commercial banks and 22% using finance companies. Commercial banks continue to be the most important source of lines of credit (80%), mortgage loans (53%), and equipment loans (48%). While the Kaufmann Firm Survey provides a look at start-up financing over a short window, the reliance of start-ups on bank financing (personal bank loans and business credit cards) for surviving firms is reported by over 40% of the respondents in that survey. This figure from Kaufmann is not that far from the average experience of existing small firms reported in the Fed's 2003 SSBF.

Mach and Wolken (2006) identify two important changes in the SSBF since the first survey in 1987. First, small firms are diversifying their providers of financial services, with an increase in importance of non-depository institutions such as finance and leasing companies – especially for larger small firms. By 2003, about 41% of the respondents to the SSBF obtain credit from the banking sector, down from 44% in 1987 (Cole et al. 1996). Between 1987 and 2003, small usage of lines of credit from banks increase to 29.5% from 19.5%, but usage falls in all other credit categories (mortgages, vehicle loans, equipment loans, capital leases). By 2003, commercial banks supply more credit lines and mortgages than non-depository institutions, but non-depository institutions supplied more vehicle loans and capital leases. These diversified sources suggest that small firms now have more choices among lending technologies (Berger and Udell 2006) that have moved beyond pure relationship lending to different types of transaction lending (e.g., leasing).

The second change Mach and Wolken (2006) noted is a big increase in the importance of business credit cards. Ou and Williams (2009) conjecture that this increased business credit card importance is related to the activity of a small number of large-bank credit card issuers. They find a decline of small banks' share of small loan markets, especially in the smallest loan markets, where small firm lending is defined as loans under $1 million in the bank call reports and the CRA reports. Using 2007 CRA data, Ou and Williams (2009) find that about 12 banks comprise 75% of the loans in the smallest category (under $100,000) and the average size in June 2007 was $3,200 compared with $20,000 from other lenders. These large credit card lenders have limited participation in other small loan markets accounting for only 3% of loans between $100,000 and $1 million.[5]

Credit cards, whether business or personal, are important to new firms. Scott (2009) reports that almost 60% of new firms in the Kauffman Firm Survey used

[5]The Small Business Administration's annual study of lending to small and micro businesses (2009) confirms these results.

credit cards in their first year of business and about one-third of the firms carried balances through the first year. Mach and Wolken (2006) report that the percent of small firms using personal credit cards remained about the same in 2003 (47%) but those firms using business credit cards increased by 14 percentage points to 48% since 1998. Confirming evidence regarding credit card usage is provided in a recent (2008) NFIB poll conducted by the Gallup Group (Dennis 2008a) where 84% of the respondents use credit cards for their business (business or personal cards). Interestingly, over one-third of the respondents with business or personal credit cards in the NFIB poll do not report any other line of credit at another financial institution. The Poll also reports that about 75% of small firms pay their balances in full every month, indicating that the credit card is more a transaction service than a line of credit. These firms that rely on credit cards without a local bank lender may contribute to findings of an increasing distance between small firms and their primary lenders over time (Petersen and Rajan 2002; Agarwal and Hauswald 2008; Brevoort and Hannan 2006; Hannan 2003; DeYoung et al. 2007). However, Brevoort (2006) finds that increases of out-of-market lending in MSAs is largely attributable to either large banks and/or smaller loans, which suggests that the impact of distance on competition may be limited to a small set of banks and borrowers that are related to credit card lending. In addition, Brevoort et al. (2009) using the 2003 SSBF find that while distances increased in the early 1990s, they decreased in the latter half and that a wide variation in distance exists depending upon the supplier of financial services.

7.4 Current Issues in Small Firm Financing

7.4.1 Bank Consolidation and Small Firm Finance

With the start of an easing in bank branching restrictions in the early-1980s, considerable consolidation in the US banking system left small firms with fewer choices among independent banks, often forcing them to a larger banking organization as their primary financial institution. Between 1989 and 2006, the number of small banking organizations decreased by 36%, while large banks' share of domestic assets increased from 66% to 80% (Jagtiani 2008). Yet at the same time, advances in information technology increased both the range of services offered, as well as the ability of financial institutions to offer credit services to small firms outside their local market. This extended reach is certainly seen in the widespread market penetration of business credit cards during the past 15 years.

Concerns over this consolidation led to a change in the call reports in the mid 1990s. A new section (currently Schedule RC-C part II) requires banks to report the number and amount of small business and farm loans. Scholars using these data initially found that the proportion of small loans in a bank portfolio declined with bank size, raising concerns that mergers reduce the supply of small firm credit (Peek and Rosengren 1998; Strahan and Weston 1998). Other papers showed that this static analysis of balance sheet proportions could be misleading and needed to take into consideration the response of other lenders in the market. For example, Berger et al. (1998) find that in markets where mergers took place and resulted in the combined banks lending less to small firms, the increase in small firm lending by banks that did not merge offset most of the merged banks' decline. Consolidation also triggers new market entry by de novo banks as documented by Berger et al. (2004).

Scott and Dunkelberg (2002), using data from the NFIB membership collected in early 1995, find that bank mergers had no significant effect on the ability of small firms to obtain a loan or the contract loan rate on the most recent loan. However, mergers are more likely to result in an increase in non-price terms and increased shopping for a new bank. A subsequent survey in 2001 confirmed the earlier findings (Scott et al. 2003).

Recent work by Berger et al. (2007) finds a more nuanced impact of market structure on the availability of new lines of credit for small firms. They document how the presence of a large-bank branch in local markets, not size or deposit concentration, affect credit availability. Along a similar line, Scott and Dunkelberg (2010) identify that lender actions, in addition to deposit concentration, affect small firm credit availability, loan terms, and non-credit service quality.

While an individual small firm may have had problems with mergers over the past 20 years, no systematic relationship can be found between credit availability with mergers and firm size, firm age, location, or industry. Part of the reason for this finding may be an increase in the number of new charters by over 2,500 between 1990 and 2008 (or over 140 per year) as well as an increase in the use of business credit cards by small firms, often issued on the basis of proprietary commercial credit-scoring models. All of these new charters are small banks by definition, and usually referred to as "community banks" in the scholarly literature as well as the statutes.[6] Community banks, typically banks with assets less than $1 billion, play a special role for small firms because of their flatter organizational structure (Berger and Udell 2002; Scott 2004). As such, they can make quicker decisions and can give private hard and soft information significantly more weight in the credit granting decision. This underwriting approach stands in stark contrast to a larger bank with a more structured, less flexible underwriting system. Several papers (e.g., Cole et al. 2004; Berger et al. 2005) show that the use of private information, the basis of relationship lending in the literature, by community banks gives them a comparative advantage over larger banks in this type of lending.

[6]The Housing and Economic Recovery Act of 2008 defined a community financial institution as one having assets less than $1 billion. Previously, the Financial Services Modernization Act of 1999 had set the threshold at $500 million, with subsequent adjustments for CPI inflation.

7.4.2 Credit Crisis of 2007–2010 and Small Firm Finance

The global credit crisis that began in the summer of 2007 and its impact on small firm financing is critical according to business press reporting. However, as noted above, there is no evidence over time that financing has become the most important problem for small firms, but the difficulty in obtaining credit has reached the highest level since in the early-1980s. The percent of small firms experiencing financing problems has crept up since mid-2007 as the duration of the recession lengthened and the net percentage not able to satisfy their credit needs in the late-2009s twice as high as it was in early 2007 (see Figs. 7.3 and 7.5). A NFIB poll conducted by the Gallup Group in early September 2008 asks a sample of small firms drawn from the Dun & Bradstreet file about their recent credit experiences as the economy, stock market, and property values headed towards a freefall (Dennis 2008b). At that time, only 32% of the sample report applying for credit, 59% report they do not want credit, and 8% reporting that do not think they can get credit. This survey identifies a somewhat higher incidence of problems with credit availability based on those who tried to get credit: 41% of small employers report obtaining all the credit they wanted, 22% most or some, while 34% report obtaining none of what they want.

The primary finding of the survey, however, is the importance of business and/or personal real estate as a source of collateral to provide capital for their business. Ninety-six percent own their personal residence, 49% own all or part of the building and/or land on which their business sits (excluding the one-quarter who operate primarily from the home), and 41% own investment real estate, excluding their residence and business.[7] Real estate, particularly home mortgages, is frequently used to finance or collateralize other business assets. Seventy-six percent have at least one mortgage on the real estate they own with 13% having three or more mortgages and 22% with at least one mortgage to finance business activities. Sixteen percent use real estate to collateralize other business assets, including 10% who use their homes as collateral. About one in 10 (9%) own at least one currently upside-down property, that is, a loan where the unpaid loan balance exceeds the market value of the property.

The widespread use of real estate collateral for business loans and the falling real estate values creates a very different problem for small firm financing than previous recessions – even in the early-1980s. More heavily mortgaged owners and those who are upside-down are less likely to obtain all the credit they wanted (for those trying to get credit) after controlling for sales growth, business size, and age. Real estate values also play a role in determining which owners report not trying for credit. After controlling for firm characteristics, more heavily mortgaged owners and those who are upside-down are more likely to report not applying for fear of being turned down (as this shows up on credit reports). In other words, owners experiencing falling real estate values self-select out of applying, knowing that they have insufficient collateral for borrowing. These results suggest that the adjustment

[7]Reynolds and Curtin (2008) report that 6% of nascent firms and 10% of new firms report asset-backed loans (primarily mortgages).

of real estate values back to their fundamental values in the most severely affected areas in the USA (California Central Valley, Las Vegas, Florida, Atlanta, Michigan, and Ohio) will be a significant obstacle for small firm access to capital.

The 2008 NFIB poll conducted by the Gallup Group was repeated in September 2009 and the results are basically unchanged from a year earlier (Dennis 2010). Fifty-one percent of small employers cite slow or declining sales as their most immediate economic problem, followed by uncertainty about the economy for 22%. Access to credit is the most immediate problem for only 8% of small employers, as was falling real estate values (8%). Fifty-five percent of the owners report applying for credit and 40% received "some" (13%), "most" (12%), or "all" (22%) of what they require. Slightly fewer than 20% are unsuccessful in obtaining the credit they required, either because of a turndown, a rejection of the terms offered, or not applying for fear of rejection. The results of these two polls show a clear disconnect between the extent to which small business credit availability is affecting their business outlook as well as the business press reporting of small business credit rationing by banks. The most telling result of the 2009 poll is that twice as many owners who could not get credit cite poor sales as the reason versus credit rationing. Credit rationing would suggest that "bankable" small firms are denied credit, whereas the reports from the NFIB polls suggest that credit may be harder to get for small firms because of the perilous state of their balance sheets.

7.5 Suggestions for Future Research

The theoretical underpinning for much of the work on small/new firm access to credit relies on the idea of information opacity and its role in creating an information asymmetry between lenders and small/new firm owners. The result of extreme information asymmetry is credit rationing where credit is not granted to otherwise creditworthy firms because the lender cannot adequately assess the risk. The nature of the information opacity that leads to information asymmetry problems needs to distinguish between business risk and management risk. Many small firms (and start-ups) are in businesses where enough data exists to estimate the probability of default and loss given default (e.g., restaurants). In other words, the source of the information opacity is unlikely to be with the characteristics of the business. In these cases, the primary uncertainty is the ability of the manager/owner to navigate the business through the challenges of start-ups and business cycle fluctuations. However, for other endeavors (such as biotechnology), business risk is very difficult to assess because the outcomes are dominated by uncertainty, not risk (Knight 1921). In these cases, both business and owner/manager uncertainty contribute to the information opacity. Future empirical work would benefit from a better model of the interaction of business versus manager risk. With such a model, testable hypotheses involving soft versus hard information could be better specified.

The association between bank size and small firm credit outcomes needs further research. While small banks have an advantage over large banks in the production of soft information and the attendant benefit in granting credit, these results may be due to the rapid consolidation of the banking system from the 1990s through the early 2000s. While consolidation is accelerating with the FDIC case resolutions attributable to the current credit crisis (2007–2009), the future pace will likely resemble the mid-2000s, rather than the frenetic pace of the mid-1990s. Large banks specialize in small firm lending but often times via credit cards or credit scoring. Presented with these opportunities, small firms could be selecting banks depending on their specific loan needs and the least cost lending technology.

A related issue with bank size is the role of technology and the importance of distance in small firm lending. Whether or not the "tyranny of distance" (Petersen and Rajan 2002) is removed because of credit-scoring and business credit cards remains to be seen. In the venture-capital market, proximity of the venture capitalist to their investment's success is still an important determinant (Chen et al. 2009). This topic can be a fruitful area for empirical research, especially focusing on how credit card use and the implementation of new credit card regulations (Credit CARD Act of 2009) might affect small firm access to capital.

Finally, the recent credit crisis has generated a tremendous amount of focus on the problems small firms have with access to capital. The data presented in this chapter show no pervasive, persistent problem with access at the same level small firms faced in the early 1980s. However, when compared to the 1990s and 2000s, the recent experience of small firms reveals a marked increase in credit access difficulty. While some firms will always have difficulty accessing capital, many of the access problems identified in the early 1980s appear to be resolved through technology, the quest for profitability (large banks focusing on small firms), or the continuing chartering of new banks (new small firm lenders). The ongoing consolidation that has increased the market share of the largest banks, along with much tighter restrictions on credit cards and small firm reliance on real estate collateral, suggests the need for a clear, data-driven analysis of small business credit availability and whether a public policy response is necessary.

7.6 Conclusions

The title of this chapter, The Changing Landscape of Small Firm Finance, is an appropriate point of departure for concluding remarks. How much has the landscape changed in the past 20 years for small firm finance? In some ways, the changes are dramatic when viewed through the lens of the number and distribution of banks and changes in lending technologies. The consolidation of the US banking system reduced the number of banking organizations by one-third over this period, many of which were small banks that served the financial needs of small firms. Yet the number of banking offices increased by almost 30,000 (www.fdic.gov/hsob) as a result of increased branching. Over the same period, the costs of information technology fell just as dramatically, enabling the rapid growth of business (and personal) credit card lending that expanded credit access to small firms, either at the business or personal level. The growth in personal credit card lines is clearly an enabler for nascent firms based on the PSED data. Unfortunately, these credit card lenders were concentrated in a few very large banks, many of which have incurred large losses resulting in a contraction in this source of funds during the Great Recession of 2008–2009.

The macro environment for small business financing is much improved since the early-1980s. The elimination of inflation in the early 1980s and the associated reduction in interest rates was a benefit to small firms. Since that time financing costs receded as an important problem for small firms. Although periodic tightening of credit by the Fed has been felt by small firms attempting to obtain credit, their difficulty is nowhere the level of the early 1980s. The recent uptick in reported problems with credit availability is not due to higher rates but reflects the impact of a weak economy on small firm financial strength. In addition, many small firms have relied on the rapid rise in real estate values as collateral for loans and the bursting of the property bubble has significantly affected their ability to offer additional business or personal collateral for loans.

But in other ways, the landscape has remained the same when viewed through the typical sources of funds for start-up firms. Personal savings and funds (equity) from friends and family still remain the most important source of start-up funding, while venture capital and other outside equity will continue to be available only for exceptional growth opportunities. Banks still remain a primary source of outside capital for new firms despite the dramatic industry consolidation during the past 25 years. The mix has changed, however, from direct lending to a mix of direct lending and credit cards, where the credit card is likely to be issued by a different bank. Despite – or perhaps because of – consolidation, approval of new bank charters by state banking regulators continues. These new banks are an important alternative to large banks for many small firms and have a comparative advantage in relationship lending that large banks cannot provide.

References

Agarwal, S., and R. Hauswald, 2008. Distance and private information in lending. Working paper.

Berger, A.N., S. Bonime, L. Goldberg, and L. White. 2004. The dynamics of market entry: The effects of mergers and acquisitions on entry in the banking industry. *Journal of Business* 77: 797–834.

Berger, A., N. Miller, M. Petersen, R. Rajan, and J. Stein. 2005. Does function follow organizational form? Evidence from the lending practices of large and small banks. *Journal of Financial Economics* 76: 237–269.

Berger, A., R. Rosen, and G. Udell. 2007. Does market size structure affect competition? The case of small business lending. *Journal of Banking & Finance* 31: 11–33.

Berger, A., A. Saunders, J. Scalise, and G. Udell. 1998. The effects of bank mergers and acquisitions on small business lending. *Journal of Financial Economics* 50: 187–229.

Berger, A., and G. Udell. 1995. Relationship lending and lines of credit in small firm finance. *Journal of Business* 68: 351–382.

Berger, A., and G. Udell. 1998. The economics of small business finance: The roles of private equity and debt markets in the financial growth cycle. *Journal of Banking & Finance* 22: 613–673.

Berger, A., and G. Udell. 2002. Small business credit availability and relationship lending: The importance of bank organisational structure. *The Economic Journal* 112: F32–F53.

Berger, A., and G. Udell. 2006. A more complete conceptual framework for SME finance. *Journal of Banking & Finance* 30: 2945–2966.

Birch, D. 1979. *The job creation process*. Cambridge: MIT Program on Neighborhood and Regional Change.

Birch, D. 1981. Who Creates Jobs. *The Public Interest* 65(Fall): 3–14.

Brevoort, K. 2006. An empirical examination of the growth in out-of-market commercial lending: The changing competitive landscape and the role of asymmetric information. Working paper.

Brevoort, K., J. Holmes, and J. Wolken. 2009. Distance still matters: The information revolution in small business lending and the persistent role of location, 1993–2003. Finance and Economics Discussion Series 2010–08, Federal Reserve Board.

Brevoort, K., and T. Hannan. 2006. Commercial lending and distance: Evidence from Community Reinvestment Act Data. *Journal of Money, Credit and Banking* 38: 1991–2012.

Chan, S. 2010. A broad U.S. push to ease credit for small business. *New York Times* (February 5)

Chen, H., P. Gompers, A. Kovner, and J. Lerner. 2009. Buy local? The geography of successful and unsuccessful venture capital expansion. Working paper.

Cole, R., L. Goldberg, and L. White. 2004. Cookie-cutter versus character: The micro structure of small business lending by large and small banks. *Journal of Financial and Quantitative Analysis* 39: 227–251.

Cole, R., J. Wolken, and L. Woodburn. 1996. Bank and nonbank competition for small business credit: Evidence from the 1987 and 1993 National Surveys of Small Business Finances. *Federal Reserve Bulletin* 82: 983–995.

Cooper, A., W. Dunkelberg, C. Woo, and W. Dennis. 1990. *New business in America*. Washington, DC: NFIB Research Foundation.

Dennis, W. 2008a. Credit cards. NFIB Research Foundation, National Small Business Poll 8, Issue 3.

Dennis, W. 2008b. Access to credit. NFIB Research Foundation, National Small Business Poll 8, Issue 8.

Dennis, W. 2010. Access to credit. NFIB Research Foundation. Working paper.

DeYoung, R., S. Frame, D. Glennon, and P. Nigro. 2007. What's driving small borrower-lender distance? Working paper.

Diamond, D.W. 1984. Financial intermediation and delegated monitoring. *Review of Economic Studies* 51: 393–414.

Dunkelberg, W., and A. Cooper. 1983. A cross-section study of small business financing. In *Frontiers of Entrepreneurship Research*. Boston: Babson College.

Dunkelberg, W., W. Dennis, and J. Scott. 2003. *Small business indicators of macroeconomic activity*. Washington, DC: NFIB Research Foundation.

Dunkelberg, W., and J. Scott. 1983, Report on the representativeness of the National Federation of Independent Business Sample. Office of Advocacy, U.S. Small Business Administration, Contract No. SBA2A-0084-01.

Dunkelberg, W., and J. Scott. 2008. The response of small business owners to change in monetary policy. *Business Economics* 44: 23–37.

Eckblad, M. 2009. Problems spring up in small business loans. *Wall Street Journal* (2 October).

Gompers, P., and J. Lerner. 1996. The use of covenants: An empirical analysis of venture partnership agreements. Journal of Law and Economics 39 (2), 463-498.

Gompers, P. 1995, Optimal investment, monitoring, and the staging of venture capital. Journal of Finance 50, 1461-1489.

Hannan, T. 2003. Changes in non-local lending to small business. *Journal of Financial Services Research* 24: 31–46.

Jagtiani, J. 2008. Understanding the effect of the merger boom on community banks. *Economic Review* 93(2): 29–48.

Kaplan, S., and A. Schoar. 2005. Private equity performance: Returns, persistence, and capital flows. *Journal of Finance* LX: 1791–1823.

Kaplan, S., B. Sensoy, and P. Strömberg. 2007. Should investors bet on the jockey or the horse? Evidence from the evolution of firms from early business plans to public companies. Working paper Journal of Finance, 2009, 64(1), 75–115. http://dx.doi.org/10.1111/j.1540-6261.2008.01429.x.

Kaplan, S., and P. Stromberg, 2003. Financial contracting theory meets the real world: An empirical analysis of venture capital contracts. Review of Economic Studies 70, 281–315.

Kaplan, S., and P. Strömberg. 2004. Characteristics, contracts, and actions: Evidence from venture capital analyses. *Journal of Finance* LIX: 2177–2210.

Knight, F. 1921. *Risk, uncertainty, and profit*. Boston: Houghton Mifflin.

Lerner, J. 1994. Venture capitalists and the decision to go public. Journal of Financial Economics 35, 293–316.

Lerner, J. 1995. Venture capitalists and the oversight of private firms. Journal of Finance 50, 301–18.

Mach, T., and J. Wolken. 2006. Financial services used by small businesses from the 2003 Survey of Small Business Finances. *Federal Reserve Bulletin* 92: 167–195.

National Venture Capital Association (14 May 2010). Venture capital industry saw short term performance improvements at the end of 2009. Retrieved from http://www.nvca.org

Ou, C., and V. Williams. 2009. Lending to small businesses by financial institutions in the United States. Small Business Administration Office of Advocacy.

Peek, J., and E. Rosengren. 1998. Bank consolidation and small business lending: It's not just bank size that matters. *Journal of Banking & Finance* 22: 799–819.

Petersen, M., and R. Rajan. 1994. The benefits of firm-creditor relationships: Evidence from small business data. *Journal of Finance* 49: 3–37.

Petersen, M., and R. Rajan. 1995. The effect of credit market competition on lending relationships. *Quarterly Journal of Economics* 110: 405–443.

Petersen, M., and R. Rajan. 2002. Does distance still matter? The information revolution in small business lending. *Journal of Finance* 57: 2533–2570.

PWC Moneytree 2009. https://www.pwcmoneytree.com/MTPublic/ns/index.jsp.

Reynolds, P., and R. Curtin. 2008. Business creation in the United States: Panel study of entrepreneurial dynamics II initial assessment. *Foundations and Trends in Entrepreneurship*4: 155–307.

Robb, A. M., J. Ballou, D. DesRoches, F. Potter, Z. Zhao, and E. Reedy. 2009. An overview of the Kauffman Firm Survey. Kauffman Foundation. Working paper.

Robb, A., and D. Robinson. 2008. The capital structure decisions of new firms. Kauffman Foundation. Working paper.

Scott, J. 2004. Small business and the value of community financial institutions. *Journal of Financial Services Research* 25: 207–230.

Scott, J., and W. Dunkelberg. 2002. Bank mergers and small firm financing. *Journal of Money Credit and Banking* 35: 999–1018.

Scott, J., and W. Dunkelberg. 2010. Competition for small firm banking business: Bank actions vs. market structure. Journal of Banking and Finance, http://dx.doi.org/10.1016/j.jbankfin.2010.06.004.

Scott, J., W. Dunkelberg, and W. Dennis. 2003. *Credit, banks and small business – The new century*. Washington, DC: National Federation of Independent Business Research Foundation.

Scott, R. 2009. The use of credit card debt by new firms. Kauffman Foundation. Working paper.

Shane, S. 2008. The importance of angel investing in financing the growth of entrepreneurial ventures. Small Business Administration contract no. SBAHQ-070Q-0016. Working paper.

Spors, K., and R. Flandez. 2008. Entrepreneurs scramble for financing. *Wall Street Journal* (2 October)

Stiglitz, J., and A. Weiss. 1981. Credit rationing in markets with incomplete information. *The American Economic Review* 71: 393–409.

Strahan, P., and J. Weston. 1998. Small business lending and the changing structure of the banking industry. *Journal of Banking & Finance* 22: 821–845.

Thirwangadam, M. 2009. Geithner calls on U.S. banks to boost lending. *Wall Street Journal* (18 November).

Chapter 8
Applications of Behavioral Finance to Entrepreneurs and Venture Capitalists: Decision Making Under Risk and Uncertainty in Futures and Options Markets

Fabio Mattos and Philip Garcia

Abstract A key dimension of entrepreneurship is risk-taking behavior, and often it is assumed that entrepreneurs exhibit a higher tolerance for risk than non-entrepreneurs. However, empirical evidence provides mixed findings, raising the question whether entrepreneur's judgment is influenced by emotion and heuristics which leads them to misperceive the risk in the market. Our findings support this idea. Empirical results indicate these investors generally take more risk than would be anticipated. Higher risk propensity is due to probability weighting and is also consistent with the idea that entrepreneurs and possible venture capitalists perceive risky situations more optimistically than non-entrepreneurs.

8.1 Introduction

Proprietary traders are market participants who trade commodities, bonds, futures and options contracts, or other financial instruments using their own resources to make profit. They are self-employed, act independently, and can be characterized as "flesh-and-blood business owner-managers" (Davidsson 2007). Patrick Arbor[1] says that "They [traders] are people who know how to take a risk and want to be in business for themselves. They embody the American spirit of entrepreneurship. These are people who come to the CBOT [Chicago Board of Trade], every day, to try to carve out a living" (Bronstein 2008, p.10).

One of the key dimensions of trading and entrepreneurship is risk-taking behavior. Trading involves decisions under conditions of uncertainty and traders can be seen as specialists who handle risk (Zaloom 2004). An important topic in the entrepreneurship

[1]Former trader and chairman of the Chicago Board of Trade.

F. Mattos (✉)
University of Manitoba, Winnipeg, MB, Canada
e-mail: fabio_mattos@umanitoba.ca

R. Yazdipour, *Advances in Entrepreneurial Finance: With Applications from Behavioral Finance and Economics*, DOI 10.1007/978-1-4419-7527-0_8,

literature is how entrepreneurs face risk. A traditional hypothesis is that entrepreneurs exhibit a higher tolerance for risk than non-entrepreneurs. However, empirical evidence provides mixed results on whether entrepreneurs exhibit higher risk propensity (Busenitz 1999; Stewart and Roth 2001; Miner and Raju 2004; Stewart and Roth 2004). The inconsistency between empirical findings and the notion of higher risk propensity among entrepreneurs motivated new approaches to explain behavior. Busenitz (1999) and Busenitz and Arthurs (2007) argue that entrepreneurs might use emotion, bias, and heuristics in their judgment, making them misperceive the amount of risk in the market. For instance, an individual may believe himself to be averse to risk but still behave in a risk-seeking manner because he misperceives the amount of risk in a given situation.

The traditional framework to investigate behavior is the Expected Utility Theory (EU). However, experimental evidence has demonstrated the EU assumptions are often violated when people make decisions under conditions of risk (Schoemaker 1982; De Bondt and Thaler 1995; Starmer 2000; Hirshleifer 2001; Barberis and Thaler 2003). As a consequence, researchers have developed alternative theories to explain choice. In financial applications Prospect Theory (PT) developed by Kahneman and Tversky (1979) and Tversky and Kahneman (1992) appears to offer the most promising non-expected utility theory for explaining decision making under risk (Barberis and Thaler 2003). Prospect theory differs from the expected utility paradigm in that choice is influenced by probability weighting and loss aversion. Probability weighting reflects the notion that decision makers use transformed probabilities rather than objective probabilities in making choices. Loss aversion posits that decisions are made in terms of gains and losses rather than final wealth, and individuals react differently to gains and losses. The choice model under prospect theory has two fundamental components: a weighting function that reflects a nonlinear transformation of probability, and a value function that incorporates loss aversion.

Several studies suggest that probability weighting plays an important role in behavior. Tversky and Kahneman (1992) discuss a fourfold pattern of decision making frequently found in empirical work, i.e., risk aversion for gains and risk seeking for losses at high probabilities, and risk seeking for gains and risk aversion for losses at low probabilities. This pattern cannot be explained solely by EU's utility function. To explain a fourfold pattern, probability weighting must be incorporated (Tversky and Kahneman 1992). In financial settings Fox et al. (1996) conduct a laboratory experiment with professional investors in stock options markets and find that their decisions exhibit probability weighting. Langer and Weber (2005) demonstrate that probability weighting can make individuals behave differently than their risk preferences suggest. They show behavior characterized by risk aversion over gains and risk seeking over losses, as implied by a typical value function in prospect theory, can change dramatically when probability weighting is taken into account. Further, they provide evidence that models incorporating probability weighting are more consistent with observed behavior, which is also in line with Blavatskyy and Pogrebna (2005), Davies and Satchell (2005), and Mattos et al. (2008).

While the importance of probability weighting in decision making is generally accepted, no attempt has been made to measure the degree to which behavior can change in its presence. A number of studies use laboratory experiments to elicit weighting functions and estimate their parameters. While estimated parameters provide information on the magnitude of deviation from objective probabilities, they do not offer a measure of how risk-taking behavior changes in the presence of probability weighting.

The objectives of this chapter are to investigate the importance of probability weighting in trading decisions and examine the degree to which risk aversion is modified when investors exhibit probability weighting. We use a group of 15 proprietary traders in the CME Group who participate in a computer experiment, whose outcomes provide information about their risk attitude and degree of probability weighting. The experiment is conducted in the form of computer-based sessions. Traders are seated in front of a personal computer and answer choice questions that appear on the screen. The trade-off method adopted by Abdellaoui (2000) and Abdellaoui et al. (2005) is used to elicit value and weighting functions under risk (when probabilities of uncertain events are known) and uncertainty (when probabilities of uncertain events are unknown). Based on their elicited value and weighting functions, risk and uncertainty premiums are calculated to identify the impact of probability weighting on behavior. Three premiums are calculated: expected utility (EU) premium, standard premium, and behavioral premium. The EU premium is the traditional risk premium, which assumes that probabilities are treated linearly. The standard premium considers the effect of probability weighting on risk attitude and reflects whether individuals perceive themselves to be risk averse or risk seeking. The behavioral premium shows actual behavior.

8.2 Theoretical Framework

Prospect theory is used to investigate trading behavior. The choice model is based on a function $V(x_i)$ with two components (Eq. 8.1): a value function $v(x_i)$ and a probability weighting function $w(p_i)$ where x is the argument of the value function, and p is the objective probability distribution of x.

$$V(x_i) = \sum_{i=1}^{n} v(x_i) \cdot w(p_i). \tag{8.1}$$

The value function measures value in terms of gains and losses (changes in wealth) with respect to a reference point. The shape that typically arises from prospect theory is S-shaped, allowing for risk-averse behavior (concavity) in the domain of gains ($x > 0$), and risk-seeking behavior (convexity) in the domain of losses ($x < 0$) (Fig. 8.1).[2] Risk seeking in the loss domain has empirical support and arises from the idea that individuals dislike losses to such a degree (loss aversion) that they are willing to take greater risks to make up their losses.

[2]Figure 8.1 assumes that the reference point is zero.

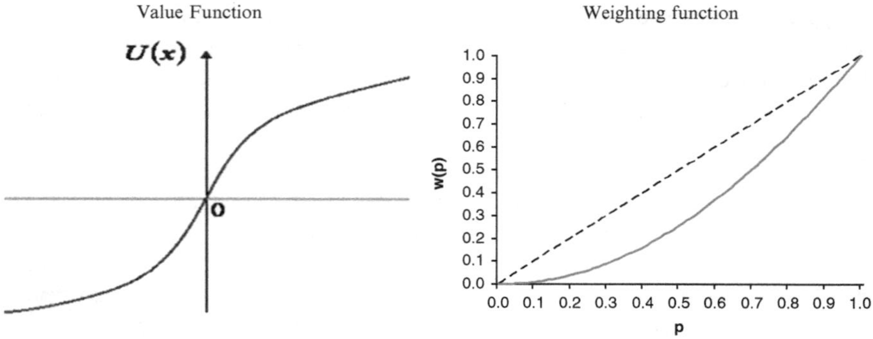

Fig. 8.1 Prospect Theory's value and weighting functions

A second component of prospect theory is a probability weighting function, which was developed from observation that individuals do not treat probabilities linearly. Empirical evidence shows probabilities can be overweighted or underweighted, meaning individuals make decisions based on perceived probabilities that are either larger or smaller than what really exist. For example, Fig. 8.1 shows the weighting function of a person who consistently underweighs probabilities, meaning that $w(p) < p$ for the whole probability scale.[3] If the individual is able to clearly distinguish probabilities and use them objectively, there is no curvature in the weighting function, represented by the linear dotted line in Fig. 8.1. In this situation, $w(p_i) = p_i$ in Eq. 8.1 and risk-taking behavior is determined solely by the risk preferences in the value function. However, when objective probabilities are not used, then $w(p_i) \neq p_i$ and decisions are based on transformed probabilities and the value function.

The effect of the weighting function in decision making depends on its structure and strength. For instance, the weighting function in Fig. 8.1 depicts an individual who underestimates the likelihood of uncertain events and thus believes that probabilities are smaller than actual. In this situation, a person is less willing to take risks. Now, consider the value function in Fig. 8.1, which shows risk aversion for gains and risk seeking for losses. In this situation, the weighting function enhances the risk aversion for gains and reduces (or eliminates) the risk seeking for losses. Consequently, in the presence of probability weighting actual behavior can differ from what might be expected based on the risk attitude observed in the value function.

8.3 Previous Studies

Empirical evidence suggests probability weighting is an important determinant of individual behavior. In financial investment settings several studies show how it can lead to patterns of behavior which differ from those based solely on risk and

[3] In empirical studies, a variety of shapes have been identified.

loss aversion. They also provide evidence that models incorporating probability weighting yield results consistent with observed behavior. Levy and Levy (2002) investigate whether risk aversion characterizes investors and the effect of probability weights on risk premium. They conclude that risk aversion is not present over the entire wealth domain, and behavior may be explained either by risk attitude or the presence of a probability function. They argue that even if individuals are risk averse, they can still act as risk-seeking investors due to probability weighting. In some situations, their results indicate that probability weights can enhance risk aversion.

Blavatskyy and Pogrebna (2005) and Langer and Weber (2005) introduce probability weighting to extend the analysis of the effect of myopic loss aversion on investment decisions. Blavatskyy and Pogrebna (2005) demonstrate that probability weighting can make investors increase the proportion of risky assets in their portfolios, which is the opposite conclusion reached by Berkelaar et al. (2004) and Hwang and Satchell (2005) who considered just the effect of myopic loss aversion. Hence in this situation, probability weighting leads the investor to buy more risky assets as opposed to buy less risky assets when only myopic loss aversion is considered. Similarly, Langer and Weber (2005) find that myopic loss-averse investors who also transform probabilities may decide to increase rather than decrease the proportion of risky assets in their portfolios.

Weighting functions for professional options investors have been investigated by Fox et al. (1996). They conduct two experiments and their findings indicate investors exhibit probability weighting. The first experiment focuses on pricing and matching prospects over gains with known objective probabilities. Their results yield a linear weighting function, which indicates investors about price-risky prospects by their expected actuarial value according to expected utility theory. A second experiment involves pricing prospects over gains with unknown probabilities and assessing the probabilities of uncertain events. The results for both decision weights and judged probabilities reveal subadditivity, meaning investors' weighting functions are not linear and expected utility theory is violated in the presence of uncertain prospects. Hence, when investors evaluate prospects weighting functions are affected by whether probabilities are known or unknown.

The reviewed studies illustrate an extensive literature that shows probability weighting is an important component of decision making. A natural extension is to explore how much probability weighting changes behavior, and Hilton (1988) and Davies and Satchell (2007) propose a theoretical framework to perform this task using risk premiums. Despite the evidence about the importance of probability weighting and the existence of a framework to investigate its impact on behavior, no attempt has been made to measure the degree to which probability weighting changes behavior using experimental data. The next section presents investor data used to investigate the importance of probability weighting and the extent to which behavior is modified in its presence. This is followed by a section that discusses procedures based on Hilton (1988) and Davies and Satchell (2007) that are used to measure the effect of probability weighting in monetary terms.

8.4 Data

Decision making is investigated in a sample of 15 professional traders. They are all male, have a college degree and trade agricultural contracts at the CME Group. Their age ranges from 23 to 54 years, with an average (median) age of 31.8 (31.0). The most experienced subject has been trading for 30 years, while the least has 5 months of market experience. The average (median) trading experience is 7.2 (5) years.

Among the traders, 12 trade futures and options, two trade only futures, and one trades only options. In terms of trading platform, eight trade only in the pit, two trade only electronic, and five trade both pit and electronic. Finally, six traders work only in corn, two trade only soybeans, two trade only soybean oil, one trades only wheat, three trade corn and soybeans, and one trades corn, soybeans, wheat, soybean oil, and soybean meal. They trade independently and only for their own portfolios, and profits are used to pay transaction and overhead costs.

Data consist of sets of value and probability points elicited using computer experiments conducted with each trader between December of 2006 and May of 2007. The trade-off method proposed by Wakker and Deneffe (1996) is used to elicit value and weighting functions in the gain and loss domains. This method is designed to elicit a sequence of outcomes $x_1,\ldots,x_n$ that are equally spaced in terms of value, and draws inferences from indifferences between two-outcome gambles (Appendix 1). The focus on decision making under risk and experimental procedure follows Abdellaoui (2000). Initially, two sequences of ten outcomes are elicited: $x_1, x_2,\ldots,x_{10}$ in the gain domain, and $x_{-1}, x_{-2},\ldots,x_{-10}$ in the loss domain. Additional sequences of nine probabilities are assessed: $p_1, p_2,\ldots,p_9$ in the gain domain, and $p_{-1}, p_{-2},\ldots,p_{-9}$ in the loss domain. So for each trader in each domain there are ten pairs of outcomes and value points $(x_i, v(x_i))$ to identify their value functions, and nine pairs of probabilities and weights $(p_i, w(p_i))$ to identify their weighting functions.

To explore decision making under uncertainty, the experimental procedure follows Abdellaoui et al. (2005). It is similar to the procedure described above, except that probabilities are not provided. Gains and losses are affected by the occurrence of uncertain events E_i and traders make their own assessment of the probabilities of those events. Thus subjects first need to judge the probability of the uncertain event, generating a choice-based probability which will differ for each individual. Then choice-based probabilities are used to elicit weighting functions. The output of this experiment is two sequences of ten outcomes: $x_1, x_2,\ldots,x_{10}$ in the gain domain, and $x_{-1}, x_{-2},\ldots,x_{-10}$ in the loss domain; and two sequences of nine choice-based probabilities: $q(E_1), q(E_2),\ldots,q(E_9)$ in the gain domain, and $q(E_{-1}), q(E_{-2}),\ldots,q(E_{-9})$ in the loss domain. So for each trader and in each domain there are ten pairs of outcomes and values $(x_i, v(x_i))$ to assess their value functions, and ten pairs of probabilities and weights $(q(E_j), w(q(E_j)))$to assess their weighting functions.

8.5 Research Method

8.5.1 Risk Premiums

Risk premiums are used to explore the effect of probability weighting on behavior. Risk premium is defined as the sure amount of money that an individual would require to be indifferent between an uncertain prospect x and a sure amount $EV(x)-r$ where $EV(x)$ is the expected value of prospect, x and r is the risk premium. Following the ideas of Hilton (1988) and Davies and Satchell (2007), we consider prospect theory's function $V(x_i)$ and a value function v. Risk premium then is calculated as the solution to $V(x)=v(EV(x)-r)$ and therefore can be represented as $r=EV(x)-v^{-1}(V(x))=EV(x)-CE(x)$, which is equivalent to the difference between the expected value of x and its certainty equivalent $CE(x)$. Intuitively, they refer to the amount of money that investors are willing to forego in order to avoid the risk associated with an uncertain prospect. A positive risk premium is associated with risk aversion since an individual requires a sure amount of money in order to take risk. In contrast, a negative risk premium is associated with risk seeking as an individual is willing to pay to take risk.

In the calculation of risk premiums a power value function with a reference point separating gains and losses (Eq. 8.2) and the weighting function $w(p)=\left[-\theta\exp\left(-\ln p\right)^{\delta}\right]$ (Prelec 1998) are adopted. Assuming a prospect x that yields outcomes x_1 with probability p and x_n with probability $1-p$, the two components of the risk premium are given by $EV(x)=px_1+(1-p)x_n$ and $v^{-1}(V(x))=v^{-1}(w(p)v(x_1)+w(1-p)v(x_n))$.

Initially we consider that there is no probability weighting ($w(p)=p$ and calculate expected utility (EU) risk premiums. EU premiums are expressed in Eq. 8.3 for gains $\left(r_G^{EU}\right)$ and Eq. 8.4 for losses $\left(r_L^{EU}\right)$ (see Appendix 2 for details of the calculation).

$$v(x)=\begin{cases} x^{\alpha} & x>0 \\ -\lambda(-x)^{\beta} & x\leq 0 \end{cases} \tag{8.2}$$

$$r_G^{EU}=px_1+(1-p)x_n-\left(px_1^{\alpha}+(1-p)x_n^{\alpha}\right)^{1/\alpha} \tag{8.3}$$

$$r_L^{EU}=px_1+(1-p)x_n+\left[p(-x_1)^{\beta}+(1-p)(-x_n)^{\beta}\right]^{1/\beta}. \tag{8.4}$$

In a prospect theory framework, two other risk premiums can be developed following the ideas of Hilton (1988) and Davies and Satchell (2007). The standard risk premium assumes that probability weighting is incorporated in the $V(x)$ component but not in the $v(EV(x)-r)$ component. It shows how individuals perceive their own risk attitude relative to the objective expected value of the prospect. Standard risk premiums are calculated for gains $\left(r_G^{S}\right)$ and losses $\left(r_L^{S}\right)$ according to Eqs. 8.5 and 8.6.

$$r_G^S = px_1 + (1-p)x_n - \left(w(p)x_1^\alpha + w(1-p)x_n^\alpha\right)^{1/\alpha} \tag{8.5}$$

$$r_L^S = px_1 + (1-p)x_n + \left[w(p)(-x_1)^\beta + w(1-p)(-x_n)^\beta\right]^{1/\beta} \tag{8.6}$$

The behavioral risk premium assumes that probability weighting is incorporated in both $V(x)$ and $v(EV(x)-r$ components, and shows risk behavior, where the evaluation of the prospect x is measured against a probability weighted expected value of x. Using Prelec's weighting function, behavioral risk premiums are calculated for gains $\left(r_G^B\right)$and losses $\left(r_L^B\right)$as in Eqs. 8.7 and 8.8.

$$r_G^B = w(p)x_1 + w(1-p)x_n - \left(w(p)x_1^\alpha + w(1-p)x_n^\alpha\right)^{1/\alpha} \tag{8.7}$$

$$r_L^B = w(p)x_1 + w(1-p)x_n + \left[w(p)(-x_1)^\beta + w(1-p)(-x_n)^\beta\right]^{1/\beta}. \tag{8.8}$$

If probability weighting is relevant in explaining behavior, then the three risk premiums will differ. In particular, the difference between the behavioral risk premium and the other risk premiums provides a reflection of how much probability weighting influences actual behavior. The difference between behavioral and standard risk premiums indicates the degree to which individuals' actions contradict their beliefs about their own risk attitude. For instance, a person may believe himself to be risk averse but still act in a risk-seeking manner. The difference between behavioral and EU risk premiums represents how much actual behavior deviates from what is predicted by expected utility theory because of probability weighting.

The three risk premiums are calculated for each trader from the data obtained in the laboratory experiment under conditions of risk. Points x_1 and x_n are the first and last points of the value function elicited in each experiment. The coefficients α and β of the value function are estimated by fitting a power function to the elicited points. The transformed probabilities $w(p)$ and $w(1-p)$ are also generated in the experiment, and coefficients δ and θ are estimated by fitting Prelec's function to the elicited probability points.

Since the magnitudes of premiums depend on the individual's risk attitude and on the distribution of outcomes, premiums calculated under different situations cannot be compared in absolute terms. Therefore, the effect of probability weighting on behavior is assessed by examining proportional risk premiums – the risk premiums expressed as a proportion of the expected value of the prospect (p, \$1,000, $1-p$, x_n). Proportional risk premiums (PRP) are calculated as $PRP_i^j = r_i^j / EV_i$, where j = EU, standard, behavioral and i = gain, loss. In the gain (loss) domain, proportional risk premiums are positive (negative) for risk-averse individuals, negative (positive) for risk-seeking individuals, and zero for risk-neutral individuals.[4]

---

[4]By construction, $EV_G>0$ and $EV_L>0$.

8.5.2 *Uncertainty Premiums*

Proportional uncertainty premiums (EU, standard, and behavioral) are also calculated for each trader in the gain and loss domains. The method to calculate uncertainty premiums is the same as explained in the previous section, except that x_1, x_n, α, β, $w(p)$, and $w(1-p)$ for each trader in Eqs. 8.3–8.8 are based on a data set obtained from the experiment under uncertainty. Thus the differences between uncertainty and risk premiums arise from distinct value and probability points elicited in each experiment, which reflect diverse behavior under conditions of risk and uncertainty.

8.6 Results

8.6.1 *Value and Weighting Functions Under Risk*

Estimation of value functions under risk reveals that traders are essentially risk averse for gains and risk seeking for losses. In the gain domain, 12 of 15 traders show concave functions, while in the loss domain 10 of 14 traders display convex functions (Table 8.1).[5] Elicited risk attitudes suggest traders follow the standard

Table 8.1 Estimated parameters of value and weighting functions under risk

	Value function		Weighting function			
			Gains		Losses	
Trader	Gains	Losses	Elevation	Curvature	Elevation	Curvature
1	0.77	1.16	1.08	1.29	0.98	0.80
2	0.74	1.31	0.09	0.00	0.52	0.53
3	0.93	0.69	0.33	1.87	1.54	1.47
4	0.58	0.75	0.83	0.43	0.39	1.04
5	0.89	0.62	0.80	0.67	0.65	0.75
6	0.81	0.73	1.73	0.73	1.46	0.65
7	0.87	0.83	0.75	0.77	1.07	0.88
8	0.78	0.83	1.26	0.73	1.43	0.91
9	–	0.71	1.00	0.09	0.83	0.70
10	1.19	1.27	1.42	1.17	0.66	0.59
11	0.82	0.93	0.92	0.75	1.01	0.63
12	0.63	–	1.29	0.49	1.00	0.00
13	0.72	0.91	0.95	0.62	0.97	0.73
14	0.81	0.66	1.98	1.03	0.70	0.77
15	1.60	1.08	1.39	0.32	0.67	0.34

Value function – gains: concave (convex) if parameter is less (greater) than 1; losses: concave (convex) if parameter is greater (less) than 1

[5] Answers to utility-elicitation questions were invalid for traders 9 (gains) and 12 (losses). Therefore 14 utility functions were elicited for each domain in the experiment, even though there were 15 traders. This problem will also affect the calculation of risk and uncertainty premiums for these two traders.

structure in prospect theory; behavior also depends on the weighting function. In the gain domain, estimation of weighting functions under risk indicates that nine of 15 traders exhibit inverse s-shaped functions. The remaining traders exhibit s-shaped curves (two traders), concave curves indicating complete overweighting of probabilities (two traders) and convex curves indicating complete underweighting of probabilities (two traders). In the loss domain, 11 of 15 traders exhibit inverse s-shaped functions. Then each of the remaining four traders exhibits an s-shaped curve, a concave curve, a convex curve, and a straight line. On balance, most traders show an inverse s-shaped curve, suggesting that small probabilities are overweighed and large probabilities are underweighted. This behavior indicates that they tend to be more willing to take small-probability risks and less willing to take large-probability risks. Nevertheless, individual results show large heterogeneity across traders (Appendix 3). Despite traders exhibiting some degree of overweighting and underweighting, the inflection points indicating the switch from underweighting to overweighting (or vice versa) vary largely across traders.

8.6.2 Risk Premiums

Three proportional risk premiums are calculated: expected utility (EU) premium, standard premium, and behavioral premium. The EU premium is the traditional risk premium which assumes that probabilities are treated linearly. The standard premium considers the effect of probability weighting on risk attitude and reflects whether individuals perceive themselves to be risk averse or risk seeking. The behavioral premium shows actual behavior. As discussed earlier, risk premiums represent the amount of money that a trader is willing to forego in order to avoid a prospect yielding x_1 with probability p and x_n with probability $1-p$, where x_1 and x_n represent monetary values elicited for each trader during the computer experiment.

Initially, proportional risk premiums are calculated based on probability $p=0.67$, which was the level used in the computer experiment. Table 8.2 shows premiums for gains and losses for each trader. Focusing first on EU and behavioral premiums, both suggest that traders are mainly risk averse for gains and risk seeking for losses (Table 8.2). However, the introduction of probability weighting indicates that behavior can be different from what expected utility theory would predict. In the gain domain behavioral premiums show that nine traders take more risk than their EU premiums suggest,[6] while five traders take less risk than their EU premiums suggest. [7] In the loss

[6]This means behavioral premiums are less positive or more negative than EU premiums. In our sample two traders switch from risk aversion to risk seeking, five become less risk averse, and two become more risk seeking.

[7]This means behavioral premiums are more positive or less negative than EU premiums. In our sample, all become more risk averse.

Table 8.2 Proportional risk premiums when $p=0.67$

	Gains			Losses		
Trader	EU	Standard	Behavioral	EU	Standard	Behavioral
1	0.10	0.17	0.10	−0.08	−0.12	−0.09
2	0.24	−1.77	−0.03	−0.02	−0.36	0.04
3	−0.04	−0.93	−0.01	0.27	0.66	0.37
4	0.38	0.16	0.33	0.11	−0.88	−0.04
5	0.04	−0.17	0.03	0.03	−0.41	−0.09
6	0.18	0.67	0.30	0.19	0.56	0.31
7	0.08	−0.22	0.06	0.11	0.18	0.12
8	0.19	0.40	0.24	0.15	0.50	0.21
9	n/a	n/a	n/a	0.03	−0.11	0.01
10	−0.09	0.24	−0.13	−0.19	−0.61	−0.11
11	0.12	0.02	0.11	0.04	0.04	0.05
12	0.07	0.45	0.25	n/a	n/a	n/a
13	0.14	0.10	0.15	0.04	0.02	0.05
14	0.17	0.76	0.32	0.15	−0.25	0.07
15	−0.15	0.09	−0.38	−0.03	−0.41	−0.02
Number of traders who exhibit:						
Risk aversion	11	10	10	4	8	5
Risk seeking	3	4	4	10	6	9

Gains: Positive (negative) premiums indicate risk aversion (seeking). Losses: Positive (negative) premiums indicate risk seeking (aversion)

domain behavioral premiums show that seven traders take more risk and another seven traders take less risk than EU premiums indicate.[8]

Contrasting behavioral and standard premiums also helps understand the effect of probability weighting on behavior by comparing how traders actually behave to how they perceive they would behave. In the gain domain ten traders are risk averse and four are risk seeking according to both behavioral and standard premiums (Table 8.2). However, in the gain domain, seven traders take more risk and another seven traders take less risk than their beliefs about their own risk attitude would suggest.[9] In the loss domain, standard premiums show that traders are mainly risk averse while behavioral premiums show that they are essentially risk seeking, suggesting while they believe themselves to be risk averse they behave in a risk-seeking manner (Table 8.2). In effect, ten traders take more risk and four traders take less risk than their beliefs about their own risk attitude would indicate.[10]

[8]For traders who take more risk, one switches from risk aversion to risk seeking, two are less risk averse and four are more risk seeking. For traders who take less risk, two switch from risk seeking to risk aversion, one is more risk averse and four are less risk seeking.

[9]For traders who take more risk, two switch from risk aversion to risk seeking and five become less risk averse. For traders who take less risk, two switch from risk seeking from risk aversion, three become more risk averse, and two become less risk seeking.

[10]For traders who take more risk, three switch from risk aversion to risk seeking, five become less risk averse, and two become more risk seeking. All traders who take less risk become less risk seeking.

The discussion can be expanded by looking at proportional risk premiums for all levels of probability. Figure 8.2 depicts the behavioral and EU premiums for trader 2. Probability p in the graphs refers to the prospect (p, \$1,000; $1-p$, x_n) where x_n varies across traders but is always positive and greater than or equal to \$1,000 in the gain domain (for losses x_n is equal to or more negative than −\$1,000). The EU premium (large dashed line) indicates that trader 2 is risk averse for gains and losses, but the behavioral premium (dark line) shows that he is risk seeking for gains and losses. Thus the introduction of probability weighting changes behavior completely. His actual behavior is consistent with his elicited weighting functions which show probability overweighting for almost all probabilities in both gain and loss domains (Appendix 3), indicating a higher propensity to take risks. Further, in the gain domain standard premium indicates that trader 2 believes himself to be more risk seeking than his behavior shows for most probability levels, while in the loss domain he believes himself to be risk averse despite behaving in a risk-seeking manner. Similar situations are found for other traders (Appendix 4), suggesting that the presence of probability weighting can make actual behavior dramatically different from what expected utility theory predicts and also from individuals' perception of their own risk attitude.

It is possible to explore the monetary effect of probability weighting by comparing the differences between proportional risk premiums. Going back to the case with $p=0.67$ (Table 8.2), in the gain domain, the expected utility theory says that trader 14 would have to receive the equivalent of 17% of the expected value to take the risky prospect, while his standard premium suggests he would require 76% to take this risk. However, his behavioral premium shows he would actually be willing to take the prospect for 32% of the expected value. Using the expected utility risk premium in the loss domain, trader 14 would be willing to pay 15% of the expected value to take the risky prospect, while using the behavioral premium he would actually be willing to pay 7% to take this risk. Differences exist for other traders along the whole range of probabilities, varying substantially across traders and also with respect to the probability adopted in the calculation (Appendix 4).

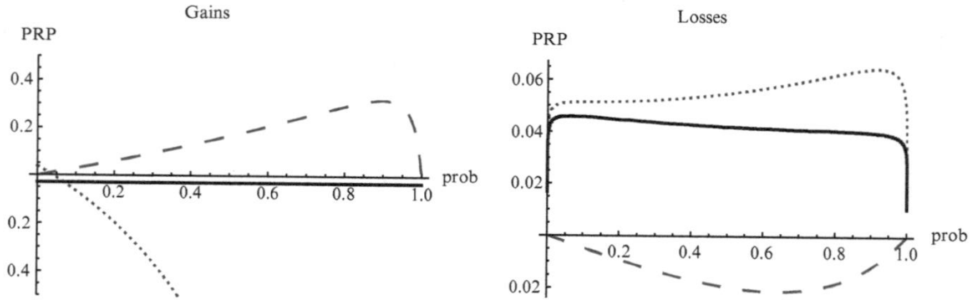

Fig. 8.2 Proportional risk premiums for trader 2. EU proportional risk premium (*large dashed line*), standard proportional risk premium (*small dashed line*) and behavioral proportional risk premium (*dark line*)

8.6.3 Value and Weighting Functions Under Uncertainty

Estimation of value functions under uncertainty reveals similar patterns to the shapes found under risk. In the gain domain, 12 of 15 traders exhibit concave curves, while in the loss domain, nine of 15 traders show convex curves (Table 8.3). Again, the risk attitudes elicited in the computer experiment suggest that most traders follow the standard behavior suggested by prospect theory, with risk aversion for gains and risk seeking for losses. On the other hand, estimation of weighting functions under uncertainty reveals a different pattern compared to the findings under risk. In the gain (loss) domain only 7 (5) of 15 traders exhibit inverse s-shaped curves, which were predominantly found under risk. Further, apparently due to the increase in uncertainty, many traders' weighting functions (five for gains and seven for losses) showed a low sensitivity to changes in probability. Consequently they tend to give similar weights to different probabilities, accounting for nearly flat curves seen in some graphs of weighting functions (Appendix 5). Finally, in the gain (loss) domain two (one) traders exhibit concave curves indicating complete overweighting, one (one) trader exhibits a convex curve indicating complete underweighting, and no (one) trader shows an s-shaped curve. As identified for situations under risk, individual results under uncertainty also show large heterogeneity across traders (Appendix 5). While most traders exhibit some degree of overweighting and underweighting along the probability range, inflection points indicating the switch from underweighting to overweighting (or vice versa) vary largely.

Table 8.3 Estimated parameters of value and weighting functions under uncertainty

			Weighting function			
	Value function		Gains		Losses	
Trader	Gains	Losses	Elevation	Curvature	Elevation	Curvature
1	0.47	0.85	0.53	0.00	0.83	0.00
2	0.70	1.85	2.48	0.28	0.57	0.30
3	0.45	0.51	0.37	0.00	0.47	0.00
4	1.11	1.29	1.14	1.00	1.11	1.00
5	0.40	0.50	0.50	0.00	0.30	0.00
6	0.67	0.98	0.78	0.19	0.43	0.43
7	0.47	0.78	0.50	1.00	0.79	1.00
8	0.78	1.09	1.21	0.02	0.81	0.00
9	0.65	3.74	0.76	0.00	0.81	0.00
10	1.25	1.10	0.99	0.04	0.56	0.00
11	0.79	0.81	0.65	0.03	0.76	0.09
12	0.46	0.54	0.38	0.00	0.33	0.00
13	0.61	0.70	0.88	0.92	1.44	2.58
14	0.83	1.00	1.20	0.01	0.99	0.58
15	1.13	0.93	1.24	0.36	0.97	0.69

Value function – gains: concave (convex) if parameter is less (greater) than 1; losses: concave (convex) if parameter is greater (less) than 1

8.6.4 Uncertainty Premiums

Three proportional uncertainty premiums are calculated: expected utility (EU) premium, standard premium, and behavioral premium. Their definitions are the same as what was discussed for risk premiums. The proportional uncertainty premiums based on probability $p=0.67$ are presented in Table 8.4.[11] Both EU and behavioral premiums reveal that traders are mainly risk averse for gains, but split between risk aversion and risk seeking for losses (Table 8.4). Again comparisons between EU and behavioral premiums point to divergences between actual behavior and what expected utility theory would predict. In the gain domain behavioral premiums show that ten traders take more risk and four traders take less risk than their EU premiums indicate.[12] In the loss domain behavioral premiums reveal that six traders take more risk and seven traders take less risk than EU premiums indicate.[13]

Comparing standard and behavioral premiums in Table 8.4 shows in the gain domain six traders are risk averse and eight are risk seeking using standard premiums,

Table 8.4 Proportional uncertainty premiums when $p=0.67$

	Gains			Losses		
Trader	EU	Standard	Behavioral	EU	Standard	Behavioral
1	0.21	–0.26	0.14	–0.07	0.10	–0.09
2	1.05	3.86	0.60	0.19	0.45	0.12
3	0.09	–0.71	–0.27	–0.19	0.36	–0.09
4	–0.04	0.09	–0.04	0.13	0.03	0.14
5	0.27	–0.25	0.18	–0.15	0.64	0.11
6	0.10	–0.06	0.12	–0.01	0.41	0.01
7	0.26	–0.29	0.13	–0.16	0.05	–0.16
8	0.14	0.43	0.21	0.03	0.22	0.04
9	n/a	n/a	n/a	0.72	0.85	0.65
10	–0.09	–0.11	–0.13	0.02	0.33	0.01
11	0.08	–0.23	0.07	–0.08	0.14	–0.09
12	0.17	–0.54	–0.06	n/a	n/a	n/a
13	0.30	0.18	0.30	–0.38	–1.05	–0.24
14	0.06	0.43	0.13	0.00	–0.01	0.00
15	–0.07	0.18	–0.09	–0.04	0.00	–0.04
Number of traders who exhibit						
Risk aversion	11	6	9	8	2	6
Risk seeking	3	8	5	6	12	7

Gains: Positive (negative) premiums indicate risk aversion (seeking). Losses: Positive (negative) premiums indicate risk seeking (aversion)

[11]Recall under uncertainty traders had to make their own assessment of probabilities, since no specific probability was provided.

[12]For traders who take more risk, two switch from risk aversion to risk seeking, five become less risk averse, and three become more risk seeking. All traders who take less risk become more risk averse.

[13]For traders who take more risk, three become less risk averse and three become more risk seeking. Among traders who take less risk, two switch from risk seeking to risk aversion, two become more risk averse, and three become less risk seeking.

in contrast to nine risk averse and five risk seeking traders using behavioral premiums. However these numbers do not fully reveal that seven traders have premiums switch signs: two move from risk aversion to risk seeking and five move from risk seeking to risk aversion when behavioral and standard premiums are compared. This comparison shows in the gain domain six traders take more risk and eight traders take less risk than their beliefs about their own risk attitude would suggest.[14] In the loss domain standard premiums indicate that 12 traders are risk seeking, while behavioral premiums present mixed evidence as six traders are risk averse, seven are risk seeking, and one is risk neutral. Eleven traders take more risk and three traders take less risk than their beliefs about their own risk attitude would indicate.[15] As can be seen in Appendix 6, examination of uncertainty premiums for all levels of probability suggests that the presence of probability weighting can lead to behavior dramatically different from what expected utility theory predicts and also from individuals' perception of their own risk attitude.

Finally, the monetary effect of probability weighting under uncertainty resembles that discussed under risk. As Table 8.4 shows for $p=0.67$, in the gain domain, expected utility theory suggests trader eight would have to receive 14% of the expected value to take the risky prospect, while his standard premium suggests he would require 43% to take this risk. However, his behavioral premium suggests he would actually be willing to take the prospect for 21% of the expected value. In the loss domain expected utility theory suggests that trader 8 would be willing to pay 3% of the expected value to take the risky prospect, while his standard premium suggests he would pay 22% to take it. His behavioral premium indicates he would actually be willing to pay 4% to take this risk. Appendix 6 illustrates the substantial degree to which traders can deviate from expected utility theory and misperceive their own risk attitude along the whole range of probabilities. These differences vary substantially across traders and also with respect to the probability adopted in the calculation, but they all show that behavior can change substantially in the presence of probability weighting.

8.6.5 Comparison Between Behavioral Premiums Under Risk and Uncertainty

Results show that proportional uncertainty premiums are generally larger than proportional risk premiums (Appendix 7). It appears that risk aversion (or risk seeking) tends to be enhanced under conditions of uncertainty compared to risk. For example, behavioral premiums for gains suggest that trader 11 is risk averse under risk and uncertainty, meaning he requires a premium in order to take risk (Fig. 8.3). However, this premium is larger when he faces uncertainty based on unknown

---

[14] For traders who take more risk, two switch from risk aversion to risk seeking, three become less risk averse, and one becomes more risk seeking. For traders who take less risk, five switch from risk seeking to risk aversion, one becomes more risk averse, and two become less risk seeking.

[15] For traders who take more risk, five switch from risk aversion to risk seeking and six become less risk averse. For traders who take less risk, one switches from risk seeking to risk neutrality, one becomes more risk averse, and one becomes less risk seeking.

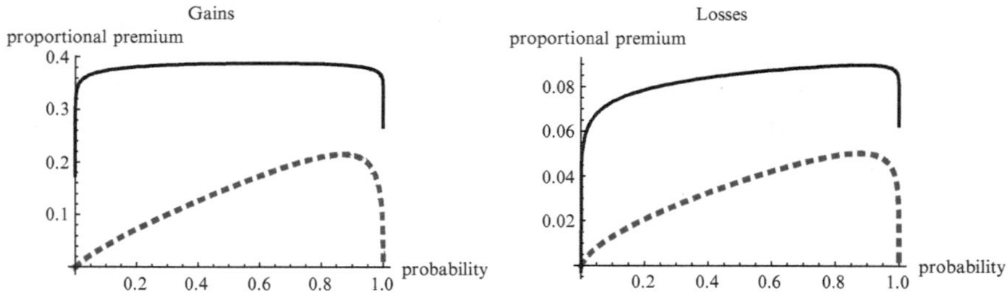

Fig. 8.3 Behavioral proportional premiums under risk and uncertainty for trader 11. The *dashed line* is the premium under risk; the *dark line* is the premium under uncertainty

probabilities than when he faces risk based on known probabilities. He requires a proportionally larger premium to take risk under uncertainty than he does under risk. Similarly, behavioral premiums for losses indicate he is risk seeking, thus he is willing to pay a premium to take risk (Fig. 8.3). The proportional premium is larger under uncertainty, implying he would pay a proportionally larger premium under uncertainty than he would under risk.

8.7 Summary and Conclusions

Three primary findings emerge from our study. First, professional traders exhibit probability weighting in their choices. This is consistent with the experiment conducted by Fox et al. (1996) under different market conditions and using different types of securities. The fact that both studies find that probability weighting is an important determinant of investment decisions emphasizes its significance in understanding the nature of risk and the resultant risk-return behavior that follows Prospect Theory. Furthermore, the implications for other types of investors such as venture capitalists and even entrepreneurs are clear.

Second, probability weighting has a substantial impact on behavior. Many situations exist in which premiums change sign when probability weighting is introduced. For instance, risk aversion (risk seeking) changes to risk seeking (risk aversion) in the presence of probability weighting. In other situations probability weighting enhances dramatically the intensity of risk aversion or risk seeking.

Third, risk-averse or risk-seeking behavior is more intense under conditions of uncertainty – a major characteristic of entrepreneurial environments – than it is under conditions of risk. This finding is consistent with previous studies including Tversky and Fox (1995), who find that the effect of probability weighting is more pronounced under uncertainty than risk. They argue that departures from expected utility theory are amplified by ambiguity. Similarly Fox et al. (1996) find that investors who participate in their experiments tend to follow expected utility theory in decisions where objective probabilities are known, but depart from expected utility theory in decisions involving a subjective assessment of probabilities.

Clearly, larger deviations from expected utility theory emerge when individuals need to make their own assessments about the likelihood of events.

Our findings support the existence of bias and heuristics when entrepreneurs and investors make decisions under conditions of risk, as suggested by Busenitz (1999) and Busenitz and Arthurs (2007). Empirical results identify investors generally take more risk than would be anticipated, since behavioral premiums tend to show a larger propensity to take risk as opposed to standard and EU premiums. In our experiment under risk (uncertainty) 9 (10) traders in the gain domain and 7 (6) traders in the loss domain take more risk than expected utility theory would predict. Seven (6) traders in the gain domain and 10 (11) traders in the loss domain take more risk than their beliefs about their own risk attitude would indicate. The higher risk propensity due to probability weighting found here is also consistent with the idea that entrepreneurs and possibly venture capitalists perceive risky situations more optimistically than non-entrepreneurs (Palich and Bagby 1995). Kliger and Levy (2010) argue that investors' optimism is reflected in their weighting functions and lead to overconfidence, making risky choices more attractive. In this context, entrepreneurs' optimism can influence their weighting function in a way that their behavior exhibits higher propensity to undertake risks.

This study also sheds light on the inconsistency between empirical findings showing mixed risk attitudes and the notion that entrepreneurs exhibit a higher risk propensity (Busenitz 1999; Stewart and Roth 2001; Miner and Raju 2004; Stewart and Roth 2004). The differences between behavioral and EU premiums indicate behavior can deviate largely from what would be expected based on risk attitudes. For example, an individual can behave in a risk-seeking manner even if his risk attitude suggests he is risk averse. This analysis can explain why empirical studies might find some entrepreneurs are risk averse even though they are involved in risk-taking activities.

Additionally, the research contributes to the literature in two ways. First, it combines two previous approaches to non-expected utility behavior – the trade-off method and behavioral risk premiums – to gather experimental data and uses them to empirically explore the importance of probability weighting. No other study has investigated the effect of probability weighting on behavior using experimental data collected from real decision makers and the risk premium concepts developed by Hilton (1988) and Davies and Satchell (2007). This combination provides a measure of how actual behavior deviates from expected utility behavior. It also allows us to assess the cost of deviating from expected utility theory, and the cost of misperceiving our own degree of risk aversion. Second, the results provide insights on the effect of probability weighting in financial decisions, which is important not only to understand market movements but also evaluating any other business opportunity such as a startup by an entrepreneurs or funding a venture by a venture capitalist. Fehr and Tyran (2005) consider the interaction between rational and irrational agents and discuss evidence that even a small degree of individual irrationality (such as probability weighting) can cause large deviations from aggregate predictions in rational models. Here, we find a high degree of heterogeneous behavior across investors, which suggest the nature and magnitude of individual irrationality may be highly diverse, making it quite difficult to predict its effect on aggregate market behavior. Importantly, understanding individual behavior is of value in its own right in many settings. For instance, a manager of professional traders may need to understand individual investor behavior to properly train and advise them. In this context, our measures can provide an indication of the value of reducing the effect of probability weighting on trading decisions.

Finally the importance of probability weighting is highly consistent with recent work by Blavatskyy and Pogrebna (2005), Langer and Weber (2005), and Davies and Satchell (2005) that also suggest behavior can change considerably in its presence. Behavior and its determinants need to be explored using these measures and possibly new methodologies to gain deeper insights into how investors and entrepreneurs, who are effectively among the major investors in their own ventures, respond. Such investigations would be in the spirit of Blavatskyy and Pogrebna (2005) and Langer and Weber (2005), who find that behavior can change dramatically when probability weighting is considered in decision-making models, and also consistent with Barberis and Thaler's (2003) call for a more integrated assessment of behavioral phenomena.

8.8 Appendix 1

The trade-off method is explained for the case of positive outcomes (gains), but its use for negative outcomes (losses) is straightforward. The first step is to determine probability p, reference outcomes R and R^*, and the starting outcome x_0. Those values are set by the experimenter such that $x_0>R>R^*$, and they are held fixed through the whole experiment. Given x_{i-1}, x_i is elicited such that the subject is indifferent between prospects (x_0, p, R) and (x_1, p; R^*). The elicitation of each outcome in the sequence $x_1,\ldots,x_n$ is obtained through an iterative procedure in which elicited outcomes are derived from observed choice rather than assessed by subjects. For example, as can be seen in Table 8.5, x_1 is the value that makes the subject indifferent between prospects (x_0, p; R) and (x_1, p; R^*). The next step is to elicit X_2 such that the subject is indifferent between prospects (x_1, p; R) and (x_2, p; R^*) (X_2, p; R^*). Outcomes $x_3,\ldots,x_n$ can be elicited by following the same steps.

The elicitation of each outcome in the sequence $x_1,\ldots,x_n$ is obtained through an iterative procedure in which elicited outcomes are derived from observed choice rather than assessed by subjects. After the sequence of outcomes $x_1,\ldots,x_n$ is obtained it is possible to use the same procedure to elicit probabilities $p_1,\ldots,p_{n-1}$. In the probability elicitation process subjects are asked a new series of choice questions, and

Table 8.5 Trade-off procedure to elicit sequence of outcomes x_1,,xn under risk

Step	Fixed values	Prospect A	Prospect B	Elicited outcome x_i	$v(x_i)$
1	R, R^*, p, x_0	(x_0, p; R)	(x_1, p; R^*)	x_1	$1/n$
2	R, R^*, p, x_1	(x_1, p; R)	(x_2, p; R^*)	x_2	$2/n$
3	R, R^*, p, x_2	(x_2, p; R)	(x_3, p; R^*)	x_3	$3/n$
4	R, R^*, p, x_3	(x_3, p; R)	(x_4, p; R^*)	x_4	$4/n$
⋮	⋮	⋮	⋮	⋮	⋮
n	R, R^*, p, x_{n-1}	(x_0, p; R)	(x_1, p; R^*)	x_n	1

Table 8.6 Tradeoff procedure to elicit sequence of probabilities $P_1, \ldots, P_{n-1}$ under risk

Step	Fixed values	Prospect A	Prospect B	Elicited probability p_i	Probability weight $w(p_i)$
1	x_0, x_1, x_n	x_1	$(x_n, p_1; x_0)$	p_1	$1/n$
2	x_0, x_2, x_n	x_2	$(x_n, p_2; x_0)$	p_2	$2/n$
3	x_0, x_3, x_n	x_3	$(x_n, p_3; x_0)$	p_3	$3/n$
4	x_0, x_4, x_n	x_4	$(x_n, p_4; x_0)$	p_4	$4/n$
⋮	⋮	⋮	⋮	⋮	⋮
$n-1$	x_0, x_{n-1}, x_n	x_{n-1}	$(x_n, p_{n-1}; x_0)$	p_{n-1}	$n-1/n$

probability p_i is determined such that the subject is indifferent between the certain outcome x_i and a prospect (x_n, p_i, x_0), as illustrated in Table 8.6. Similar to the elicitation of outcomes, the process to assess probabilities is also based on an iterative procedure in which elicited probabilities are derived from observed choice.

The design of the experiment is critical for a good assessment of values and probability weights. Hershey et al. (1982) discuss several steps for selecting an elicitation procedure in order to reduce the occurrence of bias. The choices related to the decision context and also the dimension of outcomes and probabilities are made based on conversations with the manager of the traders participating in the experiment, along with the experimental procedures adopted by Abdellaoui (2000) and Abdellaoui et al. (2005). The experiment should be as close as possible to the subjects' environment, which means that in the current study it should reflect trading decisions commonly experienced in the CME Group markets. Traders are asked to choose between two trading strategies $(x_i, p; R)$ and $(x_{i+1}, p; R^*)$ yielding different monetary outcomes, where x_i, R, x_{i+1}, and R^* represent possible gains or losses and p is the probability associated with the outcomes. Based on numbers discussed with the manager of the trading group participating in this study, small traders usually make profits (losses) in a range between US$800 and US$1,000 per trade, while large traders can make (lose) up to US$15,000 per trade. Therefore, in the initial step of the elicitation procedure x_0 is set to $1,000 (–$1,000), which then increases (decreases) from x_1 (x_{-1}) through x_n (x_{-n}) according to each trader's choices during the experiment. The values of R and R^* are set to $500 (–$500) and $0, respectively.

When the procedure is finished there is a sequence of outcomes $x_1,\ldots,x_n$ and their respective values $v(x_1),\ldots,v(x_n)$, and also a sequence of probabilities $p_1,\ldots,p_{n-1}$ and their respective weights $w(p_1),\ldots,w(p_{n-1})$. These values are used to estimate the parameters of a power value function and Prelec (1998)'s weighting function.

An extension of the experiment deals with decision making under uncertainty, and the experimental procedure in this part follows Abdellaoui et al. (2005). The procedure is very similar to the previous elicitation, except that probability p is now replaced by an event E representing some occurrence which traders are familiar with, and an extra step is added to elicit probability functions. Now participants need to infer the probability of the event based on their own capabilities. Based on Abdellaoui et al. (2005) and conversations with the trading manager of the group participating in this study, two types of events will be used. For the elicitation of $v(x_i)$ event E will be "USDA report is bullish," while for the elicitation of $w(q(E_j))$

event E will be the percentage change of the Dow Jones Industrial Average (DJIA) stock index over the next 6 months. Four elementary events will be defined based on historical performance of the DJIA: $\Delta DJIA < -4\%$, $-4\% < \Delta DJIA < 0\%$, $0 < \Delta DJIA$ 4%, and $\Delta DJIA > 4\%$. Five other events will also be defined from all unions of elementary events that result in contiguous intervals, yielding a total of nine events. The output of this second experiment will be two sequences of ten outcomes: $x_1, x_2, \ldots, x_{10}$ in the domain of gains, and $x_{-1}, x_{-2}, \ldots, x_{-10}$ in the domain of losses; and two sequences of nine choice-based probabilities: $q(E_1), q(E_2), \ldots, q(E_9)$ in the domain of gains, and $q(E_{-1}), q(E_{-2}), \ldots, q(E_{-9})$ in the domain of losses. So for each trader and in each domain there will be ten pairs of outcomes and values $(x_i, v(x_i))$ to assess their value functions, and ten pairs of probabilities and weights $(q(E_j), w(q(E_j)))$ to assess their weighting functions. Again, these values are used to estimate the parameters of a power value function and Prelec (1998)'s weighting function.

Research on Trading Behavior: Experiment in Decision Making Under Risk

Instructions

This is an experiment in the economics of decision making under risk. The experiment is simple and should take approximately 60 min. Please remember that there are no right or wrong answers in this experiment and you are expected to make decisions as honestly as possible.

During the whole experiment you will be asked to choose between two strategies. Each strategy is based on gains or losses, and all values refer to monetary amounts. You should think of those strategies as decisions you make every day in the market. Example 1 provides an example of the kind of choice you will be faced with during the experiment. If you choose strategy A you have a 67% chance to gain \$1,000 and a 33% chance to gain \$500. If you decide to follow strategy B you have a 67% chance to gain \$3,500 and a 33% chance to gain nothing.

Example 1

Strategy A		Strategy B	
Gain	Probability	Gain	Probability
1,000	67%	3,500	67%
500	33%	0	33%

In Example 2 you have strategies involving losses. If you choose strategy A you have a 50% chance to lose \$18,000 and a 50% chance to lose 1,000. If you decide to follow strategy B you have a 100% chance to lose 5,500.

Example 2

Strategy A		Strategy B	
Loss	Probability	Loss	Probability
−18,000	50%	−5,500	100%
−1,000	50%		

The two examples above provide a very accurate picture of the kind of choices you will be faced during the experiment. The experiment is computer-based and all you need to complete the experiment is to use the mouse to choose your strategies. Please don't use the keyboard.

The first few questions in the experiment are for practice purposes so that you can become more familiar with the program. Feel free to ask the researcher any questions you might have about the experiment.

Research on Trading Behavior: Experiment in Decision Making Under Uncertainty

Instructions

This is an experiment in the economics of decision making under uncertainty. The experiment is simple and should take approximately 40 min. Please remember that there are no right or wrong answers in this experiment and you are expected to make decisions as honestly as possible.

During the whole experiment you will be asked to *choose between two strategies*. Each strategy is based on gains or losses, and all values refer to monetary amounts. You should think of those strategies as decisions you make everyday in the market. Examples 1 and 2 provide an example of the kind of choice you will be faced with during the experiment.

Example 1: USDA report refers to the market(s) you trade.

Strategy A		Strategy B	
Gain/Loss	If:	Gain/Loss	If:
0	USDA report is bullish	3,500	USDA report is bullish
–500	USDA report is bearish	–1,000	USDA report is bearish

If you choose trading strategy A you will make nothing if the coming USDA report is bullish, and you will lose $500 if the coming USDA report is bearish. If you decide to follow strategy B you will make $3,500 if the coming USDA report is bullish, and you will lose $1,000 if the coming USDA report is bearish.

Example 2: ΔDJ refers to the percentage change you expect in the Dow Jones Industrial Average Index (DJ) over the next 6 months.

Strategy A		Strategy B	
Gain/Loss	If:	Gain/Loss	If:
–11,000	$\Delta DJ \leq 4\%$	–5,000	$\Delta DJ \leq 4\%$
0	$\Delta DJ > 4\%$	–5,000	$\Delta DJ > 4\%$

If you choose trading strategy A you will lose $11,000 if the DJ changes by 4% or less over the next 6 months, and you will lose nothing if the DJ changes by more than 4% over the next 6 months. If you decide to follow strategy B you will lose $5,000 either if the DJ changes by 4% or less or if the DJ changes by more than 4% over the next 6 months.

The two examples above provide an accurate picture of the kind of choices you will be faced during the experiment. The experiment is computer-based and all you need to do to complete the experiment is to use the mouse to choose your strategies. Please don't use the keyboard.

The first few questions in the experiment are for practice purposes so that you can become more familiar with the program. Feel free to ask the researcher any questions you might have about the experiment.

8.9 Appendix 2

Assuming a prospect x that yields outcomes x_1 with probability p and x_n with probability $1-p$, the two components of the risk premium are given by $EV(x) = px_1+(1-p)x_n$ and $v^{-1}(V(x)) = v^{-1}(w(p)v(x_1)+w(1-p)v(x_n))$. Considering the absence of probability weighting ($w(p)=p$) and a power value function with a reference point separating gains and losses as in Eq. 8.9, the expected utility (EU) premium can be calculated as in Eqs. 8.10–8.13 for the gain domain and Eqs. 8.14–8.17 for the loss domain.

$$v(x)=\begin{cases} x^{\alpha} & x>0 \\ -\lambda(-x)^{\beta} & x\leq 0 \end{cases} \tag{8.9}$$

$$V(x)=v\left(EV(x)-r_G^{EU}\right) \tag{8.10}$$

$$pv(x_1)+(1-p)v(x_n)=v\left(px_1+(1-p)x_n-r_G^{EU}\right) \tag{8.11}$$

$$px_1^{\alpha}+(1-p)x_n^{\alpha}=\left(px_1+(1-p)x_n-r_G^{EU}\right)^{\alpha} \tag{8.12}$$

$$r_G^{EU}=px_1+(1-p)x_n-\left(px_1^{\alpha}+(1-p)x_n^{\alpha}\right)^{1/\alpha} \tag{8.13}$$

$$V(x)=v\left(EV(x)-r_L^{EU}\right) \tag{8.14}$$

$$pv(x_1)+(1-p)v(x_n)=v\left(px_1+(1-p)x_n-r_L^{EU}\right) \tag{8.15}$$

$$p\left[-\lambda(-x_1)\beta\right]+(1-p)\left[-\lambda(-x_n)\beta\right]=-\lambda\left\{\left[p(-x_1)+(1-p)(-x_n)-r_L^{EU}\right]\beta\right\} \tag{8.16}$$

$$r_L^{EU}=px_1+(1-p)x_n+\left[p(-x_1)^{\beta}+(1-p)(-x_n)^{\beta}\right]^{1/\beta}. \tag{8.17}$$

The premiums are calculated from the data obtained in the lab experiment with traders. Points x_1 and x_n are the first and last points elicited in the experiment. The first point is always 1,000 but the last point depends on how each trader makes choices during the experiment. In the experiment for risk, x_n ranges from 4,200 to 41,900 for gains and from −2,100 to −31,500 for losses. In the experiment for uncertainty it goes from 4,500 to 38,800 for gains and −1,000 to −36,200 for losses.

8.10 Appendix 3

Figure 8.4

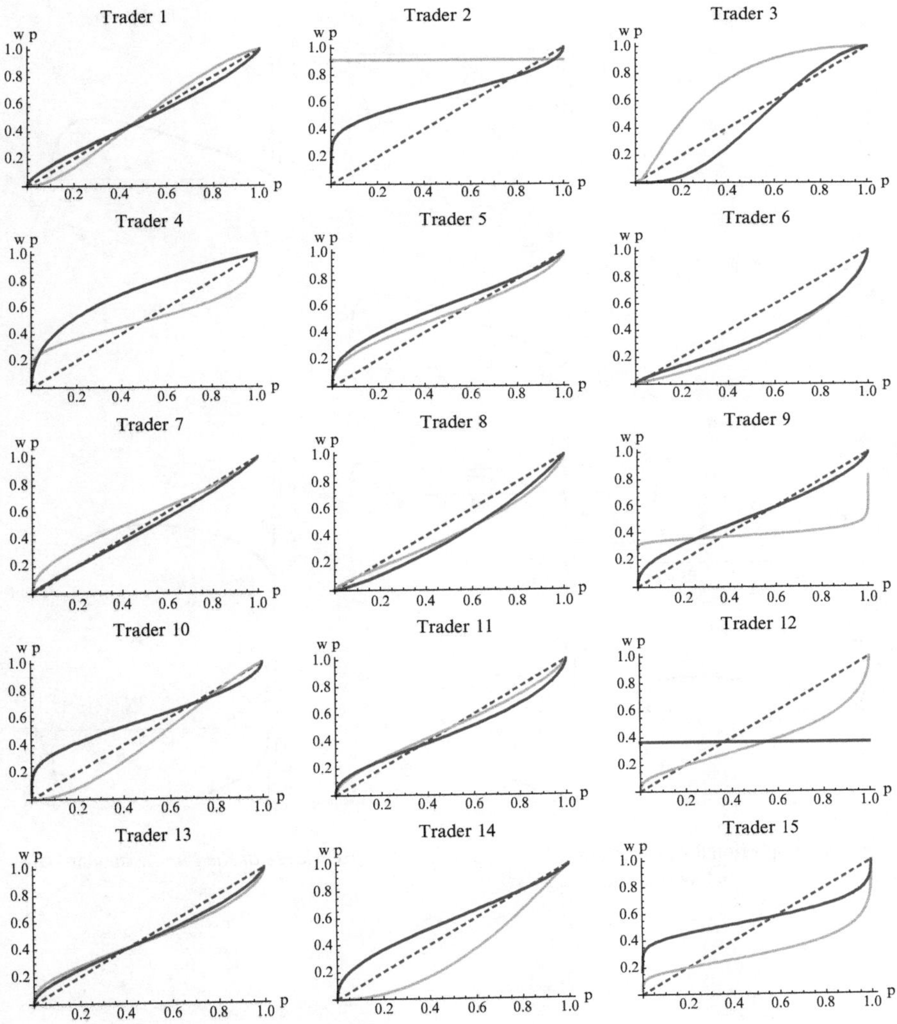

Fig. 8.4 Risk – Weighting function for gains (*gray line*) and losses (*dark line*)

8.11 Appendix 4

Figures 8.5 and 8.6

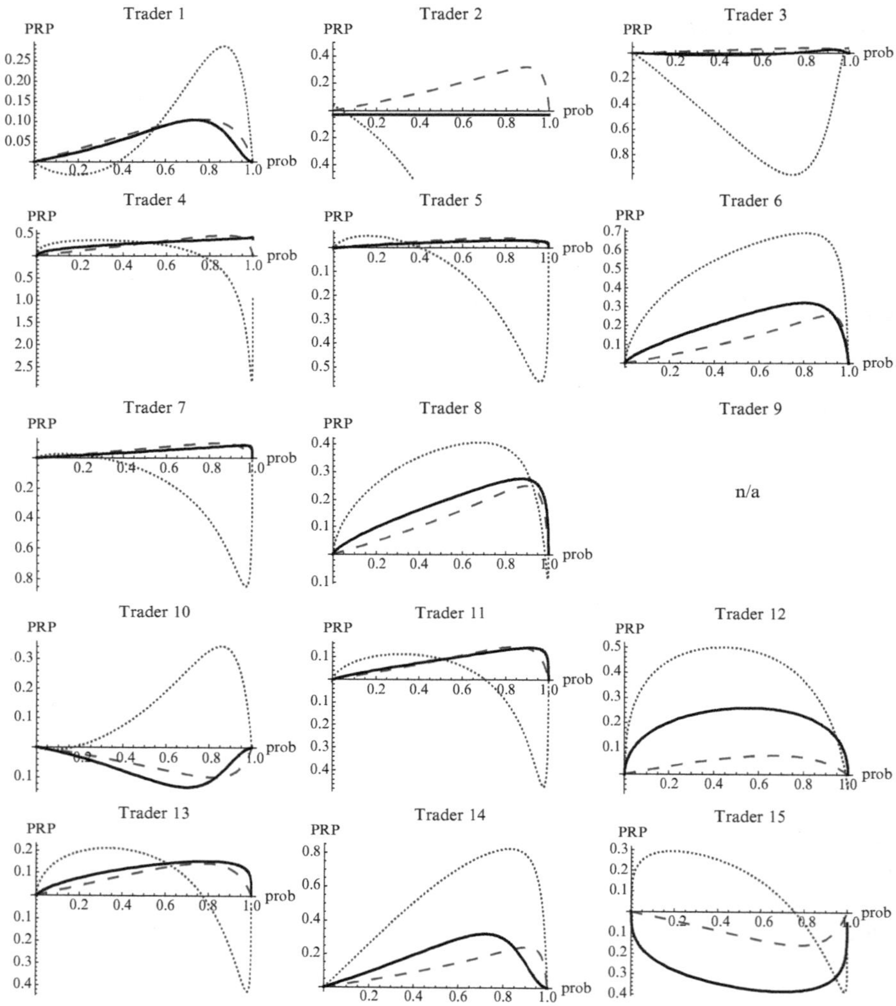

Fig. 8.5 Proportional risk premiums in the gain domain – EU (*large dashed line*), standard (*tiny dashed line*), and behavioral (*dark line*)

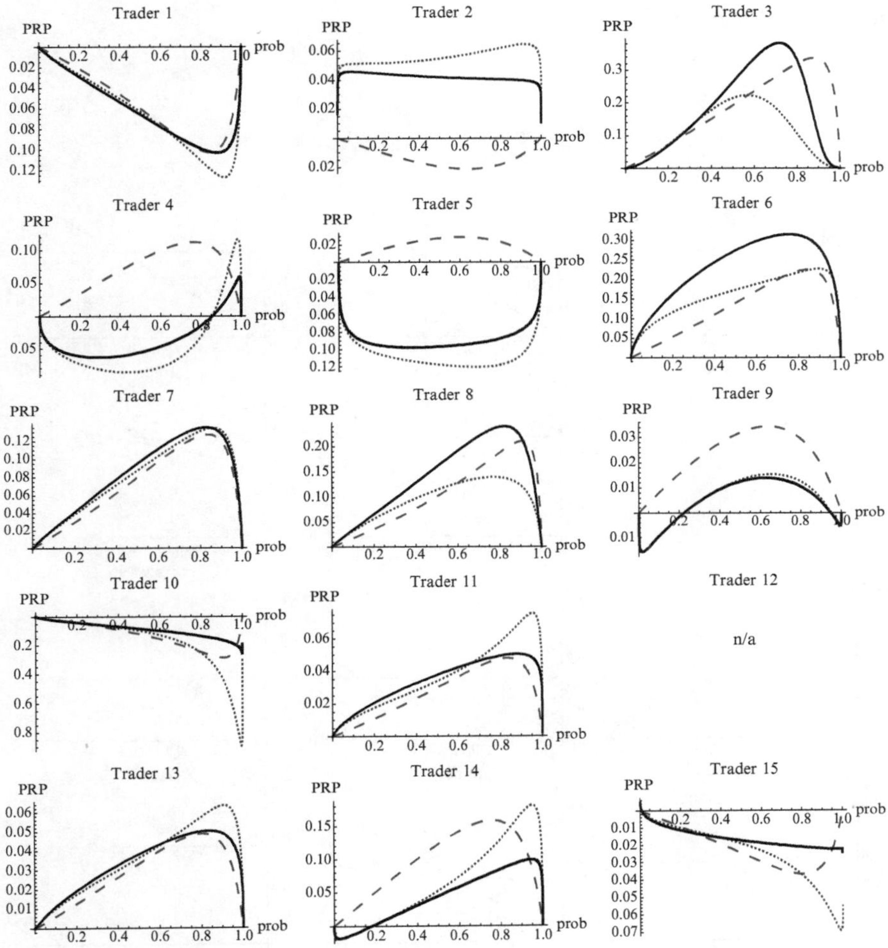

Fig. 8.6 Proportional risk premiums in the loss domain – EU (*large dashed line*), standard (*tiny dashed line*), and behavioral (*dark line*)

8.12 Appendix 5

Figure 8.7

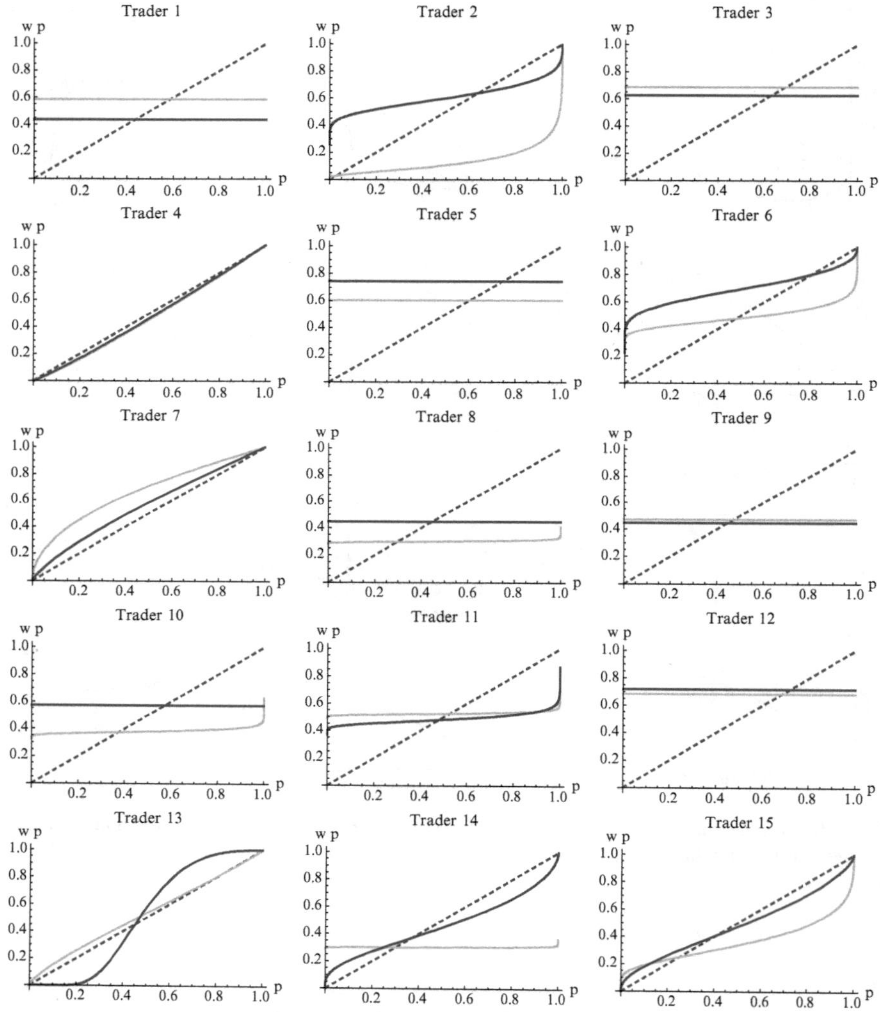

Fig. 8.7 Uncertainty – Weighing function for gains (*gray line*) and losses (*dark line*)

8.13 Appendix 6

Figures 8.8 and 8.9

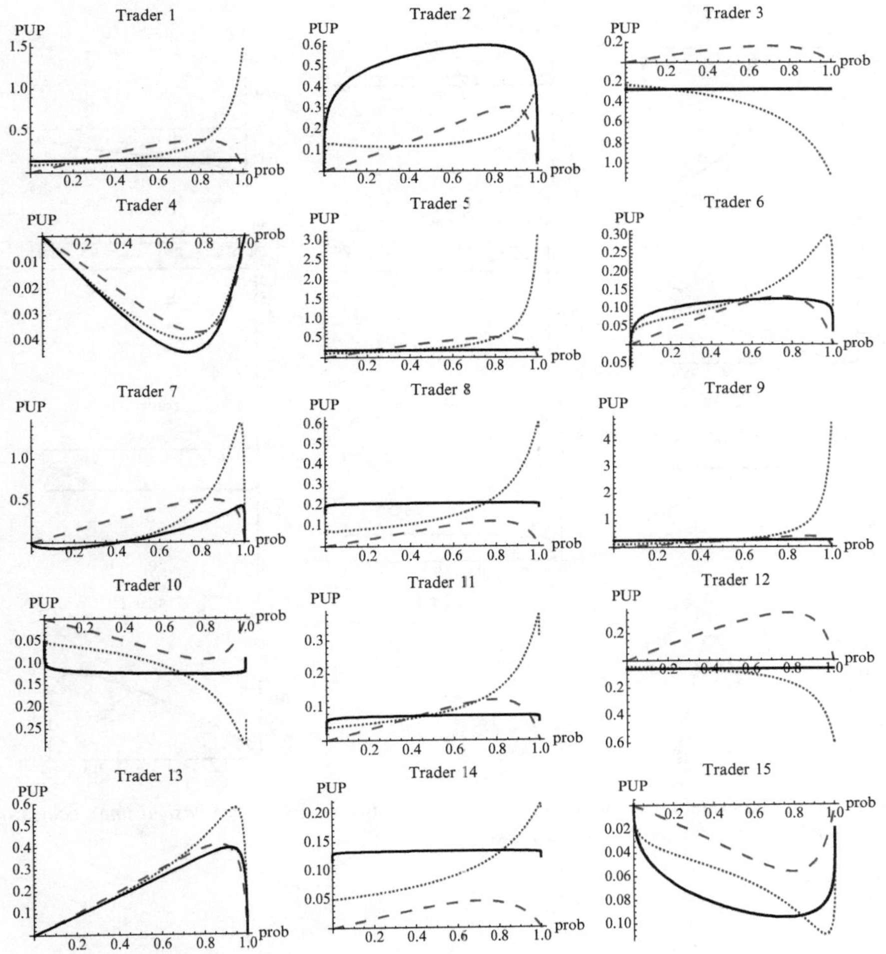

Fig. 8.8 Proportional uncertainty premiums in gain domain – EU (*large dashed line*), standard (*tiny dashed line*), and behavioral (*dark line*)

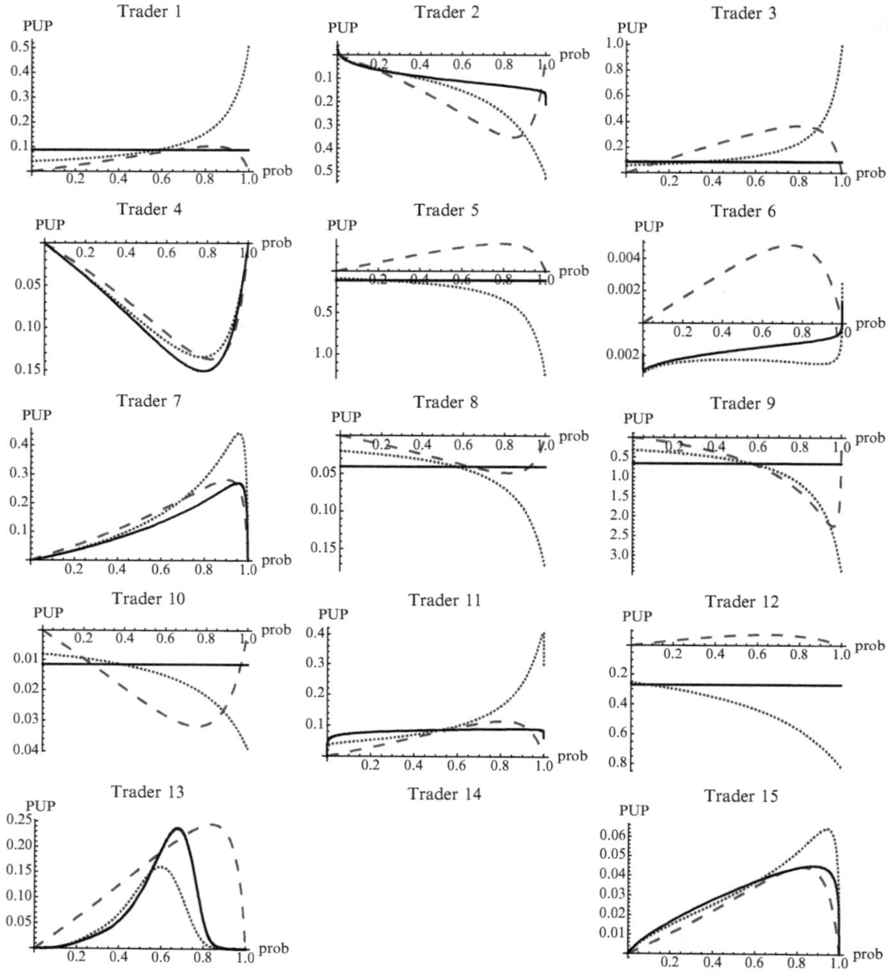

Fig. 8.9 Proportional uncertainty premiums in loss domain – EU (*large dashed line*), standard (*tiny dashed line*), and behavioral (*dark line*)

8.14 Appendix 7

Figures 8.10 and 8.11

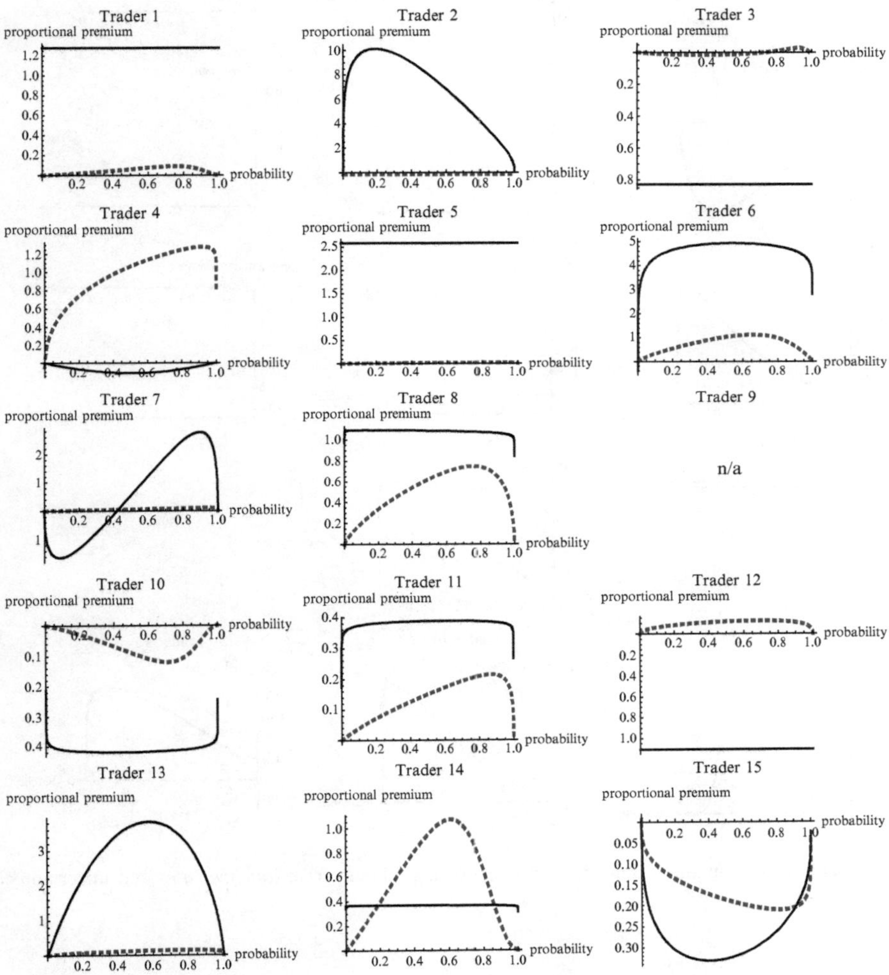

Fig. 8.10 Gain domain – Behavioral proportional premium: risk (*dashed line*) and uncertainty (*dark line*)

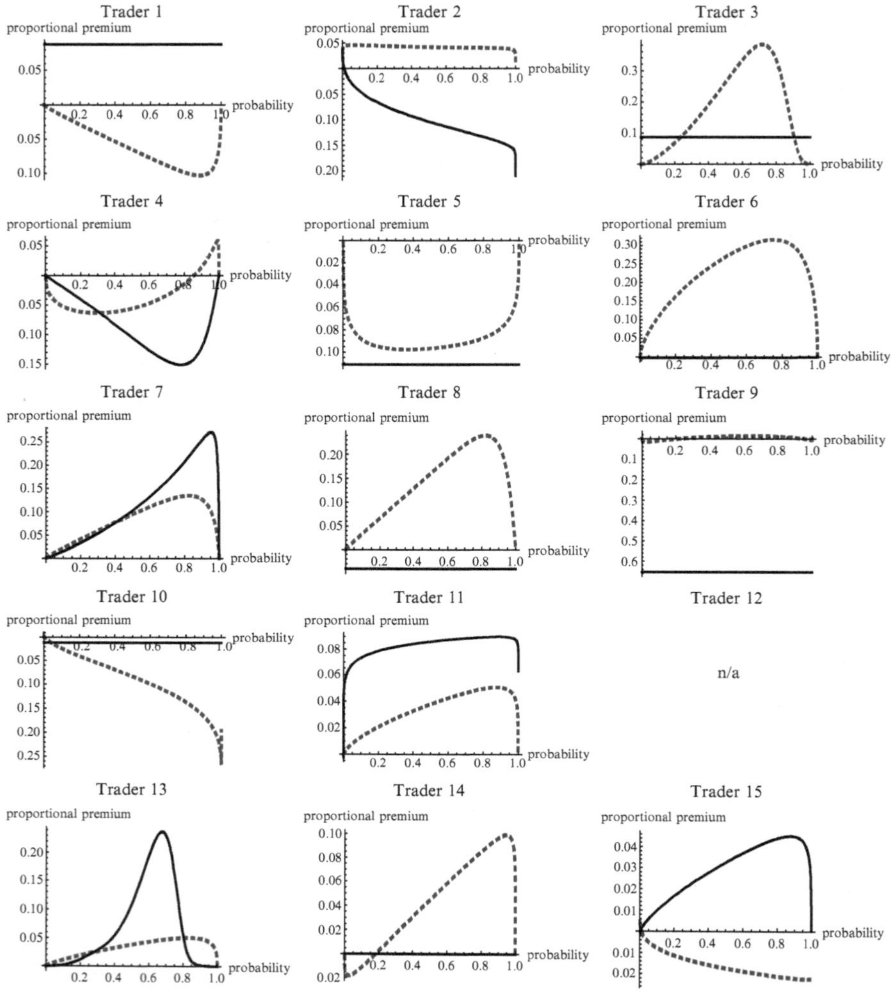

Fig. 8.11 Loss domain – Behavioral proportional premium: risk (*dashed line*) and uncertainty (*dark line*)

References

Abdellaoui, M. 2000. Parameter-free elicitation of utility and probability weighting functions. *Management Science* 46: 1497–1512.

Abdellaoui, M., F. Vossmann, and M. Weber. 2005. Choice-based elicitation and decomposition of decision weights for gains and losses under uncertainty. *Management Science* 51: 1384–1399.

Barberis, N., and R. Thaler. 2003. A survey of behavioral finance. In *Handbook of the economics of finance*, ed. G.M. Constantinides, M. Harris, and R.M. Stulz. North-Holland: Elsevier Science.

Berkelaar, A.B., R. Kouwenberg, and T. Post. 2004. Optimal portfolio choice under loss aversion. *The Review of Economics and Statistics* 86: 973–987.

Blavatskyy, P., and G. Pogrebna. 2005. Myopic loss aversion revisited: the effect of probability distortions in choice under risk, Working Paper 249. Institute for Empirical Research in Economics, University of Zurich.

Bronstein, A.M. 2008. *My word is my bond: Voices from inside the Chicago Board of Trade*. Hoboken: Wiley.

Busenitz, L.W. 1999. Entrepreneurial risk and strategic decision making: It's a matter of perspective. *The Journal of Applied Behavioral Science* 35: 325–340.

Busenitz, L.W., and J.D. Arthurs. 2007. Cognition and capabilities in entrepreneurial ventures. In *The psychology of entrepreneurship*, ed. J.R. Baum, M. Frese, and R.A. Baron, 131–150. Mahwah: Lawrence Erlbaum.

Davidsson, P. 2007. Method challenges and opportunities in the psychological study of entrepreneurship. In *The psychology of entrepreneurship*, ed. J.R. Baum, M. Frese, and R.A. Baron, 287–323. Mahwah: Lawrence Erlbaum.

Davies, G.B., and S.E. Satchell. 2005. Continuous cumulative prospect theory and individual asset allocation, Working Paper, University of Cambridge.

Davies, G.B., and S.E. Satchell. 2007. The behavioural components of risk aversion. *Journal of Mathematical Psychology* 51: 1–13.

De Bondt, W.F.M., and R.H. Thaler. 1995. Financial decision-making in markets and firms: A behavioral perspective. In *Finance handbooks in operations research and management science, Vol. 9*, ed. R. Jarrow, V. Malsimovic, and W.T. Ziemba, 385–410. North Holland: Elsevier Science B.V.

Fehr, E., and J. Tyran. 2005. Individual irrationality and aggregate outcomes, Working Paper 252. Institute for Empirical Research in Economics, University of Zurich.

Fox, C.R., B.A. Rogers, and A. Tversky. 1996. Options traders exhibit subadditive decision weights. *Journal of Risk and Uncertainty* 13: 5–17.

Hershey, J.C., H.C. Kunreuther, and P.J.H. Schoemaker. 1982. Sources of bias in assessment procedures for utility functions. *Management Science* 28: 936–954.

Hilton, R.W. 1988. Risk attitude under two alternative theories of choice under risk. *Journal of Economic Behavior and Organization* 9: 119–136.

Hirshleifer, D. 2001. Investor psychology and asset pricing. *The Journal of Finance* 56: 1533–1597.

Hwang S., and S.E. Satchell. 2005. The magnitude of loss aversion parameters in financial markets, Working Paper, University of Cambridge.

Kahneman, D., and A. Tversky. 1979. Prospect theory: An analysis of decision under risk. *Econometrica* 47: 263–291.

Kliger, D., and O. Levy. 2010. Overconfident investors and probability misjudgements. *The Journal of Socio-Economics* 39: 24–29.

Langer, T., and M. Weber. 2005. Myopic prospect theory vs. myopic loss aversion: How general is the phenomenon? *Journal of Economic Behavior & Organization* 56: 25–38.

Levy, H., and M. Levy. 2002. Arrow-Pratt risk aversion risk premium and decision weights, *The Journal of Risk and Uncertainty* 25: 265–290.

Mattos, F.L., P. Garcia, and J.M.E. Pennings. 2008. Probability weighting and loss aversion in futures hedging. *The Journal of Financial Markets* 11: 433–452.

Miner, J.B., and N.S. Raju. 2004. Risk propensity differences between managers and entrepreneurs and between low- and high-growth entrepreneurs: a reply in a more conservative vein. *The Journal of Applied Psychology* 89: 3–13.

Palich, L.E., and D.R. Bagby. 1995. Using cognitive theory to explain entrepreneurial risk-taking: Challenging conventional wisdom. *Journal of Business Venturing* 10: 425–438.

Prelec, D. 1998. The probability weighting function. *Econometrica* 66: 497–527.

Schoemaker, P.J.H. 1982. The expected utility model: Its variants purposes, evidence, and limitations. *Journal of Economic Literature* 20: 529–563.
Starmer, C. 2000. Developments in non-expected utility theory: The hunt for a descriptive theory of choice under risk. *Journal of Economic Literature* 38: 332–382.
Stewart, W.H., and P.L. Roth. 2001. Risk propensity differences between entrepreneurs and managers: a meta-analytic review. *The Journal of Applied Psychology* 86: 145–153.
Stewart, W.H., and P.L. Roth. 2004. Data quality affects meta-analytic conclusions: A response to Miner and Raju (2004) concerning entrepreneurial risk propensity. *The Journal of Applied Psychology* 89: 14–21.
Tversky, A., and C.R. Fox. 1995. Weighting risk and uncertainty. *Psychological Review* 102: 269–283.
Tversky, A., and D. Kahneman. 1992. Advances in prospect theory: Cumulative representation of uncertainty. *Journal of Risk and Uncertainty* 5: 297–323.
Wakker, P., and D. Deneffe. 1996. Eliciting von Neumann-Morgenstern utilities when probabilities are distorted or unknown. *Management Science* 42: 1131–1150.
Zaloom, C. 2004. The Productive life of risk. *Cultural Anthropology* 19: 365–391.

Chapter 9
Insights into the Psychological Profiles of Entrepreneurs

Hersh Shefrin

Abstract Entrepreneurs derive lower risk-adjusted returns than non-entrepreneurs, but are compensated through non-pecuniary benefits. This chapter reports on findings from survey evidence. The main findings are as follows: A key non-pecuniary benefit to entrepreneurs is achieving greater control over their working environment. Doing so leads entrepreneurs to report achieving higher affect and well-being than non-entrepreneurs. Entrepreneurs report that they are more skilled socially than non-entrepreneurs. This might provide a partial explanation for why entrepreneurs have a higher marriage rate and larger families than non-entrepreneurs. Entrepreneurs exhibit greater dispositional optimism than non-entrepreneurs. However, in the study sample, the difference is not statistically significant. In terms of preference for lottery-like outcomes, entrepreneurs find prospects offering high returns with low probability attractive, but regard control of their environment as more important than the preference for positive skewness.

9.1 Introduction

On the surface, entrepreneurs appear to make suboptimal financial choices. Hamilton (2000) establishes that entrepreneurs accept lower median life-time earnings than similarly skilled wage-earners. Moskowitz and Vissing-Jorgensen (2002) establish that entrepreneurs earn low risk-adjusted returns.[1] Moreover, entrepreneurs appear to hold poorly diversified portfolios. Instead they concentrate their wealth in their own private business: See Gentry and Hubbard (2001), Moskowitz and Vissing-Jorgensen (2002), and Heaton and Lucas (2000). In light of the evidence,

[1] The average return to all private equity is actually similar to that of the public market equity index. However, the risk is higher. Survival rates of private firms are only around 34% over the first 10 years of the firm's life.

H. Shefrin (✉)
Santa Clara University, Santa Clara, CA, USA
e-mail: hshefrin@scu.edu

R. Yazdipour, *Advances in Entrepreneurial Finance: With Applications from Behavioral Finance and Economics*, DOI 10.1007/978-1-4419-7527-0_9,

Bitler et al. (2004) investigate the structuring of incentives for entrepreneurs and ask why people would choose to become entrepreneurs.

Puri and Robinson (2008) provide some insight into why people would choose to become entrepreneurs. They ask whether entrepreneurs are risk-takers. They suggest that entrepreneurs might derive substantial non-pecuniary benefits from self-employment. They hypothesize that entrepreneurs might be optimistic about their entrepreneurial prospects.

Puri and Robinson's analysis of the data in the *Survey of Consumer Finances* (SCF) leads them to a series of conclusions. First, they find that entrepreneurs are more risk-loving and optimistic than the rest of the population. Second, these traits are separable in that the correlation between risk tolerance and optimism is low. Third, entrepreneurs tend to have long planning horizons, good health practices, and strong family ties. In respect to planning, entrepreneurs are almost three times more likely to indicate that they never intend to retire. Moreover, people who do not plan to retire work about 3% longer per week.

Consider how the configuration of entrepreneurs' characteristics relates to the suboptimality of the returns, which they earn. Unless entrepreneurs are actually risk-seeking, being more risk-loving than the general population does not explain why entrepreneurs earn suboptimal risk-adjusted returns.

Notably, optimism might provide part of the explanation. Puri and Robinson focus on dispositional optimism as opposed to unrealistic optimism. They point out that the psychology literature distinguishes between dispositional optimism and optimistic bias. The former views optimism as a positive personality trait associated with positive generalized expectations of the future: See Scheier and Carver (1985). The latter views optimism as a negative, domain-specific bias in expectations: See Weinstein (1980).

It is straightforward to see how optimistic bias can lead to inferior returns. Of course, dispositional optimism can also involve optimistic bias, and therefore produce inferior returns as well. This is not to say that the net impact of dispositional optimism is negative. In this regard, Bitler et al. (2004) find that effort increases firm performance.

In their analysis, Puri and Robinson (2008) focus on dispositional optimism. They do not measure optimism bias directly, but infer it from self-reported estimates of own life expectancy. This chapter extends their analysis by surveying entrepreneurs for dispositional optimism and comparing their responses to non-entrepreneurs.

Puri and Robinson (2009) is a retitled, revised version of their 2008 paper, discussing the combined effects of dispositional optimism, risk tolerance, and non-pecuniary benefits. While the combination of risk-seeking choices and optimism possibly explains why entrepreneurs earn low risk-adjusted return, to my mind it seems far more plausible that non-pecuniary benefits lie at the heart of the issue. After all, entrepreneurs work longer hours and plan to retire later than their non-entrepreneur counterparts. What might those non-pecuniary benefits be?

I suggest that a major non-pecuniary benefit for entrepreneurs is the exercise of control over their working environment, the control that derives from starting a new business and managing that business. In this regard, I hypothesize that the desire for control is a psychological need, which might be higher among entrepreneurs than non-entrepreneurs.

Puri and Robinson (2008) document that relative to non-entrepreneurs, entrepreneurs are more likely to be married and have larger families. See also Wadhwa et al. (2009). This suggests that entrepreneurs might be more socially focused than others. I hypothesize that this is the case. In particular, I test whether entrepreneurs are less anxious in social settings than non-entrepreneurs, and more aware of social cues and their own behavior.

If entrepreneurs derive significant non-pecuniary benefits from entrepreneurial activity, then it seems plausible that entrepreneurs would report being happier than their non-entrepreneurial counterparts. I test whether this is the case using two instruments, one pertaining to well-being (life satisfaction) and the other pertaining to degree of affect (positive, neutral, or negative).

The major findings of this study are as follows: Entrepreneurs exhibit more dispositional optimism than their non-entrepreneurial counterparts, although in my small sample, the difference is not statistically significant at the 95% confidence level. The most significant difference between entrepreneurs and non-entrepreneurs is the desire for control: Entrepreneurs place much more emphasis on control. Entrepreneurs appear to be more comfortable in social situations, and feel that they are more sensitive to social cues. They also report being more positive and more satisfied with their lives. Finally, entrepreneurs report that they have a preference for positively skewed returns. Taken together, these findings suggest that the non-pecuniary benefits that entrepreneurs experience are substantial.

9.2 Analysis

9.2.1 Data

The data for this study involve responses to a series of psychological surveys. The surveys relate to instruments for measuring dispositional optimism (Scheier 1985), desirability of control (Burger and Cooper, 1979), social anxiousness (Leary, 1983), self-monitoring behavior (Snyder 1974; Lennox and Wolfe 1984), life satisfaction (Diener et al. 1985), and affect (Watson and Clark 1988).

The surveys were administered to three different groups: (1) a group of entrepreneurs; (2) a group of MBA students, almost all of whom are working professionals who take evening classes; and (3) a group of undergraduate business students. The surveys were administered in the autumn of 2008 and winter of 2009. The group of entrepreneurs is affiliated to the Center for Innovation and Entrepreneurship at Santa Clara University. The students were enrolled in regular academic courses at Santa Clara University.

The demographic characteristics of the groups differed in respect to age and gender. The number of respondents who identified themselves as entrepreneurs was 53. Of these, 6 were female. The average age of the entrepreneurs was 36.9, with the standard deviation being 12.9. In contrast, the number of MBA students was 45, of which 27 were female. The average age of the MBA students was 32.3, and the standard deviation was 5.7. The number of undergraduate students was 16, of which 3 were female. The average age of the undergraduate students was 21.7.[2]

9.2.2 *Desire for Control*

Puri and Robinson (2008) classify respondents to the SCF as entrepreneurs if they own some or all of at least one privately owned business, and are full-time self-employed. It seems plausible to suggest that people who fit this description exert more control over their working environment than others, and that part of the appeal of being an entrepreneur is achieving this degree of control. Put somewhat differently, entrepreneurs possess a strong need for control, which leads them to choose a career in which they seek to meet that need.

Burger and Cooper (1979) introduce a survey instrument (DC) which is designed to measure the desirability of control. The survey instrument consists of twenty questions. Two representative questions are: "I prefer a job where I have a lot of control over what I do and when I do it," and "I would prefer to be a leader than a follower." The range of possible responses varies from 1 to 7 where 1 means "The statement does not apply to me at all," and 7 means "The statement always applies to me." For 15 of the questions, 7 is associated with the strongest desire for control, while for 5 of the questions, 1 is associated with the strongest desire for control. For sake of consistency, the score for each of the 5 questions is replaced by 8-scores.

In terms of results, the average DC score per question is 5.4 for entrepreneurs and 4.6 for students. To interpret these results, note that 4 means "I am unsure about whether or not the statement applies to me or it applies to me about half the time," 5 means "The statement applies more often than not," and 6 means "The statement usually applies to me." The difference between entrepreneurs and students is statistically significant (t statistic = 4.5). Notably, the above result is not driven by gender. For students as a whole, the desire for control is very similar for males (4.7) as for females (4.5). Hence, the difference points to an entrepreneur effect rather than a gender effect.

The results suggest that desire for control is a major non-pecuniary benefit associated with being an entrepreneur, a result consistent with the theory of motivation developed by Deci and Ryan (1985) and articulated by Pink (2009).

9.2.3 *Social Anxiousness and Self-Monitoring*

Consider psychological attributes that relate to the finding that entrepreneurs marry at a higher rate than non-entrepreneurs and have more children. This finding suggests

[2] Although the results described below feature demographic effects, meaning that gender and age are germane, demographic effects do not subsume the entrepreneurial effect.

that entrepreneurs like people. This section considers two psychological instruments that relate to interpersonal relationships. The first stems from the work of Leary (1983), who studied social anxiousness, the degree to which people are uncomfortable in social situations. The second relates to self-monitoring, a concept studied by Snyder (1974) and Lennox and Wolfe (1984).

The survey instrument used to study social anxiousness (SA) features 15 questions. Two of the questions are: "I often feel nervous even in casual get-togethers," and "I get nervous when I speak to someone in a position of authority." Responses are on a 5-point scale where 1 means "Not at all characteristic," and 5 means "Extremely characteristic."

A lower SA score signals less social anxiety. Entrepreneurs have a mean SA score of 2.0, whereas students' mean SA score is 2.9. A score of 2 means "Slightly characteristic" and a score of 3 means "Moderately characteristic." The difference between 2.0 and 2.9 is statistically significant (t-statistic = −3.5).

Self-monitoring involves being sensitive to social cues, and being able to adapt to those cues. The self-monitoring survey instrument is SM. It features questions such as the following: "I am often able to read people's true emotions correctly through their eyes." "In social situations, I have the ability to alter my behavior if I feel something else is called for." The range of possible responses comprises a 6-point scale from "Always false" to "Always true."

The mean score for entrepreneurs is 4.4 and for non-entrepreneurs is 3.9. Here 3 means "Somewhat false, but with exception," 4 means "Somewhat true, but with exception," and 5 means "Generally true." The difference between 4.4 and 3.9 is statistically significant (t-statistic = 2.4).

9.2.4 *Affect and Well-Being*

Are entrepreneurs happier than non-entrepreneurs? What makes this question especially interesting is that entrepreneurs work more than non-entrepreneurs and earn lower risk-adjusted returns on their investments. To investigate the question, I use survey instruments based on the work of Watson and Clark (1988), who study affect, and Diener et al. (1985), who study life satisfaction or well-being. I refer to the associated instruments as AF and WB, respectively.

The affect survey asks respondents to indicate how frequently they experience a variety of emotional states such as "interested," "distressed," and "excited." Responses are on a 5-point scale, in which 1 means "very slightly or not at all," and 5 means "extremely." Some states connote negative affect and some connote positive affect. An AF score of zero connotes neutral overall affect. The mean AF-score for entrepreneurs was 1.2 and the mean AF-score for students was 0.8. The difference is statistically significant (t-statistic = 2.5).

The life satisfaction survey asks respondents 25 true/false questions such as "I always seem to have something pleasant to look forward to," and "Often I get irritated at little annoyances." Of the 25 questions, 11 relate to feelings of positive life satisfaction and 14 to negative feelings. Relative to an adjusted neutral score of 0, the mean WB-score for entrepreneurs was −1.0 and for students was −1.2. Entrepreneurs score higher on the WB-survey. However, both groups' mean scores are negative responses, and the difference is not statistically significant (t-statistic = 1.7).[3]

Overall, the evidence indicates that entrepreneurs are happier than non-entrepreneurs.

9.2.5 *Optimism*

Using their life expectancy proxy for optimism, Puri and Robinson find that entrepreneurs exhibit more dispositional optimism than non-entrepreneurs. I augment their analysis by using an instrument to measure dispositional optimism: See Scheier (1985).

The optimism instrument (OP) consists of eight questions whose responses fall on a five-point scale where 1 means "strongly disagree" and 5 means "strongly agree." Two of the questions are: "I'm always optimistic about my future," and "I hardly ever expect things to go my way."

Adjusting for signs, the mean OP-score for entrepreneurs was 3.5 and for students it was 3.2. Notably, both groups feature OP-scores between Neutral and Agree, and are therefore optimistic. Although entrepreneurs appear to be more optimistic than students, the difference in scores is not statistically significant (t-statistic = 1.5). However, the results are quite similar to the larger sample described in Puri and Robinson (2008) where the differences are statistically significant.

9.2.6 *Demographics and Correlations*

The data reveal some interesting patterns about demographics and correlations. Although only 11.5% of the entrepreneur sample is female, the mean responses for males and females are similar on almost all instruments. To the extent that there are differences, females are more optimistic than males by 0.3, exhibit less social anxiousness by 0.2, and report higher social monitoring by 0.4.

The differences are interesting, but there are too few female entrepreneurs in the sample to draw meaningful conclusions from these numbers alone. Therefore, consider what information can be gleaned from the student responses. For students, the differences between male responses and female responses are small for all instruments. The major differences are across groups. Entrepreneurs are different from students. MBA students are different from undergraduate students. For every instrument, mean undergraduate responses lie between the responses for entrepreneurs and the responses for MBA students.

[3] Interestingly, the correlation between AF and WB scores is above 50% for both groups, a point to which I return below.

Table 9.1 Correlation matrices for both entrepreneurs and students

Correlation matrix for entrepreneurs						
	SM	DC	SA	AF	WB	OP
SM	100.0%					
DC	30.8%	100.0%				
SA	−23.0%	−40.9%	100.0%			
AF	23.4%	44.5%	−69.4%	100.0%		
WB	1.3%	25.4%	−41.9%	58.3%	100.0%	
OP	4.9%	25.4%	−37.8%	47.5%	44.7%	100.0%
Correlation matrix for students						
	SM	DC	SA	AF	WB	OP
SM	100.0%					
DC	21.1%	100.0%				
SA	−42.5%	−48.0%	100.0%			
AF	31.4%	56.8%	−73.5%	100.0%		
WB	31.5%	15.9%	−55.7%	53.2%	100.0%	
OP	26.8%	27.5%	−39.9%	42.8%	52.4%	100.0%

Table 9.1 below displays the correlation matrices for both entrepreneurs and students. The correlations are markedly similar across the two groups.

The correlation between affect and well-being is high enough to suggest that the two reinforce each other in respect to measuring happiness. Likewise, self-monitoring and social anxiety are negatively correlated, suggesting that these two reinforce each other as measures of social skills. Notably, optimism and desire for control are positively correlated, but the relationship is weak. Consistent with the idea that desire for control provides major non-pecuniary benefits to entrepreneurs, the correlation between DC and affect (AF) is positive and reasonably strong. Notably, desire for control is negatively associated with social anxiousness (SA), suggesting that those who are high in the desire for control are comfortable in social settings. Finding that the correlation ran the other way would be worrisome with regard to productivity.

9.2.7 *Preferences*

Puri and Robinson find that entrepreneurs are more risk-loving and optimistic than the rest of the population, although the correlation between risk tolerance and optimism is low. The analysis in this chapter suggests that desire for control is a major motivator for why people choose to be entrepreneurs, stronger than risk attitude and optimism.

In terms of risk, it is also possible that people choose to be entrepreneurs because they have a preference for lottery-type returns. To test for this possibility, I ran a supplementary survey,[4] based on the concepts in SP/A theory, which posed the following two questions to entrepreneurs:

[4] The supplementary survey is based on responses from 40 people who classify themselves as entrepreneurs. The total number of responses was 48.

1. On a scale of 1–7 where 1 is unimportant and 7 is extremely important, how important to you is upside potential as a reason being an entrepreneur?
2. On a scale of 1–7 where 1 is unimportant and 7 is extremely important, how important to you is being in control of your work world as a reason being an entrepreneur?

The mean response to the first question was 5.8 and to the second was 6.3. Clearly, both factors are important. However, between the two, control is more important.

The supplementary survey also posed qualitative questions designed to elicit features emphasized by a SP/A theory, a psychologically based framework for understanding the impact on risky choice from emotions such as fear, and hope, and the achievement of specific aspirational goals.

The responses indicate that entrepreneurs feel that fear is a weak emotion for them, hope is a moderately strong emotion, and aspirational goals are strong. Many indicate that they would accept lottery-type returns if the downside is small, but are more reluctant if the downside is not small, of if doing so significantly diminishes the probability of achieving their specific aspirations.

9.3 Conclusion

Entrepreneurs derive lower risk-adjusted returns than non-entrepreneurs, but are compensated through non-pecuniary benefits. The most important benefit is achieving greater control over their working environment. Doing so leads entrepreneurs to report achieving higher affect and well-being than non-entrepreneurs. Entrepreneurs report that they are more skilled socially than non-entrepreneurs. This might provide a partial explanation for why entrepreneurs have a higher marriage rate and larger families than non-entrepreneurs. Finally, entrepreneurs exhibit greater dispositional optimism than non-entrepreneurs. However, in my small sample, the difference is not statistically significant.[5]

Acknowledgments I thank my colleagues Jerry Burger and David Caldwell for their help with the psychological surveys used in this work. I thank Kevin Holmes, Center for Innovation and Entrepreneurship at Santa Clara University for his help in locating entrepreneurs willing to complete the survey, and for his assistance in running the survey. Financial support for this research comes from a Santa Clara University Leavey Grant.

References

Bitler, M., T. Moskowitz, and A. Vissing-Jorgensen. 2004. Testing agency theory with entrepreneur effort and wealth. *Journal of Finance* 60: 539–576.

Burger, J., and H. Cooper. 1979. The desirability of control. *Motivation and Emotion* 3(4): 381–393.

[5] Among the CIE respondents, 7% classify themselves as non-entrepreneurs. On every psychological dimension analyzed, the differences between entrepreneurs and these non-entreprenerus strongly conform to the general pattern.

Deci, Edward L., and Richard M. Ryan. 1985. *Intrinsic Motivation and Self-Determination in Human Behavior*. NY: Plenum Pres

Diener, E., R. Emmons, R. Larsen, and S. Griffin. 1985. The satisfaction with life scale. *Journal of Personality Assessment* 49(1): 71–75.

Gentry, W., and G. Hubbard. 2001. *Entrepreneurship and household saving, NBER Working Paper No. 7894*. Cambridge: NBER.

Hamilton, B. 2000. Does entrepreneurship pay? An empirical analysis of the returns to self-employment. *Journal of Political Economy* 108: 604–631.

Heaton, J., and D. Lucas. 2000. Asset pricing and portfolio choice: The importance of entrepreneurial risk. *Journal of Finance* 55: 1163–1198.

Leary, M. 1983. Social anxiousness: The constuct and its measurement. *Journal of Personality Assessment* 47(1): 66–75.

Lennox, R.D., and R.N. Wolfe. 1984. Revision of the self-monitoring scale. *Journal of Personality and Social Psychology* 46(6): 1349–1364.

Moskowitz, T., and A. Vissing-Jorgensen. 2002. The returns to entrepreneurial investment: A private equity premium puzzle? *The American Economic Review* 92: 745–778.

Pink, D. 2009. *Drive: The Surprising Truth About What Motivates Us*. New York, NY: Penguin Group.

Puri, M., and D.T. Robinson. 2008. *Who are entrepreneurs and why do they behave that way? Working Paper*. Durhum: Duke University.

Puri, M., and D.T. Robinson. 2009. *"The Economic Psychology of Entrepreneurship and Family Business," Working Paper*. Duke University.

Scheier, M. 1985. Optimism, coping, and health: Assessment and implications of generalized outcome expectancies. *Health Psychology* 4(3): 219–247.

Scheier, M.F., and C.S. Carver. 1985. Optimism, coping and health: Assessment and implications of generalized outcome expectancies. *Health Psychology* 4: 219–247.

Snyder, M. 1974. Self-monitoring of expressive behavior. *Journal of Personality and Social Psychology* 30(4): 526–537.

Wadhwa, V., R. Aggarwal, K. Holly, and A. Salkever. 2009. *The anatomy of an entrepreneur: Family background and motivation*. Kansas City: Ewing Marion Kauffman Foundation of Entrepreneurship.

Watson, D., and L.A. Clark. 1988. Development and validation of brief measures of positive and negative affect: The PANAS scales. *Journal of Personality and Social Psychology* 54(6): 1063–1070.

Weinstein, N. 1980. Unrealistic optimism about future life events. *Journal of Personality and Social Psychology* 39: 806–820.

Part III
Issues in Growth and Beyond

Chapter 10
Firm Failure Prediction Models: A Critique and a Review of Recent Developments

Richard L. Constand and Rassoul Yazdipour

Abstract This chapter first argues that the literature on financial distress and failure prediction has totally ignored the *cause* of failure – managers and owner-managers as decision makers – and instead has almost exclusively focused on the *effect* of failure, the financial data. The chapter then provides a review of the current state of the failure prediction literature. Recent studies that focus on small and medium-sized enterprises (SMEs) are covered next. We arrive at the same conclusion that after 35 years of academic inquiry into bankruptcy prediction, and despite all the sophisticated models and methodologies used in studies of the effects of firm failure, there is "no academic consensus as to the most useful method for predicting corporate bankruptcy." At the end, the chapter discusses how psychological phenomena and principles, also known as heuristics or mental shortcuts, might be utilized in building more powerful success/failure prediction models.

10.1 Introduction

If we consider that all firms, large or small, are made up of two crucial elements One, the human element, as represented by the management that makes decisions, and the other, the commerce element, where these decisions are implemented and business is conducted, then it becomes clear that almost all existing research on financial distress or business failure has focused on the commerce side of the firm. Existing research has almost completely ignored the most crucial side of the process: management's decision-making process (the cause side).[1] In fact, the way that many researchers have approached the study of business failure can be compared with the practice by a group of physicians who focus on the symptoms

[1] Studies conducted by scholars like Kahneman and Lovallo (1993), Camerer and Lovallo (1999), and Wu and Knott (2005) are among the few exceptions in this respect; as will be further discussed in this chapter.

R.L. Constand (✉)
California State University, Fresno, CA, USA
rconstand@uwf.edu

R. Yazdipour, *Advances in Entrepreneurial Finance: With Applications from Behavioral Finance and Economics*, DOI 10.1007/978-1-4419-7527-0_10,

of a given disease (the effects) while forgetting to identify the possible sources of the disease (the causes) that would provide information that can help society prevent similar cases from happening in the future.

It could be argued that a one-sided approach to the study of corporate failure that focuses only on the effects might, to some extent, make sense for large publicly traded companies since those firms are controlled by well-established business systems and processes that reduce the importance of a single person's behaviors and actions (the cause side). In addition to the diverse range of expertise available within the modern corporation, top executives at Fortune 1,000 companies can easily tap into other sophisticated talent pools for advice on key decisions by using external consultants and members of the Board of Directors, a group referred to as the "Outside View" in the behavioral finance literature.[2] Finally, the extent of easily available computerized financial information about public firms has made it a relatively easy process for researchers to access and study this data using sophisticated statistical tools ranging from MDA and LOGIT and PROBIT models to even more sophisticated artificial intelligence (AI) and expert systems (ES) approaches. By making the simplifying assumption that management in a public corporation acts to maximize shareholders' wealth, coupled with the market efficiency assumption, it is easy for researchers to focus on the effects of the management process (the financial distress), as revealed by the financial data, rather than to try to focus on the management's decision-making process that caused the financial problems in the first place.[3] Because of such unrealistic assumptions, most research has used the approaches mentioned above to attempt to make predictions about the success or failure of given publicly traded companies.[4] Such a method becomes even questionable when attempts are made by some researchers to follow the same methodology in cases of non–publicly traded firms and even recent IPO firms.

While this chapter does provide an up-to-date review of the mainstream empirical research into the financial effects associated with distress and failure, it also argues that in the future, researchers cannot ignore the human/managerial side of the equation for any company, large or small! It is obviously wrong to do so for start-ups, early-stage ventures, and even some pre-IPO companies because the majority of such companies rely heavily on individuals for both operational and strategic decisions. But in the wake of recent financial crises, it is also becoming more important to

---

[2] Theoretically, the significance of a board of directors lies in the fact that such a body can "debias" many of the top management's cognitive biases that could lead to very expensive errors in judgment, including errors leading to failure and bankruptcy. This is also an example regarding the forgotten human/managerial side in failure studies that we intend to emphasize in this chapter.

[3] We are not denying the possible roles that macro elements such as economic conditions and regulatory factors can play in a given company's failure. However, we believe our "two element-model" contains the factors that are among the most relevant for explaining why firms develop financial distress or fail.

[4] It should be noted that despite all the sophisticated models and methodologies used in studies of the effects of firm failure, it is not surprising that a comprehensive review of the related literature concludes that after 35 years of academic research into bankruptcy prediction, there is "no academic consensus as to the most useful method for predicting corporate bankruptcy." See Aziz and Dar (2006), p. 26.

realize that managerial attitudes toward risk and return and related managerial decisions in even the largest public firms can endanger the very existence of those firms. Fortunately, new theoretical and empirical breakthroughs in the field of cognitive psychology might help us to develop effective and realistic models to help predict successes or failures for not only the small and entrepreneurial firms, but also for large publicly traded corporations. Such approaches, especially if coupled with what we have already learned about failure prediction, have the potential of further enabling us to gain better insights regarding problem areas that might cause financial distress and failure later on. The present chapter first provides a review of the current state of the failure prediction literature. It then discusses the recent failure studies that focus on small and medium-sized enterprises (SMEs). Finally, the chapter discusses how psychological phenomena and principles, also known as heuristics or mental shortcuts, might be utilized in building more powerful success/failure prediction models.

10.2 Classical Statistical Models

Ever since the nineteenth century, analysts have calculated financial ratios of public and private firms, compared those ratios to industry benchmarks, and used the results of their analysis to make value judgments about the viability and future prospects of those firms. With the advent of accessible computing power and the development of statistical tools for analyzing financial data in the latter half of the twentieth century, both academic researchers and financial analysts have been developing and improving methods to analyze financial ratios and to use those ratios to forecast future firm performance.

This section focuses on the use of financial data as inputs for various classical statistical methods that are used to predict the possibility of financial distress or failure. Beaver (1966) is often cited as being the first to use a formal statistical approach applied to financial ratios for the purpose of predicting firm failure. But he, himself, cites earlier studies published in 1932, 1935, and 1942 that examine financial ratios in a systematic way.[5] Beaver builds on these earlier studies and creates a matched pair sample of 79 failed firms and 79 non–failed firms where matching is based on industry affiliation and asset size. The data come from Moody's Industrial Manual and covers 5 years. Beaver examines the ability of 30 financial ratios to discriminate between failed and non–failed firms and selects six ratios that have the best discriminating ability. The six ratios are cash flow to total debt, net income to total assets, total debt to total assets, working capital to total assets, current assets to current liabilities and something called the "no-credit interval," which is

---

[5]Beaver cites Fitzpatrick (1932), Winakor and Smith (1935), and Merwin (1942) . These studies were unavailable for review for this article but Beaver describes the Fitzpatrick and Merwin studies as comparisons of mean ratios from failed and non-failed firms and the Winakor and Smith study as an analysis of ratio trends over 10 years prior to failure.

defined as the ratio of "defensive assets minus current liabilities to fund expenditures for operations."[6] The approach Beaver employs is a univariate analysis where each ratio's relationship to failure is examined individually. At the end of his paper, Beaver suggests that a multivariate approach might provide a better predictive model than the approach he uses.

10.2.1 Multiple Discriminant Analysis

Two years after Beaver's work, Altman (1968) published the first empirical study that applied a multivariate approach to predicting firm failure using a dataset covering 66 firms (33 failed and 33 non–failed firms) with data constructed from Moody's Industrial Manuals and published annual company reports. In that paper, Altman uses multiple discriminate analysis (MDA) to define his "Z Score" model that used his coefficient estimates and the five related ratios. Altman originally examined 22 different financial ratios and he then settled on the five ratios that had the most explanatory power. His model and estimation procedure became a standard for defining such multivariate prediction models. Altman's original Z Score model with estimated coefficients for X_1–X_4 presented in decimal format (rather than as a percentage) and X_5 presented as a turnover ratio is as follows[7]:

$$Z = 0.012X_1 + 0.014X_2 + 0.033X_3 + 0.006X_4 + 0.999X_5$$

where:

X_1 = working capital/total assets,
X_2 = retained earnings/total assets,
X_3 = earnings before interest and taxes/total assets,
X_4 = market value of equity/book value of total asset,
X_5 = sales/total assets (a turnover ratio).

The resulting *Z* score allows the classification of firms on a continuum from least likely to enter bankruptcy to most likely. In Altman (2000), the author notes that over the years, this original model is usually presented in terms in which variables X_1–X_4 are presented in percentage while X_5 is still presented as a turnover ratio and is rounded to 1.0, so the discriminant function becomes:

$$Z = 1.2X_1 + 1.4X_2 + 3.3X_3 + 0.6X_4 + 1.0X_5$$

---

[6] Beaver does not explain this calculation in any detail but the "no-credit interval" is defined as "immediate assets (current assets excluding inventory and prepaid expenses) minus current liabilities, divided by total operating expenses excluding depreciation" on p. 419 of Palepu et al. (2007)

[7] Altman discusses the history and evolution of his work with classical statistical models in Altman (2000), a working paper, and provides discussions of the links between these ratios and the risk of bankruptcy.

He explains that the lower the calculated *Z* score, the higher is the risk of bankruptcy with a *Z* score of between 1.81 and 2.675 as being defined as a "zone of ignorance" where the model cannot discriminate between the two classes of firms.

Altman tested his original model's ability to correctly categorize firms destined for bankruptcy for 1–5 years before the event and used a hold-out sample for testing the ability of the model to predict out of sample results. In the years following his original work, Altman refined his original model and tested it over a number of different samples drawn from different time periods.[8] Altman (2000) also reports a reestimation of the model coefficients using a sample of private firms after replacing the market value of equity with the book value of equity in the X_4 variable and finds the model is only "slightly less" reliable than the original model.[9] The *Z* score model and estimated coefficients for the private firm data are as follows:

$$Z' = 0.717X_1 + 0.847X_2 + 3.107X_3 + 0.420X_4 + 0.998X_5$$

where:

X_1 = working capital/total assets,
X_2 = retained earnings/total assets,
X_3 = earnings before interest and taxes/total assets,
X_4 = book value of equity/book value of total asset,
X_5 = sales/total assets (a turnover ratio).

Altman et al. (1977) eventually developed what he refers to as a second-generation model called the Zeta® Credit Risk Model, which he argues is a significant improvement over his original model and coefficient estimation approach. Public information about this new model is limited since the newer version of his model is proprietary and only available through his consulting firm.

Altman's application of MDA to bankruptcy prediction created an empirical framework that became the standard for the majority of the empirical studies to follow.[10] It was the first application of a multivariate statistical model applied to the prediction of bankruptcy. Even today, many studies still use MDA as the chosen method of analysis in a number of different applications.

10.2.2 LOGIT Models, PROBIT Models, and Other Classical Statistical Models

The first major break from Altman's MDA-based approach in the literature is the LOGIT approach presented by Ohlson (1980). Ohlson argues that MDA's required

---

[8] See Altman (2000) for a summary of these developments and the predictive accuracy of the model using different samples.

[9] Altman (2000) notes his lack of a large private firm database prevented him from performing out of sample evaluations of this private firm model.

[10] See Altman (1993) for an extensive survey of this work.

assumptions on the distributional characteristics of the input data make the method less than optimal. The shortcomings of the MDA method identified by Ohlson include: (1) MDA assumes normally distributed predictor variables and this prevents the use of independent variables that are structured as dummy variables, (2) the variance-covariance matrices of the two groups under examination should be identical and this is not usually the case for failed and non–failed firms, and (3) MDA does not provide the probability of failure for a particular firm, it only provides a potential classification of "more or less likely to fail." Ohlson presents a conditional LOGIT model that avoids these problems associated with MDA and allows the determination of the probability of failure. His original model examines nine financial ratios, many of which are similar to those used by Altman, and focuses on the predictive ability 1 and 2 years before the event using data from COMPUSTAT. He also applies the MDA model to his data set and compares the performance of the two models. He concludes that the LOGIT approach outperforms the MDA approach without suffering from the theoretical shortcomings associated with MDA. His resulting "Y" score provides the logistic function probability of membership in the bankrupt group of firms. The Ohlson (1980) model is as follows:

$$Y = -1.3 - 0.4X_1 + 6.0X_2 - 1.4X_3 + 0.1X_4 - 2.4X_5 - 1.8X_6 + 0.3X_7 - 1.7X_8 - 0.5X_9$$

where:

X_1 = ln(total assets/GNP price level index),
X_2 = total liabilities/total assets,
X_3 = working capital/total assets,
X_4 = current liabilities/current asset,
X_5 = 1 if total liabilities > total assets or = 0 otherwise,
X_6 = net income/total assets,
X_7 = funds from operations/total assets,
X_8 = 1 if net income negative for 2 years or = 0 otherwise, and
X_9 = change in net income calculated as $(NI_t - NI_{t-1})/(I\ NI_t\ I + I\ NI_{t-1} I)$.

Ohlsonm's work was followed a few years later by Zmijewski (1984) who introduced the PROBIT model as an alternative method to use to predict bankruptcy. Zmijewski argues that previous empirical work is based on non–random samples, a process that results in biased estimations of model coefficients and the probability of bankruptcy. He explores this sampling issue in great detail and then using COMPUSTAT and CRSP data, he examines the ability of a PROBIT model to estimate the probability of bankruptcy for firms using the following model:

$$B^* = a_o + a_1\text{ROA} + a_2\text{FINL} + a_3\text{LIQ} + u$$

where:

B* = the probability of bankruptcy,
ROA = net income to total assets (return on assets),
FINL = total debt to total assets (financial leverage), and
LIQ = current assets to current liabilities (liquidity).

While LOGIT, PROBIT, and MDA models are the classical statistical models that still dominate the finance and accounting literature today, there are other statistical models that have been explored. For example, Linear Probability Models, pioneered by Meyer and Pifer (1970), focus on changes in financial ratios over time to predict bankruptcy. Cumulative sum procedures that use changes in the mean/variance characteristics of ratios, stock prices, or both through time to identify shifts in the data that are associated with approaching bankruptcy have been used.[11] While many other approaches have been explored, the three approaches discussed above have become standards.[12] These approaches all have shortcomings that have been discussed by a number of authors.[13] The one shortcoming of these classical approaches that is always overlooked, however, is that these models almost always rely on published financial data from public firms. The data from Moodys, COMPUSTAT, and/or CRSP are easily available and easily accessed with the statistical packages used to apply these classical methods, and so most studies focus on public firm studies and ignore the important issue of prediction of distress and failure in private firms. Newer statistical approaches are discussed in the following section, and the recent literature that focuses on SME failure is discussed in greater detail in Sect. 10.3.

10.2.3 Artificial Intelligence and Expert Systems Approaches

In the 1990s, advances in both computer speed and power and new developments in artificial intelligence and expert systems (AI/ES) software programming gave rise to a new family of failure prediction models and methods. In general, the AI/ES software programs are designed to learn from both their input data and their previous experience in solving a particular problem. In the case of bankruptcy or default prediction applications, the problem is the proper classification of a set of firm data into the proper category. The software systems actually learn and improve their prediction and categorization abilities through an iterative process as they explore the nonlinear relationships between the input data.[14] Following the research

[11] Ramaswami (1987), Dugan and Forsyth (1995), and Kahya and Theodossiou (1999).

[12] Aziz and Dar (2006) provide a table that summarizes the main characteristics of many different statistical approaches that have been used by various authors.

[13] See Balcaen and Ooghe (2006) for an extensive review of these shortcomings. See Grice and Dugan (2003) for a discussion of the problems related to LOGIT and PROBIT. See Platt and Platt (2002) for a discussion of the problems associated with the sample selection methodologies used in most studies.

[14] See Aziz and Dar (2006) for an excellent overview of these various AI/ES approaches as they are applied to bankruptcy prediction.

design approach developed in the MDA literature, most applications "train" their model on one sample and then test the model parameters on a hold-out sample or "test" set of data.

The most common AI/ES approach is that of a neural network (NN) that is designed to replicate the learning and classification processes carried out by the human brain. The NN approach is essentially nonparametric and nonlinear in the model building process. While some of the earliest applications of a NN system for failure prediction in the finance literature appeared in the early 1990s (see Coats and Fant 1993 and Altman, Marco, and Varetto 1994), many of the recent developments of these new AI/ES approaches appear in computer and operations research journals rather than finance and accounting journals.[15]

Zhang et al. (1999) provide a clear discussion of the general framework of the NN approach and how the underlying statistical theory is related to the theory supporting the use of MDA. They provide an excellent literature review of NN applications to bankruptcy prediction in the early literature, and they develop their own NN model using COMPUSTAT data. They also compare the performance of their NN model to a LOGIT model developed on the same dataset and find that the NN model outperforms the LOGIT approach.

Atiya (2001) provides another excellent survey of the literature that is more recent. He focuses his discussion on the most common AI/ES approach, that of a multilayered NN, to the prediction of bankruptcy and financial distress. He also provides a discussion on the reasons an NN approach is superior to more traditional statistical approaches based on the nonlinear characteristics of the input data typically used in prediction studies and he presents results of his own NN models that incorporate both financial and equity market information into the analysis.

Angelini et al. (2008) also provide an excellent discussion of the basics of NN design and operation (for the non-programmer) and they also develop a NN system and apply it to a sample of small firm data obtained from an Italian bank. The data represent 76 small firm clients of the bank, and the focus of the study is the prediction of bank loan defaults. Their final NN model produces a very low classification error rate that is much lower than is typical with classical statistical approaches.[16]

While neural network approaches are the most common model used, there are other AI/ES approaches that have been explored. One approach, used by Lee et al. (1996), is to build hybrid MDA/NN models where MDA is used to decide what variables to use in the NN model training stage. Another approach used by Varetto (1998) involves the use of genetic algorithms (GA) that are similar to NN in that they "learn" from the data but are different in that they are structured to follow an evolutionary logic that reflects Darwinian evolution. Etemadi et al. (1990) use another AI approach, Genetic Programming (GP), and

[15] See, for example, Salchenberger et al. (1992), Zhang et al. (1999), and Serrano-Cinca (1996).

[16] There have actually been a number of studies that apply AI/ES approaches to SME data. These studies are discussed in greater detail in Sect. 10.3.

apply it to data from the Tehran Stock Exchange in order to compare the GP approach and MDA. They report significant improvement in model prediction using the GP model over MDA. Other authors such as Dimitras et al. (1999) use "rough set" theory approach while Chen et al. (2009) build a model that incorporates both a NN and "fuzzy logic," appropriately named a "neuro-fuzzy" approach.

Some finance researchers argue that the application of these AI/ES models lacks a theoretical basis grounded in finance or accounting theory and that they do not improve on the performance of traditional statistical models.[17] Authors familiar with the statistics used in these approaches disagree. For example, Zhang et al. (1999) explain in detail the statistical theory underlying the relationship between the Bayesian classification rules and the multilinear discriminant function that is the basis of MDA when the assumption of normally distributed variables is made. They argue that since Bayesian classifiers are the basis for the training of a neural network, NN approaches are as statistically valid as MDA as a classification method. On the issue of performance, Aziz and Dar (2006) examine 89 different empirical studies that use either classical statistical methodologies, AI/ES methodologies, or other theoretical models for bankruptcy prediction. In 64% of the studies, classical statistical models were used, and in 25%, AI/ES approaches were used.[18] One of their conclusions from their analysis of these studies is as follows:

While MDA and LOGIT models are the methods of popular choice in bankruptcy prediction, it is not evident that this popularity is entirely warranted by their relative accuracy…..the IAES approach actually provides the best overall accuracy rates at 88%.[19]

Furthermore, Aziz and Dar report that the average Type I error rates from the studies examined for MDA, LOGIT and NN approaches are 15%, 15%, and 17%, respectively, indicating the classical approaches only slightly outperform NN approaches when considering the percent of failed firms wrongly classified as non–failed firms. When Type II average error rates are considered (non–failed firms classified as failed), the average error rate for NN approaches is only 6% while the MDA and LOGIT approaches exhibit average error rates of 12% and 10%, respectively.

One of the final conclusions in the Aziz and Dar paper echoes the conclusion of this discussion as well; after 35 years of academic research into bankruptcy prediction, there is "still no academic consensus as to the most useful method for predicting corporate bankruptcy."[20]

---

[17] See Altman, Sabato and Wilson (2009) for a discussion of these complaints about AI/ES approaches.

[18] The remaining studies were based on theoretical models not discussed in this paper.

[19] See Aziz and Dar (2006), p. 26.

[20] See Aziz and Dar (2006), p. 26.

10.3 Small Firm Failure Prediction Studies

10.3.1 The Early Literature

Most small firm studies focus on loan default and credit scoring models since this is the type of classification problem facing the entities that are the usual source of data from small private firms. The earliest study performed on small firm sample data was published by Edmister (1972). Using small firm financial data from a Small Business Administration's (SBA's) guaranteed loan database and Robert Morris and Associates *Annual Statement Studies* data, he constructs a number of dummy variables, some of which are designed to reflect deviations of the ratios from industry benchmarks. He then uses these variables with an MDA approach to examine the ability of his model to predict either loan repayment or loan default. His sample contains information from 42 different firms; 21 firms that repaid their loans and 21 firms that failed to repay. He examines a number of different variable construction methods including single year ratio variables as predictors, dummy variables representing the trend of changes in ratios over a 3-year period, and 3-year average ratio variables. His final model using the 3-year average ratio data is as follows:

$$Z = 0.951 - 0.423X_1 - 0.293X_2 - 0.482X_3 + 0.277X_4 - 0.452X_5 - 0.352X_6 - 0.924X_7$$

where:

$X_1 = 1$ if annual funds flow/current liabilities ratio is $<.5$, or $=0$ otherwise,
$X_2 = 1$ if equity/sales is $<.07$, or $=0$ otherwise,
$X_3 = 1$ if net working capital/sales ratio relative to the appropriate RMA benchmark ratio is $<-.02$ or $=0$ otherwise,
$X_4 = 1$ if current liabilities/equity ratio relative to the appropriate SBA benchmark ratio is $<.48$ or $=0$ otherwise,
$X_5 = 1$ if inventory/sales ratio relative to the appropriate RMA benchmark ratio is in an uptrend and still $<.04$ or $=0$ otherwise,
$X_6 = 1$ if quick ratio relative to the appropriate RMA benchmark ratio trend is down and is $<.34$ or $=0$ otherwise, and
$X_7 = 1$ if quick ratio relative to the appropriate RMA benchmark ratio trend is up or $=0$ otherwise.

Edmister finds his first three variable coefficients (X_1–X_3) are significant predictors for loan default at the .01 significance level and that the coefficients for variables X_4, X_5, and X_7 are significant at the .05 level. His final model with estimated coefficients correctly classifies 39 of 42 firms (93% accuracy).

Most of the later studies use more traditional types of financial ratios and many focus on variable sets that reflect, as closely as possible, the variables that Altman's various studies examine. Some studies, however, do examine unique predictive variables. Kallberg and Udell (2003) focus on the added value of private firm credit information available from Dun & Bradstreet Corporation (D&B) and examine whether it is of additional value to lenders when evaluating the probabilities of credit default. They use a LOGIT approach to examine 241 failed firms and 2,482 non–failed firms and in addition to the standard types of financial ratios, they include the D&B "PAYDEX" score that reflects the average number of days the firm was "past due" on any trade credit obligation. They also include dummy variables representing age, negative uniform commercial code filings, and the existence of secured lending agreements. Their results provide a model with predictive ability of about 89% in both the estimating sample and a hold-out sample and the results indicate the D&B variable adds significant predictive power above and beyond the variable constructed from public information.

In a series of papers, Keasey and Watson argue studies of small firm failure are usually driven by data availability rather than theory and they focus on the addition of non–financial data to the analysis and prediction of firm failure[21]. Abouzeedan and Busler (2004) develop a *Survival Index Value®* (*SIV®*) model that incorporates both financial and non–financial variables into the predictive process where the non–financial variables are chosen based on the Keasey and Watson work. They also provide a review of traditional MDA-based models and a good discussion of past studies that apply MDA to SMEs. While they provide an interesting discussion of the financial versus non–financial variable issue, they do not provide any comparison of the performance of their model relative to the performance of more common variable specifications and model approaches.

10.3.2 Impact of Basel II and Recent Small Firm Studies

Basel II, the recommendations on new banking regulations, were developed in the late 1990s and the final recommendations were originally published in 2004. Since then, many banking regulatory authorities around the world have been adopting the new proposed regulations. One aspect of the new regulations is that banks are allowed to use internal models to assess the risk of credits they have extended to their banking clients and to use these risk assessments to calculate their risk-adjusted capital requirements. This shift in the regulatory framework for banks has created a renewed interest in applying failure prediction models to SME data both in the US and in foreign countries.

Mramor and Valentincic (2002) examine private firm data from 19,627 very small private companies operating in 28 different industries in Slovenia in order to predict which firms will develop liquidity problems. The dataset contains both financial statement data and data on cash balances held by these firms in their banks, and they compare the performance of PROBIT, LOGIT, and MDA models

[21] See Keasey and Watson (1986), Keasey and Watson (1987), Keasey and Watson (1988) and Keasey and Watson (1991).

on industry subsamples. Their results indicate that, in general, the PROBIT and LOGIT models perform significantly better than the MDA models.

Grunert et al. (2004) examine SME credit data using client data obtained from four German banks using a PROBIT methodology and examine whether the inclusion of non–financial firm data improves the model's ability to forecast credit defaults. Their non–financial data include measures of management quality and market position. They find inclusion of these qualitative data variables significantly improves the model's predictive ability.

Pompe and Bilderbeek (2005) examine private firm data from annual reports filed with the Belgian National Bank using both an MDA approach and a NN approach. Their data contain both young firms and older, established firms. They find similar predictive results with both methods of analysis. They also report that using trends in ratios failed to increase the predictive power of the models, predictive ability is weaker when analyzing younger firms, and almost every ratio examined had some predictive power.

Altman and Sabato (2007) focus on modeling credit risk for SMEs in the US market using a LOGIT approach on a sample of over 2,000 firms that have annual sales of less than $65 million. They compare their SME model to a later version of Altman's Z score model developed in Altman and Hotchkiss (2005), which they term a "generic" corporate MDA model. While the research focus is on SMEs, the data are financial data drawn from the COMPUSTAT database. While all firms have sales of less than the cutoff mentioned earlier, detailed statistics on the final sample are not given and it is hard to determine just how representative of small firms the final sample is. Their results indicate that with a log transformation of the input variables, predictive accuracy of the LOGIT model reaches 89%, which outperforms the MDA model that they also run for comparative purposes.

Wiklund et al. (2008) focus on the factors related to SME firm failure in the first 7 years of operations. Using data from 37,782 incorporations filed with the Swedish government agency that regulates these firms, they tracked the firm performance either to the time of failure or to the end of the 7-year period. Using a discreet time LOGIT analysis, they find that greater liquidity, lower leverage, and greater profitability are extremely important determinants of early success for new firms with the importance of these factors decreasing through time.

In Altman, Sabato and Wilson (2009) the authors test the model developed in Altman and Sabato (2007) on a dataset from the UK and they expand the model to include the addition of qualitative variables to the model. Qualitative data included in the analysis represent "default events" such as court filings for unpaid debts, the timeliness of the filing of financial information with the government agency collecting the data, a dummy variable for whether the financial accounts are audited, the age of the firm, and dummy variables representing whether a firm has been recently established or has existed for more than 3 years. Their results indicate that inclusion of qualitative variables improves the predictive accuracy of the models.

Vallini et al. (2009) apply MDA, LOGIT, and NN approaches to data representing over 6,000 small Italian firms. The data are drawn from the CERVED database in Italy that contains data collected by local Chambers of Commerce on private firms throughout the country. While predictive accuracy of the models examined was low (in the 60–70% accuracy range) for the entire sample, the NN model narrowly outperformed the MDA and LOGIT approaches. When the data are partitioned by some combination of size, geographic location within Italy, and business sector, the predictive accuracy of all three methods improves but the NN predictive accuracy improves significantly more than the other approaches. For example, when partitioned by size, the NN approach provided predictive accuracy of over 71% while the MDA and LOGIT approaches only provided accuracy of 64% for the larger private firms in the sample.

Using one of the newest AI/ES approaches called Support Vector Machines (SVMs), Kim and Sohn (2010) examine both financial data and non–financial firm variables that are combined with economic variables in order to predict default rates in a sample of 4,590 Korean technology firms. The firm data examined come from a government technology credit guarantee program, and their results indicate that the SVM approach outperforms both standard neural network approaches and LOGIT models.

10.3.3 Existing Research on Small Business Failure

While there have been a number of studies using small private firm data in foreign countries, very little of the recent research has focused on small private firms in the USA. This may be partially due to the ease of access that US researchers have to large databases of public firm data such as CRSP and COMPUSTAT. Finding the necessary data to perform studies on small private firms is not always easy. There is not a central data source in the USA for small private firm data similar to the Italian data based used by Vallini et al. (2009) or the Belgian Central Bank data used by Pompe and Bilderbeek (2005). One starting point for US researchers is to look into the data sources discussed in this book written by Charles Ou. Another source of small private firm data might be large commercial banks. Researchers may be able to approach the banks and access data collected from bank's loan customers as Grunert et al. (2004) did when they created their sample from loan data supplied by German banks. Given the banking industry's new interest in modeling the credit risk of their customers, they may be more amenable to making the effort to provide researchers with data. Finally, small firm researchers need to consider incorporating the newer AI/ES modeling techniques into their research. Many studies have concluded that these newer empirical approaches are more efficient at forecasting distress and failure, so they should be considered in future research.

10.4 Psychological Phenomena as Possible Predictors of Business Success or Failure

10.4.1 The Importance of the Human Decision

As we have seen from some of the previous chapters in this book, the findings from the fields of cognitive psychology and neuroscience have fundamentally changed the way we now look at how financial decisions are made. For example, an entrepreneur might assign a low-risk assessment to an otherwise high-risk project if they particularly like that individual project and subsequently take on a riskier project then the potential return justifies. While the riskier project has a higher chance of failing, the entrepreneur does not see it that way mainly because of the affect heuristics. Since it is usually the human decision that makes or breaks a private company, our focus in this section shifts from the commerce (effect) side of failure analysis to the human/managerial (cause) side of it.

10.4.2 The Role of Heuristics

Starting, financing, managing, and growing any private venture is a rather complicated decision and if the venture is launched, it will bring further uncertainty and ambiguity for the decision maker. These types of ambiguities also exist in large publicly held corporations when, for example, a CEO contemplates entering into a new market or acquires another company. It is because of such complexities and uncertainties, and the added fact that the human brain is not wired to handle very complex scenarios, that both entrepreneurs and managers resort to a limited set of mental shortcuts (or heuristics) to simplify things and move forward. While heuristics are very beneficial in such cases and can get things accomplished, their use also introduces cognitive biases into the decision process that may lead to errors in judgment.

While arguments for shifting the focus away from the commerce (effect) side of failure analysis to its human/managerial (cause) side have some novelty, the idea of applying psychological factors and heuristics to economic activities such as business entry is not new. For example, Roll (1986), through a comprehensive literature review and analysis, forwarded "The Hubris Hypothesis of Corporate Takeovers." Cooper et al. (1988) documented the existence of overconfidence in entrepreneurs. Kahneman and Lovallo (1993) and Camerer and Lovallo (1999), respectively, suggested and directly tested the prevalence of overoptimism and overconfidence and concluded that their findings were consistent with the prediction that both phenomena would lead to excessive business entry and failure. Simon et al. (1999) tested the role that three key cognitive biases play in starting up a business. More recently, Wu and Knott (2005) discussed in detail the entrepreneur's overconfidence relative to entry decisions. While some recent work has focused on these important issues, the failure literature lacks a comprehensive framework that allows for modeling decision process variables. This is exactly the area where we see much potential for improving our failure/success prediction models.

Building upon the literature discussed above and borrowing from the findings in the field of behavioral finance and economics, it is apparent that there exists a relationship between the probability of failure at any given venture and the intensity of the cognitive biases of the entrepreneur or manager behind that venture. Recognizing that "cognitive biases" is a catch all variable that needs to be deconstructed into a subset of relevant biases that can be empirically tested, we provide a call to action for a shift in research method in future failure-oriented studies. Specifically in future business failure studies, and especially those that involve start-ups, SMEs, and IPO companies, primary attention should be placed on the individual decision maker responsible for the companies' well-being. It is only then that we can study, and possibly "debias" the decision makers' cognitive biases that could make or break their companies. Given the limited nature of our analysis here, the balance of the section will discuss some key psychological factors that prior research has shown can play an important role in the individual decision-making process, including those that could lead to business failure.[22]

10.4.2.1 The Affect Heuristic

Simply stated, the very powerful affect heuristic has been defined as a feeling state, such as "goodness or badness," when one faces an investment opportunity or a start-up potential. Affect can also be viewed as a quality, such as acceptable and unacceptable, when associated with a risky business venture. Additionally, affect can be described as behavior that places heavy reliance on intuition, instinct, and gut feeling.[23] Affect heuristic is probably among the top mental short cuts employed because it has been able to explain the otherwise peculiar negative relationship between expected risk and expected return or gain in investment situations.[24] For example, a "good feeling" toward a high-risk proposition like a start-up would lead to a higher perceived benefit in that start-up and a lower risk perception in that venture.

New research has shown that "affective reactions to stimuli (like venture proposals) are often the very first reactions, occurring automatically and subsequently guiding information processing and judgment."[25] Based on such findings, it follows that entrepreneurs start businesses they like (and not necessarily the ones they consider as

[22] This section is built upon the discussion on cognitive biases in Yazdipour (2009).

[23] For a good coverage of the latest literature on the issue see Slovic (1972), Slovic (1987), Slovic and Peters (2006), Olsen (2008) and Sheffrin (2007)

[24] Normally, in investment situations investors in high risk assets require high returns. However, from what we have learned from psychology, if an individual develops a "good feeling" (positive affect) for a high-risk investment, she/he may require low return from such an investment.

[25] Finucane et al. (2000), p.2 note that it was Zajonc (1980) who first made this argument.

high potential) and venture capitalists (VCs) finance ventures they find attractive (and not necessarily the ones they consider as highly profitable).

10.4.2.2 The Representative (Similarity) Heuristic

According to Tversky and Kahneman (1974), many of the probabilistic questions that people are concerned with can be characterized by "what is the probability that object A belongs to class B" or "what is the probability that event A originates from process B?" To answer questions like these, people utilize the representative heuristics, in which probabilities are evaluated by the degree to which A resembles B. For example, when A is highly representative of B, the probability that A originates form B is judged to be high.

In such cases, the representative heuristic assists in evaluating the probabilities dealing with objects or processes A and B. As an example, when A is highly representative of B, the probability that A originates from B is judged to be high. The problem is that representativeness (similarity) should not affect the judgment of probability. What should be considered in the judgment to probability is "prior probability" or "base rate." However, the latter is not the case in practice (violation of Bayes' rule).

The key aspects of the Representativeness Heuristic:

1. The "representativeness heuristic" is a built-in feature of the brain for producing rapid probability judgments, rather than a consciously adopted procedure.
2. As humans, we are not aware of substituting judgment of representativeness for judgment of probability.

10.4.2.3 The Availability or Recency Heuristic

To understand this judgment heuristic, it is important to understand that people disproportionately recall the salient events that they have observed; those that are very recent or those that individuals are emotionally involved with in the very recent past are considered more important. The more salient an event is, the more likely the probability that the event will be recalled. With the availability heuristics, people search their memories for relevant but recent information and data. The result is that this sort of bias prevents managers and entrepreneurs from considering other potential information and possible related outcomes that may not have occurred recently. For example, a San Francisco Bay Area entrepreneur may assess the risk of starting a new venture by recalling all the positive reports on successful start-ups that they have recently been reading about in the business section of the Silicon Valley Mercury News. The problem, however, is that not all memories are equally retrievable (or available) and this leads to error in judgment. In the above example, more recent incidences and more salient events (all positive reports on successful start-ups) will weigh more heavily than possible reports of failures and non–reported incidences and this will, in turn, lead to prediction biases that would distort one's judgment or estimate of a future outcome.

10.4.2.4 Anchoring and Adjustment

Anchoring refers to a tendency to anchor on, and stay around, an initial arbitrary value, which may be suggested by the way a proposition is presented or by some initial computation. When forming estimates and predictions, perceptions can be influenced by such prior suggestions. In addition, people adjust away from an initial value suggested to them (the anchor) insufficiently to arrive at the true value of the subject under consideration.[26] An example would be the way an investment banker uses the Relative Valuation model (multiples method) to arrive at an IPO price; or a Venture Capitalist (VC) uses the same method to price a venture capital deal. In both cases, prevailing multiples which are chosen and adjusted up or down on an arbitrary basis are used to come up with a price and this "anchored" adjustment introduces a bias. A more sensible alternative would be to look at the risks involved and the types of cash flows expected from the business and then come up with a value while ignoring anchors suggested by past experience.

From the VC's point of view, anchoring bias can be used to statistically argue that an entrepreneur may overestimate the chances of success of the business. Following Tversky and Kahneman (1973, 1974) and Minniti and Levesque (2008), it follows that starting a new venture is a conjunctive event; meaning that for a start-up to succeed, it must succeed in all the steps that are needed for its success as a whole. For example, in order for a start-up to succeed, it must first succeed in producing a working prototype, then employing the needed resources including financing to actually manufacture the product, and later to hire a marketing and sales force to bring in revenue. However, from a statistical point of view, the overall probability of a conjunctive event like a start-up is lower than the probability of each elementary component event if such events are independent. This means even if each of the steps is very likely, the overall probability of the venture's success as a whole is low. This leads to excessive optimism by entrepreneurs as they take the probabilities of elementary events as a reference point and adjust them up or down insufficiently to arrive at a desired overall probability for the venture as a whole.

10.5 Summary and Some Suggestions for Future Research

To summarize, research from the fields of cognitive psychology and neuroscience has shown that individuals, including entrepreneurs and corporate managers, use mental short cuts like the ones discussed above when the decisions are overly

[26] See Tversky and Kahneman (1973, 1974).

complex. While such heuristics simplify the decision-making process and reduce the decision maker's anxiety level, they also introduce biases that can lead to errors in judgment. This is why we encourage failure researchers to focus their attention on the decision maker, the entrepreneur and/or the manager, in addition to the financial data. Zeroing in on the commerce (effect) side of failure, as has been the case for almost all the research up to this point, only reveals to us a half-image of the foundation of the firm under consideration. To see the whole foundation, we must also consider information about the decision maker and especially her/his predisposition toward the known heuristics. The challenge, then, is to develop research methodologies that satisfy such requirements that are dictated by behavioral finance while building on the empirical methodologies that have developed in the more traditional failure prediction literature. But that task is beyond the scope of this current chapter, and hopefully, will be the subject of many research papers to come.

References

Abouzeedan, A., and M. Busler. 2004. Typology analysis of performance models of small and medium-size enterprises (SMEs). *Journal of International Entrepreneurship* 2: 155–177.

Altman, E. 1968. Financial ratios, discriminant analysis and the prediction of corporate bankruptcy. *Journal of Finance* 23(4): 589–609.

Altman, E. 1993. *Corporate financial distress and bankruptcy: A complete guide to predicting and avoiding distress and profiting from bankruptcy*. New York: Wiley.

Altman, E. 2000. *Predicting financial distress of companies: Revisiting the Z-score and ZETA® models*. New York: New York University.

Altman, E.I., and E. Hotchkiss. 2005. *Corporate financial distress and bankruptcy*, 3rd ed. New York: Wiley.

Altman, E.I., G. Marco, and F. Varetto. 1994. Corporate distress diagnosis: comparisons using linear discriminant analysis and the neural networks (the Italian experience) *Journal of Banking & Finance* 18: 505–529.

Altman, E.I., and G. Sabato. 2007. Modeling credit risk for SMEs: Evidence from the US market. *ABACUS* 43(3): 332–357.

Altman, E., R. Haldeman, and P. Narayanan. 1977. ZETA analysis: A new model to identify bankruptcy risk of corporations. *Journal of Banking and Finance* 1(1): 29–54.

Altman E., N. Wilson, and G. Sabato. 2010. The Value of Non-Financial Information in SME Risk Management. *Journal of Credit Risk* 6(2): 1–33.

Angelini, E., G. di Tollo, and A. Roli. 2008. A neural network approach for credit risk evaluation. *The Quarterly Review of Economics and Finance* 48: 733–755.

Atiya, A.E. 2001. Bankruptcy prediction for credit risk using neural networks: A survey and new results. *IEEE Transactions on Neural Networks* 12(4): 929–935.

Aziz, M.A., and H.A. Dar. 2006. Predicting corporate bankruptcy: Where we stand? *Corporate Governance* 6(1): 18–33.

Balcaen, S., and H. Ooghe. 2006. 35 years of studies on business failure: An overview of the classic statistical methodologies and their related problems. *The British Accounting Review* 38: 63–93.

Beaver, W.H. 1966. Financial ratios as predictors of failures. Empirical research in accounting: Selected studies. *Journal of Accounting Research* 3: 71–111.

Camerer, C., and D. Lovallo. 1999. Overconfidence and excess entry: An experimental approach. *The American Economic Review* 89(1): 306–318.

Chen, H., S.Y. Huang, and C.S. Lin. 2009. Alternative diagnosis of corporate bankruptcy: A neuro fuzzy approach. *Expert Systems with Applications* 36: 7710–7720.

Coats, P.K., and L.F. Fant. 1993. Recognizing financial distress patterns using a neural network tool. *Financial Management* 22(3): 142–155.

Cooper, A., C. Woo, and W. Dunkelberg. 1988. Entrepreneurs' perceived chances for success. *Journal of Business Venturing* 3: 97–108.

Dimitras, A.I., R. Slowinski, R. Susmaga, and C. Zoupounidis. 1999. Business failure prediction using rough sets. *European Journal of Operation Research* 114(2): 263–280.

Dugan, M., and T. Forsyth. 1995. The relationship between bankruptcy model predictions and stock market perceptions of bankruptcy. *The Financial Review* 30: 507–528.

Edmister, R. 1972. An empirical test to financial ratio analysis for small business failure prediction. *The Journal of Financial and Quantitative Analysis* 7: 1477–1493.

Etemadi, H., A.A. Rostamy, and H.F. Dehkordi. 1990. A genetic programming model for bankruptcy prediction: Empirical evidence from Iran. *Expert Systems with Applications* 36: 3199–3207.

Finucane, M.L., A. Alhakami, P. Slovic, and S.M. Johnson. 2000. The affect heuristic in judgments of risks and benefits. *Journal of Behavioral Decision Making* 13: 1–17.

Fitzparick, P.J. 1932. A comparison of ratios of successful industrial enterprises with those of failed firms. *Certified Public Accountant*, pp. 598–605, 656–662, 727–731.

Grice, J.S., and M.T. Dugan. 2003. Re-estimation of the Zmijewski and Ohlson bankruptcy prediction models. *Advances in Accounting* 20: 77–93.

Grunert, J., L. Norden, and M. Weber. 2004. The role of non-financial factors in internal credit ratings. *Journal of Banking and Finance* 29(2): 509–531.

Kahneman, D., and D. Lovallo. 1993. Timid choices and bold forecasts: A cognitive perspective on risk taking. *Management Science* 39(1): 17–31.

Kahya E., and P.T. Theodossiou. 1999. Predicting corporate financial distress: A time-series CUSUM methodology. *Review of Quantitative Finance and Accounting*, 13(4): 323–345.

Kallberg, J.G., and G.F. Udell. 2003. The value of private sector business credit information sharing: The US case. *Journal of Banking and Finance* 27: 449–469.

Keasey, K., and R. Watson. 1986. The prediction of small company failure: Some behavioural evidence for the UK. *Accounting and Business Research* 17(65): 49–57.

Keasey, K., and R. Watson. 1987. Non-financial symptoms and the prediction of small business failure: A test of the Argenti Hypothesis. *Journal of Business, Finance & Accounting* 14(3): 335–354.

Keasey, K., and R. Watson. 1988. The non-submission of accounts and small company financial failure prediction. *Accounting and Business Research* 19: 47–54.

Keasey, K., and R. Watson. 1991. The state of the art of small firm failure prediction: Achievements and prognosis. *International Small Business Journal* 9(4): 11–29.

Kim, H.S., and S.Y. Sohn. 2010. Support vector machines for default prediction of SMEs based on technology credit. *European Journal of Operational Research* 201: 838–846.

Lee, K.C., I. Han, and Y. Kwon. 1996. Hybrid neural network models for bankruptcy predictions. *Decision Support Systems* 18(1): 63–72.

Merwin, C.L. 1942. *Financing small corporations in five manufacturing industries, 1926-1936.* New York: National Bureau of Economic Research.

Meyer, P.A., and H. Pifer. 1970. Prediction of bank failures. *The Journal of Finance* 25: 853–868.

Minniti, M., and M. Levesque. 2008. Recent developments in the economics of entrepreneurship. *Journal of Business Venturing* 23: 603–612.

Mramor, D., and A. Valentincic. 2002. Forecasting the liquidity of very small private companies. *Journal of Business Venturing* 18: 745–771.

Ohlson, J.A. 1980. Financial ratios and the probabilistic prediction of bankruptcy. *Journal of Accounting Research* 18(1): 109–131.

Olsen, R.A. 2008. Perceptions of financial risk: Axioms and affect. *The Icfai University Journal of Behavioral Finance* 5(4): 58–80.

Palepu, K.G., E. Peek, V.L. Bernard, and E. Peck. 2007. *Business analysis and valuation: Text and cases*. London: Thompson Learning.
Platt, H.D., and M.B. Platt. 2002. Predicting corporate financial distress: Reflections on choice-based sample bias. *Journal of Economics and Finance* 26: 184–199.
Pompe, P., and J. Bilderbeek. 2005. The prediction of bankruptcy of small and medium sized industrial firms. *Journal of Business Venturing* 20: 847–868.
Ramaswami, M. 1987. Stock market perception of industrial firm bankruptcy. *The Financial Review* 22(2): 267–279.
Roll, R. 1986. The Hubris hypothesis of corporate takeover. *Journal of Business* 59(2): 197–216.
Salchenberger, L., E. Cinar, and N. Lash. 1992. Neural networks: A new tool for predicting thrift failures. *Decision Sciences* 23: 899–916.
Serrano-Cinca, C. 1996. Self organizing neural networks for financial diagnosis. *Decision Support Systems* 17: 227–238.
Sheffrin, H. 2007. *Behavioral corporate finance: Decisions that create value*. Irwin: McGraw Hill.
Simon, M., S.H. Houghton, and K. Aquino. 1999. Cognitive biases, risk perception, and venture formation: How individuals decide to start companies. *Journal of Business Venturing* 15: 113–134.
Slovic, P. 1972. Psychological study of human judgment: Implications for investment decision making. *The Journal of Finance* 27(4): 779–799.
Slovic, P. 1987. Perception of risk. *Science* 236(4799): 280–286.
Slovic, P., and E. Peters. 2006. Risk perception and affect. *Current Directions in Psychological Science* 15(6): 322–326.
Tversky, A., and D. Kahneman. 1973. Availability: A heuristic for judging frequency and probability. *Cognitive Psychology* 4: 207–232.
Tversky, A., and D. Kahneman. 1974. Judgment under uncertainly: Heuristics and biases. *Science, New Series* 185(4157): 1124–1131.
Vallini, C., F. Ciampi, and N. Gordini. 2009. Using artificial neural networks analysis for small enterprise default prediction modeling: Statistical evidence from Italian firms. *Oxford Business and Economics Conference Program*. http://www.docstoc.com/docs/21423327/Using-Artificial-Neural-Networks-Analysis-For-Small-Enterprise/.
Varetto, F. 1998. Genetic algorithms applications in the analysis of insolvency risk. *Journal of Banking & Finance* 22: 1421–1439.
Wiklund, J., T. Baker, and D. Shepherd. 2008. The age-effect of financial indicators as buffers against the liability of newness. *Journal of Business Venturing (forthcoming)*. doi:10.1016/j.jbusvent.2008.10.011.
Winakor, A., and R.F. Smith. 1935. Changes in financial structure of unsuccessful industrial companies. *Bureau of Business Research, Bulletin No. 51* Urbana: University of Illinois Press.
Wu, B. and A.M. Knott. 2005. Entrepreneurial risk and market entry. Working Paper, U.S. Small Business Administration.
Yazdipour, R. 2009. What can venture capitalists and entrepreneurs learn from behavioral economists? *Journal of Strategic Change Management* 18: 241–247.
Zajonc, R.B. 1980. Feeling and thinking: Preferences need no inferences. *The American Psychologist* 35: 151–175.
Zhang, G., M.Y. Hu, B.E. Patuwo, and D.C. Indro. 1999. Artificial neural networks in bankruptcy prediction: General framework and cross-validation. *European Journal of Operational Research* 116: 16–32.
Zmijewski, M.E. 1984. Methodological issues related to the estimation of financial distress prediction models. *Journal of Accounting Research (Studies on Current Econometric Issues in Accounting Research)* 22: 59–82.

Chapter 11
The Evolution of Entrepreneurs and Venture Capitalists

Martin Sewell

Abstract We have evolved "as if" reproduction is the sole goal for which human beings were "designed," and everything else is a means to that end. However, natural selection is a slow process, and *Homo sapiens* originated about 200,000 years ago, so our minds today are adapted to maximize gene replication in the Pleistocene. Meanwhile, an investor seeking to maximize wealth, *Homo economicus*, should behave according to expected utility theory. Aspects of the behavior of *Homo sapiens* that differ from *Homo economicus* include the endowment effect, loss aversion, risk aversion, overconfidence, optimism, the representativeness heuristic, the availability heuristic and herding. This chapter speculates how these heuristics and biases may have evolved, and focuses on their effect on entrepreneurs and venture capitalists.

11.1 Introduction

11.1.1 Background and Overview

Taking an evolutionary psychology perspective informs us that our minds today are adapted to maximize gene replication in the environment of evolutionary adaptedness (the Pleistocene). Meanwhile, an investor seeking to maximize wealth should behave according to the normative model from economics, expected utility theory. In practice, the key to maximizing wealth lies in identifying the differences between the (descriptive) behavior exhibited by *Homo sapiens* and the (normative) behavior exhibited by the hypothetical and rational *Homo economicus* (or *Economic man*), and seeking to avoid the uncovered cognitive biases (so-called behavioral "anomalies") so that behavior is consistent with the normative model.

M. Sewell (✉)
University of Cambridge, Cambridge, UK
e-mail: mvs25@cam.ac.uk

R. Yazdipour, *Advances in Entrepreneurial Finance: With Applications from Behavioral Finance and Economics*, DOI 10.1007/978-1-4419-7527-0_11,

In common with all individuals, entrepreneurs and venture capitalists (VCs) are susceptible to cognitive biases, and likely exhibit behavior that distinguishes them from other individuals, which may exacerbate or mitigate the various biases. This chapter speculates how various heuristics and biases may have evolved, and focuses on their effect on entrepreneurs and VCs. The exposition implicitly provides a prescriptive approach for both groups for overcoming biases and maximizing wealth.

11.2 Normative Model

11.2.1 Uncertainty

First, we must decide how best to deal with *uncertainty*. A *Dutch book* is a gambling term for a set of odds and bets that guarantees a profit, regardless of the outcome of the gamble. At the very least, one who practices self-consistent reasoning should not be susceptible to having a Dutch book made against them. If an individual is not susceptible to a Dutch book, their previsions are said to be *coherent*. A set of betting quotients is coherent if (Ramsey 1926; de Finetti 1937; Shimony 1955) and only if (Kemeny 1955; Lehman 1955) they satisfy the axioms of probability. On this basis, it is my view that probability is both necessary and sufficient when dealing with uncertainty. This is the philosophy of a Bayesian. A person is said to be well *calibrated* if his or her subjective probabilities match observed relative frequencies.

11.2.2 Expected Utility Model

From the field of economics, *expected utility theory* (also known as *von Neumann–Morgenstern utility*) (Bernoulli 1738; von Neumann and Morgenstern 1944; Bernoulli 1954) is a normative model of decision making under risk. Expected utility theory states that when making decisions under risk, people choose the option with the highest utility, where utility is the sum of the products of the utility of each potential outcome and the probability of occurrence of the outcome. For an investor, an outcome would be final wealth. In terms of how an investor should behave, he must determine his utility function and evaluate probabilities.

11.2.3 Risk Attitude

The problem of how to maximize growth of wealth has been solved (maximize the expected value of the logarithm of wealth after each period (Kelly 1956; Breiman 1961), but most investors are unwilling to endure the volatility of wealth that such a strategy entails. For this reason, a compromise between an optimal growth strategy and the security of holding cash has been suggested (MacLean et al. 1992). In contrast, McDonnell (2008) recommends combining the use of logarithms for maximum growth of wealth (Kelly 1956) with the logarithmic utility function (Bernoulli 1738), resulting in an iterated log function, $\log_e(1+\log_e(1+r))$, where r is return.

11.3 The Evolution of Cognitive Biases

11.3.1 Evolutionary Psychology

Evolutionary psychology (Buss 2008) proposes that human psychology can be better understood in the light of evolution. *Homo sapiens* originated about 200,000 years ago, and natural selection is a slow process, so human beings today are better equipped to solve the problems faced by our ancestors. The environment to which a species is adapted is known as the *environment of evolutionary adaptedness* (the *EEA*) which, for modern man, is the Pleistocene (which lasted from 1.8 million to 12,000 years before the present) where we lived in hunter-gatherer tribes on the African savannah. From a gene's eye view, evolution is survivorship bias, so our minds have adapted to ensure that we propagate our genes in an environment that dealt with predators, food acquisition, interpersonal aggression, diseases, mate choice, child rearing, etc. For example, in the present, we are more afraid of snakes and spiders than cars, despite the fact that cars cause more deaths and injuries than creatures in developed countries.

It should not be overlooked that the most significant feature of humans that distinguishes them from other animals is their high intelligence. Such high intelligence was likely sexually selected (Miller 2001), and leads to greater complexity among heuristics and biases.

Evolutionary psychology is the study of human universal nature, but also sex-specific male human nature and female human nature. When compared to the simplicity of asexual reproduction, sexual reproduction seems inefficient. More precisely, as they don't give birth to offspring, what is the point of males? Atmar (1991) posits that the purpose of males in most species is to act as a genetic filter with the function of eliminating deleterious genetic material from the lineage. In this sense, it should be of no surprise that in relative terms, the majority of men fail, while a small minority succeed. Correspondingly, the distribution of success (e.g. wealth) of men has a positive skew.

11.3.2 Risk Preferences

What sort of biases are likely to have evolved? Firstly, why are we generally risk averse? In order to propagate our genes, we need to survive. By definition, I have survived thus far, everything that I have already experienced cannot be fatal because I am alive. I have never eaten that berry before, and I have survived, so why should I risk eating it? The most fundamental bias, therefore, is the *status quo bias* (also known as *conservatism*). Haselton and Nettle (2006) demonstrate the evolutionary benefits of paranoia. Sinn and Weichenrieder (1993) considered the evolution of risk preferences and showed that it is better to have 4 offspring rather than 2 or 6 (because $4^n > 2^{n/2} \times 6^{n/2}$ for $n \in \mathbf{Z}^+$), thus justifying risk aversion for gains. Similarly, when wealth is generated by a multiplicative process such as a financial market, it is $\log_e$(wealth) that is additive. If one is risk neutral in terms of $\log_e$(wealth), because the log utility function is concave, it follows that one must exhibit a small degree of risk aversion regarding wealth. We also exhibit a preference for known risks over unknown risks, that is, we prefer known probabilities.[1] This is known as *ambiguity aversion*.

The status quo bias can lead to another cognitive heuristic, known as *anchoring* (Tversky and Kahneman 1974), which describes the common human tendency to make decisions based on an initial "anchor." We prefer relative thinking to absolute thinking. The conservatism/anchoring/status quo bias can cause *underreaction*.

The idea of *loss aversion* is that losses and disadvantages have a greater impact on preferences than gains and advantages. The *endowment effect* (Thaler 1980) is the phenomenon in which people value a good or service more once their property right to it has been established. In a reversal of the cause and effect in previous hypotheses, Gal (2006) proposes that the status quo bias explains the endowment effect and risk aversion, and that the principle of loss aversion should be abandoned, in other words, apparent "loss aversion" is actually due to a preference for the status quo. Living in groups meant that respect for private property would have likely evolved as a Nash equilibrium, and Gintis (2007) shows how the evolution of private property gave rise to the endowment effect, and thus loss aversion. To summarize, I hypothesize that the endowment effect, an example of the status quo bias, leads to both loss aversion and risk aversion. It could be that we are merely conservative.

The most cited paper ever to appear in *Econometrica*, the prestigious academic journal of economics, was written by the two psychologists Kahneman and Tversky (1979). They present a critique of expected utility theory as a descriptive model of decision making under risk and develop an alternative model, which they call *prospect theory*. Kahneman and Tversky found empirically that people underweight outcomes that are merely probable in comparison with outcomes that are obtained with certainty; also that people generally discard components that are shared by all prospects under consideration. Under prospect theory, value is assigned to gains and losses rather than to final assets; also probabilities are replaced by decision weights. The value function is defined on deviations from a reference point and is normally concave for gains (implying risk aversion), commonly convex for losses (risk seeking) and is generally steeper for losses than for gains (loss aversion). Decision weights are generally lower than the corresponding probabilities, except

[1]As the subjective Bayesian Bruno de Finetti famously noted, "probability does not exist," but the point here is that we prefer to assign a subjective probability with ease.

in the range of low probabilities. The theory – which they confirmed by experiment – predicts a distinctive fourfold pattern of risk attitudes: risk aversion for gains of moderate to high probability and losses of low probability, and risk seeking for gains of low probability and losses of moderate to high probability.

Tversky and Kahneman (1992) superseded their original implementation of prospect theory with *cumulative prospect theory*. The new methodology employs cumulative rather than separable decision weights, applies to uncertain as well as to risky prospects with any number of outcomes, and it allows different weighting functions for gains and for losses.

Note that there are two fundamental reasons why prospect theory (which calculates value) is inconsistent with expected utility theory. Firstly, while utility is necessarily linear in the probabilities, value is not. Secondly, whereas utility is dependent on final wealth, value is defined in terms of gains and losses (deviations from current wealth). However, Harrison and Rutström (2009) propose a reconciliation of expected utility theory and prospect theory by using a mixture model. More recent developments have improved upon cumulative prospect theory, such as the transfer of attention exchange model (Birnbaum 2008).

Risk preferences may vary across time. As, ultimately, men are competing with other men, and women with other women, it is our status or wealth relative to others that counts. In that sense, it seems reasonable that our risk tolerances should also be dependent on the wealth and risk preferences of those against whom we are competing with, so may vary over time. For example, appetite for risk may vary according to whether a nation is in a period of prosperity, or going through a recession.

11.3.3 Overconfidence and Optimism

Due to conflicts between predator and prey, group living, and the competition for reproduction, deception has evolved under natural selection; and as a consequence, so has the capacity to detect deceit (Cosmides 1989). The easiest way of avoiding detection is to effectively lie to ourselves. This is known as *self-deception*. So, not only do we wish to appear (genetically) fitter than others (this has obvious advantages when it comes to sexual selection), but we actually believe that we are. We will also attribute successful outcomes to our own skill but blame unsuccessful outcomes on bad luck, this is known as *self-attribution bias*. An apparently genuine belief that we can provide a rosy future is another trait that increases our fitness. Self-deception leads to *overconfidence* and *optimism*.

Due to sexual dimorphism vis-à-vis parental investment, men and women do not differ in degree but differ in kind. In all species, the relative investment that is made by the male and the female in their offspring determines the degree of discrimination exercised by the individual when selecting a mate. In humans, females give birth to their offspring, while men do not, so females can be expected to be the more discriminating sex. Females limit the reproductive success of males, and men compete with other men for access to women. Men form a dominance hierarchy, while women exist in a more equitable social network. Men are forced into a lifetime of competing for status in order to attain a high-fitness mate. See Moxon (2008) and Sewell (2008). The need for men to maximize their rank in the dominance hierarchy led to greater overconfidence (via self-deception) in men than women (Barber and Odean 2001). For a classic text on the evolution of optimism, see Tiger (1995).

To clarify the difference between optimism and overconfidence, consider the following contemporary example: if you believe that the stock market will rise, you are an optimist; if you believe that you can forecast the stock market with greater accuracy than you actually can, then you are overconfident. Overconfidence causes individuals to overestimate how well calibrated they are.

11.3.4 Representativeness

Recall from your school days that the finite frequency theory of probability defines the probability of an outcome as the frequency of the number of times the outcome occurs relative to the number of times that it could have occurred. A quick count of the number of predators approaching is likely to be a useful heuristic for survival, which may explain why we make fewer errors when dealing with relative frequencies than when we are faced with (Bayesian) probabilities. Fast and frugal frequency-based probability, rather than Bayesian methods, has evolved (Gigerenzer and Hoffrage 1995; Cosmides and Tooby 1996). This leads to failing to take sufficient account of, or even ignoring, prior probabilities, which is known as *base rate neglect*.

Base rate neglect combined with overconfidence can lead to decisions being made based on how representative a given individual case appears to be independent of other information about its actual likelihood. This is the cognitive heuristic known as *representativeness* (or *similarity*) (Tversky and Kahneman 1974) and is essentially stereotyping. Representativeness, via underweighting the base rate, is likely to cause *overreaction*.

11.3.5 Availability

What is the effect of newspapers and other media reporting news? News, by definition, is unpredictable (otherwise, it would have been reported yesterday). If we cannot predict something, it will be a surprise. So news is surprising, the most likely to be reported news, therefore, is the most surprising. This means that rare events, such as a man being killed by a shark, are likely to be heavily reported. While, for example, dying of diabetes is much more common, but goes unreported. In other words, the media creates a biased impression of the world around us. Our ancestors lived without the luxury of the media, and the ease with which they remembered an event would have been more representative of the probability of it recurring. Of course, "extreme" events have always been more memorable than mundane events, but in the EEA, one would only experience or witness events (whether surprising or mundane) taking place within the environment of one's own tribe, so it made sense to remember the extreme or important events. To summarize, modern man is far more likely than his ancestors to recall events that he is unlikely to experience (such as an airplane crash). I hypothesize that this is how *availability* (or *saliency*) (Tversky and Kahneman 1973) evolved. Availability is a cognitive heuristic in which we rely upon knowledge that is readily available, rather than examine other alternatives or procedures. That is, we make decisions based on how easily things come to mind (which is usually something that is likely to be newsworthy).

11.3.6 Underreaction and Overreaction

There are occasions when different biases can work against each other. For example, as we have seen, the conservatism/anchoring/status quo bias causes *underreaction*, while representativeness is likely to cause *overreaction*. If "strength" represents the extremeness of some information, and "weight" represents the credence or reliability of the information, Griffin and Tversky (1992) have shown that, in general, a combination of high strength and low weight will generate overreaction, whereas a combination of low strength and high weight tends to lead to underreaction. There is also evidence that we expect underreaction to news, but an overreaction to a series of good or bad news (Barberis et al. 1998).

11.3.7 Herding

The aforementioned biases can affect individuals in isolation; in contrast, the following bias concerns an individual's response to their peers, so addresses group behavior. There is both greater safety and improved efficiency with task sharing in numbers, so human beings have always tended to live in groups. The size of social groups was likely to have been constrained by the information-processing capacities of the brain, with 150 people being a good average. This led to the type of conversation that helped our ancestors, such as information about food sources, dangers, or (most importantly) other people – tips and recommendations.[2] Today, due to faster and wider means of communication, such behavior can lead to *information cascades* and create *herding* (the *crowd effect*) with many people behaving in a similar manner, all following the *trend*.

---

[2]Gossip was of great importance from an evolutionary perspective, see Dunbar (1996).

11.4 The Effect of Cognitive Biases

11.4.1 Entrepreneurs

The task of an entrepreneur is seemingly straightforward: to search for a profit opportunity and exploit it. Until recently, economists had little to say about entrepreneurs, possibly because the behavior of entrepreneurs is inconsistent with the models of neoclassical economics. If entrepreneurs' behavior is irrational in this sense, it makes them ripe for studying in terms of behavioral economics. Below, we consider what characteristics and traits entrepreneurs exhibit that set them apart from nonentrepreneurs, and how the various previously discussed evolved heuristics and biases affect entrepreneurs.

Risk taking is at the heart of entrepreneurialism. Unlike risk-averse employees, entrepreneurs bear the risks associated with the business. Indeed, Sahakian et al. (2008) studied the brains of entrepreneurs and managers and found that, compared to their managerial counterparts, entrepreneurs are highly risk tolerant. Relative to others, entrepreneurs seem unlikely candidates for the conservatism/anchoring/status quo bias, but if susceptible are likely to underreact to news. As an example of the endowment effect, entrepreneurs are strongly attached to their companies, and habitually talk about their "babies".

Globally, the majority of entrepreneurs are male (Bosma et al. 2009). Sixty percent of small businesses fail within the first 6 years (Headd 2003), which is consistent with Atmar (1991)'s theory of males functioning as a "genetic filter" leading to many men failing.[3] Note that even if nine out of ten entrepreneurs lost $10,000, so long as one in ten entrepreneurs made $100,000, a risk-neutral individual would still consider becoming an entrepreneur a good bet. This would be consistent with the majority of men failing, and a positive skew of success.

If intelligence is the ability of an individual to perform a novel cognitive task, and an entrepreneur is "somebody who offers an innovative solution to a (frequently unrecognized) problem" (*The Economist* 2009), intuitively one would expect successful entrepreneurs to be of above average intelligence. Hartog et al. (2007) found that an individual's level of general intelligence increases both entrepreneurs' and employees' incomes to the same extent. Interestingly, there is a higher incidence of dyslexia in entrepreneurs than in both the normal corporate management population and the population as a whole (Logan 2009).

Although entrepreneurship has a reputation for excitement, successfully finding a gap in the market may be better achieved by focusing on something mundane. For example, in the USA, Fred Smith built a billion-dollar business by improving the

[3]Another important implication of the failure rate is that any study of entrepreneurs suffers from survivorship bias.

delivery of packages, and in the UK, Peter Jones became a multimillionaire in the mobile phone industry, not through mobile phone innovation, but by focusing on the distribution of the phones.

Entrepreneurs exhibit greater overconfidence than managers in large organizations (Busenitz and Barney 1997), and this is likely to lead entrepreneurs to overestimate how well calibrated they are. Bernardo and Welch (2001) argue that overconfident individuals (entrepreneurs) persist because they broadcast valuable private information to others. Excess overconfidence among males in particular is consistent with the larger proportion of male entrepreneurs.

Entrepreneurs exude optimism (Cooper et al. 1988; Cassar 2010). Optimism naturally creates a "bullish" tendency, so increases the number of entrepreneurs, as they have an often irrational belief that their new business venture will prosper. Brocas and Carrillo (2004) argue that optimism among entrepreneurs can be optimal as it avoids inefficient procrastination.

The availability bias could, for example, cause entrepreneurs to start a company selling a product because it has been featured in the media, when there would likely be less competition selling other products. To counter this, the customers may well be susceptible to the same bias and purchase the product on that basis. Traditionally, companies first established themselves in their local markets and then expanded abroad slowly, while more recent entrepreneurs sometimes span the globe from the very beginning.

Entrepreneurs manifest the representativeness bias more extensively in their decision-making than managers within large organizations (Busenitz and Barney 1997), so have a tendency to overgeneralize from limited information.

William Baumol, one of the leading economists in the area of entrepreneurial finance, defined an entrepreneur as "the bold and imaginative deviator from established business patterns and practices," which seems to imply that entrepreneurs are less prone to exhibit herding almost by definition. Indeed, it seems reasonable to assume that entrepreneurs exhibit herding to a lesser degree than the population as a whole. However, herding can lead entrepreneurs to create a bandwagon effect, with entrepreneurs mimicking each other. This would cause a particular market to become saturated, while other opportunities would be missed. Entrepreneurs may be more independent than the usual company employees who follow the rules, but they almost always need social networks to succeed. However, entrepreneurs are surprisingly unlikely to have (business) partners (Cooper and Saral 2010). Entrepreneurship flourishes in clusters. A third of American venture capital flows into two places, Silicon Valley and Boston, and two thirds into just six places, New York, Los Angeles, San Diego, and Austin as well as the Valley and Boston (*The Economist* 2009). One of the effects of entrepreneurial clusters may be that the increased networking and contact among the entrepreneurs works to create a culture that normalizes a more risk-tolerant type of decision making.

An entrepreneur's success will likely depend on the degree to which his probabilistic reasoning is calibrated and the degree to which his decision making is consistent with the normative expected utility theory.

11.4.2 Venture Capitalists

A venture capitalist's job is to select entrepreneurs according to their assessment of the potential performance of the business conditioned on the VC's own contribution, while considering the opportunity cost (in terms of both money and time) and their personal risk profile. The VC must also consider if and how the performance of a business will be correlated with his existing business interests, as positively correlated businesses increase risk.

Another term for "venture capital" is "risk capital," which gives a clue as to how the industry is perceived with regard to risk tolerance. However, the conservatism/anchoring/status quo bias is likely to prevent VCs from investing in risky ventures, so would work against the optimism bias.

VCs are overconfident (Zacharakis and Shepherd 2001). Overconfidence is likely to lead VCs to overestimate how well calibrated they are and therefore underestimate their chances of choosing start-ups that fail. As was the case with entrepreneurs, excess overconfidence among males is consistent with the larger proportion of male VCs (over 90% of VCs are male) (Brush et al. 2004).

VCs are less likely to be as optimistic as entrepreneurs, as they are taking the other side of the contract, and their overconfidence lies in their own talent, not in that of their entrepreneurs. However, optimism would lead VCs to overinvest in entrepreneurs, as they would expect a rosy future, which would include being bullish about potential start-ups.

The availability heuristic could lead to VCs investing in entrepreneurs in industries or markets that they are familiar with, which is quite rational, but could also mean that VCs ignore those in other markets or countries, potentially missing lucrative start-ups.

Representativeness leads VCs to predict future events by looking for familiar patterns and taking a short history of data and assuming that future patterns will resemble past ones. For example, a VC may invest in a particular industry because their last venture in the same industry did well, when the market may now be saturated.

There is evidence of herding by VCs (Lerner 2002). In the 1990s, Silicon Valley's VC's believed that they should invest "no further than 20 miles from their offices," and most venture capital goes into just a small number of business sectors: computer hardware and software, semiconductors, telecommunications, and biotechnology (*The Economist* 2009). Herding can lead VCs to chase after the same entrepreneurs, with the risk of missing out on less popular but profitable new ventures.

In common with that of an entrepreneur, a VC's success will likely depend on the degree to which his probabilistic reasoning is calibrated and the degree to which his decision making is consistent with the normative expected utility theory.

11.5 Conclusion and Implications

It should now be clear that the unboundedly rational economic man who seeks to maximize utility is consistent with *Homo sapiens* if and only if his utility coincides with gene replication. Wealth is a proxy for the mate value of males, so economics is an approximation of psychology. Economics is certainly a science as it focuses on first principles, and science is the pursuit of knowledge that allows us to generalize, so first principles, such as general laws, are key.

This chapter contains some messages important for future research and implications for actual entrepreneurs and venture capitalists. We have seen that the success of both entrepreneurs and VCs will likely depend on the degree to which his or her probabilistic reasoning is calibrated and the degree to which their decision making is consistent with the normative expected utility theory.

The research explicated here is based on theory, only some of which has empirical support. A lot of what we believe about the Pleistocene and evolutionary psychology is probably wrong (although in the absence of any viable alternative hypotheses, the broad hypothesis that our minds are the product of evolution is not controversial). The research would be strengthened by more empirical data supporting some of the predictions.

References

Atmar, W. 1991. On the role of males. *Animal Behaviour* 41: 195–205.

Barber, B.M., and T. Odean. 2001. Boys will be boys: Gender, overconfidence, and common stock investment. *The Quarterly Journal of Economics* 116: 261–292.

Barberis, N., A. Shleifer, and R. Vishny. 1998. A model of investor sentiment. *Journal of Financial Economics* 49: 307–343.

Bernardo, A.E., and I. Welch. 2001. On the evolution of overconfidence and entrepreneurs. *Journal of Economics & Management Strategy* 10: 301–330.

Bernoulli, D. 1738. Specimen theoriae novae de mensura sortis. *Co-mentarii Academiae Scientiarum Imperialis Petropolitanae* 5: 175–192.

Bernoulli, D. 1954. Exposition of a new theory on the measurement of risk. *Econometrica* 22: 23–36. English translation of Bernoulli (1738) by Sommer L.

Birnbaum, M.H. 2008. New paradoxes of risky decision making. *Psychological Review* 115: 463–501.

Bosma, N., Z.J. Acs, E. Autio, A. Coduras, J. Levie. 2009. Global entrepreneurship monitor: 2008 executive report.

Breiman, L. 1961. Optimal gambling systems for favorable games. In *Proceedings of the fourth Berkeley symposium on mathematical statistics and probability*, vol. I, ed. J. Neyman, 65–78. Berkeley: University of California Press.

Brocas, I., and J.D. Carrillo. 2004. Entrepreneurial boldness and excessive investment. *Journal of Economics & Management Strategy* 13: 321–350.

Brush, C., N. Carter, E. Gatewood, P. Greene, and M. Hart 2004. Gatekeepers of venture growth: A Diana Project report on the role and participation of women in the venture capital industry. Ewing Marion Kauffman Foundation, Kansas City.

Busenitz, L.W., and J.B. Barney. 1997. Differences between entrepreneurs and managers in large organizations: Biases and heuristics in strategic decision-making. *Journal of Business Venturing* 12: 9–30.

Buss, D. 2008. *Evolutionary psychology: The new science of the mind*, 3rd ed. Boston: Pearson Higher Education.

Cassar, G. 2010. Are individuals entering self-employment overly optimistic? An empirical test of plans and projections on nascent entrepreneur expectations. *Strategic Management Journal* 31: 822–840.

Cooper, D.J., and K.J. Saral. 2010. Entrepreneurship and team participation: An experimental study. Working paper. Florida State University, Tallahassee.

Cooper, A.C., C.Y. Woo, and W.C. Dunkelberg. 1988. Entrepreneurs' perceived chances for success. *Journal of Business Venturing* 3: 97–108.

Cosmides, L. 1989. The logic of social exchange: Has natural selection shaped how humans reason? Studies with the Wason selection task. *Cognition* 31: 187–276.

Cosmides, L., and J. Tooby. 1996. Are humans good intuitive statisticians after all? Rethinking some conclusions from the literature on judgment under uncertainty. *Cognition* 58: 1–73.

de Finetti, B. 1937. La prévision: Ses lois logiques, ses sources subjectives. Annales de l'Institut Henri Poincaré 7: 1–68. Translated into English as Foresight: Its logical laws, its subjective sources. In *Studies in Subjective Probability*, eds. H.E. Kyburg Jr, and H.E. Smokler, pp. 93–158. New York: Wiley, 1964.

Dunbar, R. 1996. *Grooming, gossip, and the evolution of language*. London: Faber and Faber.

Gal, D. 2006. A psychological law of inertia and the illusion of loss aversion. *Judgment and Decision Making* 1: 23–32.

Gigerenzer, G., and U. Hoffrage. 1995. How to improve Bayesian reasoning without instruction: Frequency formats. *Psychological Review* 102: 684–704.

Gintis, H. 2007. The evolution of private property. *Journal of Economic Behavior & Organization* 64: 1–16.

Griffin, D., and A. Tversky. 1992. The weighing of evidence and the determinants of confidence. *Cognitive Psychology* 24: 411–435.

Harrison, G.W., and E.E. Rutström. 2009. Expected utility theory and prospect theory: One wedding and a decent funeral. *Experimental Economics* 12: 133–158.

Hartog, J., J. van der Sluis, and M. van Praag. 2007. Returns to intelligence: Entrepreneurs versus employees. University of Amsterdam, Amsterdam.

Haselton, M.G., and D. Nettle. 2006. The paranoid optimist: An integrative evolutionary model of cognitive biases. *Personality and Social Psychology Review* 10: 47–66.

Headd, B. 2003. Redefining business success: Distinguishing between closure and failure. *Small Business Economics* 21: 51–61.

Kahneman, D., and A. Tversky. 1979. Prospect theory: An analysis of decision under risk. *Econometrica* 47: 263–292.

Kelly Jr., J.L. 1956. A new interpretation of information rate. *The Bell System Technical Journal* 35: 917–926.

Kemeny, J.G. 1955. Fair bets and inductive probabilities. *The Journal of Symbolic Logic* 20: 263–273.

Lehman, R.S. 1955. On confirmation and rational betting. *The Journal of Symbolic Logic* 20: 251–262.

Lerner, J. 2002. When bureaucrats meet entrepreneurs: The design of effective 'public venture capital' programmes. *The Economic Journal* 112: F73–F84.

Logan, J. 2009. Dyslexic entrepreneurs: The incidence; their coping strategies and their business skills. *Dyslexia* 15: 328–346.

MacLean, L.C., W.T. Ziemba, and G. Blazenko. 1992. Growth versus security in dynamic investment analysis. *Management Science* 38: 1562–1585.

McDonnell, P. 2008. *Optimal portfolio modeling: Models to maximize returns and control risk in Excel and R + CD (Wiley Trading)*. Hoboken: Wiley.

Moxon, S. 2008. *The woman racket: The new science explaining how the sexes relate at work, at play and in society*. Exeter: Imprint Academic.

Miller, G. 2001. *The mating mind: How sexual choice shaped the evolution of human nature*. London: Vintage. Originally published: 2000, London: William Heinemann.

Ramsey, F.P. 1926. Truth and probability. In *The foundations of mathematics and other logical essays*, Chapter VII, ed. R.B. Braithwaite, 156–198. London: Kegan, Trench, Trübner, 1931.

Sahakian, B., A. Lawrence, L. Clark, J.N. Labuzetta, B. Sahakian, and S. Vyakarnum. 2008. The innovative brain. *Nature* 456: 168–169.

Sewell, M. 2008. Gender (*sic*) equality (*sic*). *Opticon1826*, 4.

Shimony, A. 1955. Coherence and the axioms of confirmation. *The Journal of Symbolic Logic* 20: 1–28.

Sinn, H.-W., and A.J. Weichenrieder. 1993. The biological selection of risk preferences. In *Risk is a construct: Perceptions of risk perception*, ed. B. Rückversicherung, 67–83. Munich: Knesebeck.

Thaler, R. 1980. Toward a positive theory of consumer choice. *Journal of Economic Behavior & Organization* 1: 39–60.

The Economist. 2009. A special report on entrepreneurship, 12 March 2009.

Tiger, L. 1995. *Optimism: The biology of hope*. New York: Kodansha. Originally published: 1979, New York: Simon & Schuster.

Tversky, A., and D. Kahneman. 1973. Availability: A heuristic for judging frequency and probability. *Cognitive Psychology* 5: 207–232.

Tversky, A., and D. Kahneman. 1974. Judgment under uncertainty: Heuristics and biases. *Science* 185: 1124–1131.

Tversky, A., and D. Kahneman. 1992. Advances in prospect theory: Cumulative representation of uncertainty. *Journal of Risk and Uncertainty* 5: 297–323.

von Neumann, J., and O. Morgenstern. 1944. *Theory of games and economic behavior*. Princeton: Princeton University Press.

Zacharakis, A.L., and D.A. Shepherd. 2001. The nature of information and overconfidence on venture capitalists' decision making. *Journal of Business Venturing* 16: 311–332.

Chapter 12
Statistical Databases for Research on the Financing of Small and Start-Up Firms in the United States: An Update and Review*

Charles Ou

Abstract Academic and policy makers' interest in start-up business financing originated from two areas of concern – capital requirements for a start-up and the availability of external sources of private financing for a start-up. The former is important because underestimation of capital requirements has been mentioned by most small business management professional as one of the most critical deficiencies in start-up planning affecting the prospect for success or survival of a start-up (Studies on "new firm creation" using the Panel Study Entrepreneur Dynamics (PSED) data concluded that majority of nascent entrepreneurial start-ups failed to become operational businesses (Reynolds 2007).) Many nascent entrepreneurs have lost their lifetime savings in starting a business by being overly optimistic about the time and the resources it takes to develop and operate a viable business. The amount of capital required relative to the availability of internal resources will determine the need for external sources of capital. (Internal resources include monetary resources such as personal savings, other income (from the spouse as well), personal credit lines, as well non-monetary resources such as an office/work place at home, office equipment and telecommunication facilities, and personal transportation.) Unavailability of external sources of financing from private capital markets has been blamed for the high failure rate among start-ups.

This chapter updates information about the databases available for researchers in conducting financial research on small and startup firms. Three major databases on startup financing are discussed in detail, including comments on the strengths and weaknesses of each of the three major databases regarding their uses for conducting different types of research. It is followed by a review of major data

*This chapter is an updated version of the author's work previously published in the *Journal of Entrepreneurial Finance & Business Ventures* (Now *Journal of Entrepreneurial Finance*), Ou, C. Statistical Databases for Economic Research on the Financing of Small Firms in the United States, December, 2005 Journal of Entrepreneurial Finance and Business Ventures 10(3), 35–61.

C. Ou (✉)
Office of Advocacy, The US Small Business Administration, Washington, DC, USA
e-mail: ou3family@veriton.net

R. Yazdipour, *Advances in Entrepreneurial Finance: With Applications from Behavioral Finance and Economics*, DOI 10.1007/978-1-4419-7527-0_12,

sources for small firm financing, including time-series information, on activities in specific financing markets for small firms.

12.1 Introduction

Research on small business financing issues has been much hampered by the lack of statistics. Financial data come from the users of financial services – the small business borrowers – and/or the suppliers – the lenders and investors. Small firms are reluctant to provide information about their finances, and lenders/investors have been unwilling or unable to provide lending data classified by the size of the borrowing businesses. Except in the case of data compiled from administrative records and reports submitted by businesses and financial institutions, obtaining information on small firms' financing activities usually requires special surveys.

Policymakers and researchers need information to answer a variety of questions concerning the financing of small- and medium-sized enterprises: What is the structure of the financial market for small firms? Who are the participants, and how important are they to the lenders and borrowers? What are the costs? What factors affect participants' decisions in the market? How are the markets responding to changes in external conditions, such as economic conditions, deregulation, reregulation, etc.? How are the markets performing? How are the markets serving subgroups of borrowers such as minority- and women-owned firms, and start-up firms? Are there financing gaps and if so, what are the causes of the market imperfections – discrimination by the suppliers, underdevelopment of the market, high transaction costs as a result of high search costs? What has the government done to help? How successful have any such efforts been?

Different kinds of data are needed to investigate different issues. Cross-sectional data on the types of borrowers and lenders, the classes of products, geographic distribution, etc. are most useful for profiling the structure and characteristics of the market and its participants. A longitudinal or panel-type database is needed to examine a firm's decision and actions at different life-cycle stages. A cross-sectional database updated regularly over time with consistent data collection criteria and methods for a defined population offers opportunities for time-series analysis.[1]

Another issue that impinges on the availability of data is confidentiality. Micro-firm data enable researchers to investigate individual firms' decision-making processes – a firm's borrowing decision and a lender's lending decision. But many statistics collected by government agencies come as part of administrative records such as tax returns and unemployment insurance program filings, and are made available only in aggregate statistics.[2] It has been difficult to obtain permission to

---

[1] A database conducive to time-series analysis requires consistency in both the definition of variables and the statistical methodology of data collection.

[2] Preserving the privacy of the subjects of research – avoiding revealing the identity of individual reporting units – is a major concern of statistical collection agencies.

access micro-data because of confidentiality issues. Some public use files have been created by these agencies to make the micro-firm data available to the public for research, however.[3]

This chapter will provide a survey of statistical databases available for research on small business financing in the USA.

12.1.1 What Is a Statistical Database?

A statistical database is a database for a well-defined population. Populations can be of varying sizes as long as they are well defined. The Office of Advocacy estimates that there are 23 million small firms, but only 5.7 million small "employer" firms, based on estimates from the Bureau of the Census.[4] There are subgroups of small firms – by race, industry, and special business characteristics. For example, statistics are regularly collected for members of one of the largest small business trade associations in the USA, the National Federation of Independent Business (NFIB).

Information for a population can be collected from all known members of the population – so-called census data – or from a statistically representative sample of the population that the data are intended to describe or depict. A statistically representative sample requires that a generally acceptable survey methodology has been utilized to generate unbiased estimates of the population. The sampling methodology should meet requirements such as that the respondents are randomly selected rather than self-selected, nonresponse bias is known, etc. In short, the estimation must be capable of being duplicated.

The information collected must be for a specific time frame – during a certain time period (for flow information) or at a certain point in time (for stock information).[5]

In addition, the variables to be estimated should be defined and interpreted consistently by the respondents and data-collection organizations. This is especially important with financial data from small firms as many small business owners are unfamiliar with financial terminology. For example, a business's net worth is obtained by subtracting the value of debts from total assets owned by the business. This value does not exist until the business owner takes account of the firm's assets

[3]Examples include IRS Statistics of Income Division's individual income tax public use files and the Bureau of the Census Business Information Tracking Series files.

[4]US Small Business Administration, Office of Advocacy, *Small Business by the Numbers*.

[5]For example, flow information might include output, sales, and profits during a given quarter or a given year, as contrasted with stock-type information on the number of employees, value of total assets, or value of debts outstanding as of a certain date. This is one reason statistics collected in many commercial databases are not used by researchers as aggregated statistics for comparisons over time. For example, employment data from the Dun & Bradstreet file are not suitable for analysis of job creation over time by small firms in the USA.

and liabilities. Moreover, the value of net worth can vary since assets can be based on either cost or market value.[6]

The present chapter includes two main parts. Part I discusses three major data sources for research in startup financing in the United States. (Sections 12.2.1 to 12.2.3). Part II provides a comprehensive summary of major statistical databases available in the USA for financial research on small businesses in the United States. (Sections 12.4.1–12.5.8).

12.2 Major Statistics on Start-up Financing in the USA

12.2.1 The Kauffman Firm Survey (KFS)

The KFS is a longitudinal survey of new businesses in the USA (Table 12.1). This survey collected information on some 5,000 firms that started in 2004 and have been surveyed for additional years since the 2004 baseline survey (conducted in 2005). The database contains detailed information on the characteristics of both the firm and the business owners (for up to ten owners per firm) on their age, gender, race, ethnicity, education, previous industry experience, as well as their previous start-up experience. Detailed business information on industry group, physical location, employment, profits, intellectual property for the firms were also collected. For financial condition, financial capital (for both equity and debts) used at the start-up year and several follow-up years were collected as well as major items on a firm's balance sheet (on the firm's assets and liabilities) and the income statement (on revenues and expenses items).[7]

In the KFS survey, a business start-up is defined operational as a firm's first appearance on a "registry list" as follow:

> To be eligible for inclusion in the KFS, at least one of the following activities had to have been performed in 2004 and none performed in the prior year: a. Payment of state unemployment (UI) taxes; b. Payment of Federal Insurance Contributions Act (FICA) taxes; c. Presence of a legal status for the business; d. Use of an Employer Identification Number (EIN); and e. Use of Schedule C to report business income on a personal tax return.

While this definition of a business start did not use those specific economic or business events discussed in Part II, detailed business and financial information collected

---

[6]In this respect, data collected through interviews are more accurate than that obtained through mail surveys, unless the questions in the mail survey are simple and easily understood. Data collected in the SCF and SSBF are examples – all terms were well defined and interviewers were well trained to explain the terms when necessary.

[7]For more information about the KFS survey design and methodology, please see Ballou et al. (2007). A public use dataset is available for download from the Kauffman Foundation's website and a more detailed confidential dataset is available to researchers through a secure, remote access data enclave provided by the National Opinion Research Center (NORC). For more details about how to access these data, please see www.kauffman.org/kfs.

Table 12.1 Kauffman Firm Survey (2004)

Unit of analysis	Businesses
Data type	Micro-data from individual firms Longitudinal data (for 2004 through 2007: additional years of follow-up data will be collected) Time-series analysis – not possible
Population	All small business start-ups identified from the D&B Business Profile file (in 2004)
Coverage: population or sample	A sample of 4,928 firms
Definition of start-up	A start-up with fewer than 100 employees meeting the definition as specified
Data elements on small business financing	Sources and the amount of equity investment and debt funding from internal and external sources during the first year and the subsequent years in 2005, 2006, and 2007; sales/revenues and major expenses; profits during first and subsequent years; major assets and debts items at the end of the survey year. (Balance sheet data)
Time frame:	
a. Collection frequency	One time (2004)
b. Time period/date	Subsequent surveys of panel firms every year until 2012
Time lag in data availability	
Source	www.kauffman.org/kfs
Remarks	

under the longitudinal data collection approach allows a researcher to adopt a different start-up definition.

Strengths and weaknesses of the KFS

Strengths:

- A survey of "start-up" firms defined based on very specific criteria; although there are arguments about the appropriateness of the definition used;
- A longitudinal survey for at least 3 years since start-up (it has been decided that the panel firms will be surveyed for a total of 8 years beginning in 2004);
- All sources of "financial" resources were asked – formal, informal, inside, and external sources;
- Additional financial information are collected – e.g., income and expenses of business operation, during the start-up and subsequent years, were collected as well as major balance sheet items (on assets and debts).
- A very large sample of "nationally" representative start-ups; though there are major disagreement about the coverage of firms in the D&B Business population[8]

[8] The D&B business master list is one of the most comprehensive privately maintained business registry in the USA (some 10 million business entries). However, there are 25 million businesses in the USA in 2004 and many of these businesses are non-employer firms (19.5 million of them) and majority of them had annual revenues below $10,000. See Office of Advocacy, US Small Business Administration, The Small Business Economy-2008, Table A.1, July, 2009.

Weaknesses:

- A start-up as defined, an entry to the registry directories, will omit much information on start-up financing for those pre-start-up" stages.[9] Although, there was a question on the amount of cash and other assets the business had at the "start-up time" the sources of these cash and other assets would not be known because no question on the sources was asked; a question on the detailed sources of these assets would be most revealing;
- Little information was asked about the uses of non–monetary resources before (and even after) the start-up – non–monetary resources such as personal and household assets used for business purposes as well as non–paid labor services contributed by the owner(s). The availability or unavailability of these resources affects the success or failures of many business start-ups.[10]

To conclude, this database will provide much-needed information on start-up financing for a large sample of start-ups in the USA, especially for start-up financing information since and after the start-up year (as defined in the data collection project).

12.2.2 Panel Study of Entrepreneurial Dynamics (PSED II)

The first Panel Study of Entrepreneurial Dynamics (PSED I) is a multiyear effort to follow a representative sample of 685 people who were involved in the business formation process in 1998 and 1999, and who were surveyed in 1999 and were recontacted at 12, 24, and 36 months after the initial survey.[11] Limited information was collected on start-up financing items, though, for a detailed analysis of start-up financing issues. The second Panel Study (PSED II), a replication of PSED I, was initiated in 2005 under the support of Kauffman Foundation, and was designed to collect more detailed information about start-up outcomes, including both business and financial outcomes.[12] Similar to the approach adopted under the PSED I, the database was developed in three stages – first, a random sample of some 32,000 households was screened (with landline phones) to identify "nascent entrepreneurs active in the start-up phase"; second, 60-min phone interviews on the start-up-up initiative (for 1,214 respondents) were conducted; finally, two follow-up surveys (12 and 24 months after the initial survey) were conducted to collect information on "start-up effort outcome."

[9] Those nascent entrepreneurs that never become a start-up as defined by KFS will, of course, not be covered at all.

[10] The ability of the owner(s) to carry out a time-consuming start-up with no monetary compensation is much more constrained to a low-income, unemployed potential nascent business owners.

[11] The survey collected detailed information for a comprehensive assessment of the business creation process by a nascent entrepreneur. Data collected included factors that affect an entrepreneur's decision to create a business as well as those factors that "may be associated with completing the start-up process with a new firm" (Reynolds 2007).

[12] Reynolds (2009).

Though not as adequate as a national statistical source to derive national estimates on the magnitudes of start-up financing for small businesses in the USA, much insight can be gained from the survey's collection of information on start-up financing. Particularly useful is the survey's broad definition of a start-up, i.e., covering all stages of start-up operations from start-up preparation – possibly business birth, and pre-start-up financing. For example, detailed questions were asked about the amount and the sources of financing to the start-up before it establishes as a legal entity, to the new business as a legal entity, and to the new business 12 and 24 months after the start-up.[13]

Strengths and weaknesses of PSED (II)

Strengths:

- Though the "start-up" was defined as a firm established as a legal entity, detailed information on pre-start-up period were asked;
- A longitudinal survey for the base year and two follow-up years was conducted. This allowed for the collection of additional start-up financing information during the long process of start-up operation;
- Information on financial resources used as well as other information on financial outcome income and expenses of the business during the survey year were collected (though these are not as detailed as those collected by the KFS).

Weaknesses:

- Small sample size for subsequent surveys (in 2006 and 2007) makes this survey an inadequate database to provide accurate national estimates on the magnitudes and the uses of start-up capital by start-up firms in the USA.[14]
- Small sample size also makes it difficult to provide start-up analysis for subsectors/groups such as women, minority, etc.
- It is a cost inefficient approach to collect start-up financing data because it is very expensive to identify and collect information from those "nascent" entrepreneurs; the marginal costs of collecting start-up financing data on the very early stage of start-up process are very high.To summarize, this database provides useful insights about the importance of collecting detailed information on start-up activities over a relatively long period. However, although detailed information on start-up financing was collected after entry year through two follow-up surveys, the large fall-off in the sample size from 1,200 to 660 makes it difficult for using the survey for finding national estimates of the sources and the uses of capital by start-up firms in the USA. A larger sample and possibly an effort to recapture those missing firms, especially those failed, would make this survey more useful (Table 12.2).

[13] With questions on: additional equity provided by the start-up team members; additional loans to business from such sources as personal asset backed loans; lease commitments on physical assets; working capital loans; supplier credit;owners' personal loans; personal loans from of spouses, relatives, kin personal loans; employee and other persons; credit card debt to the new business; bank loans to the new business; and government agency loans.

[14] See Reynolds (2009).

Table 12.2 Panel study on entrepreneur dynamics (PSED II)

Unit of analysis	Nascent entrepreneurs
Data type	Micro-data from nascent entrepreneurs/business owners; Longitudinal data (for two additional years in 2006 and 2007); Time-series analysis – not possible
Population	All nascent small business start-ups identified from a population of households with landline phones in the USA
Coverage: population or sample	A final sample of 1,218 nascent entrepreneurs (for base year)
Definition of start-up	A nascent entrepreneur; an additional definition was introduced to include that "a legal entity is established";
Data element on small business financing	Sources and the amount of equity investment and debt funding from internal and external sources before, during the start-up, and two follow-up years after start-up)
	Sales/revenues and major expenses; profits during first and subsequent years; Major assets and debts items at the end of the survey year (Balance sheet data).
Time frame:	
a. Collection frequency	One time (2005)
b. Time period/date	Follow-up surveys of panel firms for 2006 and 2007
Time lag in data availability	12 months
Source	www.psed.isr.umich.edu
Remarks	Data available in either SAS transport file or in ASCII flat file.

12.2.3 Survey of Business Owners (SBO) 2002

The SBO is a consolidation of two prior surveys, the Surveys of Minority- and Women-Owned Business Enterprises (SMOBE/SWOBE), and the inclusion of questions from a survey discontinued in 1992 on Characteristics of Business Owners (CBO). As part of the Economic Census (of the Bureau of Census), the SBO is conducted every 5 years, for years ending in "2" and "7." The 2007 SBO is in the final stage of preparation and is ready for the field test.[15]

Types of Available Data

The 1992 CBO is the first national survey that provided very detailed information on both the characteristics of business owners as well as the characteristics of their businesses. As a replication, the SBO collected detailed statistics that describe the characteristics of business owners – e.g., gender, race, veteran status,

[15] SBO statistics describe the characteristics of US businesses by ownership category, i.e., by gender, Hispanic or Latino origin, and race of principal owners; by geographic area at the national, state, and sub-state regional levels; by 2-digit industry sector based on the 2002 North American Industry Classification System (NAICS); and by size of firm (employment and receipts). Summary reports of the 2002 SBO include – the Company Summary, released on September 14, 2006, and two additional reports on Characteristics of Businesses and Characteristics of Business Owners, released on September 27, 2006. (www.census.gov/econ/sbo/index.html), See also Fairlie and Robb (2008).

immigrant versus native born, the owner's age, education level, and business experience as well as their primary function in the business – the employment status in the business and their business interest. The SBO also collected detailed information about the characteristics of the businesses the owner(s) owned.[16] Information on businesses' characteristics and activities such as family-based versus home-based businesses, types of customers and workers, sources and purposes of financing are collected and made available in the report(s).

To obtain information on start-up financing, three questions were used:[17]

- First to identify the start-up – "In what year was this business originally established? (For owner(s), the year the ownership was established through "start-up, purchased, or inherited");
- Second, the sources of start-up capital used – "(for the owners) as of December 31, 2007, what was the source(s) of capital used to start or to acquire this business?";
- Third the amount of "start-up capital" used – "for the owners as of December 31, 2007, what was the total amount of capital used to start or to acquire this business (capital includes savings, other assets, and borrowed funds of owner(s)?"

Strengths and weaknesses of the SBO

Strengths:

- A national survey of a very large statistically representative sample of small business owners and the firms they owned; high response rates were achieved for this mail survey because it is mandatory survey from a government agency, (the Bureau of Census of the US Department of Commerce).
- Availability of administrative records (on sales, etc.) to supplement the survey collected data.
- A very large sample of start-ups, though with a vaguely defined "start-up year"

Weaknesses:

- Difficulties in collecting useful financial data from a one-time mail survey, as was discussed in the previous sections, because most start-up processes occur over an extended time period and many of them require additional capital injection years after the "start-up" year, however defined.[18]

---

[16] However, several important pieces of information on the characteristics of start-up firms and their owners asked in 1992 CBO were omitted in the SBO (2002) (see also Fairlie and Robb 2008). Since information about the owners was derived from the business populations based on the tax returns files, basic business information such as business organization forms, etc. was collected from administrative records.

[17] The questions on start-up financing asked in 2002 survey were found deficient in collecting the needed information on various sources of financing, in addition to the problems related to defining a "start-up" in an one-time survey. Though improved, problems remain in the new survey instrument for the upcoming 2007 SBO.

[18] Some 10% of "start-ups" in the PSED-II became "new firms" (initial profitability) after two follow-up interviews (i.e., 24 months after entry to start-up process). See Reynolds (2009). Consequently, the majority of the start-ups will continue to require injection of additional capital several years after the start-up year, however, defined.

- A vaguely defined and/or understood "start-up time" with no reference to specific start-up events created much doubt regarding the usefulness of the start-up financing data collected. A question such as "in what year was this business originally established (i.e., started, purchased, or inherited)?" is likely to be interpreted differently by different respondents. As a result, the capital requirements estimated from information provided by the respondents could widely differ because of the different start-up definitions used.
- Without collecting other information about financial conditions and activities of the owners/business at start-up, financing information collected under this survey will be difficult to interpret.To conclude, start-up financing information collected by SBO (in 2002 and the upcoming survey for 2007) may not provide much useful information to enhance our understanding of start-up financing in the USA. A reconsideration of the methodology and the approaches in collecting this information is warranted (Table 12.3).

12.3 Conclusions

The availability of Kauffman Firm Survey provides small business financial researchers with a most promising database on financing of business start-up in the USA. Many aspects of start-up financial research cannot be carried out because of the unavailability of panel data—a micro-firm database that traces financial developments of individual firms overtime. Financial information made available in the

Table 12.3 Survey of Business Owners (2002)

Unit of analysis	Business owners and their businesses
Data type	Micro-data from individual owners. However, it is difficult for researchers to access the micro-data at the Census; No longitudinal data Time-series analysis – not possible
Population	All business owners in the IRS
Coverage: population or sample	A sample of 20,561 business owners
Definition of small firm	
Small business data elements	Information on the characteristics of business owners and their businesses; Sources of financing used at start-up and during the year of survey (2002)
Time frame:	
a. Collection frequency	Irregular years (1992 and 2002)
b. Time period/date	End of the survey year and for the survey year
Time lag in data availability	3–4 years after data collection
Source	www.census.gov/econ/sbo/
Remarks	Data available in tabulated format. Special request to Bureau of Census for special tabulation can be considered

Kaufman Firm Survey enable an examination of the life cycle patterns of small growing firms.

In the following sections, a detailed review of key statistical databases for financial research on small firms in the USA will be provided.

12.4 Major Statistical Databases for Small Firm Financial Research in the USA—A Summary

Six major statistical databases will be described first in this section in terms of their coverage, the regularity of data collection, and strengths and limitations with respect to various small business research efforts. They include:

1. The Survey of Small Business Finances (NSSBF, 1987 and 1993 and SSBF, 1998)
2. Statistics on Loans to small businesses by depository institutions – a. call reports (June edition) and b. Community Reinvestment Act (CRA) reports (since 1997)
3. Consumer Finance Survey (by the Board of Governors of the Federal Reserve System)
4. Tax return data from the Statistics of Income (SOI) division of the Internal Revenue Service (IRS)
5. The National Federation of Independent Business (NFIB) studies of Credit, Banks, and Small Business, a survey of a special group of small firms – the members of the NFIB.

   This will be followed by brief discussions of several time series databases (in sections 12.5.1–12.5.8).

12.4.1 Survey of Small Business Finances (NSSBF, 1987 and 1993 and SSBF, 1998)

The Survey of Small Business Finances (formerly National Survey of Small Business Finances) collects information on small business finances from a nationally representative sample of small firms with fewer than 500 employees in the USA. The Board of Governors of the Federal Reserve System conducted three national surveys on small business finances in 1988 (using 1987 information), 1994–1995 (using 1993 information), and 1999–2000 (using 1998 information) (Table 12.4).[19]

[19] The first two surveys were called the National Survey of Small Business Finances (NSSBF). The Small Business Administration co-sponsored the first two surveys in 1988 and 1993. The Federal Reserve Board conducted a new survey covering information for the year 2003 during 2004–2005. The 2003 SSBF has been available for public use since 2007. For details, please visit www.federalreserve.gov/pubs/OSS/OSS3/nssbftoc.htm

Table 12.4 Survey of Small Business Finances (1998)

Unit of analysis	Businesses
Data type	Micro-data from individual firms
	Cross sectional;
	No longitudinal data
	Time-series analysis – possible with a carefully designed research methodology
Population	All small businesses in the D&B Business Profile file (5.2 million in 1998)
Coverage: population or sample	A sample of 3,561 firms
Definition of small firm	A firm with fewer than 500 employees
Small business data elements	Uses of financial services and credit with link to the suppliers; detailed information on the most recent loan applied/used; financial statement data
Time frame:	
a. Collection frequency	Once every 5 years (1987; 1993; 1998)
b. Time period/date	End of the survey year and for the survey year
Time lag in data availability	1 and 1/2 years after data collection
Source	www.federalreserve.gov/boarddocs/surveys/
Remarks	Data available in either SAS transport file or in ASCII flat file.

The SSBF (or NSSBF) is the most comprehensive source of data available on small businesses' use of financial services and the suppliers of these services. The survey collects detailed information about a firm's uses of all types of services and credit and their respective suppliers; characteristics of the firm and its primary owner (for example, firm and owner age, industry, and type of business organization); and the firm's income statement and balance sheet. The survey also asks for information about the firm's most recent borrowing experience, as well as its use of trade credit and capital infusions in the most recent period.

For the 1998 SSBF, a cross-sectional sample of 3,561 for-profit, non-financial business enterprises responded to the telephone interview (compared with 4,637 for 1993). These firms are a sampling of about 5.2 million small businesses in operation at the end of 1998.[20]

A consistent definition and a majority of identical questions used across all three of the NSSBF/SSBF surveys permits an analysis of changes over time. However, as with other data collections of general purpose statistics, the NSSBF/SSBF database will not provide information to investigate many other financing issues that are of interest to researchers and policymakers.

A small final sample is one of the major deficiencies of the 1998 SSBF.[21] This deficiency makes a detailed investigation of the financing issues for subgroups

[20] See Bitler et al. (2001). See also US Small Business Administration (September 2003).

[21] Despite an extra effort extended to increase the response rates for minority-owned firms in the 1998 survey, the outcome was a disappointment to the Federal Reserve Board's project director. The final count of small minority-owned firm respondents was 273 African-American owned firms, 214 Asian-origin firms, and 260 Hispanic-origin owned firms.

such as small firms owned by African-Americans, Asians, etc., difficult, if not impossible. Another problem with the survey, a problem faced by all surveys directly collecting financial information from small firms, is the long average interview time. In a survey for a comprehensive profile of a firm's financing sources, this is inevitable. However, high costs have reduced the likelihood of increasing the frequency of conducting the survey, say, every 2 or 3 years instead of every 5 years.[22]

Interim surveys using a shorter questionnaire covering more up-to-date developments in small business financing would be a very useful supplement to the present data collection effort. More information on lenders, especially commercial banks, could be included in the public use database. Finally, questions could be revised to obtain better information on the uses of equity capital.

Financial researchers at the Federal Reserve Board and the Federal Reserve Banks have utilized extensively the survey data, supplemented by internally available banking data for research on small business financing issues. The Office of Advocacy of the US Small Business Administration has also sponsored contract research with special emphasis on utilizing "large database," including this survey.[23] For a listing of research conducted using this database by researchers at the Federal Reserve, the Small Business Administration, and other small business researchers, see the "Survey of Small Business Finances abstract" www.federalreserve.gov/publs/oss/oss2/abstract.html/

12.4.2 Loans to Small Businesses by US Depository Institutions

Two databases are available for statistics on loans to small businesses by insured depository institutions (banks and thrifts or savings and loans). They are the Reports of Condition and Income (the call reports) submitted by all insured institutions and reports submitted under the Community Reinvestment Act requirements (the CRA reports) by larger depository institutions.

12.4.2.1 June Call Reports on Lending to Small Firms

Since 1993, the Federal Reserve Board and other regulatory agencies have required all insured depository institutions to report on small business lending in mid-year

---

[22] It is always expensive to collect financial information from small businesses – because of the high costs of reaching the potential respondents, obtaining successful responses, editing the responses, etc. The costs are belied to have amounted to several hundred dollars per successful response for the 1998 and 2003 surveys. High cost has been one of the major considerations in the Federal Reserve Board's decision on conducting this survey.

[23] www.sba.gov/advo/research/

Reports of Condition and Income (June call reports).[24] These data are collected to measure the extent of insured depository institutions' lending to small businesses. In June 2002, there were 7,949 commercial banks submitting the reports (Table 12.5).

In the June edition of the call reports, insured depository institutions report on two types of business loans: (1) commercial and industrial loans outstanding to US businesses and (2) loans secured by non-farm non-residential properties, by loan size. That is, the annual June reports cover, for each type of business loan, the number and amounts outstanding for loans with origination amounts of less than \$100,000, \$100,000–\$250,000, and \$250,000 to less than \$1 million.[25]

Attractive features of the call report data set are:

1. It is an administrative record submitted by all institutions under reporting requirements.[26]
2. It is fairly timely; data are available within 3–4 months.
3. With a well-defined population, annual data can be collected over time to permit a time-series analysis of small business lending activities;

Table 12.5 Call reports submitted by banks and thrifts to regulatory authorities

Unit of analysis	Depository institutions – banks and thrifts
Data type	Micro-data from individual institutions Cross sectional Longitudinal data possible but only with great effort Suitable for time-series analysis
Population	All insured depository institutions in the USA
Coverage: population or sample	All reporting insured institutions
Definition of small firm	By loan size, not by borrower size.
Small business data elements	Loans outstanding; number and dollar amounts of business loans; commercial and industrial and non-residential mortgage loans by three loan sizes (<\$100,000; \$100,000 to <\$250,000; and \$250,000 to <\$1 million)
Time frame:	
a. Collection frequency	Once a year in the June edition of the call reports
b. Time period/date	End of June
Time lag in data availability	4 months after report submission
Source	www.chicagofed.org/economic_research_and_data/commercial_bank_data.cfm
Remarks	Knowledge and experience in accessing and manipulating data files are essential in efficiently conducting statistical research using this and related files

[24] Major reporting problems occurred in the first year (1993), but since 1994, the data have been mostly reliable.

[25] Origination amounts are the larger of the loan extension, loan commitment, or total loan value if the extension is part of a loan participation.

[26] However, a member of a bank holding company (BHC) can file a separate report or report its activities in the consolidated report filed by the parent BHC.

4. Longitudinal studies could be attempted by creating panel data. However, extensive efforts would be required, including the uses of other banking files maintained by the federal regulatory institutions – the Federal Reserve System, the Federal Deposit Insurance Corporation, etc. because of extensive merger and acquisition activities of major banks during the past two decades.[27]

12.4.2.2 The Community Reinvestment Act (CRA) Database

The Community Reinvestment Act (CRA), enacted in 1977, was intended to encourage and monitor banks to meet the credit needs of the local communities from which they obtain deposited funds. The geographic location of loans made by the depository institutions is identified in the reports submitted to federal financial regulatory agencies. In 1994, the federal banking supervisory agencies revised the regulations implementing the CRA. The revisions included a requirement that banks report data on small business lending by census tract (Table 12.6).[28]

Table 12.6 CRA reports submitted by banks and thrifts to regulatory authorities

Unit of analysis	Depository institutions – banks and thrifts
Data type	Micro-data from individual institutions Cross sectional Longitudinal data possible for selected institutions; Time-series analysis – not yet
Population	Large insured depository institutions in the USA
Coverage: population or sample	All large reporting institutions – 900 larger banks and BHCs, 2002
Definition of small firm	By loan size, not by borrower size; also, small firms with receipts of less than $1 million.
Small business data elements	Amount of loans for the year. Number and dollar amounts of business loans; C&I and non-residential mortgage loans by three loan sizes (<$100,000; $100,000 to <$250,000; and $250,000 to <$1 million)
Time frame:	
a. Collection frequency	Once a year
b. Time period/date	Calendar year
Time lag in data availability	May or June in the following year.
Source	Federal Financial Institution Examination Council; website (http://www.ffiec.gov/cra/default.htm).
Remarks	In ASCII flat file.

[27] See, KeyPoint Consulting, LLC, (by Hancock, Wilcox, and Peek) the Effects of Mergers and Acquisitions on Small Business Lending by Large Banks, a report prepared for the US Small Business Administration, Office of Advocacy (March 2005). www.sba.gov/advo/research/banking.html

[28] For more information about the history of the CRA, see Home purchase lending in low-income neighborhoods and to low-income borrowers, *Federal Reserve Bulletin*, 71–105, February 1995, and New information on lending to small businesses and small farms: the 1996 CRA data, *Federal Reserve Bulletin*, 1–35, January 1998.

To minimize the paperwork burden on small banks, the bank regulatory authorities require only banks with assets over $250 million or any member banks of a bank holding company (BHC) with assets over $1 billion to provide this information. For 2001, some 900 banks and BHCs filed CRA reports. These banks made 73% of the small business loans under $ 1million. However, they accounted for 86 percent of total domestic assets and 87 percent of all business loans (based on June 2002 call reports for these banks).[29]

A Comparison of the Two Data Sets. The call report and CRA data complement each other, but are not comparable, in that they provide different kinds of loan information, are identified differently by location, and cover different banks (not all banks are required to report under the CRA program) (Table 12.7).

CRA data reflect the loans being made during a given year (the flow of credit), while the call reports cover all the loans outstanding as of June 30 of the year (the stock of credit). The call reports attribute all lending of a banking organization to the state where the headquarters of the reporting bank is located,[30] while the CRA data report actual lending in a given census bloc.[31]

One major limitation of the banking data is that only very limited information is available about the loan contracts – nothing about the business borrower, loan type, loan terms (including maturity, loan costs, etc.), or the location where the loans were made (for call report data). Small loan size is used as a proxy for lending to small firms.[32]

Table 12.7 Comparison of the call report and CRA databases

	Call report data	CRA data
Loan information provided	Stock of business loans outstanding, for example, as of June 2002	Flow of business loans over entire calendar year, for example, for 2001
How location is identified	Bank headquartered in the state	Lending activity in the state by a CRA reporting bank or BHC
Categories of banks covered	All reporting commercial banks and bank holding companies	Banks with $250 million or more in assets or members of BHCs with more than $1 billion in assets

29 See Table G in US Small Business Administration (December 2003).

30 Given the recent increase in interstate mergers, call report data become less relevant and CRA data become more relevant in understanding the lending activity in a given state.

31 For example, in the call report database, Wells Fargo is shown as located in California, but the CRA database shows Wells Fargo lending in all 50 states. Consequently, CRA data are important in analyzing the state-by-state lending behavior of the larger banks.

32 However, this assumes that small loans are initiated with small firms. In some situations, this assumption may not be tenable. The 1997 revision to the CRA required banks to report loans to businesses with annual revenues under $1 million. This should provide useful reference information.

Second, depository institutions make loans to small businesses through different channels – indirectly through personal loans to business owners in the forms of home equity lines, home equity loans, and personal credit cards or credit lines, as well as directly through loans to businesses *per se*. Personal loans used for business purposes will not be booked as commercial and industrial loans or non-farm, non-residential property loans.

Additional problems arise in attempts to use the CRA database for time-series analysis. As the number of reporting banks and the component banks of a BHC changes over time, the reporting population is not defined. Caution is needed to conduct a time-series analysis of aggregate trends in small business lending by CRA-reporting banks.

Another major problem is that the CRA database provides only loan data. Other information about a bank's lending activities and performance can be obtained by linking the CRA data files to the call report files. While it is easier now to link the two databases, the results have not been totally successful.[33]

Comparisons of figures in the two databases are also difficult, as CRA data reflect annual flows, and call report data reflect loans outstanding as of June 30, and there is no information about the maturity structure of the loans made.

Finally, the number of credit card loans issued by major banks has been increasing. The amount of these loans reflects line limits, while the loans outstanding are amounts drawn down. Since many banks do not report credit card operations separately (for example, Wachovia, US Bankcorp, Wells Fargo, and others), the relationship between loan flows and loans outstanding becomes rather complex.

Of course, the data would be more useful if firm size rather than loan size is available. In addition, for banks that issue considerable credit in the form of business credit cards and that maintain separate accounting operations for these activities, credit card activities should be reported separately from other C&I lending.

Despite the limitations of these data, a sizeable body of literature has used the call reports and the CRA database to examine issues centering around bank consolidation and the effects of bank size on small business lending. Examples: papers by Peek and Rosengren (1998); Strahan and Weston (1998); Berger et al. (1998); Walraven (1997); Kolari (2003) Symolic and Avery (2002); Avery, Bosatic, and Canner on CRA Special Lending Programs, *Federal Reserve Bulletin*, November 2000.[34]

12.4.3 The Survey of Consumer Finances (SCF)

The Survey of Consumer Finances (SCF) is a triennial household survey sponsored by the Federal Reserve Board with cooperation from the Statistics of Income

[33] In the 2000 version of *The Bank Holding Company Study,* matching was successful so that both the Call Report and CRA information on BHCs could be ranked using Advocacy's four-variable methodology.

[34] Data became available in 1997. See also annual analyses of banks' lending to small firms by the US Small Business Administration (December 2003), and editions for years from 1994 through 2001.

Division (SOI) of the Internal Revenue Service (IRS). Detailed data are collected on household finances – sources of household income and expenses, details of holdings of assets and debts, as well as employment status, household characteristics, and risk-taking attitudes. The most recent survey, the 2001 SCF, collected information between June and December of 2001 (Table 12.8).

While most interviews were obtained in person, about 35% were conducted by telephone, generally as an accommodation to respondents' preferences.[35] Since data are collected on certain items that are not always widely distributed in the population (e.g., ownership of privately held businesses or tax-exempt bonds), the SCF combines two techniques for random sampling. The sample is selected from a dual frame that is composed of a standard, multistage area-probability (AP) sample and a list frame.[36]

SCF is the best database to investigate the financial behavior and investment activities of owners of, and investors in, privately held businesses in the USA. It allows the researchers to develop a profile of household heads that own and invest in privately held businesses, including the number and changes in the number of households that own privately held businesses; profiles of different types of business owners and non-business owners, including multiple business owners/investors and career-oriented self-employed individuals. (The table provides a brief

Table 12.8 The survey of consumer finances, 2001

Unit of analysis	Households – head of the household; Job of the spouse also
Data type	Micro-data from individual firms
	Cross sectional
	Longitudinal data – No
	Time-series analysis – possible for certain topics
Population	All households in the USA (110 million households in 2001)
Coverage: population or sample	A sample of 4,449 households
Definition of small firm	"Privately" held businesses
Small business data elements	Holdings of various assets and debts of business owners and "investors" in privately held businesses.
Time frame:	
a. Collection frequency	Once every 3 years (1988; 1992; 1995, 1998, and 2001).
b. Time period/date	End of the survey year and/or the survey year;
Time lag in data availability	1 and 1/2 years after data collection
Source	www.federalreserve.gov/boarddocs/surveys/
Remarks	Data available in either SAS transport file or in ASCII flat file.

[35] For the 2001 Survey of Consumer Finances, the median-length interview required approximately 79 min, although complicated cases took substantially longer.

[36] See Kennickell and McManus (1993) for a discussion of the sample design. The list frame is based on statistical records derived from tax returns. The list sample is designed to over-sample relatively wealthy families (excluding the Forbes' 400 wealthiest in the USA). Of the 4,449 completed interviews in the 2001 survey, 2,917 families came from the AP sample and 1,532 came from the list sample. The response rate for the AP sample was about 68%. The overall response rate for the list sample was about 30%.

description of these owners for 1989 through 2001).[37] Since the SCF included questions on detailed household financial transactions – investment in personal and business assets as well as the sources of financing – it is an invaluable source of information on the intermingling of owners' personal and business finances. (See Avery and Haynes on wealth as collateral versus uses of personal financing sources (HELC), etc. for business purposes).[38]

Since the unit of observation is the head of a household, information collected has more relevance to the activities of the business owner than to the business(es) they own. While the survey also collects information about the businesses households own – including the number of employees, type of business, industry, gross revenues, net income, how and when the business was acquired – the database is not an important source of information on the small business population (privately held businesses) in the USA. The data provide a profile of the "first" businesses identified by the business owners for the 1998 survey. Of a total of 13 million first businesses owned by 13 million business owners, 6.5 million are sole proprietorships – 3.75 million non-employer sole proprietorships and 2.8 million sole proprietorships with employees. That is, of a total of 7.23 million employer firms identified as the first business owned, 2.8 million were sole proprietorships. In 1998, the US business population had 5.2 million employer firms, fewer than the 7.2 million identified in the SCF. Apparently, many businesses have multiple owners and many business owners owned multiple businesses.[39]

For working papers and articles using the SCF, visit the Federal Reserve Board website at www.federalreserve.gov/pubs/oss/oss2/methods.html/ See also Haynes (2003), and Ou and Haynes (2003).

12.4.4 Tax Return Data from the Statistics of Income Division of the Internal Revenue Service

Tax returns submitted by business taxpayers containing statements of revenue and expenses and balance sheet statements (for assets and liabilities) are the most comprehensive data on the financial conditions of businesses in the USA.[40] The Internal Revenue Service's Statistics of Income division annually conducts a sampling of

[37] See Haynes and Ou (November 2003) (www.sba.gov/advo/research/).

[38] See also Haynes et al. (1999).

[39] The database could be an useful source of information on small sole proprietorships owned by American households—those that have yet to be captured in the Census Bureau file. In the 2010 Survey, the Federal Reserve has included an extensive survey on the sources and the uses of financing the businesses owned by business owners. The 2010 SCF data should be available to the public in 2011.

[40] Internal Revenue Service, Statistics of Income Division, *Sole Proprietorship Returns*, various years; *Partnership Returns*, various years; *Corporation Income Tax Returns*, various years, and *Corporate Source Book*, various years. However, no balance sheet information is required in the sole proprietorship tax filings. See also the SOI Division's *SOI Bulletin* for articles about these publications, as well as an analysis of the developments in these sectors.

tax returns (for different company organizations) for information on the financial condition of business operations in a given calendar or fiscal year for the business (Table 12.9).[41] Aggregate data are tabulated by industry code and by firm size and are made available to the public through publication of the reports.

The SOI database has been used by various federal statistical agencies as the basis for estimates of various economic and business activities in the USA.[42] Various traditional financial ratios have been computed for use by financial analysts (for corporations and partnerships that are required to file balance sheet statements with the IRS).[43]

Overall, the database is not very useful for doing research on issues related to the availability of financing to small firms and the role different suppliers play in

Table 12.9 Corporation source book of the internal revenue Service[a]

Unit of analysis	C and S corporations
Data type	Micro-firm analysis – no Cross-sectional analysis Longitudinal – no Time-series analysis by size and industry[b]
Population	All corporations submitting tax returns to the IRS (4.7 million in 2000)
Coverage: population or sample	A sample of about 12,000 tax returns
Definition of small firm	Asset size of corporations – varying asset sizes provided
Small business data elements	Major items in the income/expense statement and major assets and liabilities in the balance sheet plus tax-related variables
Time frame:	
a. Collection frequency	Once every year (fiscal or calendar year depending upon company accounting practices)
b. Time period/date	Calendar or fiscal year
Time lag in data availability	2 to 2 1/2 years after tax filing
Source	*SOI Bulletins*, various issues, and SOI Division of IRS www.irs.gov/taxstats/index.html?portlet=5
Remarks	No micro-data on business tax returns is available for public uses. Requests to the Office of Statistics of Income division (SOI) for special tabulations are accepted.

[a]See also Corporation Tax Returns, Partnership Returns and Sole Proprietorship Returns prepared by the US Department of the Treasury, Internal Revenue Service, Statistics of Income Division
[b]See Dynamics of Women-Operated Sole Proprietorships – 1990–1998, Office of Advocacy, US Small Business Administration, March 2003

[41] The sample sizes are around 12,000 for corporate tax returns and 50,000 for sole proprietorship returns.

[42] The US Department of Commerce's Bureau of Economic Research and Bureau of the Census have made much use of the SOI database. SOI data on corporations have also been essential for reaching high-income households in the USA for the Survey of Consumer Finances.

[43] Prentice Hall, Financial ratios for US Business, various years (until 1985?).

the small business financing markets. One major limitation of the database is that since the data are for tax filing purposes, the asset and liability items are grouped in a general purpose accounting format – e.g., debts in the balance sheets filed are grouped with reference to maturity – current, short-term, and long-term debts (with maturities of over 1 year), and by debt type such as bonds, trade debts, or mortgage-related debt. No reference is made to other debt types, such as credit lines, or to debt sources or suppliers of the funds.

The database also offers limited information about the sources of equity capital for small firms. Only one source of internal equity – retained earnings – can be identified from these annual statements.[44] Moreover, the value of net worth is not well defined because it is a residual item in accounting, defined after both the values of total assets and liabilities are established.[45] This also explains why a large number of small corporations show negative net worth in the tax returns, even though these corporations continue to operate with positive cash flows and vitality.

Finally, confidentiality (and disclosure) issues remain a major obstacle hindering researchers' access to more details or microdata in the SOI databases.

12.4.5 NFIB Survey of Credit, Banks, and Small Business

The National Federation of Independent Business (NFIB) initiated a survey on credit market activities and attitudes of its members in 1980. Subsequent surveys were conducted in 1982, 1984, 1987, 1995, and late autumn of 2001. The findings of the recent survey appear in *Credit, Banks, and Small Business—the New Century* (Table 12.10).[46] This constitutes the longest time series on small business finances, longer than the National Survey of Small Business Finances conducted by the Federal Reserve Board (beginning in 1987). While there is some overlap in content between these two perspectives on small business finances, they are on the whole complementary. The NFIB credit and banking survey is designed more to collect information for investigation of the changing market conditions and their impact on small business financing. The Federal Reserve Board survey collects statistics on broader areas of small business financing – detailed information on the uses of all types of credit and financial services, with specific links to the suppliers.

From the beginning, the survey sample for *Credit, Banks, and Small Business* has been drawn from the NFIB membership, and this is also true of the 2001

[44] See *The State of Small Business: A Report of the President, 1987*, Chap. 2, 72–74.

[45] Consequently, it is not very meaningful to calculate one important indicator – the debt-to-equity ratio. The broad NAICS industry grouping does not help either.

[46] NFIB Research Foundation, *Credit, Banks, and Small Business – the New Century,* at www.nfib.org

Table 12.10 NFIB survey of credit, banks, and small firms, 2001

Unit of analysis	NFIB member firms
Data type	Cross-sectional analysis Time-series analysis for many variables
Population	Over 500,000 members of the trade association (NFIB)
Coverage: population or sample	A sample of about 12,500 for the 2001 survey; A response rate of 18% for 2,220 responses
Definition of small firm	NFIB members
Small business data elements	Detailed items on the uses of credit by member firms, especially their experience; demographic characteristics of firms
Time frame:	
a. Collection frequency	Once every 3–7 years
b. Time period/date	Most current year and/or during the past year of past 3 years.
Time lag in data availability	1 ½ to 2 years
Source	www.nfib.org/research

edition.[47] More attention has been devoted to obtaining information on borrower and lender characteristics, changes in credit market conditions and lending practices, and the experience of small business owners in the banking markets. Information collected covers sources of financing for small firms; types of financing, such as credit cards, trade credit, and other products and services; technology and product/service use; credit availability and terms; the credit search, including the effects of mergers and acquisitions on banking competition; and the prices for and quality of the financial services used by small firms.

12.5 Statistics for Time-Series Analysis of Small Business Financing Issues in the USA

The data described above are more comprehensive data-collection efforts, intending to provide a more detailed description of the markets – market activities as well as factors that affect the behaviors of the market participants. Most of these databases

[47] NFIB, "*The Credit, Banks...*" micro-data are available for researchers wishing to use them. While the NFIB membership is large and generally reflects the broader population, the sample inevitably creates questions about whether it is representative of the small business population in the USA. The authors of the studies discussed weighting the data in response. A set of weights appears in the dataset for those who are more concerned about whether the sample is representative and less concerned about change over time. The weights were created by the authors from a three-axis matrix consisting of employee size of the business (four classifications), industry (eight major SIC codes), and geographic region (seven regions). The matrix was produced by the Office of Advocacy of the U.S. Small Business Administration.

are not designed to provide time-series information for the analysis of trends and cyclical fluctuations in the market activities. It is true that there are enough years of annual call report data to portray some trends, but not cyclical changes. Because of the short duration of recessions in the US economy over the past 30–40 years, only quarterly data permit an analysis of small business financing issues during these periods.[48]

Data have been collected and estimates made for financing activities in some specific markets used by small firms to examine trends and cyclical changes in the credit conditions confronted by small businesses. For example, quarterly data are available only on a very limited basis from the Flow of Funds Accounts data prepared by the Federal Reserve Board. Quarterly surveys on the banks' lending conditions and small firms' perceptions of credit availability are conducted by the Federal Reserve Board and the NFIB (from their member survey). Quarterly estimates are now also available for venture capital funding.

Some of these databases are collected with a lower degree of comparability with other comprehensive databases – that is, with different small business definitions, a less comprehensive small business population, and for some, the sample may not be statistically representative, etc. The data collected, or estimates provided, however offer more current information about developments in the markets and changes in activities in the markets for small business financing. These series include:

1. Federal Reserve Board, "Flow of Funds Accounts"
2. Federal Reserve Board, "Senior Loan Officer Opinion Survey"
3. Federal Reserve Board, "Survey of Terms of Business Lending' (Statistical Release E2) on bank loan rates by loan size
4. US Department of Commerce, Bureau of the Census, Quarterly Financial Reports
5. National Federation of Independent Business (NFIB), quarterly (and monthly) surveys of business expectations
6. National Venture Capital Association (NVCA)/Thomson Financial Corporation, Venture Capital Yearbook
7. Center for Venture Research, University of New Hampshire, angel capital
8. Thomson Financial, initial public offerings (IPOs) of small issuers

12.5.1 *Flow of Funds Accounts for Non-farm, Non-corporate Business in the USA*

The Federal Reserve Board's Flow of Funds data provide estimates of the sources and uses of funds by non-financial corporate businesses and by non-farm, non-corporate businesses. Commercial mortgage loans and bank loans not elsewhere

---

[48] See Joel Popkin and Company (July 2003), and PM Keypoint (June 2003).

classified are identified as the sources of funds in the flow of funds accounts. Since no breakdown for small corporations is available in the non-financial corporation accounts, only the information on accounts for non-farm, non-corporate businesses is useful for understanding the small business financial markets.[49]

For more information, see Board of Governors of the Federal Reserve System, "Flow of Funds Accounts," various issues. (www.federalreserve.gov/releases/)

12.5.2 Senior Loan Officer Opinion Survey on Bank Lending Practices

The Senior Loan Officers' Survey, conducted quarterly by the Federal Reserve Board, solicits, among other things, information on changes in bank-lending policies toward small- and medium-sized to large firms.[50] Small firms are defined as firms with less than $50 million in annual sales. The sample consists of approximately 60 large domestic banks and 24 US branches and agencies of foreign banks. The three questions relevant to small business borrowers relate to loan standards, the spread of the lending rate over the banks' cost of funds, and the demand for loans.

One major limitation of the survey is that since only loan officers of large banks (and branches of foreign banks in the USA) are included in the survey, and small businesses are defined as those with annual sales of under $50 million, information collected in this survey does not cover the majority of small businesses in the USA.

For more information, see www.federalreserve.gov/boarddocs/surveys/

12.5.3 Survey of Terms of Business Lending

The Survey of Terms of Business Lending collects data on details of the terms of borrowing for gross commercial and industrial (C&I) loan extensions made by commercial banks during the first full business week in the middle month of each quarter (February, May, August, and November). The authorized panel size for the survey is 348 domestically chartered commercial banks and 50 US branches and agencies of foreign banks. However, the estimates reported here are not intended to measure the average terms on all business loans in bank portfolios.

---

[49] The usefulness of this account is further diminished by its "residual" nature – that is, many of the estimates are derived from the subtraction of other accounts from the total. The result is that larger than average estimates are observed for several items in the accounts after revision of the estimates.

[50] The Federal Reserve Board generally conducts the survey quarterly, timing it so that results are available for the January, May, August, and November meetings of the Federal Open Market Committee. The Federal Reserve occasionally conducts one or two additional surveys during the year – for example, in 1998 and 2001.

The sample data are used to estimate the terms of loans extended during that week at all domestic commercial banks and all US branches and agencies of foreign banks. Information collected is reported by loan size (under $100,000, $100,000 to under $1 million, $1 million to under $10 million, and over $10 million) and by risk category of the loans.[51] The variables provided in the statistical release include: maturity/repricing interval, risk category of loans; weighted-average effective loan rate (percent); total value of loans; average loan size; weighted-average maturity; and percent made under commitment, secured by collateral, subject to prepayment penalty, index based, etc.

The survey is the only source for information on the terms of bank loans to small firms (or small loans) by commercial banks in the USA. Since loan volumes are also estimated, it is tempting to attempt to compare the estimates with the loan estimates derived from the CRA reports. But as readers are cautioned, the estimates are not intended to measure total business loans in the banks' portfolios.

For more information, see *Federal Reserve Bulletin*; Statistical Release E.2 of the Board of Governors of the Federal Reserve System and www.federalreserve.gov/releases/.

12.5.4 Bureau of the Census, Quarterly Financial Reports

The Census Bureau's Quarterly Financial Reports provide the most up-to-date information on the financial positions of US corporations.[52] Based upon a sample survey, the QFR presents estimated statements of income and retained earnings, balance sheets, and related financial and operating ratios for manufacturing corporations with assets of $250,000 and over; and mining, wholesale trade, and retail trade corporations with assets of $50 million and over. The statistical data are classified by industry and by asset size.[53] The data collected are the basis for the Bureau of Economic Analysis' quarterly estimates of economic activity in the USA. While estimates of financial activities for small manufacturing corporations continue to be provided in the report, information for small firms became less useful after 1985, when an effort to reduce reporting burden for small companies substantially reduced the sample size. Consequently, many variables for small manufacturing corporations were estimated, rather than collected quarterly. The data collection efforts have been transferred from the Federal Trade Commission to the Bureau of the Census.

[51] Research staff at the Federal Reserve Board have usually been very receptive to suggestions about doing special tabulations on the database for use by the Small Business Administration.

[52] The survey was conducted by Federal Trade Commission before 1984 when the Bureau of the Census took over the collection and publications of the database.

[53] However, data are provided only on small manufacturing corporations with assets under $10 million. Moreover, because of the small number of respondents in the survey with a shorter questionnaire, estimates were made for several variables in place of data collected.

For more information, see US Department of Commerce, Bureau of the Census, *Quarterly Financial Reports.* (www.census.gov/csd/qfr/)

12.5.5 NFIB Survey on Small Business Trends

In addition to the survey of credit, banks, and small business as discussed in the previous section, the NFIB Research Foundation conducts several other surveys. One survey that results in time-series statistics for current business conditions and business attitudes of small firms is the quarterly survey of small business activities and attitudes as reported in Small Business Economic Trends.[54]

The quarterly survey collects detailed information on members' past business activities – sales, employment, etc., as well as their expectations of business conditions in the immediate future. Questions about credit conditions include those on credit availability, interest rates paid, and whether financing is a factor in business-related expectations and decisions.[55] In general, the questions asked in the survey are subjective – for example, questions as to whether current conditions in business or investment are better or worse than in the past or whether certain conditions are expected to get better or worse in the future. Time periods referenced in the questions are not uniform, but most questions refer to the past or the next 3 months. (Source: www.nfib.org/research)

12.5.6 National Venture Capital Association (NVCA)/Thomson Financial Venture Capital Yearbook www.pwcmoneytree.com/moneytree/index.jsp

For a small number of emerging companies with fast growth potential, external equity capital plays a very critical role in financing their birth and growth. While private investment in dynamic ventures is very popular, very limited information is available about the magnitude of private equity investment. Only investment by formally organized institutions, venture capital funds, has been attempted since the mid-1970s.[56]

[54] In fact, monthly surveys are conducted by NFIB with larger sample size for the end of the quarter months. The other two are: (1) Small Business Poll (special issues faced by small business) and (2) Survey of Small Business Problems and Priorities. Note that the Small Business Poll solicits information from a nationally representative sample of small firms (conducted by the Gallup Organization) rather than from the members of NFIB.

[55] For an effort to test a possible relationship between these variables and small business economic conditions, see Joel Popkin and Company (July 2003).

[56] SBA's Small Business Investment Company program (SBIC) was initiated in 1963, providing a training ground for many promising venture capitalists.

Estimates of investment by private venture capital companies, financial intermediaries that accept private money for equity investment in fast growth companies, have been made and published in the Venture Capital Journal since mid-1970s.[57] However, statistics were collected only from "independent" venture capital companies, mostly limited partnerships.[58] What are missing were corporate-sponsored venture capital funds, which were very active during the IT-telecom and equity investment boom of late 1990s, and some public venture capital funds. Quarterly estimates are available by sector and by geographic location (as made available in the Moneytree survey). Detailed information on the source of funds is available in the annual edition published by NVCA – including sources of capital commitments, records of exits through IPO and acquisitions, and fund performance.[59]

12.5.7 Center for Venture Research, University of New Hampshire, Angel Capital

As discussed in the previous section, even less information is available for external equity from informal investors – the angel investors.[60] The market has developed significantly during the last half of the 1990s when equity investment were yielding high returns and with the emergence of a significant number of technology entrepreneurs-turned-investors. As the market developed, more structured, "semi-formal" organizations were formed for angel investing – the formation of angel clubs.

Effort to estimate the flow of angel capital investment has been made by VRC at University of New Hampshire under the direction of Professor Jeff Sohl. It was estimated that informal investment amounted to $15.7 billion in 2002, about 50%

[57] Dr. Stanley Pratt was the prime mover of this database effort. *The Venture Capital Journal* kept track of the developments in the venture capital industry beginning in the mid-1970s. The company has since been acquired by Thomson Financial Co. and the data collection was performed by PriceWaterhouse-Cooper (in the MoneyTree project). The National Venture Capital Association co-sponsored this data collection effort and published the *Venture Capital Yearbook*.

[58] The number of VC firms increased from 87 (in 1980) to 892 (in 2002) with VC capital under managed rose from $3 billion to $253 billion in 2002. See *2003 National Venture Capital Association Yearbook* (2002 data) prepared by Thomson Venture Economics for NVCA.

[59] See *2003 National Venture Capital....* Op.cit. See also, The MoneyTree Survey, a quarterly study of venture capital investment activity in the USA, a collaboration between PricewaterhouseCoopers, Thomson Venture Economics and the National Venture Capital Association (www.moneytree.com).

[60] The angel investors invest in private businesses without the use of investment professionals such as partners and their associates in VC companies. They rely on informal networks and contacts for investment opportunities.

of the amount of $30 billion in 2001.[61] Some 30,000 ventures received financing from angel clubs.

12.5.8 *Thomson Financial, Initial Public Offerings (IPOs) of Small Issuers*

Finally, equity capital was provided to small firms from the public equity market. Only IPOs registered with US Securities Exchange Commission (SEC) are available.[62] IPOs by venture capital-funded companies are also available. Offerings in the limited offering markets – Reg A offering, small business offerings, etc. – are not available when the SEC discontinues recording the filing information in digital format.[63]

12.6 Conclusion

Researchers have come far in locating statistical information about small business financing activities. Comparing the statistical sources used in the discussions in the financing chapters of The State of Small Business reports of the early 1980s to those of the past several years, one realizes the significant progress made over the past 25 years. Availability of the Kauffman Firm Surveys, a panel database, provides great promise for many interesting researches on startup financing. However, data on financial conditions and the financing behaviors of small businesses are still very limited. Many aspects of small business financial research cannot be carried out because of the unavailability of data. For example, limited panel data are available on most small and growing firms for an examination of the life cycle patterns of small growing firms; limited information is available about the costs of financing and its impact on small firms during high interest-rate periods; little is available on the risk and profitability of small business lending

[61] See "The Angel Investor Market in 2002: Investment Activity and Growth Prospects" in www.unh.edu/cvr/ Information was obtained through mail survey of managers of angel club/alliances and individual investors. Of 108 confirmed angel clubs, 45 surveys were returned, representing a response rate of 42%. The respondents represented a diverse set with respect to geographic location and organizational structure and as such, the sample appears to adequately represent the disbursement of angel activity in the USA.

[62] See Table "Common Stocks Initial Public Offerings by All and Small Issuers" in "The State of Small Business – A Report of the President," various years.

[63] SEC used to public information on these offerings for presentation at the annual Small Business Capital formation Forum. See US Securities and Exchange Commission, Directorate of Economic and Policy Analysis, "Small Business financing Trends" various years.

and investment, etc. Information is also lacking on many aspects of small business equity financing, especially on the demand and supply of internal and external equity. Finally, there is very limited information about the lending behavior of another major supplier of small business financing – finance companies. As an industry not subject to federal regulatory supervision, finance companies provide very limited information about the cost and the availability of credits supplied in different small business credit markets.

The situations could be in at least two ways: by continuing the effort to create new databases through more surveys and by expanding and/or revising existing database collection efforts. The Federal Reserve Board, the Bureau of Census, and the Kauffman Foundation are three major organizations with resources that are active in this effort.

Among actions that can be taken to improve existing databases, the following suggestions are made.

12.6.1 Survey of Small Business Finances

More information on lenders, especially commercial banks, from administrative records such as call reports, etc., could be included in the public use database.[64] In addition, questions on the uses of equity capital could be revised to obtain better information. Finally, an interim survey (between the comprehensive surveys) on the most recent financing activity could be initiated (using a shorter questionnaire) for more up-to-date developments in small business financing. This might help reduce the number of questions and the average interview time to improve the response rates of the comprehensive survey.

12.6.2 Call Reports and CRA Data

One immediate item of interest to banking researchers is information on small business credit card activity. Banks that actively extend credit in the form of business credit cards and that maintain separate accounting operations for these activities should be required to report the statistics separately from other C&I lending. Also, in the CRA report, one loan category, loans to small firms with receipts under $1 million, could be improved to make the data more useful. In fact, a small panel of data users could be organized by the financial regulatory agencies to review the two databases for possible improvements in data collection efforts.

[64] The Federal Reserve Board should be able to design a data dissemination approach that can resolve the privacy issues in public use database.

12.6.3 Survey of Terms of Business Lending

As the only source of nationwide information of the terms of small business borrowing from commercial banks, the Survey of Terms of Business Lending could be expanded in its coverage to make it more useful to study the costs and the pricing of small business borrowing/lending. Expanding the numbers of banks participating in the survey, either to include all the CRA reporting banks or to increase the sampled banks from around 300 to, for example, 450, would allow for better understanding of the pricing and competition in different local markets.

12.6.4 Survey of Consumer Finances

More questions on intermingling of business and personal finances of business-owning households would be most useful. The survey is already constrained by the lengthy interview time required. One solution would be to economize on questions that are less important to make space for additional questions. Adding supplementary surveys are another alternative. The SCF survey is also a cost-effective way to provide a national profile of private business investors – angel investors – through a supplemental interview on investment activities of angel investors in the USA.

12.6.5 Finance Company Survey

The Federal Reserve's survey of finance companies, which has been conducted every 5 years, should be expanded to obtain information on their lending to small firms.

Finally, administrative records in two government agencies – the Statistics of Income Division of the Internal Revenue Service (SOI/IRS) and the Securities and Exchange Commission (SEC) – should be better utilized. A concerted effort to explore the best ways to utilize tax return data collected by SOI/IRS as the source of small business financial information is urgently needed. The SOI office has the most comprehensive financial information on American businesses – sole proprietorships, partnership, and corporations. The Master Business Files and information on business receipts and income have long been the basis of economic and business statistics of government statistical and research agencies such as the US Treasury, the Bureau of the Census, the US Department of Commerce's Bureau of Economic Analysis, etc. In addition to providing benchmark statistics on small firm financial activities, a public use file of data on small business taxpayers would contribute much to small business financial research efforts in the USA. The SEC receives all the applications for public offerings (and limited public offerings) in the USA and has financial information on the most dynamic business groups in this country. However, since the late 1980s, the SEC has stopped generating information for public on applications for public offerings.

References

Ballou, J., D. DesRoches, Z. Zhao, and F. Potter. 2007. Meeting the challenges of designing the Kauffman Firm Survey: sampling frame, definitions, and questionnaire development, and respondent burden. *Third international conference on establishment surveys*, June 18–21, 2007. Montreal: Mathematica Policy Research.

Berger, A., A. Saunders, J. Scalise, and G. Udell. 1997. The effects of bank mergers and acquisitions on small business lending, revised draft, May 1997.

Berger, A., A. Saunders, J. Scalise, and G. Udell. 1998. The effects of bank mergers and acquisitions on small business lending, Journal of Financial Economics, 50: 187–229.

Bitler, M., A.M. Robb, and J.D. Wolken. 2001. Financial services used by small businesses: evidence from the 1998 survey of small business finances. *Federal Reserve Bulletin* 87(4): 183–205.

Canner, G., et al. 1998. New information on lending to small businesses and small farms: the 1996 CRA data. *Federal Reserve Bulletin, January* 84(1): 1–35.

Dynan, K.E., K.W. Johnson, and S.M. Slowinski. 2002. Survey of finance companies, 2000. *Federal Reserve Bulletin, January* 2002: 1–14.

Fairlie, R. and Alicia Robb. 2008. Entrepreneurship, self-employment, and business data: in introduction to several large nationally-representative datasets. Discussion paper, IZA Discussion paper series. The Institute for the Study of Labor (IZA), Bonn, Germany.

Haynes, G.W. 1995. Finance companies and small business borrowers: who are they, what financial services do they buy, do they pay higher prices, a report prepared for the US Small Business Administration (SBA Contract Number – SBA-8029-OA-93).

Haynes, G. 2001. Wealth and income: how did small business fare from 1989 to 1998? A report submitted to the Office of Advocacy, US Small Business Administration, June 2001.

Haynes, G. and C. Ou. 2002. Income and wealth: how did small business owners fare in the 1990s, United States Association of Small Business and Entrepreneurship/SBIDA 2000 Proceedings.

Haynes, G. and C. Ou. 2003. A profile of owners and investors of privately-held businesses in the US 1989–1998; Advocacy working paper series; Nov. 2003. Office of Advocacy, US Small Business Administration (www.sba.gov/advo/research/)

Haynes, G., and M. Watts. 1997. Finance companies and small business borrowers: an empirical investigation. *Journal of Entrepreneurial and Small Business Finance* 5(1): 17–42.

Haynes, G.W., R. Walker, B. Rowe, and S. Hong. 1999. The intermingling of business and family Finances in family-owned businesses. *Family Business Review* 12(3): 225–240.

Haynes, G.W., B.R. Rowe, R. Walker, and G.S. Hong. 2000. The differences in financial structure between women- and men-owned family businesses. *Journal of Family and Economic Issues* 21(3): 209–226.

Joel Popkin and Company. 2003. Small business during the business cycle, a report prepared for US Small Business Administration under the contract No. SBAHQ-01-R-0011 (July 2003).

Keaton, W. 1996. Do bank mergers reduce lending to businesses and farmers? The Federal Reserve Bank of Kansas City. *Economic Review* 81: 63–75.

Kennickell, A. and D. McManus. 1993. Sampling for Household Financial Characteristics Using Information on Past Income SCF Working papers, Federal Reserve Board. (www.federalreserve.gov/pubs/oss/oss2/methods.html)

Kolari, J. 2003. Assessing the profitability and riskiness of small business lenders in the banking industry, contract. No. SBAHQ-01-R-0005 prepared for the U.S. Small Business Administration, Office of Advocacy.

Kolari, J. and A. Zardkoohi. 1996. A report prepared for the Office of Advocacy of the US Small Business Administration, contract No.

NFIB Research Foundation. 2003. Credit, Banks, and Small Business – the New Century www.nfib.org/research-foundation/

Ou, C. 1991. Available financial data bases for research on small business. In *Advances in small business finance*, ed. R. Yazdipour, 169–179. Netherlands: Kluwer Academic Publishers.

Ou, C. 2005. Statistical Databases for Economic Reasearch on the financing of small firms in the United States. Journal of Enterpreneurial Finance and Business ventures.

Peek, J. 1995. The effects of interstate banking on small business lending, a report prepared for the Office of Advocacy, US Small Business Administration, cont No. HQ-95-C-0024.

Peek, J. and E. Rosengren. 1997. Bank consolidation and small business lending: it's not just bank size that matters, presented at the *Conference on the economics of small business financing, Stern School of Business*, New York: New York University, May 22–23.

Peek, J. and E. Rosengren. 1998. The Evolution of Bank lending to small business, New England Economic Review, March/April, 27–36.

PM Keypoints. 2003. The impact of tight money and/or recession on small business. A report submitted to US Small Business Administration Cont No. SBAHQ-01-C-0152 (June 2003).

Reynolds, P. 2007. New firm creation in the United States: a PSED I overview. *Foundations and Trends in Entrepreneurship* 3(1): 155–307.

Reynolds, P. 2009. Informal and early formal financial support in the business creation process: exploration with PSED II data set. A paper presented at *Workshop on Entrepreneurial Finance* co-sponsored by Kauffman Foundation and FRB Cleveland, Cleveland, Ohio, March 12–13.

Strahan, P. and J. Weston. 1997. Small business lending and the changing structure of the banking industry (mimeographed).

Strahan, P. and J. Weston. 1998. Small business lending and the changing structure of the banking industry, Journal of Banking and Finance, v.22, pp. 821–45.

Symolic, K. and R. Avery. 2002. Bank consolidation and small business lending: The role of Community Banks. Paper presented at Conference on Community Banking: Whither the Community Bank? organized by the Federal Reserve Bank of Chicago, March 13–14, in Chicago, IL.

US Securities and Exchange Commission, Directorate of Economic and Policy Analysis, "Small Business financing Trends" materials presented at Annual Capital Formation Forum sponsored by the SEC. various years before 1994. (See also www.sec.gov/info/smallbus/sbforum.htm)

US Small Business Administration. 2003/2004. Office of Advocacy, Small Business by the Numbers.

US Small Business Administration. 2003a. Office of Advocacy, financing patterns of small firms: findings from the 1998 Survey of Small Business Finance (September, 2003).

US Small Business Administration. 2003b. Office of Advocacy, small business and micro business lending in the United States, 2002 edition, (December 2003).

US Small Business Administration. 2003c. Office of Advocacy, dynamics of women-operated sole proprietorships – 1990–1998, (March, 2003).

US Treasury, Internal Revenue Service, Statistics of Income Division. Publications include: sole proprietorship returns (various years); Partnership Returns (various years); Corporation Income Tax Returns (various years), and Corporate Source Book various years. See also, SOI Bulletin, various issues (www.irs.gov/taxstats/index.html?portlet=5)

Venture Capital Journal, various issues, by Capital Publishing Corporation, then by Venture Economics; and then by Thomson Venture Economics.

Walraven, 1997. Notes on Banking consolidation, an unpublished manuscript, Federal Reserve Board, Washington, D.C.

Wolken, J.D. 1998. New data sources for research on small business finance. *Journal of Banking and Finance* 22(6–8): 1067–1076.

Author Index

R. Yazdipour, *Advances in Entrepreneurial Finance: With Applications from Behavioral Finance and Economics*, DOI 10.1007/978-1-4419-7527-0,

Subject Index

R. Yazdipour, *Advances in Entrepreneurial Finance: With Applications from Behavioral Finance and Economics*, DOI 10.1007/978-1-4419-7527-0,

FSC
www.fsc.org
MIX
Papier | Fördert
gute Waldnutzung
FSC® C083411

Kolibri 360 GmbH
Ferdinand-Jühlke-Straße 7
99095 Erfurt, Deutschland
produktsicherheit@kolibri360.de